STATE OF THE
WORLD
1986

Other Norton/Worldwatch Books

STATE OF THE WORLD
1986

A Worldwatch Institute Report on Progress Toward a Sustainable Society

PROJECT DIRECTOR
Lester R. Brown

ASSOCIATE PROJECT DIRECTOR
Edward C. Wolf

EDITOR
Linda Starke

SENIOR RESEARCHERS
Lester R. Brown
William U. Chandler
Christopher Flavin
Sandra Postel
Edward C. Wolf

RESEARCHER
Cynthia Pollock

W·W·NORTON & COMPANY
NEW YORK   LONDON

The text of this book is composed in Baskerville, with
display type set in Caslon. Composition and
Manufacturing by The Haddon Craftsmen, Inc.

ISBN 0-393-02260-9

ISBN 0-393-30255-5 {PBK}

W. W. Norton & Company, Inc., 500 Fifth Avenue, New York, N.Y. 10110
W. W. Norton & Company Ltd., 37 Great Russell Street, London WC1B 3NU

234567890

132037

Acknowledgments

Although *State of the World 1986* is concerned with the ominous implications of debts of various kinds, it is a pleasure to begin by acknowledging our own debts to the many people who have made the book possible. We are especially grateful to Rockefeller Brothers Fund President William Dietel for his untiring efforts on behalf of this series. The Rockefeller Brothers Fund, David Rockefeller, and the Winthrop Rockefeller Trust provided the initial three-year funding that launched the *State of the World* series. *State of the World* also draws on ongoing research funded by the Geraldine R. Dodge, William and Flora Hewlett, Edna McConnell Clark, Andrew E. Mellon, and Edward John Noble Foundations and the United Nations Fund for Population Activities.

Several individuals deserve special recognition for their assistance. Orville L. Freeman, Chairman of the Worldwatch Board of Directors, strongly supported the concept of an annual assessment from the beginning. Iva Ashner, who anchors our relationship with W.W. Norton, has always been a delight to work with. Andy Marasia, who manages the printing of *State of the World* at Norton, puts us on the fast track, producing printed copies within weeks of receiving the word processing disks.

A book encompassing so many topics is necessarily an amalgam of many perspectives and opinions. While acknowledging an intellectual debt to many others, the authors especially thank the following for their generous assistance and thoughtful reviews of chapter drafts at various stages of maturity: Ray Anderson, Edward Ayensu, Leonard Berry, Douglas R. Bohi, Robert A. Bohm, Robert Browne, Frank Cardile, Luther Carter, Duane Chapman, Michael Dow, Charles K. Ebinger, Mohamed El-Ashry, Henry Elwell, Norbert Engel, Peter Erickson, Carl Feldman, Andrea Fella, Howard Geller, Robert Goodland, Kenneth Hare, Linda Harrar, Hans Hurni, Judith Jacobsen, Marvin Jensen, Karl Kronebusch, Jeffrey Lewis, John H. Lichtblau, Philip Metzger, Norman Myers, Farrokh Najmabadi, Sharon Nicholson, Donald A. Norman, Rick Piltz, David Pimentel, Bob Pollard, R.T. Ravenholt, James L. Repace, R. Neil Sampson, Allan Savory, Stephen H. Schneider, Saidi Shomari, J. Shukla, S. Fred Singer, Jyoti Singh, Maurice Strong, Theodore Taylor, Bassirou Touré, J.A.N. Wallis, Charles E. Weiss, Lee Wilson, and Phyllis Windle. The authors, of course, accept responsibility for any errors that remain.

Capable and creative research assistance make an author's task immeasurably easier. The authors owe special thanks to Angela Coyle (Chapters 8 and 10), Marion Guyer (Chapter 9), Jodi Jacobson (Chapters 1, 2, and 11), and Cynthia Pollock (Chapters 3, 5, and 6), who did much more than gather research materials; their many contributions and comments proved central to the analytic work throughout *State of the World*.

As editor and production coordinator, Linda Starke managed to distill consistency and unity from the work of six authors. Making the simultaneous stylistic, graphic, and logistical decisions that allow accelerated production of *State of the World*, Linda drew on skills befitting an air traffic controller. Readers and authors both share a debt to her literary and aesthetic judgments. In addition, Bart Brown provided a thorough index that enhances the book's usefulness as a reference.

State of the World could not be produced at all, let alone each year, without the talented and spirited Worldwatch Institute staff. Pamela Berkeley, Jodi Johnson, and Susan Norris handled a flood of drafts and revisions with grace and humor. Colleen Bickman, with help from Susan and Jodi, coordinated a publication sales and marketing effort that would make Japanese managers envious. David Macgregor, now with the World Resources Institute, designed an international outreach strategy for *State of the World,* while editing the regular series of Worldwatch Papers. Brian Brown managed the countless office tasks that kept information flowing smoothly, duties that did not stop him from placing fifth in the U.S. National Whitewater Kayak Championships.

Worldwatch Vice President Blondeen Gravely and Treasurer Felix Gorrell provide the administrative and financial leadership that makes all our work easier. Along with the guidance of our Board of Directors, Blondeen's skillful management frees the research staff to pursue the standards of quality and independence that we hope distinguish *State of the World.*

Production of this year's book was punctuated in mid-October by the arrival of Trace William Norris, born to Susan and Bob Norris. He reminded us all of the timeless human notion that the next generation deserves nothing less than our very best care and commitment. We wish Trace well.

Lester R. Brown and Edward C. Wolf

Contents

Tables and Figures

LIST OF TABLES

LIST OF FIGURES

Foreword

In the first two annual assessments in this series, *State of the World-1984 (SOTW-84)* and *SOTW-85*, we concentrated on the relationship between the economy and its environmental support systems. Specifically, we looked at how the economic demands of a world population approaching 5 billion were affecting the earth's natural systems and resources. In turn, we analyzed the effect of a deteriorating resource base on the economic system.

In *SOTW-86*, we maintain this analytical framework, but expand it to embrace threats to security as well. Although national governments have defined security in military terms, the environmental and economic dimensions of security are becoming increasingly apparent. While traditional analyses often overlook the new threats to national security, the integrated or interdisciplinary approach employed in *State of the World* brings them into focus.

When we launched this series, we hoped, of course, that such an approach would generate interest among those dissatisfied with the more specialized analyses, but we underestimated the response. For example, when *SOTW-84* was released, we did not anticipate that there would soon be 117,000 copies in print in nine languages.

Worldwide distribution of the *State of the World* series is progressing on several fronts. Our U.S. publisher, W.W. Norton, distributes in the United States and Canada, and, through its London sub-sidiary, in the United Kingdom and the English-speaking Commonwealth. The international distribution of *State of the World* in major languages has been greatly aided by the worldwide network of our New York literary agent, Curtis Brown.

The Spanish rights have been purchased by Fonda de Cultura Economica, a large Mexico City publishing house that markets throughout Latin America. Negotiations are under way for a Portuguese edition in Brazil. If this contract is signed, as we anticipate, it will complete coverage in the western hemisphere.

In Asia, *State of the World* is being published in Chinese, Japanese, Indonesian, Thai, and Malay. In addition, a special English edition is being printed in India for distribution in the subcontinent. In Europe, along with distribution of the English edition from London, we expect to sign publishing contracts shortly for German and Italian. In Eastern Europe, we have a Polish edition and are discussing publication in the Soviet Union with the Soviet Academy of Sciences.

With the recent signing of a contract for an Arabic edition, the only remaining gap among the major languages is French. We are now seeking a French edition that would be published in Paris and marketed both in France and in the French-speaking countries of Africa.

Perhaps the most exciting development to date has been a proposal from the producers of the public television series NOVA that we collaborate on a 10-part television series based on *State of the World*. To the best of our knowledge, this is the first time that a research institute has teamed up with public broadcasting to produce a major television series. Our goal is a timely and informative series that will be aired throughout the world.

We hope that one day the printed and film versions of *State of the World* will reinforce each other, not only in the United States, but worldwide in countries as diverse as China, Brazil, and West Germany. Together, the print and film versions of the *State of the World* series could underpin an unprecedented worldwide public education effort on the relationship between the global economy and its environmental support systems.

One of the most rapidly growing markets for the *State of the World* report is the college classroom. For example, *SOTW-85* was adopted for course use during the 1985 fall semester in at least 170 U.S. colleges and universities. In some, it was used in several different departments, including agriculture, demography, ecology, economic development, geography, and international affairs. The list is led by the University of California, where it was used in eight courses on seven campuses, and by the University of Wisconsin, where it was used in five courses on the Madison campus alone.

Among national governments, those of the United States and China are the two leading users of Worldwatch publications. Indeed, the Chinese first printing of 59,000 copies of *State of the World* is even larger than the English first printing. In addition, the Institute for Scientific and Technical Information of China has launched a series patterned after the Worldwatch Papers, entitled "The Development Papers." Among the first dozen papers, three are reprints from Worldwatch.

The U.S. government typically purchases Worldwatch Papers in bulk. For example, the Department of Agriculture purchased for internal use 250 copies of the Institute's report on soil erosion. The Agency for International Development purchased 125 copies of Worldwatch Paper 65, *Reversing Africa's Decline*, for use in the Africa Bureau. In cases where demand is particularly strong, reprint rights have been purchased, such as for the Worldwatch Paper on photovoltaics, which the U.S. Department of Energy incorporated into its own publication series.

Among international agencies, the World Bank, the U.N. Fund for Population Activities, and the United Nations Environment Programme are among the leading users of Worldwatch research. The World Bank, for example, has purchased and distributed 900 copies of *Reversing Africa's Decline*. It has also translated the paper into French, in order to reach key policymakers in francophone Africa.

When we started the Institute a decade ago with the help of William Dietel and the Rockefeller Brothers Fund, we expected to earn some income from publication sales. What we did not anticipate was the strength of the market for integrated public policy research. We certainly did not foresee that income from publication sales, including royalties and reprint rights, and the interest on savings from this earned income would cover 54 percent of our costs, as they did in 1985.

The strong market demand for Worldwatch publications appears to stem from their interdisciplinary character. In this sense, the analyses reflect the world that policymakers face. Decision makers cannot view the world exclusively in economic, ecological, or political terms. Responsible policy requires pulling information together across many fields of knowledge.

As in the past, we welcome ideas and suggestions. The more feedback we get, the more useful *State of the World* will be.

Lester R. Brown
  Project Director

Edward C. Wolf
  Associate Project Director

Worldwatch Institute
1776 Massachusetts Avenue, N.W.
Washington, D.C. 20036

December 1985

STATE OF THE
WORLD
1986

1

A Generation of Deficits

Lester R. Brown

For 40 years, the United States and the Soviet Union have been engaged in an arms race, an unremitting contest that has sapped the energies and resources of both countries. Each is determined to gain a strategic military advantage, regardless of cost. This competition has dominated not only relations between the two countries, but a generation of world affairs as well.

For both superpowers, the costs are far higher than any fiscal reckoning would suggest. And they range far beyond the disproportionate share of national product devoted to military purposes. Claims on the time of political leaders in Washington, Moscow, and elsewhere have been heavy, diverting policymakers from other issues, including emerging new threats to security.

The U.S. decision to accelerate the arms race in the early eighties has pushed military spending to a new level. Unwilling to raise taxes or cut other ex-

penditures, the United States has run up massive fiscal deficits to finance this unprecedented peacetime military expansion. Mounting federal deficits since 1980 have made the Treasury the dominant borrower in capital markets, competing with private firms for investment capital. This in turn has led to record-high real interest rates and contributed to a dollar that is overvalued against other currencies, making U.S. exports less competitive in world markets.

For the United States, declining competitiveness and higher capital costs are discouraging investment in new industrial capacity, and contributing to industrial decline. Basic industries such as steel are being overwhelmed by imports produced in more efficient, modern plants abroad. Since the onset of the massive U.S. fiscal deficits, 2 million jobs in basic industries have been lost to imports.[1]

All major sectors of the U.S. agricultural and industrial economy are affected by the deteriorating competitive position. The overvalued dollar is reduc-

Units of measurement are metric unless common usage dictates otherwise.

ing the ability of American farmers to compete in world markets, thus depressing commodity prices and reducing agricultural income. A portion of the farm debt—$213 billion at the end of 1985—will never be repaid. Farm foreclosures, at the highest level since the Great Depression, are weakening the U.S. banking system in a way that alarms federal banking regulators.[2]

A portion of the farm debt—$213 billion at the end of 1985—will never be repaid.

In the Soviet Union, the arms race is exacting a heavy toll on living standards and diverting political energies from the sorely needed modernization. To maintain its position in the arms competition, the Soviet Union, with an economic output only half that of the United States, devotes twice as much of its gross national product (GNP) to the military effort. Now the economy is in deep trouble. As the Soviet Union tries to move beyond the early stages of industrial development toward a highly diversified modern economy, the shortcomings of state control are becoming more apparent. For Mikhail Gorbachev, the young, reform-minded Soviet leader, the difficulty of launching the needed economic reforms if the arms race is not slowed is obvious.

Preoccupied with each other, the two military superpowers apparently have failed to notice that global geopolitics is being reshaped in a way that defines security more in economic than in traditional military terms. While the United States and Soviet Union have concentrated on military competition, Japan has been challenging both nations on the economic front.

Following its defeat in World War II, Japan was both sheltered under the U.S. defense umbrella and barred from the arms race by the Allied powers' stipulation that its militarization remain limited to a small, lightly armed self-defense force. Without an imposing military sector to sap investment capital and scientific and managerial talent, Japan is moving toward a position of global economic supremacy. High domestic savings plus negligible military expenditures have combined to boost investment in new plant and equipment, giving Japan the world's most modern, technologically advanced economy.

Measured by ability to compete in world markets and by investment abroad, Japan is steadily improving its position relative to the superpowers. Per capita income in Japan surpassed that in the Soviet Union in the mid-sixties and is approaching that in the United States. In trade, Japan's exports are nearly double those of the Soviet Union. And if recent trends continue, before 1990 Japan will supplant the United States as the world's leading trading power.[3]

Japanese investment abroad has also surged in recent years. With only modest net foreign assets of less than $12 billion as recently as 1980, Japan's net external holdings now exceed $120 billion. The United States, long the world's leading overseas investor, with net assets abroad of $147 billion as recently as 1982, has now become a debtor nation—a precipitous, and unprecedented, fall from leadership. Its once-vast net foreign assets have been wiped out almost overnight.[4]

In the international economic arena, Japan is thus now in a class by itself. The combination of international trade and rapidly growing investment abroad gives the nation a direct international economic involvement that the United States can no longer claim. In 1985 Japan's exports totaled $174 billion. Combined with its net foreign assets of

$125 billion, this gives Japan a total economic involvement abroad of $299 billion. By comparison, U.S. exports of $217 billion and net foreign assets of minus $120 billion yielded a total of $97 billion, just one third that of Japan.[5]

Japan, initially barred from the international arms race, now has mastered the new geopolitics, recognizing that in the nuclear age military power is of limited value and that political influence derives more from the economic strength of a highly productive, internationally competitive economy. U.S. governors and mayors now compete vigorously for Japanese attention and industrial investment. And Third World delegations seeking investment and technology from abroad journey to Tokyo. For developing countries, the Japanese model is far more attractive than either the problem-ridden Soviet economy or the debt-ridden American one.[6]

Another country that has grasped the new geopolitics is China. Although it shares a 3,000-kilometer border with the Soviet Union, it has unilaterally decided to reduce military expenditures, cutting them from some 14 percent of GNP a decade ago to 7.5 percent in 1985. At the same time, the leaders in Beijing have increased investment in agriculture and the manufacture of consumer goods and have stepped up the effort to restore and protect the economy's environmental support systems by increasing expenditures on reforestation, desert reclamation, and, most importantly, family planning. In effect, China is defining security in economic and ecological terms.[7]

Unfortunately, the two superpowers that are perpetuating the arms race are not its only victims. To the extent that the arms competition diverts attention from the Third World debt that is weakening the international financial system, or from the ecological deterioration that is undermining the global economy, the entire world suffers.

DEFICITS AND DEBT

Seldom if ever have deficits and debt so dominated public attention. The United States has accumulated almost as much debt over the past six years as during the preceding two centuries. The external debt of the Third World, particularly in Latin America and Africa, now threatens international financial stability. Although rising oil prices contributed to debt accumulation on both these continents, economic mismanagement underscored by a deteriorating ecosystem and declining rainfall raised African debt to unmanageable levels. This combination—the growing U.S. federal debt, now in excess of $2 trillion, and the Third World's external debt, now over $800 billion—will plague the world economy for decades to come.[8]

The burgeoning U.S debt, driven primarily by the growth in defense spending, is of concern to economic policymakers throughout the world. As the U.S. government's preoccupation with the arms race heightened during the eighties, spending in this sector rose dramatically. As recently as 1980, U.S. defense expenditures totaled $174 billion (in 1985 dollars). (See Figure 1–1.) Those for 1986 are projected at $272 billion. Unfortunately, these increases, which accounted for much of the growth in the budgetary deficit, were not matched by increases in tax revenues. Consequently, the gap between federal expenditures and revenues has widened, approaching $200 billion annually in recent years.[9]

As a result, the U.S. federal debt has grown at an unprecedented rate. (See Figure 1–2.) Escalating debt, the associated high interest rates, and an overvalued dollar are creating a host of economic problems for both the United States and the rest of the world. Among other things, the deficit is being financed in part by an influx of capital from other

Billion
Dollars

(1985 dollars)

Source: U.S. Census Bureau

Figure 1-1. U.S. Military Expenditures, 1950-85

countries. For perhaps the first time in history, the savings of people in lower-income countries are being used to finance the growth in consumption of an affluent society.[10]

The Third World debt problem received worldwide recognition only after the financial insolvency of debtor nations had reached crisis proportions. Mexico brought the crisis to center stage in August of 1982, when Mexico's Finance Minister, Jesus Silva Herzog, "showed up on our doorstep and turned his pockets inside out," in the words of a U.S. Treasury official.[11] As foreign affairs analyst Karin Lissakers has noted, "His arrival marked the beginning of an international debt crisis that by Christmas had swept through a dozen debtor countries and a thousand creditor banks and placed more than $300 billion in international loans in jeopardy."[12] Mexico was not the first Third World country unable to meet the payments on its debt, but it was the first large enough to threaten the international financial system.

Part of the growth in Third World external debt was attributable, directly and indirectly, to the oil price hikes of the seventies. Consumers and government policymakers, accustomed to the easy

growth that cheap oil made possible during the quarter-century following World War II, were reluctant to adjust their life-styles and consumption patterns to new realities. In an effort to offset the effect of rising oil prices and to keep their economies growing faster than their populations, the majority of Third World governments borrowed heavily during the late seventies and early eighties. They were encouraged in this by the international lending institutions, which were seeking ways of "recycling" massive deposits of petrodollars.

Indirectly, higher oil prices slowed global economic growth, and hence growth in raw material markets. They also set in motion energy conservation programs that involved increased recycling of materials, including aluminum and copper, both major Third World foreign-exchange earners. The net effect of these shifts was weaker prices for raw material exports. Necessary though the oil price hikes were to wean the world from its oil-wasteful ways, they left many painful adjustments in their wake.

The key to the financial crisis plaguing Third World countries is the relationship of debt-service payments (principal plus interest) to export earnings. Tradi-

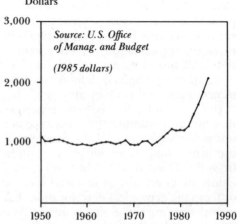

Billion
Dollars

Source: U.S. Office
of Manag. and Budget

(1985 dollars)

Figure 1-2. U.S. Gross Federal Debt, 1950-86

tionally, international banks avoided lending when debt-service payments exceeded 20 percent of export earnings.[13] Heavy borrowing, combined with rising interest rates and a global recession in the early eighties, has pushed many Third World countries far beyond this threshold. Several financially troubled nations, such as Argentina, Bolivia, Egypt, Pakistan, and Sudan, have not only exceeded this limit—they are allocating more than half their export earnings merely to pay interest on their debts. (See Table 1–1.)

The current strategy for coping with excessive Third World debt, developed by the International Monetary Fund (IMF) with the cooperation and support of the international banks, has three main components. The first is to expand

markets for Third World exports through sustained growth in the industrial economies. The second requires structural improvements in Third World economies in exchange for debt reschedulings. Typically, the changes include reductions in imports and government spending, and increases in savings and exports, with currency devaluation frequently used to improve trade balances. The third component, which is expected to follow improved economic conditions, involves a resumption of net capital inflows from lender countries.[14]

This approach has succeeded insofar as it has avoided massive defaults that would have jeopardized the international banking system. The trade deficits of most major debtor nations also have been remedied, with some, such as Brazil, even running moderate trade surpluses. And the time bought with the IMF approach has allowed international banks to increase their reserves against Third World loans and thus reduce their risk.[15]

But this strategy has not restored sustained growth in debtor countries. In nearly all of the heavily indebted ones, incomes are lower today than when the crisis began four years ago. The ratio of debt servicing to exports has not declined as projected. And, finally, capital flight from most countries continues, signaling a failure to restore investor confidence.

A compilation by the Morgan Guaranty Trust Company shows that real gross domestic product per capita declined in 9 of the 10 major debtor countries from the peak level of 1980–81 to 1985. (See Table 1–2.) The declines ranged from 5.6 percent in Brazil to 25 percent in Nigeria. For the 10 countries as a group, per capita incomes fell by one tenth during this brief span of years. Even worse, with existing external debt burdens, there is little prospect of once again steadily improving living standards.

Table 1-1. Selected Debtor Countries Where Interest Payments on External Debt Exceed 20 Percent of Export Earnings, 1984

Country	Total External Debt	Share of Export Earnings to Pay Interest[1]
	(billion dollars)	(percent)
Sudan	9	80
Argentina	48	56
Bolivia	5	48
Chile	20	44
Brazil	102	38
Mexico	97	36
Peru	14	33
Philippines	26	28
Ecuador	7	24
Morocco	13	23

[1]Percentages are much higher if principal payments are included.
SOURCES: Morgan Guaranty Trust Company, New York, private communication, November 6, 1985; Sudan data from U.S. Department of Agriculture, Economic Research Service, *Agricultural Outlook*, Washington, D.C., October 1985.

Table 1-2. Change in GDP Per Capita from 1980–81 Peak to 1985 in 10 Major Debtor Countries

Country	Change
	(percent)
Argentina	−17.1
Brazil	− 5.6
Chile	−14.4
Ecuador	− 6.3
Mexico	− 9.4
Peru	−13.7
Venezuela	−17.1
Nigeria	−25.0
Philippines	−14.1
Yugoslavia	+ 1.5
Average	− 9.8

SOURCE: Morgan Guaranty Trust Company, *World Financial Markets,* New York, September/October 1985.

As of early 1986, the IMF's plan for managing Third World debt is not working as intended. What once appeared to be a temporary slowdown in global economic growth now appears to be chronic. In addition to the constraints imposed by the end of the era of cheap energy, a deteriorating natural resource base is affecting the economic prospects of scores of Third World countries. (See Chapter 2.)

In Africa, food deficits are adding to trade deficits throughout the continent. With some 40 percent of Africans living in countries where cropland productivity is lower now than it was 30 years ago, excessive soil erosion is contributing to growth in external debt. The continent's cereal import bill climbed from $600 million in 1972 to $5.4 billion in 1983, a ninefold increase.[16]

Further complicating efforts to repay Third World bills is the growing U.S. debt. This promises not only a continuation of record or near-record real interest rates in world money markets, but also a weakened U.S. economy and, consequently, a smaller market for Third World exports. In addition, it undermines the capacity of the United States to lead in any effort to resolve the debt issue.

It is time to go back to the drawing board. Sudan's Foreign Minister, Ibrahim Taha Ayoub, expressed the sentiments of many in the Third World when he said, "It is becoming glaringly evident that we cannot service and repay these debts and succeed at the same time in providing our people with the minimum requirements of survival."[17] Ayoub is describing a new reality for his country and dozens of others that the world has not yet come to grips with.

ECOLOGICAL DEFICITS

Economic deficits may dominate our headlines, but ecological deficits will dominate our future. Accounting systems signal when a country begins to run up an economic deficit, but they do not indicate when the sustainable yield threshold of a biological resource, such as a forest, has been crossed. Ecological deficits such as a loss of tree cover or of topsoil often go unnoticed until they begin to affect economic indicators. But by that time, excessive demand may be consuming the resource itself, converting a renewable resource into a nonrenewable one.

When historians analyze this era of debt, they will discover that excessive economic and ecological deficits have similar roots, for they reflect similar values and processes. Occasionally, these are a result of miscalculations. But more commonly they result from a loss of social discipline, from a decision to satisfy today's needs and desires at the expense of tomorrow—in effect, a decision to "charge it" to our children. Carried to excess, this weakens the economy itself, leading to economic decline.

Though similar in cause, economic and ecological deficits differ in their effect. The former do not reduce immediately an economy's inherent productivity. Ecological deficits, however, actually diminish the resource base on which the productivity of the economy depends. For example, a farmer in debt may eventually lose the farm, as the local bank forecloses on the mortgage. But the farm does not lose its productivity; it merely changes hands. If, however, the farmer is incurring an ecological deficit, losing topsoil through erosion, then the farm becomes worthless and the land must be abandoned.

Ecological deficits occur when the demands on a natural system exceed its carrying capacity. (See Table 1–3.) If the amount of wood removed from a forest exceeds the new growth, the forest begins to shrink, and will eventually disappear. Likewise with a fishery: When the catch begins to exceed the sustainable yield, the fish stocks decline. If the excessive catch continues, the fishery will collapse. If the demand on a system continues to expand once the sustainable yield threshold is crossed, the resource base will shrink with each passing year. In the absence of action to correct the growing excess of demand over sustainable yield, the pace of resource destruction will accelerate, leaving society little time to act.

Of all the excessive demands on the earth's natural resources, that on forests is the most visible. Land clearing for agriculture, firewood gathering, and harvesting by lumber and paper industries are all taking a toll. As of the mid-eighties, every country in Africa is losing tree cover. Indeed, forest deficits are now the rule throughout the Third World. Only South Korea and China appear to be planting more trees than they are harvesting.[18]

At the same time, forests in industrial countries are beginning to suffer from excessive chemical stress. As fossil fuel combustion has expanded over the past generation, the discharge of sulfur dioxide and nitrogen oxides has also grown, as have ozone levels. Across the northern tier of industrial countries—North America, Europe, and the Soviet Union —air pollution and acid precipitation are now damaging and destroying forests. No industrial country is escaping this destruction, though some, such as Czechoslovakia, Poland, and West Germany, are suffering more than others.[19]

The same demographic forces that are increasing pressure on Third World forests are also multiplying pressures on grasslands. With livestock herds growing almost as fast as human populations, grasslands are deteriorating in Africa, the Middle East, the Indian subcontinent, and Central America. In some countries, grassland deterioration has reached the point where herd liquidation is now the only feasible response.[20]

Economic deficits may dominate our headlines, but ecological deficits will dominate our future.

Throughout most of history, the human demand for seafood did not even remotely approach the sustainable yield of oceanic fisheries. But as our numbers have nearly doubled since mid-century, claims on many fisheries have become excessive. From 1950 to 1970, the world fish catch expanded at 5 percent per year, as fast as or even faster than the global economy. This changed abruptly after 1970, when annual growth dropped to 1 percent. Overfishing, which had been the exception, was becoming the rule, and a lead sector in global economic growth began to lag.[21]

Perhaps the most worrisome loss is that of topsoil. Soil erosion is a natural process, but when it exceeds the rate of new soil formation, as it now does on 35 percent of the world's cropland, then the

Table 1-3. Resource Depletion That Is Adversely Affecting Global Economy

Resource	Extent of Depletion
Forests	World's tropical forests disappearing at 2 percent per year. Far faster in West Africa and southeast Asia, where moist tropical forests will have virtually disappeared by end of century. Previously stable forests in temperate zone now suffering from air pollution and acid rain. Dead and dying forests plainly visible in West Germany, Czechoslovakia, and Poland.
Grasslands	Excessive pressure on grasslands, closely paralleling growing pressure on forests and soils, has led to deterioration, which is most advanced in Africa and Middle East. Herd liquidation in pastoral economies of Africa now commonplace.
Fisheries	Rapid growth in world fish catch during fifties and sixties now history; overfishing often the rule, not the exception. Fish catch per person, including from fish farming, down 15 percent since 1970. Biggest consumption cuts in Third World countries such as Philippines.
Soil	Soil erosion exceeding new soil formation on 35 percent of world's cropland. World losing an estimated 7 percent of topsoil per decade. Effects most evident in Africa, where 40 percent of people live in countries where land productivity is lower than it was a generation ago.
Water	Growing water demand exceeding sustainable supplies in many locations, leading to scarcity. Falling water tables now found on every continent and in key food-producing regions. In some areas, including portions of the United States, water being shifted out of irrigated agriculture to satisfy growing residential demands.
Oil	Increases in the price of oil, the principal commercial fuel, sharply reduced world economic growth since 1973. Part of decline is due to ill-conceived responses to oil price hikes, notably the heavy borrowing by Third World countries. Progress in developing renewable alternatives is lagging.

SOURCE: Worldwatch Institute, based on various sources.

land's inherent productivity begins to decline. The cumulative loss of topsoil, now affecting industrial and developing countries alike, is beginning to also affect the economics of food production. Industrial societies can often offset such a loss with increased fertilizer use, but in some 14 Third World countries—mainly in Africa—soil loss is reducing land productivity.[22]

Water, too, is becoming scarce in some parts of the world, constraining growth in both agriculture and industry.

In most situations, scarcity results from a growth in demand that exceeds locally available supplies. In others, it stems from a reduction in supplies, as deforestation, other losses of vegetation, and land degradation increase rainfall runoff, thus reducing both aquifer recharge and evaporation. Reduced aquifer recharge lowers water tables, and reduced evaporation and transpiration may lower rainfall. Countries experiencing a rapid growth in water demand, diminished aquifer recharge, and less rainfall can find themselves in a water crisis almost overnight.

Whether they occur with forests, soils, fisheries, or water supplies, ecological deficits—like fiscal ones—represent a borrowing from the future. The price for our shortsighted choice to live beyond our means will be paid by our children and grandchildren.

Reducing Oil Deficits

While economic and ecological deficits are growing, oil import deficits have been reduced. Petroleum being shipped into the United States, the world's largest importer, has declined from an all-time high of 8.7 million barrels per day in 1977 to 5.4 million in 1984, a reduction of 38 percent. Western Europe's imports have dropped from the peak of 15.4 million barrels in 1973 to 8.6 million in 1984, a fall of 44 percent. Although less impressive, Japan's imports have also fallen, from a high of 5.6 million barrels daily in 1979 to 4.3 million in 1984.[23]

This reduced dependence on imported oil has helped stabilize petroleum prices and virtually eliminated any threat of embargoes, at least for the near term. As discussed in Chapter 5, reduced imports are largely the product of increased worldwide efficiency of oil use; of a shift to other energy sources, such as coal, natural gas, hydropower, wood fuel, and nuclear power; and of impressive oil production gains in countries that are not members of the Organization of Petroleum Exporting Countries (OPEC). The trend toward less reliance on oil is well established and will likely continue for the foreseeable future.

The combination of more-efficient oil use and fuel substitution is steadily reducing the oil intensity of world economic activity, reversing the historical trend. The oil used per $1,000 of economic output increased from 1.3 barrels in 1950 to 2.3 barrels in 1973, where it leveled off through 1979, before beginning the decline that continues today. With the sixth consecutive year of declining oil intensity in 1985, the world was using 21 percent less oil per unit of economic output than in 1979. (See Table 1–4.)

Since 1973, all western industrial countries and China have sharply reduced the oil intensity of their economic activity. Oil efficiency gains in the centrally controlled economies of Eastern Europe have been much less impressive, however. Indeed, the oil intensity of the Soviet economy has continued to rise during the eighties.[24]

Worldwide, lowered oil intensity is due more to energy efficiency gains than to fuel substitution, though this varies by sector. Within the United States, for example, gains in the fuel efficiency of new automobiles marketed since 1973 have reduced automotive fuel use by nearly one tenth. Between 1973 and 1985, the official fuel efficiency ratings, which overstate somewhat the "on-road" fuel economy, show miles traveled per gallon of gasoline used in new cars increasing from 14 to 27, a gain of some 90 percent. (See Table 1–5.) For the fleet as a whole, fuel efficiency during the same span improved more slowly, from just over 13 miles per gallon to more than 17. Stated simply, the average American car traveled 32 percent farther on a gallon of gasoline in 1985 than in 1973.

By contrast, fuel substitution has played only a negligible role in the auto sector. Two countries, South Africa and Brazil, have effectively broken the automobile's dependence on oil, but at a high cost. South Africa, using a coal liquefaction process, and Brazil, producing alcohol from sugarcane, are now running close to half their fleets with

Table 1-4. Oil Intensity of World Economic Output, 1950–85

Year	Oil Used Per $1,000 Of Output[1]
	(barrels)
1950	1.33
1955	1.46
1960	1.67
1965	1.90
1970	2.17
1971	2.21
1972	2.23
1973	2.27
1974	2.13
1975	2.05
1976	2.15
1977	2.16
1978	2.14
1979	2.15
1980	2.00
1981	1.91
1982	1.85
1983	1.79
1984	1.74
1985	1.69

[1]1980 dollars.
SOURCES: Worldwatch Institute estimates based on data from British Petroleum Company, *BP Statistical Review of World Energy* (London: 1985); International Monetary Fund, *International Financial Statistics* (Washington, D.C.: various issues); and Herbert R. Block, *The Planetary Product in 1980* (Washington, D.C.: U.S. Department of State, 1981).

Table 1-5. United States: Automobile Fuel Efficiency, 1970–85

Year	New Cars	Total Fleet
	(miles per gallon)	
1970	14.8	13.6
1971	14.4	13.6
1972	14.5	13.5
1973	14.2	13.1
1974	14.2	13.4
1975	15.8	13.5
1976	17.5	13.7
1977	18.3	13.9
1978	19.9	14.1
1979	20.3	14.3
1980	23.5	15.1
1981	25.2	15.5
1982	26.1	16.2
1983	25.9	16.7
1984	26.5	17.0
1985	26.9	17.3

SOURCES: Motor Vehicle Manufacturers Association, *Motor Vehicle Facts and Figures, '85* (Detroit, Mich.: 1985); U.S. Census Bureau, *Statistical Abstract of the United States 1984* (Washington, D.C.: U.S. Government Printing Office, 1984); Federal Highway Administration, U.S. Department of Transportation, Washington, D.C., private communication.

these alternative fuels. In both countries, the costs in government subsidies have been high, with the benefits of these subsidies going to the small minority who own automobiles.[25]

The changing outlook for oil—the ideal transport fuel—and the less bullish world economic outlook have markedly altered the long-term prospect for the automobile industry. Between 1950 and 1973, annual world automobile output expanded from 8 million to 30 million, or roughly 100,000 per working day, closely paralleling the spectacular five-fold growth in oil output of that period. After 1973, automobile production dipped for a few years, then recovered, reaching an all-time high of 31 million in 1978. Following that, it fell for four consecutive years. As real oil prices declined during the eighties, automobile output turned upward in 1983 and 1984. Yet there is little indication today that the growth in automobile manufacturing, which was so impressive from 1950 to 1973, will ever be resumed.[26]

In contrast to the automotive sector, the dramatic reduction of oil used in electrical generation is largely the result of substituting other fuels, principally coal, nuclear power, natural gas, and hydropower. In the United States, the amount of oil used to generate electricity has fallen by two thirds or more since 1978, a pattern typical of other oil-importing industrial countries.[27]

The historical shift from coal to oil, which was under way when this century began, weakened with the 1973 oil price hike, and was decisively reversed after that of 1979. (See Figure 1–3.) Coal has been the principal fuel substitute for oil in the electric utility and other industrial sectors in oil-importing countries.[28]

More recently, natural gas has been extensively substituted for oil—again, largely for economic reasons. The principal substitutions are occurring in the Soviet Union and in Eastern and Western Europe, with all countries drawing on vast Soviet reserves of natural gas. As these reserves are linked to European markets by an international network of pipelines, this substitution is likely to continue. In contrast to the shift from oil back to coal, that from oil to natural gas generates less air pollution.[29]

In addition to coal, the 3 percent yearly growth in hydroelectric generation since 1979 has helped curb the amount of oil used in electrical generation in many Third World countries. The most dramatic hydropower expansion is occurring in Latin America and Asia, where there is a vast undeveloped potential. Canada and the Soviet Union are also developing large-scale hydroelectric projects, with the former planning to sell its swelling surplus of electricity to the United States. China, too, is making a major push on hydropower as it attempts both to industrialize and to bring electricity to the countryside.

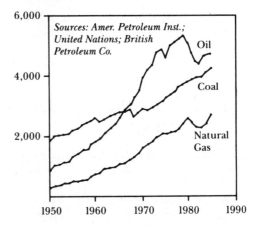

Million
Metric
Tons

Sources: Amer. Petroleum Inst.; United Nations; British Petroleum Co.

Figure 1-3. World Production of Coal, Oil, and Natural Gas (in Coal Equivalent), 1950-85

Small but rapidly growing amounts of other renewable energy sources such as geothermal energy, solar collectors, and wind power are also being substituted for oil in electrical generation. (See Chapter 6.)

Oil prices have stabilized in the short run, but at considerable long-term expense. The growth in non-OPEC oil production, a key to oil market stability in the eighties, is not likely to be sustained for much longer. North Sea production is expected to peak and turn downward within the next few years. The apparent peaking of Soviet oil production in 1983 follows the high point in U.S. output by 13 years, and almost certainly assures an overall decline in non-OPEC oil output.[30]

As non-OPEC oil reserves dwindle, and as production declines during the early nineties, control of world oil supplies and prices will shift back to the handful of Middle Eastern OPEC members who will control an even greater share of world oil output than they did during the price-raising seventies. (See Chapter 5.) In effect, the stability in the world oil market that is being bought with expanded non-OPEC oil production during the eighties will be paid for with increased dependence on Middle Eastern OPEC oil during the nineties.

DIVERGING FOOD SECURITY TRENDS

The contemporary world consists overwhelmingly of food-deficit countries, with over 100 of them importing grain from the United States alone. But this figure does not tell the whole story, since two countries, China and India—which together contain over one third of humanity—have recently attained cereal self-sufficiency.[31]

Some of the 100 or so national food deficits are intentional, but most are the result of excessive population growth, land degradation, or agricultural mismanagement, or some combination of these. Important exporters of grain can be counted on the fingers of one hand—Argentina, Australia, Canada, France, and the United States. In recent years, grain deficits have worsened in Africa and the Middle East, but have declined or disappeared in Western Europe, China, and India.

Over the past decade, growth in food output has slowed markedly and regional food production trends have diverged. The slowdown in food output dates to the first oil price increase. Between 1950 and 1973, grain production increased at 3.1 percent per year, easily outstripping population growth. (See Table 1–6.) During the dozen years since, production has expanded at only 2.2 percent per year, dramatically narrowing the margin between the growth in food production and that of population. The per capita production trends

for individual regions, all moving upward until around 1970, have begun to diverge since then, with some now declining.

Nowhere is the regional contrast greater than between Western Europe and Africa. In Africa, per capita grain production in 1985 was still down by one fifth from its 1967 peak, though up from the depressed harvests of 1983 and 1984. In Western Europe, by contrast, per capita grain production has more than doubled over the past generation, climbing from 235 kilograms in 1950 to 495 kilograms in 1985. Spurred by producer price incentives well above the world market level, Western Europe's farmers have vigorously expanded output, even though some countries have lost cropland through conversion to nonfarm uses. With population growth now at a near standstill, nearly all the increased output can be exported. (See Figure 1–4.)

While Western Europe has been achieving broad-based gains on the food front, the Soviet Union and Eastern Europe have been backsliding. Since 1978, Soviet grain production has fallen in absolute terms, marking the first time in the postwar period that a major food-producing country has experienced a sustained production decline. Such a

Table 1-6. Annual Growth in World Grain Production, Total and Per Capita, 1950–73 and 1973–85

Period	Grain Output	Population	Grain Output Per Capita
	(percent)		
1950–73	3.1	1.9	1.2
1973–85	2.2	1.8	0.4

SOURCES: U.S. Department of Agriculture, Economic Research Service, *World Indices of Agricultural and Food Production, 1950–85* (unpublished printout) (Washington, D.C.: 1985).

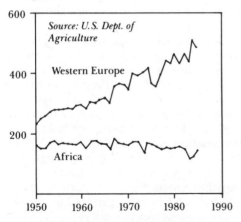

Figure 1-4. Per Capita Grain Production in Western Europe and Africa, 1950-85

drop is difficult to explain in agronomic terms alone, suggesting that low farm-labor morale may be affecting productivity. In addition to Africa and the Middle East, Latin America has also experienced a downturn in per capita grain production. For this area, the production peak came in 1982, the year the debt crisis surfaced. Foreign-exchange restrictions on the import of agricultural inputs in countries such as Brazil and Mexico and the overall weakening of demand since that year have both played a role in the downturn.

For the Indian subcontinent, home to one fifth of humanity, the trends have been mixed. India's per capita grain production has increased enough to eliminate grain imports, but not enough to markedly raise per capita grain consumption, which has gone up scarcely 5 percent over the past generation. Consumption of leguminous crops, a key source of protein in the largely vegetarian diet of most Indians, has fallen by one third during this period. The big, bright spot in the world food economy over the last decade has been China. With 22 percent of the world's people, it has achieved cereal self-sufficiency,

dramatically raised per capita food consumption, and largely eliminated malnutrition.[32]

Regional trends in food consumption are influenced not only by production trends, but by other economic and social forces as well. Per capita consumption of grain, a useful yardstick of dietary quality, ranges from a low of roughly 180 kilograms per year in Africa to some 800 kilograms per year in North America and the Soviet Union. At the lower level, nearly all grain is consumed directly, while at the higher level, the bulk is consumed indirectly in the form of livestock products.

Some more-affluent societies have apparently reached the saturation point in consumption of livestock products. For example, the trend in per capita beef consumption in the United States has abruptly reversed over the past decade. (See Figure 1–5.) Between the early fifties and the mid-seventies, per capita beef consumption in the United States doubled. But after reaching 94 pounds in 1976, it began declining, falling to 77 pounds in 1985.[33]

Grain deficits have worsened in Africa and the Middle East, but have declined or disappeared in Western Europe, China, and India.

Prior to the downturn, the U.S. Department of Agriculture (USDA) had projected that per capita beef consumption would continue to climb through the end of the century. But this decade-long decline, which reflects a widening concern over the health effects of diets rich in high-fat livestock products, may well continue. The combination of diet modification in affluent industrial societies, such as the United States and Canada, and the decline in purchasing

Pounds

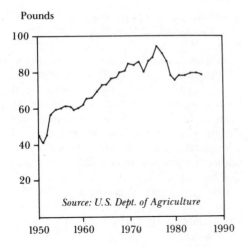

Source: U.S. Dept. of Agriculture

1950   1960   1970   1980   1990

**Figure 1-5. U.S. Beef Consumption
Per Capita, 1950-85**

power in key parts of the Third World
has contributed to a much more modest
growth in the world demand for grain in
recent years.

Reflecting these various changes, the
pattern of world grain trade has shifted
dramatically over the last 35 years. At
mid-century, most of the grain that
crossed national borders flowed across
the Atlantic from North America to
Western Europe. (See Table 1–7.)
Today the largest flow of grain between
continents is that across the Pacific, from
North America to Asia, now the world's
leading importer. North America re-

mains the world's breadbasket, but it is
Asia, not Europe, that is now the principal market.

Perhaps the most striking development in world grain trade has been the
recent shift of Western Europe from import to export status. It is the only region
that has moved decisively to the surplus
side of the grain trade ledger in recent
history. The combination of little or no
population growth and of output driven
by advancing technologies and high support prices has firmly established Western Europe as a grain exporter.

Most of Europe's exportable surplus
comes from France. Until recently, much
of the French surplus was absorbed by
the grain-deficit members of the European Community, but with recent Com-
munity-wide production gains, these
deficits have diminished or disappeared,
forcing France to seek outside markets,
such as North Africa or Eastern
Europe.[34]

While Western Europe has moved to
the export side of the ledger, Eastern
Europe, including the Soviet Union, is
now solidly on the deficit side, second
only to Asia. Indeed, the Soviet Union,
which has shifted from buying grain
abroad only during poor crop years to
doing so consistently, is now importing
more grain than any country in history.

Africa's position in world grain trade

Table 1-7. The Changing Pattern of World Grain Trade, 1950–85[1]

Region	1950	1960	1970	1980	1985[2]
		(million metric tons)			
North America	+23	+39	+56	+131	+103
Latin America	+ 1	0	+ 4	− 10	+ 1
Western Europe	−22	−25	−30	− 16	+ 11
E. Eur. and Soviet Union	0	0	0	− 46	− 35
Africa	0	− 2	− 5	− 15	− 29
Asia	− 6	−17	−37	− 63	− 72
Australia and New Zeal.	+ 3	+ 6	+12	+ 19	+ 21

[1]Plus sign indicates net exports; minus sign, net imports.   [2]Preliminary.
SOURCES: United Nations Food and Agriculture Organization, *Production Yearbook* (Rome: various years);
U.S. Department of Agriculture, *Foreign Agriculture Circulars,* various issues.

has also been changing. Although the region was virtually self-sufficient in grain as recently as 1970, its imports have climbed steadily since then, reaching some 29 million tons in 1985. In contrast to East Asia, where growing grain imports are the result of economic gains, Africa's situation stems from the failures of its agricultural and population policies. Declining per capita food production since 1967 has created a situation where national food deficits in Africa are now the rule, not the exception.

IDEOLOGY AND AGRICULTURE

Few relationships between political systems and economic conditions have held as consistently during the last half of the century as that between socialism and national food deficits. Under socialist systems, agriculture has invariably gone downhill. Until recently, a socialist economy was, almost by definition, a food importer. China, Cuba, East Germany, Ethiopia, Poland, Romania, the Soviet Union, and Vietnam are obvious examples. China recently altered this relationship, however, when it broke ideological ranks and replaced its state-controlled agricultural system with a market-oriented one, in a successful move to achieve food self-sufficiency.

A comparison of farm production trends in China and the Soviet Union, the world's largest food-producing countries after the United States, graphically illustrates the influence of ideology on agricultural productivity. In a recent review of Chinese agricultural development, China analyst Frederick Surls observed that by the late seventies, "the [agricultural] policies of nearly two decades had created indifference among farmers; misuse of land, fertilizers and other inputs; and declining productiv-

ity."[35] This same language could have been used to describe Soviet agriculture.

Though plagued with similar lethargy and indifference among those working the land, the two governments responded differently. The Soviets recognized the need to restructure agriculture, but they were unable to introduce effective reforms because the party bureaucracy was unwilling to relinquish control of agriculture. Meanwhile, Chinese agriculture underwent a profound restructuring, providing the world with a real-life experiment in the transition from a state-controlled to a market-oriented system.

After the 1949 revolution in China, Beijing sought to collectivize agriculture along Soviet lines. In some ways adopting an even more strictly collectivist approach, the government organized the entire rural population into communes and production teams. The leadership concentrated on the redistribution of land to production brigades, formation of Agricultural Producer Cooperatives, and the adoption of central planning. From 1950 through the mid-seventies, grain production in the Soviet Union and China were closely parallel. (See Figure 1–6.) Only when Chinese food production fell sharply during the Great Leap Forward and its aftermath in 1958–62, or when Soviet output was sharply depressed by weather, as in 1975, did the two diverge markedly.[36]

Under socialist systems, agriculture has invariably gone downhill.

As agriculture modernizes, however, it becomes increasingly dependent on a range of off-farm physical inputs and support services and on the authority of those working the land to make on-the-spot decisions. Providing the appropri-

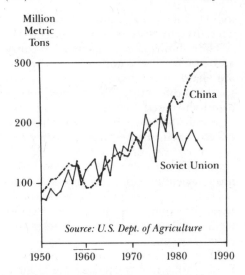

Million
Metric
Tons

300

China

200

Soviet Union

100

Source: U.S. Dept. of Agriculture

1950   1960   1970   1980   1990

**Figure 1-6. Grain Production in the Soviet Union
and China, 1950-84**

ate inputs in the proper amounts at the right times and being able to respond to continually changing farm conditions is virtually impossible when decision making is centralized. Individual farmers making day-to-day decisions in response to market signals, changing weather, and the conditions of their crops have a combined intelligence far exceeding that of a centralized bureaucracy, however well designed and competently staffed.

Recognizing this, in 1978 the Chinese decided to restructure their agricultural sector, shifting from tightly controlled production units to reliance on market forces, price incentives, and individual initiative. In addition, procurement prices for farm products were raised an average of roughly 20 percent, shifting the terms of trade between rural and urban areas in favor of the countryside. The resulting divergence in production trends could not be more dramatic. Soviet grain production, suffering from systemic agricultural failures, has declined by easily one fifth from its 1978 high. Meanwhile, Chinese agricultural production has surged ahead, surprising even leaders in Beijing with its vigor.[37]

Production of basic crops such as grains, soybeans, and cotton increased at record rates, as did production of fruits, vegetables, and livestock products. Rural incomes rose, and diets improved measurably. Production gains led to a sharp curtailment of wheat imports, which had once averaged close to 10 million tons per year. As recently as 1980, China was the world's largest cotton importer; today, it is a leading exporter, shipping a million bales abroad annually.[38]

In addition to the extensive use of animal and human wastes, the Chinese sharply boosted chemical fertilizer use during this period. Central to this increase has been a rapid rise in the availability of this product. The large nitrogen fertilizer plants imported from the West in the mid-seventies doubled China's fertilizer production capacity, making it the third largest producer, after the United States and the Soviet Union. Combined with rising imports, this pushed fertilizer consumption from less than 9 million tons in 1978 to nearly 18 million tons in 1984, one of the few cases where use is expanding rapidly. As fertilizer use rises and returns diminish, which they inevitably will, the record agricultural growth of recent years is likely to slow somewhat, however.[39]

These structural changes have transformed the Chinese countryside, unleashing energy and spurring innovation among the hundreds of millions who work the land. As of 1985, households have become the principal production unit, replacing collectives. USDA China analyst Terry Taylor reports: "In effect, the responsibility system has all but done away with collectivization. Labor organization and the management of production and distribution have been left largely in the hands of individual families."[40]

As individual initiative takes over in the Chinese countryside, it is simultaneously spurring production and increasing the efficiency of resource use. In 1985, the Chinese produced 100 million more tons of grain than they did a decade earlier, one of the most spectacular production surges ever recorded. But they achieved this impressive record on 8 percent less land, as they reversed the environmentally destructive policy launched by Mao Zedong of plowing marginal land for grain. While the land used was declining, irrigation expanded only moderately, but fertilizer use increased dramatically. The net effect of shifting to the "responsibility system" has been an impressive across-the-board increase in the efficiency of agricultural resource use, a gain that has boosted per capita food consumption by nearly half and that has eliminated China's food deficit.

In stark contrast to this record, grain production in the Soviet Union has fallen from a high of 229 million tons in 1978 to 190 million tons in 1985. Unable to introduce effective reforms due to an intransigent party bureaucracy, the Soviet Union now imports one fifth or more of its grain supplies. Bringing in some 35–55 million tons of grain yearly since 1978, the lion's share from the United States, the Soviet Union must now import massive quantities of grain continuously. The 1985 massive crop shortfall, the seventh consecutive one, signals a systemic deterioration of Soviet agriculture that, in the absence of reform, assures grain deficits far into the future.[41]

Discussions of Soviet agriculture, whether by Soviet officials, the Soviet press, or Western commentators, tend to focus on specific shortages and shortcomings. But these are symptoms of a more fundamental problem—the nature of the system itself. The principal weakness of Soviet agriculture, with its giant state farms, is that there is little incentive for those who live on the land to work hard and to innovate. Merely appointing more competent farm managers, as Mik-

hail Gorbachev has done in his early months as leader, may boost output marginally, but it will not revitalize Soviet agriculture. There is an inherent conflict between a centrally planned, state-controlled agricultural system and a highly productive, modern one. The more the Soviets try to modernize their agriculture, the more obvious the conflict will become.[42]

RETIRING OUR DEBTS

The world's economic difficulties—especially the proliferation of unmanageable debts plaguing countries in every region and at every income level—provide ample evidence of ill-conceived policies and misplaced priorities. Enforced austerity nearly always falls most heavily on those least able to bear the burden of a decline in living standards—the poor, and particularly women and children. Ironically, the countries with the brightest prospects, such as Sri Lanka and China, are those that have placed highest priority on improving the lives of just these groups.

Few countries in the Third World have ignited an economic improvement as rapid and broad-based as that now under way in China, one of the few Third World countries that has no external debt to speak of. While many developing and industrial economies have stagnated or declined over the last decade, China's economic expansion has accelerated. Campaigns in family planning, rural health care, primary education, and female literacy in the seventies laid the foundation for the economic reforms in 1978 that boosted the nation's growth rates. At the same time that leaders in Beijing have fashioned policies to slow population growth and push harvests ahead, they have cut the military share of the country's budget by nearly half.[43]

Even though average incomes in China are still lower than in most Third World countries, levels of health and longevity are comparable to those in industrial societies. Indeed, the country's birth rate, infant mortality rate, and life expectancy at birth rank closer to those of the United States than to the remainder of the Third World. (See Table 1–8.) Its birth rate of 19 is only slightly above that in industrial countries. Its infant mortality rate of 38 is close to that in some American cities. And life expectancy, at 65 years, denotes lasting conquest of major childhood diseases. Sri Lanka's infant mortality rate of 37 and life expectancy of 69 indicate equally impressive progress, and with an average income of scarcely $300 per year.[44]

China's low birth rate has allowed the country to concentrate on providing better opportunities for its children. Ninety-five percent of Chinese children are enrolled in primary school, and the country's 80 percent literacy rate is among the highest in the Third World. Women have perhaps gained most from these advances. Nine girls out of ten are enrolled in school, and Chinese women can expect to live to age 69, longer than in any other developing country.[45]

Sustainable economic growth has eluded societies that neglect these basic indicators of well-being. The consequences of this neglect cannot be offset by deficit financing, as Latin America's principal debtor countries demonstrate. Brazil has incurred its $104-billion debt without noticeably reducing its infant

mortality rate of 70, among the highest in the region. In addition, its income distribution is one of the world's least equitable: The average income of the wealthiest one fifth of the population is 33 times higher than that of the poorest fifth.[46]

Widespread environmental decline only exacerbates Africa's steadily deteriorating financial position.

Mexico, $97 billion in debt, is in much the same position. With an infant mortality rate of 50 and an income disparity of 20 to 1, painful adjustments lie ahead. Such fundamental social inequities may prove incompatible with the kind of economic recovery needed to manage even partial repayment of Latin American debts.[47]

Africa's principal deficits are agronomic and ecological, but widespread environmental decline only exacerbates the continent's steadily deteriorating financial position. Even though sustained economic recovery in Africa does not appear imminent, China and Sri Lanka demonstrate that basic improvements in living standards and the environment do not depend on high incomes.

Effective soil conservation and reforestation efforts, based on people rather than on capital, can stabilize Africa's land and restore the hydrological cycle,

Table 1-8. Basic Economic and Social Indicators for Industrial World, China, and Rest of Third World, 1985

	Industrial World	China	Rest of Third World
Per Capita GNP (dollars)	9,380	290	880
Birth Rate (per 1,000 population)	15	19	36
Infant Mortality (per 1,000 live births)	18	38	101
Life Expectancy at Birth (years)	73	65	56

SOURCE: Population Reference Bureau, *1985 World Population Data Sheet* (Washington, D.C.: 1985).

laying a foundation for better harvests. In virtually every African country today, forests are in decline and croplands are eroding; China, meanwhile, has begun increasing its tree cover while boosting harvests.

One region of the world where economic trends are not clear-cut is the Indian subcontinent, whose population will reach 1 billion within a matter of years, barring an unanticipated decline in birth rates. By some measures India, by far the most populous country in the region, is doing well; by others, it remains in jeopardy. India has achieved food self-sufficiency, but it has done so by ending imports with per capita grain consumption of a rather meager 185 kilograms, barely above subsistence needs. This contrasts with China, which ended food imports when per capita consumption was at 290 kilograms, a level that largely eliminates undernutrition. India has attained the economic base needed for rapid progress, but the weight of an additional 16 million people each year threatens to undermine economic and social improvements.[48]

Although the expectation of a longer life is one of the most heartening indicators of progress toward improved living standards, mortality trends sometimes reveal astonishing gaps in well-being even in the wealthiest societies. For example, in the United States, smoking-related diseases now kill some 375,000 people each year.[49]

Cigarettes brought premature death to 1 in every 640 Americans in 1985—a rate that, if adjusted for population, approaches the death toll of Africa's famine of roughly 1 in 540. Starvation's victims are disproportionately children; in contrast, the victims of cigarette-linked heart attacks and cancer, nearly always adults, often die in their economic prime. (See Chapters 8 and 9.) Both these tolls are preventable; neither should be considered tolerable in modern society.

When life spans shortened by smoking and other "life-style" diseases go unattended long enough, the premature mortality may begin to erase the gains in life expectancy achieved by assuring child survival. The Soviet Union may be the first industrial country to suffer such a reversal: Soviet men now have a shorter life expectancy than they did just a few years ago. Although an official explanation has not been offered, 65 percent of Soviet men smoke, nearly twice the U.S. rate. Smoking-related deaths are compounded by widespread alcoholism. Although a national campaign was inaugurated in 1985 to curb excessive drinking, no such effort has yet been aimed at cigarettes.[50]

Deficits of many kinds plague the world in 1986. We have begun to recognize that Third World debts are not exclusively a Third World concern, and that solutions will require a partnership of debtors and creditors. Another key point needs to be acknowledged—that the many fiscal, ecological, and social debts we incur today come at our children's expense. We can begin to retire our debts by recognizing that policies that take seriously the interests of the next generation usually best serve the current generation as well.

2

Assessing Ecological Decline

Lester R. Brown and Edward C. Wolf

Ecologists have long lamented the world's casual approach toward altering ecosystems with scant understanding of the consequences. Two recent studies— one by the World Bank on Ethiopia's deteriorating agricultural ecosystem, and one by a Yale University researcher on the effects of air pollution and acid rain on northeastern U.S. forests—have assessed the effect of growing stress, physical or chemical, on ecosystems. Both trace the stages of deterioration as pressures intensify. Each reaches the same conclusion: If the stresses are great enough, the ecosystem will deteriorate and eventually collapse.[1]

For a number of scientists, this comes as no surprise. A small community of ecologists have been warning for years that the stresses caused by population growth and pollution can lead to ecosystem deterioration. Such deterioration is now adversely affecting economic trends in scores of countries, mostly in the Third World. And for some governments, coping with the economic consequences of ecological deterioration has become a full-time challenge.

PROFILES OF ECOLOGICAL DECLINE

Accumulating evidence from ecology, agronomy, and hydrology indicates that sustained overuse of biological systems can set in motion changes that are self-reinforcing. Each stage of deterioration hastens the onset of the next. When destructive ecological change is coupled with rapid human population growth in subsistence economies, the stage for human tragedy is set.

World Bank energy analyst and ecologist Kenneth Newcombe has described how complex, interrelated systems unravel through several stages. His model, based on fieldwork in Ethiopia, portrays a cascading decline in biological and economic productivity triggered by loss of tree cover. According to Newcombe, as people seek new agricultural land, natural forests retreat before the plow. Without trees, mineral nutrients are no longer recycled from deep soil layers. As this nutrient cycle is breached, soil fertility begins to decline. In this first stage, wood supplies remain sufficient and the gradual erosion of cropland fertility is imperceptible.[2]

As rural and village populations grow, markets appear for wood, both for construction and for household fuels. Cutting wood from remnant forests generates income for peasant families, who generally burn crop residues and animal dung in their own households. This in turn interrupts two more nutrient cycles: Removing crop residues and diverting dung from fields degrades soil structure and leaves the land more vulnerable to erosion. On sloping fields, annual soil erosion of 50–100 tons per hectare is common. The depletion of remaining forests then accelerates, and the loss of soil fertility begins to reduce crop yields.

Once nearby stands of trees are gone, dung and crop residues turn up in local markets where formerly only wood was sold. The steady loss of nutrients and organic matter from croplands severely limits crop yields and the ability of pastures to support livestock. A greater share of family cash income comes from the sale of dung than from that of food crops, for erratic crop yields prove barely sufficient even for subsistence.

Eventually, cow dung becomes the main fuel source in villages and thus the main cash crop from nearby farms. Rural families use crop residues for cooking and as fodder for their livestock, which can no longer be supported by grazing land. Pervasive topsoil depletion leaves farmers vulnerable to total crop failure during even routine dry seasons. In markets, both food and fuel prices rise rapidly.

When this final stage is reached in a subsistence economy, biological productivity is destined to collapse. Families can no longer produce enough food for themselves or their livestock, let alone for markets. A massive exodus from rural areas begins, often triggered by drought that could formerly have been tolerated. Famine is widespread; peasants' lack of purchasing power is compounded by absolute shortages of food at any price.

This model of an accelerating cycle of degradation is now being confirmed in portions of Africa. A joint U.N. Development Program/World Bank report points out that "this transition from the first to the final stage is in process right across Ethiopia and has reached the terminal phase in parts of Tigre and Eritrea."[3] At a World Bank workshop in Botswana in March 1985, Newcombe warned "There is evidence that [the final stage] has already been reached in some areas of several countries in Southern Africa and that virtually every country has areas that have reached [the point at which wood gathering has overtaken land clearing as a cause of deforestation]."[4]

Once nearby stands of trees are gone, dung and crop residues turn up in local markets where formerly only wood was sold.

The cascading effect Newcombe describes results from disruption of the self-regulating mechanisms of natural systems on which humans depend. The distinct stages of decline, and the event that pushes the system into instability, can be identified. Newcombe believes a critical point occurs in subsistence economies when more trees are cut for fuel than to make way for farmland.

The U.N. Food and Agriculture Organization (FAO) estimates that 60–70 percent of the outright clearing of forests and woodlands in tropical Africa is for agriculture. In many countries, however, wood collection for fuel and other uses exceeds the sustainable yield of remaining accessible forests. A 1980 World Bank study of West Africa showed that fuelwood demand exceeded estimated sustainable yields in 11 of the 13 countries surveyed. Only in Senegal and Ghana was the annual growth of remaining woodlands believed sufficient to satisfy demand.[5]

The degree of imbalance between demand and sustainable yields of wood varies widely. For example, in both semiarid Mauritania and mountainous Rwanda, firewood demand is 10 times the sustainable yield of remaining forests. In Kenya, the ratio is 5 to 1; in Ethiopia, Tanzania, and Nigeria, demand is 2.5 times the sustainable yield, and in Sudan, it is roughly double.[6]

Sudan's wood imbalance illustrates the interaction between rapidly expanding populations and their biological support systems. Estimates based on World Bank data indicate that national fuelwood consumption crossed the sustainable yield threshold somewhere around 1965. From then on, fuelwood consumption exceeded new tree growth, gradually diminishing both the forest stock and each year's growth.[7] (See Figures 2–1 and 2–2.)

During the first few years after the sustainable yield threshold was crossed, forests in Sudan changed little. After 20 years, forested area had contracted by about one fifth. In the next 20 years, however, expanding demand is likely to deplete all the remaining woodlands. During the first half of this 40-year span there is little evidence of the problems coming in the second half. But once the mid-point is passed, only extraordinary efforts in family planning and tree planting can halt the system's complete collapse.

An analysis of chemical stress on forest ecosystems in the northeastern United States by ecologist F.H. Bormann of Yale University's School of Forestry resembles Newcombe's analysis of physical stress on rural ecosystems in Africa. Specifically, Bormann addressed the effects of air pollution and acid rain.

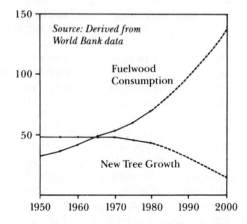

Figure 2-1. Fuelwood Consumption and New Tree Growth in Sudan, 1950-80, With Projections to 2000

Like Newcombe, he identified several stages in the deterioration of forests. At first, pollution stress is minimal, and effects on the forest ecosystem are negligible. As pollution levels increase, the more sensitive species begin to suffer, and the overall structure of the forest

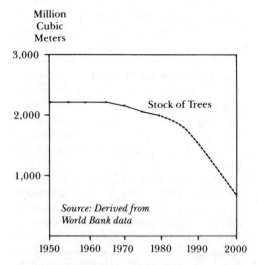

Figure 2-2. Standing Stock of Trees in Sudan, 1950-80, With Projections to 2000

ecosystem begins to change. Typically, the larger species are the first to go, followed by shrubs and herbs. Over time, as pollution stress accumulates, productivity drops. And the ability of the ecosystem to repair itself diminishes.[8]

As the vegetative density is reduced, so too is the amount of nutrients held in the system. At this point, increases in rainfall runoff and the erosion of soil become noticeable. The export of soil and nutrients to adjacent streams and lakes can be severely disruptive. In the absence of human intervention to remove the source of chemical stress, the ecosystem will continue to deteriorate, and eventually collapse. As graphic illustrations of this final stage of ecosystem collapse, Bormann cites the degraded ecosystems that now exist around strong sources of air pollution, such as Copper Hill, Tennessee, and Sudbury, Ontario.

The pollution-related deterioration of forest ecosystems is difficult to analyze partly because pollutants are varied and wide-ranging. Seemingly healthy forests may act as a sink for pollutants over a long period of time before showing stress. On the other hand, chemical stress often weakens the more sensitive species, making them more vulnerable to natural events such as drought, frost, attacks by insects, or disease. An unprecedented insect outbreak, for example, could be the result of a physiological weakening of the plant species, leaving it open to exploitation by insects.

Another study that charted pressures on ecosystems dealt with grasslands in nine countries of southern Africa that are being degraded by physical stress. (See Chapter 4 for further discussion of this ecosystem.) The problem is particularly noticeable in Africa, where livestock numbers have expanded nearly as fast as the human population. In 1950, Africa had 219 million people and a livestock population of 295 million. Since then, the continent's population has in-

creased two and a half times, reaching 513 million in 1983. Meanwhile, livestock numbers have expanded by three fourths, increasing to 518 million.[9]

Because little grain is available for feeding livestock, the continent's 176 million cattle, 190 million sheep, and 152 million goats are supported almost entirely by grazing or browsing. Everywhere outside the tsetse fly belt, livestock are vital to the economy. But in many countries, herds and flocks are destroying the grass resource that sustains them.[10]

The U.N. report, by FAO, reveals the extent of overgrazing in the nine nations of southern Africa: "For some countries and major areas of others, present herds exceed the carrying capacity by 50 to 100 percent. This has led to deterioration of the soil—thereby lowering the carrying capacity even more—and to severe soil erosion in an accelerating cycle of degradation."[11] Heavy grazing, combined with declining rainfall, gradually changes the character of rangeland vegetation and its capacity to support livestock.

As grazing and wood gathering increase in semiarid regions, rapidly reproducing annual grasses replace perennial grasses and woody perennial shrubs. The loss of trees such as the acacias in the Sahel (the band of semiarid savanna that extends across Africa south of the Sahara) means less forage in the dry season, when the protein-rich acacia pods formerly fed livestock on otherwise barren rangeland. Annual grasses that come to dominate the landscape are far more sensitive to water stress than perennials, and may not germinate at all in drought years. A range already shrinking as cultivated land expands can no longer sustain local herds, even in wet years.

As Africa's grasslands deteriorate, the composition of its livestock population is changing. From 1950 to 1970, the conti-

Table 2-1. Changes in Africa's Cattle, Sheep, and Goat Populations, 1950–70 and 1970–83

| | Average Annual Change ||
	1950–70	1970–83
	(percent)	
Cattle	+2.15	+0.83
Sheep	+1.67	+2.36
Goats	+1.67	+2.19

SOURCE: U.N. Food and Agriculture Organization, *Production Yearbook* (Rome: various years).

nent's cattle herd grew over 2 percent per year, somewhat faster than that of either sheep or goats. (See Table 2–1.) Since 1970, herd growth has been halved, while that of the sheep and goat populations has actually accelerated. This shift toward livestock dependent on woody foliage reflects a period of unrelenting rainfall decline that has diminished forage grasses, which in turn intensifies pressure on the woodlands that also supply household fuel.

Although environmental deterioration has now reached the point where it is visibly shaping Africa's economic future, little effort has been devoted to systematically measuring changes in the continent's support systems. One notable exception to this is a survey done for the United Nations Environment Programme by Leonard Berry of Clark University. (See Table 2–2.) Initially undertaken for 14 countries and covering the period 1977–84 (see *State of the World-1985*), the assessment has since been expanded to cover some 20 countries and updated through 1985. The inclusion of eastern and southern Africa confirms the sobering findings of the earlier study.

The countries included in the latest assessment, representing a cross section of the continent, have a combined population of 281 million people, just over half Africa's total. The survey focused on five manifestations of ecological deterio-

ration: sand dune encroachment, the deterioration of rangelands, forest depletion, the deterioration of irrigation systems, and problems in rainfed agriculture. Not one of the 100 indicators—5 for each of the 20 countries—showed any improvement. Roughly one fifth of the readings did not change significantly during the eight years under review. Almost half of the measurements showed a moderate deterioration. And over a quarter revealed serious deterioration, indicating a marked reduction in the ecosystem's capacity to support economic activity.

The climatic, ecological, economic, and demographic trends reflected in Berry's survey are interdependent and continuously interacting. All show signs of the self-reinforcing deterioration that Kenneth Newcombe has also documented, a cycle of degradation that progressively robs the land of its resilience and reduces the economic choices open to people who depend on it.

Economic Costs

Ecological deterioration, an insidious process resulting from mismanagement of resources, eventually affects economic development adversely. Real production costs and imports rise, while land and labor productivity, output, exports, and tax revenues fall. Whether the evidence is regional water shortages in the United States, firewood shortages in India, or food shortages in Africa, the relationship between wasted and abused resources and economic stresses has become readily apparent. Even more apparent is the tendency of ecologically induced economic decline to ignore national boundaries.

Excessive pressures on land and land mismanagement have led to widespread

Table 2-2. Desertification Trends in Selected African Countries, 1977–85

Country	Sand Dune Encroachment	Deterioration in Rangelands	Forest Depletion	Deterioration of Irrigation Systems	Rain-fed Agriculture Problems
Botswana	+	+	o	o	o
Burkina Faso	o	+	+	+	++
Cameroon	o	+	+	o	+
Chad	++	++	+	++	++
Ethiopia	+	++	++	+	+
Guinea	o	o	+	+	++
Kenya	o	++	+	o	+
Lesotho	n.a.	+	++	o	++
Mali	+	++	++	+	+
Mauritania	+	++	++	+	+
Niger	+	++	+	++	+
Nigeria	o	+	++	o	+
Senegal	+	++	+	+	++
Somalia	+	+	+	++	+
Sudan	++	+	+	+	o
Swaziland	n.a.	+	++	o	++
Tanzania	n.a.	++	+	n.a.	++
Uganda	o	++	o	o	+
Zambia	n.a.	n.a.	n.a.	+	+
Zimbabwe	n.a.	++	+	+	++

Key: o = stable, + = some increase, ++ = significant increase, n.a. = not available or not applicable.
SOURCE: Adapted from Leonard Berry, "Desertification: Problems of Restoring Productivity in Dry Areas of Africa," presented to the 1985 Annual Meeting Symposium, African Development Bank, Brazzaville, Congo, May 8, 1985.

cropland degradation on every continent. Worldwide, agricultural output has more than doubled over the past generation, though trends in cropland productivity have varied widely. At the upper end of the spectrum, some countries have tripled land productivity. Others have actually experienced a decline. In addition to the degradation of land already under cultivation, average crop yields have also been reduced by the extension of agriculture onto shallow soils, steeply sloping land, or the arid fringe of cropping regions.[12]

Since mid-century, the combination of advancing technology and rising investment in agriculture has enabled most countries to override the negative effects of land degradation. But some 14 nations have failed to do so. (See Table 2–3.) Ranging in size from tiny Guyana in Latin America to Nigeria, the most populous country in Africa, they have experienced an average decline in grain yields of roughly one fifth.

Of these 14 countries, the most pronounced decline occurred in Sudan, where the average yield in 1982–84 was 44 percent below that of 1950–52. This is somewhat ironic, because as recently as the late seventies this country was slated to become the breadbasket for the Middle East, an area in which its food-deficit, capital-surplus neighbors could invest. Instead, land degradation and declining rainfall in the region have con-

Table 2-3. Countries with Declining Grain Yields Per Hectare, 1950–52 to 1982–84

Country	1950–52	1982–84	Decrease
	(kilograms)		(percent)
Sudan	780	436	−44
Tanzania	1,271	900	−29
Niger	458	379	−17
Mozambique	610	521	−15
Zambia	952	819	−14
Ghana	764	686	−10
Lebanon	869	786	−10
Rwanda	1,122	1,010	−10
Nigeria	760	694	− 9
Guyana	2,231	2,099	− 6
Iraq	703	657	− 6
Kampuchea	1,002	939	− 6
Algeria	648	613	− 5
Zaire	902	878	− 3

SOURCE: U.S. Department of Agriculture, Economic Research Service, *World Indices of Agricultural and Food Production, 1950–84* (unpublished printout) (Washington, D.C.: 1985).

verted Sudan, one of the world's poorest countries, into a nation of refugee camps and feeding stations.

Nigeria, the most populous country to experience a decline in land productivity, is one of three oil-exporting countries with falling yields. Clearly, the mere availability of capital does not necessarily prevent land degradation. And political conflicts, such as the war between Iraq and Iran, can divert both capital and human resources from agriculture on a scale that affects land productivity.

Iraq's yields have declined 6 percent since the early fifties. Waterlogging and salting of its soils bode ill for future land productivity, yet agriculture is not getting the attention it deserves. Yields in Iran have increased by only 5 percent, compared with the global average of 97 percent. The war is hindering agricultural development and contributing to environmental degradation in both nations.[13]

The countries listed in Table 2–3 are not necessarily those with the most serious land degradation; they are only the ones where the advances in agricultural technology have not been sufficient to override the negative effects of such deterioration or of the addition of marginal land to the cropland base. In many countries, cropland degradation is being offset by the heavy use of chemical fertilizer. Over time, as energy becomes more costly, this substitution of artificial for natural fertility will become more difficult.

Just as cropland degradation reduces food supplies in Third World countries, degradation of woodlands reduces fuel supplies. After a point, the loss of tree cover translates into firewood scarcity and rising prices, a trend that can clearly be seen in Addis Ababa. During the 13 years from 1970 through 1983, firewood prices in Addis Ababa more than tripled, but even this was modest compared with some other parts of Africa and even with other locations in Ethiopia. In the eco-

Table 2-4. India: Prices of Firewood in Selected Cities, 1960, 1975, and 1983 (current prices)

City	1960	1975	1983	Ratio of 1983 to 1960
	(rupees per 100 kilograms)			
Bangalore	4.7	21.0	50.0	10.64
Indore	5.7	24.3	60.0	10.53
Bombay	8.5	36.1	85.7	10.08
Kanpur	6.1	21.0	52.3	8.57
Delhi	10.1	—	85.0	8.42
Hyderabad	6.6	23.2	55.0	8.33
Madras	8.2	25.4	59.1	7.21
Calcutta	9.3	—	61.3	6.59
Ahmedabad	9.0	28.3	55.5	6.17

SOURCE: Based on data in Centre for Science and Environment, *The State of India's Environment, 1984–85* (New Delhi: 1985).

logically devastated provinces of Eritrea and Tigre, fuelwood prices in the early eighties were roughly double those in Addis.[14]

India, too, is facing a fuelwood shortage. As firewood becomes more scarce, India's urban centers import wood from ever greater distances. Delhi, for example, now ships firewood from the states of Orissa, Bihar, Maharashtra, and Assam, the latter some 1,000 kilometers away. Even with these imports from distant states, the number of firewood rail wagons unloaded in Delhi plummeted from 12,424 in 1981–82 to 7,577 just two years later. This decline in deliveries helps explain why firewood prices in Delhi were eight times higher in 1983 than in 1960. (See Table 2–4.) Bombay and Bangalore experienced even greater price hikes during the same period.[15]

A survey undertaken in the late seventies in Madhya Pradesh, an Indian state with a population of 52 million, located in the geographic center of the Indian subcontinent, showed that 26 of its 45 districts faced a fuelwood deficit. Following this survey, the state—India's leading exporter of firewood—banned such exports in August 1981. In contrast with OPEC export embargoes, this ban did not aim to raise firewood prices elsewhere, but to bring down the price paid by the state's residents.[16]

In some Third World countries, urban dwellers spend one fourth of their income on cooking fuel. Government officials in New Delhi already question where India's projected year 2000 population of 994 million will find the fuel to cook their food. The shift from firewood to cow dung and crop residues that invariably accompanies a loss of tree cover is well under way in India, as data for Madhya Pradesh indicate.[17] (See Table 2–5.)

Although widespread air pollution and acid rain are recent compared with

Table 2-5. Household Fuel Consumption in the Indian State of Madhya Pradesh

Fuel	Quantity
	(million tons)
Cow Dung	9.64
Firewood	9.47
Crop Residues	6.93

SOURCE: Centre for Science and Environment, *The State of India's Environment, 1984–85* (New Delhi: 1985).

soil erosion, some of their costs are beginning to surface. A study by the Czechoslovakian Academy of Sciences estimated annual damage from acid rain to be at least $1.5 billion, with the loss of forests accounting for most of the total. With this Academy report, Czechoslovakia became one of the first countries to recognize the effect of air pollution and acid rain on farm productivity, thus linking fossil fuel combustion and agricultural output.[18]

The Czechoslovakian Academy of Sciences estimated annual damage from acid rain to be at least $1.5 billion.

According to the Academy, increasing soil acidity and air pollution are adversely affecting crops, preventing the full gains in yields expected from the tripling in fertilizer use since 1960. Referring to soil poisoning from acid rain, the report noted that increased acidity was altering soils by chemically tying up nutrients essential to plants and releasing aluminum and other toxic metals. The Academy estimated that arresting this process in severely affected woodlands would require spreading lime at the rate of 5 to 10 tons per hectare.[19]

West Germany is deeply concerned with both the aesthetic and economic costs of losing its forests to air pollution and acid rain. As early as 1983, the Bavarian Agricultural Ministry estimated the loss of trees in southern Germany at $1.2 billion. Ironically, in the short run, damage to German forests is expected to increase harvesting and reduce timber prices. Over the longer term, however, timber prices will rise as the forested area dwindles and trees become scarce.[20]

The loss of tree cover and land degradation, whether from excessive firewood cutting or from air pollution (chemical stresses), also affect the hydrological cycle. As land is degraded, its ability to absorb and retain water diminishes, and the share of rainfall that runs off, returning directly to the ocean, increases. One consequence is a reduction in aquifer recharge and falling water tables.

A project undertaken at Hatcliffe Research Station in Zimbabwe shows how land use changes affect rainfall runoff when a natural grassland is cleared for cultivation. Agronomist Henry Elwell measured the runoff from test plots on gently sloping savanna land under different cover, ranging from undisturbed natural vegetation to bare soil. (See Table 2–6.) He found that as the ungrazed savanna was replaced by bare land, the share of rainfall running off increased from 1 percent to 35. The 4.5 percent slope of the test plots at Hatcliffe is gentle compared with land under the plow in many Third World countries.

Another consequence of increased runoff is a greater frequency and severity of floods. The Swedish Red Cross reports that the number of floods worldwide classified as severe jumped from 15 in the sixties to 22 in the seventies, an increase of one half. The annual death toll from these disasters climbed sixfold,

Table 2-6. Rainfall Runoff Under Varying Land Uses at Hatcliffe Research Station, Zimbabwe (4.5 percent slope)

Vegetative Cover	Share of Annual Rainfall Running Off
	(percent)
Natural Vegetation[1]	1
Clipped Grass	8
Soybeans	20
Bare Soil	35

[1]Mostly tall grass, ungrazed.
SOURCE: Personal communication with H.A. Elwell, Institute of Agricultural Engineering, Ministry of Agriculture, Harare, Zimbabwe, May 2, 1985.

a reflection of the greater severity of the flooding and a growth in size of vulnerable populations.[21]

Some countries have recently lost valuable stocks of tropical timber to fire, until recently a rare phenomenon in a tropical rain forest. Such areas are normally resistant to fire, but they have been dried out from tightening slash-and-burn cycles, from tree cutting for timber, or from firewood gathering, and they have consequently become vulnerable in drought years. In the spring of 1983, a forest fire in Kalimantan burned for three months, eventually consuming 2 million hectares of tropical rain forest.[22]

The Ivory Coast also experienced a massive forest fire in that year. Like the one in Kalimantan, the triggering event was a sharp reduction in rainfall. Before it was over, the fire in the Ivory Coast had destroyed some 450,000 hectares of forest, much of it high-value tropical hardwoods. In neighboring Ghana, forest fires during the same period consumed an estimated 10 percent of the country's cocoa plantations, reducing the earnings from the country's principal export crop.[23]

Declines in rainfall affect not only rain-fed agriculture but also irrigated agriculture and hydroelectric generation. For example, the World Bank observed that in 1984 Ghana's generation of electricity from hydropower, its principal source of this power, was three fourths lower than the level of just two years earlier. This led to a shutdown of Ghana's aluminum smelter, which reduced export earnings by some $18 million in 1983. When added to the loss of cocoa exports, estimated at some $76 million, and the need for increased food imports as a result of the decline in rainfall, the adverse balance-of-payments effect easily exceeds $100 million.[24]

The energy sector of the Ivory Coast was also deeply affected by the decline in rainfall. In December 1983, this nation that normally obtains some two thirds of its electricity from hydropower generation had to switch entirely to thermal power plants, costing the electricity company an estimated $100 million. These examples illustrate how a decline in rainfall can markedly reduce output of both the agricultural and energy sectors.[25]

The livestock sector, too, has been greatly affected by the deterioration of grasslands and the disruptions associated with rainfall declines. The World Bank reports, for example, that Botswana lost 600,000 head of cattle in 1983 and 1984, sharply reducing its long-term capacity to export livestock products. Lesotho lost 58,000 head of cattle and 243,000 sheep. During the same period, Zimbabwe lost an estimated 50,000 head of cattle. At least a dozen other African countries have experienced similar herd reductions during the eighties, and for the same reasons. In many situations herds will be rebuilt, but in some, where rangeland degradation is severe and topsoil has been lost, the liquidation may be final.[26]

In Africa, where 40 percent of the people live in countries with falling land productivity, ecological deterioration is slowing economic growth and in some cases causing economic decline. On a continent where agriculture is the primary livelihood, this decline has contributed to the roughly one-fifth reduction in per capita income since 1970. As long as Africa's population continues to expand rapidly, ecological degradation is likely to continue, and its economic consequences will no doubt worsen.[27]

THE SOCIAL CONSEQUENCES

Of all the social consequences of ecological deterioration, falling per capita food production and the increase in malnutrition and mortality that often follows are undoubtedly the most serious. Some countries have offset declines in per capita food production with commercial imports or food aid, but in many others, belt-tightening is the only possible response. For those living in countries where average consumption is already close to the subsistence level, further reductions lead to increased malnutrition, rising death rates, and, in severe cases, famine of the sort that has plagued many African countries in the mid-eighties.

Failed or nonexistent population policies can both expand demand for food and undermine agricultural support systems.

The unprecedented technological advance and economic progress of the past generation notwithstanding, more than 40 developing countries are producing less grain per person in the mid-eighties than they did in the early fifties. (See Table 2–7.) The declines range widely, from 85 percent in Lebanon to 2 percent or less in Bangladesh and Costa Rica. Not by coincidence, the great majority of the countries are in Africa, the Middle East, Central America, and the Andean region—areas where ecological deterioration is proceeding most rapidly. Together, these nations are home to over 700 million people, some 15 percent of the world total.[28]

In a few industrial countries, such as Japan and Taiwan (not included in Table 2–7), declines follow a planned shift of labor to the nonfarm sector. Japanese agricultural policy has been designed to maintain essential self-sufficiency in rice, the national food staple, while greatly increasing imports of the feedgrains consumed by its burgeoning livestock and poultry industries. Taiwan is following similar policies.

The decline in per capita grain production in most countries is not exclusively due to ecological deterioration. Inattention to population policy and the overall neglect of agriculture have also contributed. Failed or nonexistent population policies can both expand demand for food and undermine agricultural support systems. In essence, population growth hastens the process of ecological decline.

Virtually all the countries with falling land productivity (see Table 2–3) also experienced a decline in per capita grain production. The only exceptions were Zambia, Tanzania, and Guyana, where the cultivated area grew faster than the population and more than offset the decline in land productivity.

Although the spotlight in recent years has focused on the agricultural decline in Africa, the Middle East has experienced an even greater fall in per capita grain production. Iraq, Jordan, and Lebanon have experienced declines since mid-century that range from 61 to 85 percent. In almost every Middle Eastern country, the growth in agricultural output is falling further behind population growth with each passing year.

This situation has attracted less attention than Africa's because the falling grain output per person has been offset by growth in oil-financed grain imports. As long as oil exports are available to finance rising food deficits in the Middle East, agricultural deterioration can be ignored. But some day these countries will find themselves with far larger populations, with little oil remaining to finance food imports, and with a thoroughly degraded agricultural resource base.

The two principal exceptions to the agricultural deterioration in the Middle East are Israel and Saudi Arabia. Israel has worked hard to restore its agricul-

Table 2-7. Developing Countries with Declining Grain Production Per Person, 1950–52 to 1982–84

Country	1950–52	1982–84	Decrease
	(kilograms/year)		(percent)
North Africa			
Algeria	219	79	−64
Libya	106	69	−35
Morocco	258	177	−31
Tunisia	196	154	−21
Sub-Saharan Africa			
Mozambique	97	36	−63
Mali	242	134	−45
Angola	81	45	−44
Kenya	226	139	−38
Nigeria	171	111	−35
Ghana	66	44	−33
Uganda	155	107	−31
Guinea	131	95	−27
Rwanda	58	43	−26
Zaire	39	32	−18
Benin	124	103	−17
Senegal	139	118	−15
Cameroon	112	97	−13
Togo	121	108	−11
Liberia	153	139	− 9
Niger	286	260	− 9
Sudan	114	104	− 9
Sierra Leone	155	143	− 8
Ethiopia	202	189	− 6
Burkina Faso	181	177	− 2
Middle East			
Lebanon	54	8	−85
Jordan	138	44	−68
Iraq	269	105	−61
Syria	315	215	−32
Iran	193	176	− 9
Turkey	472	446	− 5
Latin America			
Haiti	135	75	−44
Honduras	194	133	−31
Nicaragua	188	136	−28
Panama	174	136	−22
Chile	192	153	−20
Peru	105	85	−19
El Salvador	142	129	− 9
Cuba	55	52	− 5
Costa Rica	142	141	− 1
Asia			
Kampuchea	401	267	−33
Afghanistan	417	324	−22
Nepal	296	243	−18
Bangladesh	240	235	− 2

SOURCE: U.S. Department of Agriculture, Economic Research Service, *World Indices of Agricultural and Food Production, 1950–84* (unpublished printout) (Washington, D.C.: 1985).

tural productivity to the levels that once existed in the region, literally converting desert into gardens. Its achievements demonstrate the potential for reversing the worsening situation in the Middle East and elsewhere if the political commitment exists.

Saudi Arabia has also achieved impressive agricultural advances in recent years, but with exorbitant investments of oil money. For example, it has greatly expanded wheat production through the use of costly water drawn from aquifers far beneath the earth's surface. Unfortunately, this may not be financially sustainable over the long term, since it is based on a wheat support price of $28 a bushel—seven times the 1985 world price of $4 per bushel.[29]

The Middle East is unique in that it is experiencing simultaneously some of the most severe ecological degradation and worst political turbulence of any region. The longstanding conflicts between Israel and its Arab neighbors, the internal disintegration of Lebanon, and the war between Iran and Iraq that has stretched on for some five years are exacting a heavy long-term cost.

In North Africa, per capita grain production is falling in the entire northern tier of countries except Egypt. Ironically, these countries occupy the lands that were once the granary of the Roman Empire. Algeria and Libya now import over half the grain they consume. In sub-Saharan Africa, the great majority of people live in countries where per capita food production is falling. In seven countries, with about a third of the continent's population, per capita grain production has declined between one third and one half since mid-century.

The comparison of yield data for the early fifties and mid-eighties in Table 2–7 does not fully convey the gravity of the situation in Africa, since in many countries—indeed, for Africa as a whole —grain production per person actually rose from mid-century through the late sixties. Thus the declines since the late sixties have been even more precipitous than those shown for the longer time period covered in the table.

There are nine countries in Latin America and the Caribbean with falling per capita grain production. They tend to be the smaller nations, concentrated in Central America and the southern Andes. Of the three countries astride the southern Andes, grain production per capita in two, Chile and Peru, has declined by one fifth since mid-century. Only Bolivia was able to eke out any gain at all.

As a continent, Asia has fared well on the food front, largely because of production gains in China and India. Of the four countries where per capita grain production has fallen, Kampuchea and Afghanistan have been torn by war for the last several years. The other two— Nepal and Bangladesh—are suffering from severe ecological degradation. Indeed, the deforestation of Nepal is not only increasing soil erosion and undermining agriculture there, it is contributing to the severity of floods that destroy crops and trigger famine downstream. In Bangladesh, which ranks with Ethiopia, Chad, and Mali as one of the world's poorest countries, famine is never more than one flood away.

Assessing the effect on nutrition of land degradation and falling per capita food production is hindered by the paucity of research on this linkage. One of the few studies that links population pressure with soil erosion and nutrition is a World Bank report by William Jones and Roberto Egli. They note that in the Great Lakes Highlands of Rwanda, Burundi, and Zaire: "As population densities have increased, particularly where land is most scarce, farmers have turned to tubers as a starch source. Statistics show a consistent and continuous displacement of grains and legumes by tubers, which yield more starch per hectare."[30] As farm sizes grow smaller and land productivity declines, farmers plant cassava, yams, or potatoes in place of corn to maximize the number of calories, rather than the amount of protein, that their fields produce. In effect, they switch from an agricultural system based on marketable crops to one aimed at meeting bare subsistence needs.

POLITICAL FALLOUT

In addition to the economic and social effects of ecological deterioration, governments must contend with the political fallout as well. Among the more worrisome of these consequences are food riots and the forced migration of people in search of sustenance, both of which are becoming distressingly frequent. Both are politically destabilizing, exerting a heavy claim on the time of political leaders.

Perhaps the most visible political stress are the riots and demonstrations that break out in response to food shortages and price increases. (See Table 2–8.) In extreme cases, the overthrow of a government can be the result, a sequence that was dramatically illustrated in Sudan in the spring of 1985.

With its land productivity declining for close to two decades, and its food deficit and external debt rising as a result, Sudan's foreign debt reached $9 billion in 1985. One of the austerity

Table 2-8. Food-Related Riots and Demonstrations, 1981–85

Country	Date	Triggering Event
Bolivia	July 1983	Drought-induced food shortages
Brazil	Summer 1983	Food shortages in northeast
Dominican Republic	Spring 1984 January 1985	Food price increases Sharply increased prices for basic foodstuffs
Egypt	May 1984	Increased bread prices
Haiti	May, June 1984	Food shortages
Jamaica	January 1985	Food price increases
Morocco	January 1984	Cuts in government food subsidies
Philippines	January 1984	50 percent increase in food prices
Sierra Leone	Spring 1981	Scarcity of rice and increased retail food prices
Sudan	March 1985	Food price increases
Tunisia	December 1983	Sharply increased prices for wheat and wheat products

SOURCES: U.S. Department of Agriculture, *Outlook and Situation Reports,* Washington, D.C.; various news articles.

measures imposed on it by the international financial community in exchange for new loans was the abandonment of the food subsidies that favor city dwellers. The resulting food price increases in the spring of 1985 led to riots and demonstrations in Khartoum. While President Nimeiry was in Washington seeking additional financial assistance, this civil unrest paved the way for a military takeover of the government.[31]

If the massive flow of refugees across the border with Senegal continues, in a matter of years more Mauritanians will live in Senegal than in Mauritania.

Nearly all the countries in Table 2–8 are essentially agrarian economies. And nearly all have experienced extensive ecological deterioration—deforestation, soil erosion, land degradation, rangeland deterioration, and increases in rainfall runoff. In half the countries, grain production per person is lower today than it was at mid-century.

Food subsidies are a common governmental response to growing food deficits and rising food prices. They often merely postpone the day of reckoning, however, because eventually the size of the subsidy becomes unmanageable. The government of Tunisia, faced with a growing trade and budget deficit, announced in December of 1983 that it would reduce the government supports on wheat and wheat products. The resulting 85 percent price increase precipitated a week of rioting, which ended only when President Bourguiba restored the subsidies.[32]

Brazil has been plagued with more food riots than any other country. In the summer of 1983, hungry people descended on stores and supermarkets in the towns of the ecologically devastated northeast. The food shortages were a result of prolonged drought, land degradation, and the associated lack of water-absorptive capacity that contributed to the severity of the crop shortfalls.[33]

Ecological degradation is also causing a swelling tide of refugees fleeing famine, disaster, and poverty. For centuries, political refugees have migrated to other countries, and in recent decades, people in search of jobs have crossed international borders in large numbers. Now, ecological deterioration in Africa is generating millions of migrants, who are leaving their villages in record numbers in search of food and water. African farmers and herders are converging on cities and emergency relief camps.

In February 1985, the United Nations estimated that more than 10 million Africans had left their homes in search of food, frequently crossing national borders in their desperate quest. Hundreds of thousands of Ethiopians have crossed into Sudan, heading for relief camps. (See Table 2–9.) Mozambicans have moved into Zimbabwe in droves to escape the guerilla warfare, ecological deterioration, and social disintegration of their homeland.[34]

Mauritanian nomads have moved into Senegal and The Gambia, attempting to escape the Sahara as it pushes southward. In the Mauritanian capital of Nouakchott, residents must spend the early hours of each day shoveling the sand away from doors and off streets and sidewalks so that they remain passable. If the massive flow of refugees across the border with Senegal continues, in a matter of years more Mauritanians will live in Senegal than in Mauritania.[35]

Sudan, now host to 1.1 million refugees from neighboring countries, has become one huge relief camp. As of mid-1985, the country had absorbed 775,000 Ethiopians, 250,000 Ugandans, and

Table 2-9. Distribution of Refugees in Africa by Country of Refuge, 1984

Country of Refuge	Number of Refugees	Primary Countries of Origin
Sudan	1,100,000	Ethiopia/Uganda/Chad
Somalia	700,000	Ethiopia
Zaire	304,000	Angola/Uganda
Tanzania	180,000	Burundi/Zaire
Algeria	167,000	Western Sahara
Uganda	132,000	Rwanda/Zaire
Zambia	104,000	Angola/Zaire
Angola	96,000	Namibia/Zaire
Rwanda	49,000	Burundi/Uganda
Zimbabwe	44,000	Mozambique
Ethiopia	40,000	Sudan
Djibouti	23,000	Ethiopia
Kenya	8,000	Uganda/Ethiopia
Central African Rep.	7,000	Chad
Egypt	5,000	Ethiopia

SOURCES: U.S. Committee for Refugees, *World Refugee Survey 1984* (New York: American Council for Nationalities Service, 1984); U.N. Office of Emergency Operations in Africa, *African Emergency Bulletin,* July 15, 1985.

120,000 Chadians. In addition to wrestling with its own massive food shortfalls, the Sudanese government must confront such logistical questions as how to truck enough water to refugee camps where wells have gone dry. Declining rainfall and the closely associated deterioration of local life-support systems were the principal forces driving people into Sudan, although civil strife in the originating countries also played a role.[36]

In Chad, a combination of drought and civil war have displaced an estimated 2.2 million of a total population of 4.8 million, the great majority of them still within the country. This extensive dislocation of a national population—46 percent—may be a record. Such massive displacement means that economic development has been replaced by economic decline, as food output falls.[37]

Whether people are migrating to another part of their own country or across national borders, the process is politically stressful and economically disruptive. People are losing their livestock and being separated from the land, their means of livelihood. Cultivators and nomads are descending on cities and relief camps, unable to sustain themselves. Even when drought eases, agricultural recovery is slow. People are far removed from their land, have lost their draft animals, and have eaten the seed normally saved for replanting.

As these experiences in many countries indicate, the relationship between ecological deterioration and political stresses is real. Walter Truett Anderson, a political scientist specializing in biological issues, has focused on this particular relationship in Central America: "At this point, with tree cutting proceeding far more rapidly than tree planting, Central America is moving rapidly toward an ecological deterioration that will make it difficult to establish any stable social order."[38] His point applies to all of the Third World countries that are undergoing rapid ecological deterioration.

THE NEED FOR INTEGRATED ANALYSIS

With only occasional exceptions, policy analysts and decision makers have failed to adopt an integrated and multidisciplinary approach for analyzing the relationship between ourselves and our environmental support systems. Although specialization is essential to the systematic advancement of knowledge, there is also a need for generalists who can integrate across fields of knowledge, particularly across the social and natural sciences.

This specialization of knowledge and mission without a counterbalancing, integrating mechanism is proving to be socially costly. In key policy areas, such as population, agriculture, and economics, policies and priorities often rest on such a narrow information base that they prove counterproductive. This is perhaps truest of national security, where the policymaking process is even more isolated from other fields.

Perhaps the greatest single need for intellectual integration is between economics and ecology. Throughout much of the period of rapid global economic expansion since World War II, economists have been able to ignore ecological concepts such as carrying capacity, largely because the human demands on biological systems were well below their sustainable yields. With the quadrupling of world economic activity since mid-century, however, human demands are beginning to exceed sustainable yield thresholds in country after country. Unfortunately, most Third World planning

commissions are staffed largely, if not entirely, by economists—at a time when long-term economic planning is impossible without a command of basic ecology.

This weakness is evident in most global economic policymaking models. These are essentially macroeconomic, assuming unlimited ecological capacities, and they thus produce unrealistic economic forecasts. For example, agricultural supply and demand projections invariably include projections of cropland area, but ignore entirely the effect of soil loss on land productivity. Nor do these models incorporate key relationships between the hydrological cycle and the loss of vegetation so widespread in the Third World.

One of the central issues in development planning is how to respond to the effect of population growth and associated changes in land use on the hydrological cycle. Given the obvious importance of this issue, an extensive collaborative exploration of these relationships by demographers, hydrologists, and meteorologists should be a priority. So far, few meteorologists are looking at how land use changes affect climate, and they are not translating their findings into policy recommendations.

For Africa, the question central to any assessment of the continent's future is whether changes in land use and the loss of vegetation and soil associated with population growth are reducing rainfall. Are the 18 consecutive years of below-normal rainfall in Africa since 1967 just another of many historical climatic oscillations? Or do they presage a long-term gradual decline that will likely continue as long as populations expand and land use changes? According to French meteorologist Robert Kandel, "Plant cover in general and forests in particular may have virtues going beyond the microclimate and extending to the regional scale circulation.''[39] In a review of desertification in West Africa, World Bank forester Jean Gorse writes: "The current 17-year dry period is most worrying. With population growing faster than ever before, the proposition that there is now a trend towards increasing aridity deserves a special research effort.''[40]

Unless at least an informed assumption can be made about the relationship between ecosystem change and the hydrological cycle, devising an intelligent development strategy for Africa is impossible. For example, in reforestation planning, there may be a vast difference between the scale of tree planting needed merely to satisfy future firewood demands and that which would be required to restore the hydrological cycle of a generation ago. The latter could easily require 10 times as many plantings as the former. Likewise with agricultural research: Without some understanding of whether Africa's rainfall decline is temporary, it is impossible to know whether to concentrate research efforts on a widely grown crop, such as maize, or on traditional staples that are better adapted to low rainfall conditions, such as sorghum.

Population projections also suffer from a narrow base of information that is almost exclusively demographic. Population projections by U.N. or World Bank demographers are essentially abstractions. There are no feedback loops in their models to incorporate the effect of population growth on the local resource base. The effects of deforestation, soil erosion, cropland abandonment, and freshwater scarcities are entirely omitted from these projections.

Unfortunately, many policymakers, including Third World political leaders, assume that these are "real world" projections that may materialize.

Most Third World planning commissions are staffed by economists —at a time when long-term economic planning is impossible without a command of basic ecology.

Closely related to this analytical challenge is that of assessing the effect of reinforcing trends. At what point does ecological deterioration begin to contribute to political disintegration? And at what point does political disintegration undermine efforts to manage ecological systems intelligently? Lebanon's per capita food production, for example, declined 87 percent since 1950. Most of the reduction has come in recent years, a time marked by social fragmentation and a breakdown of political structures. Clearly, political disintegration is affecting the agricultural prospect. But to what extent did ecological deterioration and agricultural decline contribute to the social stresses that led to political disintegration?

Separating the effects of ecological deterioration from economic neglect and political instability or social unrest is analytically difficult. But without an integrated information and analytical base, formulating policies responsive to the circumstances of an earth with 5 billion human inhabitants may not be possible.

3

Increasing Water Efficiency

Sandra Postel

Despite modern technology and feats of engineering, a secure water future for much of the world remains elusive. Farmers in several key food-producing regions face limited and, in some cases, dwindling water supplies, threatening future food production. In recent years, millions of residents have had their household water rationed because of supply shortfalls in such climatically diverse cities as Newark, New Jersey; Corpus Christi, Texas; Managua, Nicaragua; and Tianjin, China.[1] Water planners in many corners of the world—in humid climates as well as dry, in affluent societies as well as poor ones—are projecting that within two decades water supplies will fall short of needs.

Historically, water management has focused on water development—building dams, reservoirs, and diversion canals—and has aimed at supplying water wherever and in whatever amounts

desired. Governments often built and financed large water projects to encourage agricultural and economic expansion. In the United States, for example, the 1902 Reclamation Act aimed to settle the western frontier by offering family farmers cheap water and power. The act established a separate agency, the Bureau of Reclamation, explicitly charged with developing the West's rivers for irrigation and later for hydropower. Since 1902, hundreds of dams have been erected, and the Bureau has built or authorized more than 160 irrigation projects. Collectively, these facilities supply water to about one quarter of the West's irrigated land.[2]

Viewed as a key to economic growth and prosperity, water development in much of the world has expanded virtually unchecked. Where people drilled their own wells, pumping was regulated minimally, if at all. Cities and farms sprawled across virtual deserts, and water was brought to them. Soaring demands were met by ever larger dam and diversion projects, and planners often

An expanded version of this chapter appeared as Worldwatch Paper 67, *Conserving Water: The Untapped Alternative.*

projected future water needs without considering whether available supplies could sustainably meet them. Rarely did the notion of adapting to a limited supply enter into planning scenarios.

Today's water institutions—the policies and laws, government agencies, and planning and engineering practices that shape patterns of water use—are steeped in a supply-side management philosophy that is no longer appropriate. Aquifer depletion, falling water tables, and streamflows diminished to ecologically damaging levels are increasingly widespread. Though the conventional approach of continuously expanding supplies may work when water is abundant, it is not well suited for an era of growing scarcity, rising water development costs, and damage to the environment.[3]

Most Third World countries have not developed their water sources as extensively as industrial countries have, and they face some special challenges in a time of scarce and costly water. Third World economies are still largely agrarian, and irrigated agriculture claims 85–90 percent of their developed water sources. Supplying an expanding urban and industrial base while meeting the food needs of growing populations will require much additional water. But these nations now confront far greater capital and energy constraints to water development than did those undergoing industrialization earlier this century. Few can afford to double water withdrawals within two decades, as, for example, the United States did between 1950 and 1970.[4]

By increasing water productivity—the benefit gained from each liter used—food production, industrial output, and cities can expand without a parallel increase in water demands. Investments in water efficiency, recycling, and conservation can increasingly yield more usable water per dollar than can conventional water supply projects. But their potential is severely undermined by pricing policies and water laws that encourage inefficiency and waste. Removing these institutional barriers is crucial in order to expand the many new water-conserving methods now in limited use. Only by managing water demand, rather than ceaselessly striving to meet it, is there hope for a truly secure and sustainable water future.

WATER-SAVING IRRIGATION METHODS

Since 1950, irrigated area worldwide has nearly tripled, now totaling about 270 million hectares. Along with fertilizer and high-yielding seed varieties, irrigation helped spur the Green Revolution that spread during the sixties and seventies. In the drive to expand irrigation, however, comparatively little attention has been paid to the efficiency with which irrigation systems operate. Much water is lost as it is conveyed from reservoirs to farmlands, distributed among farmers, and applied to fields. Worldwide, the efficiency of irrigation systems is estimated to average only 37 percent. Some of this "lost" water returns to a stream or aquifer where it can be tapped again, provided the necessary infrastructure is available. But much is rendered unproductive or becomes severely degraded in quality as it picks up salts, pesticides, and toxic elements from the land.[5]

Besides accounting for about 70 percent of water withdrawals worldwide, agriculture consumes the largest share of most nations' water budgets. Whereas 90 percent or more of the water supplied to industries and homes is available for reuse, return flows from agriculture are often only half the initial withdrawal. The rest is consumed through evaporation and transpiration, which depletes the local water supply. Though water can be saved only by reducing consumption, reducing withdrawals—whether they are consumed or not—can make a given reservoir or aquifer supply last longer or serve a larger area. (Throughout this chapter, the terms water withdrawal, use, and demand are used interchangeably; water consumption will be distinguished.) Raising irrigation efficiency by 10 percent in the Indus region of Pakistan, for example, could provide enough water to irrigate an additional 2 million hectares.[6]

Most farmers still irrigate the way their predecessors did 5,000 years ago—by flooding or channeling water through parallel furrows. Water flows by gravity across a gently sloping field, seeping into the soil along the way. These gravity systems (also called surface systems) are typically the least expensive to install and by far the most common method in use today. Unfortunately, most fail to distribute water evenly. Farmers must often apply an excessive amount of water to ensure that enough reaches plants situated on higher ground or on the far side of the field. Some areas receive more water than the crops can use, and the excess percolates out of the root zone or simply runs off the field.[7]

Most farmers still irrigate the way their predecessors did 5,000 years ago.

Because of these problems, many gravity systems are less than 50 percent efficient: Only half the water applied to the field actually benefits the crops. Yet a number of practices can greatly improve their performance. Probably the most universally applicable is leveling the land so that water gets distributed more evenly. To sufficiently water crops sitting just 3 centimeters higher than the surrounding surface, farmers may have to apply as much as 40 percent more water to the entire field. Precise leveling can thus greatly reduce water needs, besides alleviating waterlogging, curbing erosion, and raising crop yields. It can be done with traditional equipment—a tractor or draft animals pulling a soil scraper and land plane—but most farmers will require training and assistance in carrying out the initial field surveys and leveling operations. In recent years, farmers in the United States and elsewhere have begun to use lasers to guide the leveling process, which can raise the efficiency of surface systems to as high as 90 percent.[8]

Over the last two decades, much new land has been brought under irrigation with a variety of high-pressure sprinkler designs. Sprinklers tend to irrigate more uniformly than gravity systems, and efficiencies typically average about 70 percent. But much water can be lost to evaporation, especially in windy, dry areas. A new method, known as LEPA—for low-energy precision application—offers substantial improvements over conventional designs. Rather than spraying water high into the air, the LEPA method delivers water closer to the crops by means of drop tubes extending vertically from the sprinkler arm. When used in conjunction with water-conserving land preparation methods, LEPA irrigation can achieve efficiencies as high as 98 percent. Since the system operates at low pressure, energy requirements may drop by 20–30 percent. A key advantage is LEPA's suitability for retrofitting existing sprinklers. For many farmers, a LEPA retrofit would pay for itself in reduced pumping costs in 5–7 years.[9]

For fruits, vegetables, and orchard crops, a group of thrifty irrigation techniques collectively known as microirrigation has rapidly expanded over the last decade. The most common micro method is drip (also known as trickle) irrigation, in which a network of porous or perforated piping, installed on or below the soil surface, delivers water directly to the crops' roots. This keeps evaporation and seepage losses extremely low. To provide sufficient water to a crop, drip systems may apply 20–25 percent less water to a field than conventional sprinklers would and 40–60 percent less than simple gravity systems.[10]

Although the principles behind drip irrigation date back more than a century, the emergence of inexpensive plastic following World War II spurred the technology's commercial development. By the mid-seventies, a half-dozen countries—Australia, Israel, Mexico, New Zealand, South Africa, and the United States—were irrigating substantial areas by drip methods, and drip area worldwide totaled about 56,000 hectares. Since then its use has steadily spread. (See Table 3–1.) Israel now waters 73,200 hectares by drip methods, up from 6,000 just a decade ago. Together, drip systems and microsprinklers water more than 109,000 hectares, nearly half that nation's total irrigated area.[11]

In the United States, drip systems still water a negligible share of total irrigated area. But their use greatly expanded over the last decade—from 29,000 hectares in 1974 to more than 226,000 hectares in 1983. California accounts for nearly half the U.S. total, and Florida for about a fifth. Today, microirrigation systems water more than 475,000 hectares worldwide, less than 1 percent of total irrigated area, yet an impressive eightfold increase since the mid-seventies.[12]

Though new technologies can do much to reduce water withdrawals for agriculture, many are too costly and complex to benefit farmers in the Third World. Incorporating the principles behind these modern techniques into technologies affordable and appropriate for developing countries should be a high

Table 3-1. Use of Microirrigation Worldwide and in Selected Countries, 1974 and 1981–82[1]

Country	1974	1981–82[2]
	(hectares)	
United States	29,060	185,300
Israel	6,070	81,700
South Africa	3,480	44,000
France	—	22,000
Australia	10,120	20,050
Soviet Union	—	11,200
Italy	—	10,300
China	—	8,040
Cyprus	160	6,600
Mexico	6,470	5,500
All Other	1,010	21,970
Total	56,370	416,660

[1]Includes primarily surface and subsurface drip methods and microsprinklers. [2]See text for selected more recent estimates.
SOURCES: 1974 estimates from Don Gustafson, "Drip Irrigation in the World—State of the Art," in *Israqua '78: Proceedings of the International Conference on Water Systems and Applications* (Tel Aviv: Israel Centre of Waterworks Appliances, 1978); 1981–82 estimates adapted from J.S. Abbott, "Micro Irrigation—World Wide Usage," *Bulletin of the International Commission on Irrigation and Drainage*, January 1984.

research priority. One method, for example, known as "pitcher irrigation," incorporates properties somewhat akin to drip systems. Vegetable or fruit seeds are planted around a baked earthen pitcher buried in the soil. Farmers fill the pitcher with water, which then gradually seeps through the porous walls into the root zone. As with drip systems, evaporation and water losses remain very low. Locally manufactured in many developing countries, the pitchers offer an inexpensive and efficient water-delivery method. Experiments in India in the early seventies showed pitcher irrigation to work well with pumpkins and melons; more recently, a local association of farmers in the Brazilian state of Piauí began using the technique.[13]

With investment needs for new large-scale irrigation projects in the Third World averaging about $5,000 per hectare, most experts agree that near-term efforts should focus on increasing the efficiency of systems already in place. Better management alone could reduce water withdrawals for most surface canal systems by at least 10–15 percent, allowing new land to be brought under irrigation for much less than it would cost to develop new supplies. The World Bank estimates, for example, that reducing the water loss from systems supplying 13 million hectares in Pakistan from 50 percent down to 30 percent would recapture for productive use as much water as three Tarbela Dams could store—the equivalent of a $9-billion investment.[14]

More than 80 percent of the world's cropland is still watered only by rainfall.

What constitutes "better management" varies from project to project. Typical problems include the large water losses resulting from canal seepage as water is conveyed from reservoirs to fields, poor mechanisms for distributing water among farmers served by a particular project, and the farmers' inability to control the timing and amount of water applied to fields. Consequently, often less land is irrigated than was originally planned in a project design, contributing to the low rate of return from many irrigation investments. Some farmers get too much water, while others get too little, and few apply water to their crops in optimal amounts.

These shortcomings diminish not only the productivity of the water supply, but food production and farmers' livelihoods. An analysis of the Rajangana irri-

gation project in Sri Lanka, for example, found that farmers located near the tail end of the system—who therefore had last access to water in the irrigation canal —had average incomes one fifth lower than those near the head, where the supply was plentiful. Despite ample application of fertilizer, rice yields from most farmers' fields were far below their potential.[15]

Only if farmers are assured of an adequate and reliable supply of water will they invest in other inputs that can boost productivity, such as fertilizer and high-yielding seeds. Many large canal systems now deliver water according to a rigid schedule that gives farmers little control over their supply. Robert Chambers of the University of Sussex cites farmers in Gujarat, India, who were willing to pay seven to nine times more for pumped groundwater than for canal water because the former was more reliable.[16]

Whatever the type of system used— flood or furrow, sprinklers, or drip methods—farmers everywhere can conserve water by scheduling irrigations to more closely coincide with their crops' water needs. This requires periodically monitoring soil moisture and irrigating just before crops would become stressed by lack of water. Farmers with limited financial resources may do fairly well by extracting a soil sample from the appropriate depth and estimating moisture content by its consistency. If data on evapotranspiration and rainfall are available, growers can keep a water budget, irrigating when their calculations show that their crops will soon need more water. Of the many devices available to measure soil moisture, gypsum blocks are probably the least costly and simplest to use. When buried in the root zone, the blocks acquire a moisture content roughly equal to that of the surrounding soil. They connect to a meter that measures electrical resistance, which tells the farmer how moist the soil is. On test plots of alfalfa and corn, irrigation scheduling using gypsum blocks led to water applications respectively 14 and 27 percent below neighboring control plots.[17]

Especially where irrigation systems are extremely inefficient, as in much of the Third World today, substantial water productivity gains can be made for a small price. A case in point is the Claro River valley in Chile, where the Chilean Ministry of Civil Works, aided by technical experts from West Germany and the Catholic University of Chile, launched a study to determine the benefits of some simple and inexpensive irrigation improvements. Investigations showed that irrigation efficiencies were averaging only about 20 percent, drainage was poor, and nutrients were being leached out of the root zone—all contributing to low crop yields.[18]

On selected plots, the research group modified traditional furrow and flood irrigation methods to get a more even distribution of water throughout the field. Soil moisture was monitored, and crops were irrigated when moisture in the root zone had been depleted by about half. For a total annual cost of only $25–30 per hectare, the irrigation improvements led to some dramatic results. (See Table 3–2.) Half the controlled irrigations achieved efficiencies of 60 percent or higher, whereas only 15 percent did in the uncontrolled fields. Yields of alfalfa doubled compared with those in the unimproved plots, potato yields were two thirds higher, and barley yields, 43 percent higher. Water productivity—measured as crop yield per unit of water applied to the field—was boosted 30–136 percent.

Table 3-2. Chile: Water Productivity Gains in the Claro River Valley

| Crop | Crop Yield Per Cubic Meter of Water | | Change |
	Without Improvements	With Improvements[1]	
	(kilograms)		(percent)
Alfalfa	0.28	0.66	+136
Barley	0.30	0.58	+ 93
Beans	0.10	0.13	+ 30
Potatoes	0.25	0.55	+120

[1]Annual cost for improvements did not exceed $30 per hectare.
SOURCE: Gaston Mahave and Jorge Dominguez, "Experiments at Farm Level to Introduce Technology in Irrigation: Its Influence on Production and Water Resources," in Brazilian National Committee, *Transactions of the 1st Regional Pan-American Conference*, Vol. 1, Salvador (Bahia), Brazil, October 1984.

NEW CROPPING PATTERNS

Though the spread of irrigation has fostered a tremendous surge in crop production over the last generation, more than 80 percent of the world's cropland is still watered only by rainfall. These lands produce two thirds of the global harvest and provide the subsistence diets for many growing Third World populations. Some of this land can and will, in time, be brought under irrigation. But given the high cost of new irrigation projects—often $10,000–15,000 per hectare in much of Africa—expanding irrigation may in many cases not be a feasible near-term solution to raising food production. Effective water management is as crucial to increasing crop yields in nonirrigated agriculture as it is in irrigated areas. Yet with irrigation occupying center stage in recent decades, the potential to improve water productivity on rain-fed farmland has been largely neglected.[19]

Rain-fed farming (often called dryland farming in arid and semiarid regions) is inherently a risky enterprise. Regardless of what historical rainfall records may show, dryland farmers have no guarantee that rain will sufficiently water their crops throughout the growing season. In a dry year, the quality of water management in dryland production can mean the difference between a field of withered crops and a successful harvest. Capturing and retaining rainwater on the land, reducing the amount lost to evaporation, and selecting crops suited to regional rainfall patterns are the keys to enhancing productivity. According to U.S. Department of Agriculture researchers B.A. Stewart and Earl Burnett, these components of sustainable dryland farming have been known for centuries, but "progress in adapting them to specific areas and situations has been slow."[20]

Wherever water is the only factor limiting crop production, a crop's yield varies directly with the amount of water available for evapotranspiration. A sorghum plant, for example, might yield an additional 15 kilograms of dry matter for each additional millimeter of water its roots absorb. By increasing the amount of moisture stored in the root zone, farmers can thus increase their crop yields.[21]

Making effective use of the fallow period—the time between one crop's harvest and the next one's planting—can substantially increase soil moisture storage. While fields lie idle, rainwater accumulates in the root zone, helping fill the gap between the next crop's water requirements and the amount of rain that falls during its growing season. Researchers have found that yields under well-planned crop-fallow rotations can increase dramatically compared with those under continuous cropping, which in some cases may more than compensate for the smaller number of harvests. Yields of wheat, for example, have doubled or tripled after a year of fallow compared with continuous cropping.[22]

Conservation tillage, which helps farmers cut energy costs and curb soil erosion, is among the most effective water-conservation measures. This practice, also known as minimum tillage, involves leaving crop residues and stubble on the field after harvest, which then trap rainwater, slow runoff, and reduce evaporation from the soil, thereby increasing soil moisture storage. One study in the southern U.S. High Plains found that both soil water storage and sorghum yields increased in proportion to the amount of residue left during an 11-month fallow. (See Table 3–3.) With eight tons of residue per hectare, 44 percent of the precipitation falling during the fallow period was retained in the soil, compared with only 23 percent on cleared fields. Sorghum yields on fields with the eight tons of residue were double those on the cleared fields—a tremendous gain as a result of conserving natural rainfall.

As many as 4,000 years ago, farmers practiced "runoff agriculture," in which rainwater is captured and channeled to fields to provide enough water for crops to grow in an otherwise hostile environment. These methods allowed some ancient farming cultures to thrive where annual rainfall averaged only 100 millimeters (4 inches), and they became widely used throughout the Middle East, North Africa, China, India, northwest Mexico, and the American Southwest. If combined with today's knowledge of crop water needs and local rainfall patterns, modern variants of runoff agriculture could increase dryland production in semiarid regions and greatly lessen the risk of crop failure.[23]

One promising method for small-scale subsistance crop production is microcatchment farming. The terrain around each cultivated plant is shaped so that rainfall from a larger area gets directed to a small basin in which the plant grows. Water retained in the basin seeps through the soil, and the crop gets a greater supply than it would from rain-

Table 3-3. Effects of Conservation Tillage on Water Storage and Sorghum Yields in the Southern U.S. High Plains

Amount of Residue Left Per Hectare on the Field	Share of Fallow-Period Precipitation Stored in the Soil	Sorghum Yield Per Hectare
(tons)	(percent)	(kilograms)
0	23	1,780
1	31	2,410
2	31	2,600
4	36	2,980
8	44	3,680
12	46	3,990

SOURCE: B.A. Stewart and Earl Burnett, "Water Conservation Technology in Rainfed and Dryland Agriculture," paper presented at the International Conference on Food and Water, College Station, Tex., May 26–30, 1985, based on data in P.W. Unger, "Straw-Mulch Rate Effect on Soil Water Storage and Sorghum Yield," *Soil Science Society of America Journal,* Vol. 42, 1978.

fall alone. Experiments in Israel's Negev Desert indicate construction costs of only $10–40 per hectare, depending on the catchment size needed to supply the crop sufficiently. Despite their applicability to labor-intensive, subsistence cropping systems, which characterize much of Third World agriculture, microcatchments are only in limited use. Since they work especially well with tree crops, microcatchments could bolster reforestation efforts that combine production of food, fodder, and fuelwood— an urgent need, for example, in sub-Saharan Africa.[24]

As water becomes an increasing constraint on food production, more attention must be given to exploiting crop characteristics and selecting cropping systems that make optimum use of the water available. Crops vary, among other things, in their resistance to drought, their tolerance of salinity, the total amount of water they consume from planting to harvest, and the length of their growing season. In dryland production, for example, farmers can help secure a good harvest by setting the planting date of a crop so that its growing season corresponds with the maximum probability of it getting sufficient moisture. They can also switch to crops and farming techniques better suited to their particular growing conditions.

In regions prone to drought, or where water supplies are otherwise unreliable, crops less sensitive to water stress can help guard against devastating yield reductions. Among the common grains, corn and rice are highly sensitive to water deficits, whereas sorghum and wheat, for example, are comparatively tolerant. Although both corn and sorghum are likely to suffer yield reductions during a prolonged drought, corn yields would drop by a greater percentage, other things being equal.[25] Research directed at boosting the yields of drought-resistant crops could thus greatly benefit areas where irrigation is limited or unavailable, including much of Africa.

A graph of any crop's seasonal water consumption typically has a bell shape, starting out low when plants are young, reaching a peak at some point in the growing season, and tapering off as harvest approaches. In general, crops are more sensitive to water deficiencies during their flowering or reproductive stage than during their vegetative or ripening stages. For example, if corn's water needs are not met during its silking and tasseling period, yields can drop by half. Though sorghum, cotton, and soybeans are more drought-tolerant, their yields can fall by a third or more if stressed by lack of water at critical growth stages.[26]

Where lack of developed supplies makes full irrigation impossible, the limited water available could be used to irrigate crops during their most sensitive periods. Especially in the Third World, where minimizing the water stress of crops can help avert famine, training farmers to apply water at the most critical times for their particular crops—and making supplies available during those times—could greatly enhance food security.

Another exploitable crop characteristic of growing importance is salt tolerance. Barley, cotton, sorghum, soybeans, sugar beets, and wheat are among the common crops at least moderately tolerant of salinity. This trait is especially useful for desert regions, such as the Middle East, where a large share of the extractable groundwater supply is quite salty. To conserve high-quality water for drinking, the Saudi Arabians frequently use water with a salt concentration exceeding 2,000 parts per million (ppm) to grow barley, sugar beets, cotton, spinach, asparagus, and date palms.[27] (For comparison, ocean water has a salinity of about 35,000 ppm, water with a salinity of 1,000 ppm or less is considered fresh, and the recommended limit for drinking water in the United States is 500 ppm.)

Some scientists see a promising future for the commercial production of halophytes—plants physiologically adapted to a salty environment. Researchers at the University of Arizona's Environmental Research Laboratory in Tucson have collected several thousand halophyte specimens representing some 800 species. Of the small portion screened so far, a number appear promising as providers of livestock feed or plant oil.

Chickens, for example, can tolerate feed with a halophyte content of 10–20 percent. Of course, before any halophyte crop is grown on a commercial scale, it must prove to be economical to seed, cultivate, harvest, and sell.[28]

Over the long term, water constraints could prompt the spread of new crop varieties. One that has attracted some recent attention is amaranth, a broad-leaved plant that produces an edible cereal-like grain. Native to Mexico, Guatemala, the southwestern United States, and the Andean highlands of South America, amaranth is a hearty, drought-resistant crop that appears readily adaptable to new environments. About 20 farmers are growing it in the United States, and some with several years' experience see a potentially large role for the crop in the High Plains. According to one Kansas grower, amaranth weathered the recent dry years better than sorghum. However, given its comparatively low yields and some technical problems that make planting costly, amaranth will not supplant substantial acreages of the common cereals without much additional research and development.[29]

RECYCLING AND REUSE

Water supplies for cities and industries are typically taken from a river, lake, or aquifer, used in a factory or home, and then released as "wastewater" to the nearest watercourse. Treating this wastewater before it is discharged to the environment not only protects the quality of rivers, streams, and aquifers, it sets the stage for water recycling and reuse. By using water several times, cities and industries can get more production out of each liter, thereby lessening the need to develop new supplies. Water pure

Table 3-4. United States: Water Recycling Rates in Major Manufacturing Industries, 1954–78, With Projections for 1985 and 2000

Year	Paper and Allied Products	Chemicals and Allied Products	Petroleum and Coal Products	Primary Metal Industries	All Manufac- turing
	(number of times each cubic meter used)				
1954	2.4	1.6	3.3	1.3	1.8
1959	3.1	1.6	4.4	1.5	2.2
1964	2.7	2.0	4.4	1.5	2.1
1968	2.9	2.1	5.1	1.6	2.3
1973	3.4	2.7	6.4	1.8	2.9
1978	5.3	2.9	7.0	1.9	3.4
1985	6.6	13.2	18.3	6.0	8.6
2000	11.8	28.0	32.7	12.3	17.1

SOURCES: U.S. Department of Commerce, Bureau of the Census, *Water Use in Manufacturing* (Washington, D.C.: U.S. Government Printing Office, 1981); projections from Culp/Wesner/Culp, *Water Reuse and Recycling: Evaluation of Needs and Potential*, Vol. 1 (Washington, D.C.: U.S. Department of the Interior, 1979).

enough to drink serves many functions that do not require such high quality. Much wastewater can therefore be used again within a given factory, home, or business (usually called recycling) or collected from one or more sites, treated, and redistributed to a new site (called reuse).

In the United States, manufacturing industries took in some 49 billion cubic meters of water in 1978, the last year for which a comprehensive survey is available. On average, each cubic meter was used 3.4 times before being discharged, eliminating the need to withdraw 120 billion cubic meters from the nation's water sources. More than 80 percent of water use in U.S. manufacturing occurs in just four industries—paper, chemicals, petroleum and coal, and primary metals—and each has fairly steadily increased its water recycling rate over the last few decades. (See Table 3–4.) Each cubic meter supplied to paper mills, for example, is now used an average of 7.2 times, and for the paper industry as a whole, the average recycling rate has climbed from 2.4 in 1954 to 5.3 in 1978. Petroleum refineries use water about 7

times, chemical product manufacturers 2.9 times, and primary metal industries —dominated by steelmaking—1.9 times.

Despite impressive progress, water recycling's potential in manufacturing has barely been tapped. Many industrial pollution control processes recycle water by design. Also, because wastewaters must be treated to a high quality to meet environmental regulations, recycling partially treated water within a plant becomes more economical than paying the high costs of treating discharges to the levels required. As pollution control standards get more stringent, recycling rates thus tend to increase.

By using water several times, cities and industries can get more production out of each liter.

The projected 1985 rates in Table 3–4 are probably overestimates, since compliance with pollution control requirements has lagged. But by the year 2000, the recycling rates in both the primary metals and paper industries are expected to rise to about 12, in chemicals to 28, and in petroleum to more than 30, with an average for all manufacturing industries of 17. If these levels are reached, total water withdrawals for manufacturing in the year 2000—taking into account expected economic growth —will be 45 percent lower than they were in 1978.[30]

In the Valley of Mexico, 4 out of every 10 liters pumped from local aquifers are not replaced by recharge.

Some industrial plants are already operating close to these recycling levels, attesting to the technical feasibility of attaining them. An Armco steel mill in Kansas City, Missouri, that manufactures steel bars from recycled ferrous scrap draws into the mill only 9 cubic meters of water per ton of steel produced, compared with as much as 100–200 cubic meters per ton in many other steel plants. Besides cutting its total water needs by using recycled iron scrap rather than new metal in its production, the Armco plant uses each liter of water 16 times before releasing it, after final treatment, to the river. One paper mill in Hadera, Israel, requires only 12 cubic meters of water per ton of paper, whereas many of the world's mills use 7–10 times this amount. In water-short regions of the Soviet Union, six oil refineries are now using closed water systems; wastewater is continuously treated and reused so that none is discharged.[31]

In deciding how much to recycle, any industry weighs the combined costs of getting water and treating it prior to disposal with those of treating wastewaters for reuse within the plant. In most industries, recycling offsets its costs by recovering valuable materials, such as nickel and chrome from plating operations, silver from photographic processing, and fiber from papermaking. As water and wastewater treatment costs rise, recycling thus begins to pay. One California paper mill, for example, when required by state authorities to curb its release of pollutants into the Pacific Ocean, found that internally treating and recycling its wastewater was the least expensive way to meet the state's requirements. Water use was cut by 15 percent, and, by annually reclaiming $548,000 worth of fiber that otherwise would be discarded, the system essentially pays for itself.[32]

If encouraged, industrial recycling can make a dramatic difference in a region's water use and quality. In Sweden, strict pollution control requirements have led to widespread adoption of recycling in the pulp and paper industry, which accounts for 80 percent of the nation's industrial water use. Between the early sixties and late seventies, the industry halved its water use while doubling production, a fourfold increase in water efficiency. Not only were Sweden's rivers and streams much cleaner, the nation's total water use in the mid-seventies was only half the level projected a decade earlier.[33]

The Israeli government sets water use standards for industry, allocating to each factory only as much water as necessary to achieve its production target. As new technologies are developed, the standards become more stringent. This forced efficiency has greatly increased water productivity. (See Table 3–5.) In just two decades, the inflation-adjusted value of industrial output per cubic meter of water used rose 3.3 times.[34]

Along with industrial recycling, reusing municipal supplies can reduce demands for high-quality water. Most of the world's cities have opted for centralized sewer systems that collect household and commercial wastewater via an

Table 3-5. Israel: Water Productivity in Selected Industries, 1962–82

Industry	Value of Output Per Cubic Meter		Change
	1962	1982[1]	
	(constant Israeli pounds)		(percent)
Rubber and Plastic Goods	107.5	333.3	+210
Food	84.7	166.7	+ 97
Textiles	66.7	142.9	+114
Wood Products	55.2	500.0	+806
Chemicals	35.3	111.1	+215
Paper Products	15.7	71.4	+355
Mining and Quarrying	6.8	20.0	+194
All Industries	50.0	166.7	+233

[1]Preliminary estimates.
SOURCE: Saul Arlosoroff, "Water Management Policies Under Scarce Conditions," presented at Water for the 21st Century: Will It Be There? Southern Methodist University, Dallas, Tex., April 1984.

extensive piping network, transport it to a central treatment plant, and then dispose of it to the ocean, a bay, or a nearby river. Treatment progresses in stages, starting with physical processes that remove solids, followed by biological methods that reduce organic matter, and then by chemical treatment for further upgrading. The level of treatment given usually depends on the water quality controls in effect. In the United States, federal laws stipulate that most wastewaters be treated at least through the second stage before being released to the environment. Such treatment generally makes the water suitable for use where people will not directly contact it—in industrial cooling or pasture irrigation, for instance. More-extensive treatment can make the water safe for a wide variety of other functions.

By setting and enforcing pollution control standards and encouraging reuse of existing supplies, policymakers can lessen the need to import costly new supplies from a distant river basin or to overexploit underground aquifers. Especially in many Third World cities, incorporating water reuse into plans for

water and wastewater services can help meet rising household water demands, which in some cities may double or triple over the next two decades.

In the Valley of Mexico, for example, 4 out of every 10 liters pumped from local aquifers are not replaced by recharge. Portions of the land already are sinking from the overpumping, and few affordable options exist to import more fresh water. In the region known as the Federal District, which includes about 70 percent of the Mexico City metropolitan area population, treated wastewater provides about 4 percent of current water use, mainly watering public parks and filling recreational lakes. Planners have set the year 2000 as a target for reusing 17 percent of the wastewater generated in the district, which, if accomplished, would meet about 12 percent of projected water demands.[35]

In Israel, where virtually no freshwater supplies remain untapped, all new demands will be met by treating and reusing wastewater. Reclaimed water will replace one fourth or more of the fresh water currently used in agriculture, releasing high-quality supplies for growing cities and industries. By the year 2000, treated wastewater is expected to supply 16 percent of the nation's total water needs, up from 4 percent in 1980.[36]

In the United States, despite federal water quality laws that expressly encourage reuse, reclaimed wastewater represents only 0.2 percent of total annual water use. Most communities have chosen the conventional treat-and-dispose types of systems. A survey in the late seventies showed that 536 reuse projects were under way, collectively using about 937 million cubic meters of treated wastewater annually. Over 60 percent of it was used for irrigating crops, parks, and landscapes; a third for industrial cooling and processing; and the remainder for recharging groundwater and various recreational functions.[37]

California, which leads the United States in the number of reuse projects, has promoted wastewater reclamation as an integral part of its water management plans. Collectively, the state's 380 individual sites now supplied with reclaimed water (versus 283 sites identified in the late seventies' survey) return to productive use more than 271 million cubic meters of water annually—a volume equal to the yearly household needs of 1 million people.[38]

Many cities will experience more frequent shortages if steps toward conservation and greater water efficiency are not taken.

Though typically viewed as "pollutants," most wastewater constituents are nutrients that belong on the land, where they originated. Farmers and gardeners spend millions of dollars on fertilizers to give their crops the nitrogen, potassium, and phosphorus that urban wastewater contains in large amounts. According to one calculation, it would take 53 million barrels of oil—worth $1.4 billion—to replace with petroleum-based fertilizers the amount of nutrients yearly disposed of in U.S. wastewaters.[39]

Provided harmful constituents are removed and monitored, such payoffs can be powerful incentives for the land-treatment approach to water reuse. Would-be pollutants become valuable fertilizing agents; the irrigated land returns benefits, such as revenue from marketable crops or a green landscape for a park; and the reclaimed water is a reliable, nearby source of supply.

In *Future Water,* John R. Sheaffer and Leonard A. Stevens cite some impressive successes with land-treatment designs. For example, one system that has been serving Muskegon County, Michigan, for a decade (and which Sheaffer codesigned) handles 159,000 cubic meters of wastewater per day and irrigates 2,145 hectares of cropland. In 1981, the county earned $1.2 million by selling wastewater-irrigated corn for feed, and the treatment system turned a $250,000 profit.[40]

Incomplete knowledge of the health effects of various pollutants remains a barrier to water reuse. Ways to reduce and monitor levels of bacteria in wastewater are well understood, but much is unknown about viruses, heavy metals, and organic chemicals. Where wastewater is used for irrigation or is otherwise applied to the land, crops must be selected carefully. Not only do they differ in their ability to take up nitrogen, phosphorus, and potassium—and thus to adequately treat the water—but some are harmed by or may concentrate heavy metals, such as cadmium, copper, nickel, and zinc.[41]

Unless removed, heavy metals could accumulate in the soil or percolate to groundwater, possibly contaminating a community's drinking water supply. Pathogenic organisms can survive biological (secondary-level) treatment, which is the maximum now required at most U.S. facilities. Moreover, many community treatment plants do not consistently operate properly, and sometimes fail to meet specified quality standards.[42] Stricter enforcement of standards could eliminate many of these risks and uncertainties. But where they persist, treated wastewater must be used cautiously, and only where human exposure to it is limited.

In very special circumstances, wastewater reclaimed to an exceptionally high quality may be used to supplement a city's drinking water supplies. Though expensive, the most advanced biological and chemical treatment processes can virtually eliminate harmful pathogens and dangerous pollutants. Windhoek, in Namibia, was the first city to add reclaimed water to its public supply, and has been doing so for more than a decade. In the United States, Denver, Colorado, is operating a demonstration plant to study this idea, and in the spring of 1985, the Texas city of El Paso began injecting highly treated wastewater into the aquifer used as its primary public water supply—the first such project in the nation. Much should be learned in the years ahead from these pioneering efforts in water-short areas.[43]

CONSERVATION IN CITIES

Though accounting for less than a tenth of water withdrawals worldwide, urban areas face severe physical and financial constraints on adequately meeting their residents' water needs. The reservoirs, canals, pipes, sewers, and treatment plants that make up a modern water and wastewater system require vast amounts

of money to build, expand, operate, and maintain.

In the Third World, the challenge is to develop and install affordable technologies to meet the basic water supply and sanitation needs of the millions of people who now lack them. As urban populations expand, this challenge becomes more and more formidable. Peru-based engineers Carl R. Bartone and Henry J. Salas write that "the explosive urbanization in the Latin American countries has given rise almost overnight to peripheral communities that severely strain the ability of water and sewage authorities to provide even minimal services."[44]

Cities in the industrial world, on the other hand, face spiraling demands associated with affluence and growth—thirsty green lawns in sprawling suburban areas, swimming pools, additional cars to wash, and houses filled with water-intensive appliances. With increasing constraints on expanding their supplies, many cities will experience more frequent shortages if steps toward conservation and greater water efficiency are not taken.

Conservation has many times pulled communities through short-term crises, such as drought-induced shortages. Putting conservation to work in meeting long-term water needs, however, is a relatively new idea. Planners have typically projected future water demands based on the historical rate of growth in per capita water use and the projected future population. They then plan to meet this estimated demand by drilling more wells or building new reservoirs and by expanding the capacity of their water and wastewater treatment plants. Rarely have planners focused on reducing demand as a way to balance the long-term supply/demand equation.

Only a few cities have broken the historical rise in per capita water use. Because of conservation and water reuse, Tucson, Arizona, now plans for a per capita level of freshwater use 25 percent lower than in the early seventies. Like most water systems, Tucson's was designed to meet the city's peak day demand. For most western U.S. cities, this occurs on one of the hottest days of summer, and can be two to four times greater than the year-round average daily demand. A mid-seventies study found that with peak demand nearing the system's capacity, if the city's growth and pattern of water use continued, $145 million would have to be invested by 1983 to drill more groundwater wells and build larger transmission pipes.[45]

Until that time, the policy of Tucson Water, the municipally owned water utility, was like that of most water suppliers —to plan to meet projected demands by developing new water sources and expanding the supply system. But faced with such large capital costs, the city chose to shift its strategy from simply meeting the demand to managing it, and it set a goal of postponing the need for some 30 percent of projected new capital requirements.[46]

Hefty water price increases caused an initial dramatic drop in Tucson's per capita use between the middle and late seventies. In June 1977, the city initiated its "Beat the Peak" program, aimed at cutting outdoor water use. Each summer, residents are asked not to water more than every other day, and never between the hours of 4:00 and 8:00 p.m. Desert landscaping is promoted as a replacement for green lawns. Largely because of altered outdoor water use patterns, Tucson Water's peak day pumpage dropped by 26 percent in less than a decade, from nearly 568,000 cubic meters in 1976 to 420,000 cubic meters in 1984. Moreover, year-round average daily demand fell by 27 percent, to about 570 liters per person—still high by many nations' standards, but low for a western U.S. city. Besides helping to slow the depletion of its aquifers, Tuc-

son's comparatively modest investment in conservation allowed it to defer $45 million in capital costs that would have been needed to meet an otherwise unmanaged demand.[47]

Conservation requires creativity; there is no ready-made package that will prove effective and economical for every community. But successful efforts to permanently curb per capita demand invariably include some combination of water-saving technologies, economic incentives, regulations, and consumer education. These measures are mutually reinforcing, and they are most effective when implemented jointly. Higher water rates, for example, encourage consumers to install water-saving devices in their homes and apartments and to opt for native landscaping when purchasing a new home. Education is crucial to gain support for conservation, and to make people aware of the easy and cost-effective ways they can save water.[48]

Many water-using technologies, especially those adopted in the United States, were not designed with water efficiency in mind. A typical U.S. toilet—the biggest water user in the home—turns about 19 liters (5 gallons) of drinking-quality water into wastewater each time it is flushed. This is an extravagance few water and wastewater utilities will long be able to afford—and a needless waste of costly, high-quality water. For comparison, most toilets in West Germany work well with only 9 liters, and in Scandinavia, 6-liter toilets have been routine since 1975.[49]

In recent years, U.S. manufacturers have designed a variety of fixtures that can greatly reduce water use indoors. (See Table 3–6.) Substituting the most common water-saving varieties—many of which are now widely installed in western homes—for conventional American models can reduce total household water use by a fifth. The fixtures that use extremely little water that are now available from some manufacturers cut existing levels by as much as 50–70 percent. Many cities, including those in the eastern United States forced to ration water in 1985, could benefit by setting water-appliance efficiency standards and instituting programs to retrofit existing fixtures with inexpensive water-saving devices. Simply getting toilets to operate at 13 liters per flush, instead of the typical 19 liters, could cut total residential water use by at least 10 percent.

Since conserving water indoors reduces sewage flows, plans to expand wastewater treatment facilities can be delayed or scaled down in size, again reducing investment needs. One study for the California Department of Water Resources found, for example, that reducing household water use in both new and existing homes to the economically optimum level would cut statewide capital requirements for wastewater treatment by more than $200 million. Saving water also saves energy, because less water needs to be pumped through the urban system—from source, to treatment plant, to homes, and finally to the wastewater plant. Direct energy costs account for about 20 percent of the total operating budgets of most water and waste-

Table 3-6. United States: Potential Water Savings with Available Water-Efficient Household Fixtures

Fixture	Water Use	Water Savings Over Conventional Fixtures
	(liters/use)	(percent)
Toilets		
Conventional	19	—
Common low-flush	13	32
Washdown	4	79
Air-assisted	2	89
Clothes Washers		
Conventional	140	—
Wash recycle	100	29
Front-loading	80	43
	(liters/minute)	
Showerheads		
Conventional	19	—
Common low-flow	11	42
Flow-limiting	7	63
Air-assisted	2	89
Faucets		
Conventional	12	—
Common low-flow	10	17
Flow-limiting	6	50

SOURCES: Figures for common low-flush and low-flow fixtures from Brown and Caldwell (Inc.), *Residential Water Conservation Projects* (Washington, D.C.: U.S. Department of Housing and Urban Development, 1984). All others from Robert L. Siegrist, "Minimum-Flow Plumbing Fixtures," *Journal of the American Water Works Association,* July 1983.

water utilities, so cutting the volume of flow can significantly lower utility costs.[50]

Rounding out conservation's benefits are energy savings in the home. Since about 15 percent of the total energy used in a typical household is for heating water, measures that save hot water can significantly lower energy costs. In most cases these energy savings pay back the cost of the water-conserving fixture within a few years at most. For example, simply installing a low-flow showerhead can reduce the year's electricity bill for a family of four with an electric water heater by about $100.[51]

Besides encouraging their consumers to conserve, urban water suppliers can stretch existing supplies through improved management techniques. Water agencies in the Washington, D.C., metropolitan area, faced with a growing imbalance between projected demand and supplies, explored such an approach after failing to agree on a strategy to build more dams and reservoirs. They calculated that with a combination of measures—including higher fees for higher rates of water use, public education, improved hydrologic forecasting, new institutional arrangements for more efficiently operating the water-delivery network, a reallocation of some flood storage capacity to water supply, and the construction of one small dam—existing reservoirs could meet the area's needs until the year 2030. Spending $250 million for new reservoirs, the previous recommendation, became unnecessary.[52]

Investing in leak detection and repair is one of the most universally cost-effective conservation measures urban suppliers can undertake. Especially in older or poorly maintained water systems, a large share of the supply often seeps out through broken pipes and other faults in the distribution network. Many of the world's major cities are losing as much

as 25–50 percent of their water supplies in this way. These are costly losses because this "unaccounted-for water" is secured, stored, treated, and distributed, but it never reaches a billable customer.[53]

Except where leakage is extremely low, finding and fixing leaks will usually pay. In Vienna, Austria, such an effort returned to productive use 64,000 cubic meters per day—roughly enough to meet the household needs of 400,000 people—and allowed the city to postpone new capacity investments. In the Philippines capital of Manila, water losses from an aging and poorly maintained supply network were averaging 50 percent in the seventies. A 1983 pilot project cut water losses in one northern area by a fifth, and the city's goal is to reduce losses to less than 30 percent throughout the metropolitan area. The repairs are expected to salvage enough water to serve an additional 1 million people.[54]

Though conservation and better management can benefit growing Third World cities, the more urgent need is to develop water and sanitation technologies that can improve health standards while requiring less water, energy, and financial resources than the conventional technologies used in the industrial world. Few Third World cities can afford to adopt the kinds of water-intensive practices used in the United States today. Supplying the projected population growth in most Latin American cities, for example, will require that levels of water use not rise much above their present range: 75–150 liters per person per day.[55]

Many intermediate technologies for urban sanitation exist between the simple pit latrine and the water-borne piped sewage system. Ventilated and lined pit latrines, toilets that use only 3 liters, septic tanks that serve several houses, and waste stabilization ponds combined with systems for reusing treated wastewaters are all being studied in various projects in Latin America. The African nations of Botswana, Lesotho, Tanzania, and Zambia are each implementing low-cost urban sanitation programs, some aided by bilateral and multilateral lending agencies. Such projects can help develop new models of affordable water and sanitation services.[56]

As incomes rise in the Third World, efficiency must be built into water-using fixtures and appliances. Residents of Beijing, China, now use an average of 145 liters per person daily, but some high-quality apartments register levels between 300 and 450 liters. And certain tourist hotels equipped with modern Western facilities reportedly use water at the extraordinary rate of 2,000 liters per person a day. A recent assessment of Beijing's water situation concludes that "the prospect for the city to have a stable, sustained, and adequate water supply for domestic and industrial use looks bleak. Unless remedial measures are taken immediately and implemented on a sustained basis, sooner or later the city will run out of water."[57] A widespread increase in demand even approaching these higher water use levels would surely thwart the region's economic growth.

BALANCING THE WATER EQUATION

Though the technical means exist to increase water efficiency greatly, technology alone cannot close the growing gap between regional demands and supplies. Unless the policies, laws, and institutions that govern water use begin to foster efficiency rather than discourage it, projected water shortages will worsen.

Pricing policies that promote wastefulness still prevail in most countries. Many governments pay all or most of the capital costs for major irrigation projects. Even in the United States, where western agriculture is arguably overdeveloped, farmers supplied with water from federal projects pay on average only one fifth of the water's true cost. A 1982 U.S. Department of Agriculture study found that nearly 80 percent of the water from federal Bureau of Reclamation projects was priced at $12 per 1,000 cubic meters (5¢ per 1,000 gallons) or less, too low to make most efficiency investments economical. These prices reflect the set of lenient repayment terms for irrigation projects that evolved earlier this century, including no interest charges, repayment periods as long as 60 years, and use of an "ability to pay" criterion in determining the share of costs beneficiaries would bear.[58]

In the United States, farmers supplied with water from federal projects pay on average only one fifth of the water's true cost.

In Third World and industrial countries alike, farmers invariably will irrigate more efficiently if charged more for water. A study in Mexico, for example, found that where charges increased with the amount of water used, irrigation efficiencies averaged 20 percent higher than where farmers paid a fixed fee unrelated to their usage.[59]

Water prices should reflect the cost of supplying the next increment of water—called the marginal or replacement cost—so that consumers get accurate signals about water's true value. Government policies to subsidize water obviously deviate from this economic tenet. But even most urban water utilities set charges to cover their yearly revenue requirements, which are based on historical average costs, not marginal costs. As industry analyst Loren Mellendorf points out, pricing water below its true cost is tantamount to accepting "an inability to meet tomorrow's demands."[60]

Of the 122 billion cubic meters pumped from the U.S. groundwater supply each year, 26 billion— one fifth—are nonrenewable.

In most countries, the water rights and laws that shape patterns of water use are also biased against conservation. In many European countries and U.S. jurisdictions, the right to an allotted quantity of water may be lost if the full allotment is not "beneficially" used. Since conservation is not a beneficial use, farmers and other water consumers are encouraged to use their full entitlements—even if they could economically reduce their water use. Contractual arrangements may restrict beneficiaries of government projects from transferring water use either to a different location or a different function. If the savings from conservation cannot in some way be marketed, water users again have little incentive to invest in efficiency. Rather than buying water that a conserving farmer could profitably offer, new water consumers pressure state and federal governments to build more water supply projects, and water demands and costs incessantly rise.[61]

A number of jurisdictions have acted to remove these barriers to efficiency, but institutions change slowly. In 1983, officials in New South Wales, Australia, adopted a plan allowing water transfers between irrigators, though it applied only for the 1983–84 irrigation season. In the United States, a few jurisdictions,

including the states of California and Colorado, have taken steps to at least partially remove the conservation disincentive inherent in the "use it or lose it" principle of western water rights.[62]

With proper incentives and institutional reforms, many prospective "water crises" could disappear. The Metropolitan Water District (MWD) in southern California, which indirectly serves 12.6 million people, has estimated that its supplies could fall 14 percent short of demand by the year 2000, and consequently has pushed for greater imports of water from northern California. East of the MWD's service area, farmers in the Imperial Irrigation District (IID) irrigate 200,000 hectares with highly subsidized water from a federal reclamation project.[63]

A 1983 analysis by the Environmental Defense Fund suggests that if the MWD paid for conservation in the irrigation district in return for the water thereby saved, both parties would gain. It shows that such a conservation/transfer scheme could supply the MWD with more water than each of two proposals to increase diversions from the north— at a marginal cost respectively 27 percent and 42 percent lower. (See Table 3–7). By choosing the conservation alternative over conventional supply strategies, the MWD could save an estimated $710 million over 20 years.[64]

In mid-1985, the IID retained a private firm, the Pasadena-based Parsons Corporation, to study further conservation's potential and the market for conserved water. Whether carried out by a private company or the MWD itself, conservation investments appear a cost-effective way to balance supply and demand in southern California, and should be explored elsewhere.[65]

Large-scale water development in the Third World began several decades later than in most industrial countries and is much less extensive. Yet given the inor-

Table 3-7. Southern California: Estimated Costs of Water Supply and Conservation Alternatives

Representative Alternatives	Annual Yield	Marginal Cost
	(thousand cubic meters)	(dollars/thousand cubic meters)
Conserve/Transfer Irrigation Water	370,200	545
Develop Groundwater Basins	236,900	575
Reclaim and Reuse Wastewater	299,500	648
Conserve/Transfer Irrigation Water[1]	493,600	665
Build Newville Reservoir/Increase Diversions of Northern Water	271,500	750
Build Los Vaqueros Reservoir/Increase Diversions of Northern Water	327,000	943

[1]Includes lining a major canal in addition to the measures of the first conservation alternative.
SOURCE: Adapted from Robert Stavins, "Trading Conservation Investments for Water," Environmental Defense Fund, Berkeley, Calif., March 1983.

dinate investment requirements to expand irrigation, and the growing problems of land degradation from poor water management, attention must already turn to raising the efficiency and productivity of existing systems. According to Sadiqul I. Bhuiyan of the International Rice Research Institute in Manila, failure to address the inefficiency, inequity, and unreliability of irrigation systems will set back the momentum in Third World food production. Throughout Southeast Asia, he points out, the share of irrigation project budgets devoted to operation and maintenance is diminishing. Project staff are inadequately trained and are not sufficiently accountable for the system to manage it responsibly. British irrigation specialist W.R. Rangeley echoes these concerns, suggesting the need for national or international training programs in irrigation management.[66]

Without adequate monitoring and regulation, intensive use of groundwater can lead to aquifer depletion, falling water tables, land subsidence, and saltwater intrusion. The pervasiveness of these problems is a clear sign that existing institutions fail to foster sustainable groundwater use. Of the 122 billion cubic meters pumped from the U.S. groundwater supply each year, 26 billion —one fifth—are nonrenewable.[67] Those pumping this water pay only the private costs of their water use, not the public costs. They are charged nothing for the right to deplete a water reserve, even though such depletion diminishes the nation's future food and water security. Placing a tax on groundwater pumping wherever aquifers are being depleted would help equate private and social costs, and would encourage conservation. Similarly, where water tables are dropping, taxing or otherwise limiting withdrawals can restore a balance between pumping and recharge.

A model attempt to balance water budgets in the United States is Arizona's 1980 Groundwater Management Act. It calls for each of the state's four most critical areas of groundwater overdraft to develop strategies to reduce groundwater pumping to the level of recharge by the year 2025. It requires conservation, calls for taxes on groundwater withdrawals, and, if it appears by the year 2006 that balance will not be achieved, allows the state to begin buying and retiring farmland. Projections for both the Phoenix and Tucson areas show that most of the balancing will come from shifting water out of agriculture to supply urban and industrial growth. Whether the act's goals can be achieved without limiting the burgeoning populations of these cities remains to be seen.[68]

Standards can help encourage efficiency when the market fails to do so, or where water is critically scarce. In Israel, which is now using virtually all its available supplies, each farm and factory is allotted only the minimum amount of water necessary, assuming up-to-date conservation measures are in place. As new technologies are developed, more stringent water use standards are set, ensuring that water efficiency continually increases.[69]

Several American states now have laws requiring that fixtures installed in new homes, apartments, and offices meet specified water efficiency standards. But this transition could be greatly expanded—and made more quickly and uniformly—if standards were set at the federal level. The government set similar standards in the mid-seventies to boost auto fuel economy, and new cars are now twice as fuel-efficient as the average car on the road a decade ago. If even modest water efficiency standards were set for toilets, showerheads, faucets, and dishwashers, residential water demands by the year 2000 could be reduced by 1.5 billion cubic meters annually—a volume that would meet the yearly residential needs of nearly 10 million people.[70]

Planners facing projected water shortages should consider conservation and increased efficiency as alternatives to traditional water supply strategies. The Soviet Union has reportedly decided to proceed with a long-debated project to divert water from Siberian rivers into Soviet central Asia. The project's main purpose is to expand irrigation, both to increase yields and to ensure greater output during dry years. With an estimated capital cost of $36.4 billion—or $15,700 for each of the 2.3 million hectares expected to come under irrigation—and uncalculated environmental risks, the diversion appears less desirable than a water efficiency strategy that might achieve the same goals.[71]

According to Soviet researchers, some 5 million hectares of irrigated land in central Asia are badly in need of upgrading. Water withdrawals for these farms is excessive—often two to three times greater than those on experimental plots where irrigation systems have been modernized. Consequently, the output from each unit of water diverted to fields in the region is low. At $7,000 per hectare, modernizing all 5 million hectares would require an investment of $35 billion—roughly equal to that of the diversion.[72]

Yet the returns from such an investment should be far greater. Yields would increase, and land degradation from waterlogging and salinization would be greatly lessened. Just a 30 percent reduction in water withdrawals for those 5 million hectares—which modernization should achieve given the current high rates of water use cited by Soviet researchers—could free as much water to expand irrigation as would be supplied by the Siberian diversion: 25 billion cubic meters per year. Moreover, since these savings would begin to accrue in just a few years, farmers might bring new land under irrigation long before any water from Siberia would arrive.[73]

Writing in the journal *Soviet Geography*, researchers from the Soviet Institute of Geography point out "there will obviously be a time when the water resources of the Aral Sea basin will be fully used up and water from Siberia will not yet be available. . . . Until the arrival of Siberian water, southern Kazakhstan and Central Asia will have to rely on their own resources." They further state that the pace of reconstructing irrigation systems in the region is "obviously inadequate."[74] If the Soviet government cannot simultaneously invest in both the Siberian diversion and increasing water efficiency, the efficiency strategy—though institutionally more difficult to implement—appears the sounder choice.

In the United States, similar decisions face the state of Texas, where depletion of the Ogallala aquifer threatens the lucrative High Plains farming economy. With no action taken on long-standing, multibillion-dollar proposals to divert water into the region from distant rivers, Texas Agriculture Commissioner Jim Hightower has proposed a strategy of state investments in water efficiency. By offering 10 percent purchase rebates, at a one-time cost to the state of $37 million, the plan would leverage the transition to more efficient irrigation methods on 1.3 million hectares of farmland. It reasonably assumes that farmers will buy cost-effective, water-conserving technologies, if they are helped over the cash-flow hurdle.[75]

Including technical assistance and low-interest loans to stimulate other conservation investments, the complete plan would cut agricultural water use by an estimated 17 percent, or 2.46 billion cubic meters per year. This is 30 percent *more* water than would be supplied by a $10-billion cross-Texas diversion scheme examined by the Army Corps of Engineers. As Hightower says, "we can generate more water resources for much less money by making an investment in water conservation."[76]

High costs, environmental risks, and tight budgets will make large water projects increasingly unattractive and hard to implement for some time to come. Yet few officials and water managers have replaced their strategies of increasing supplies with ones geared toward reducing demand. This gap in policy, planning, and commitment can only lead to worsening water deficits and economic disruption.

The transition to a water-efficient economy will not be easy or painless. But it has begun, and it should be fostered. With the technologies and methods now available, even modest expenditures on conservation and efficiency could make unnecessary many of the inordinately expensive, ecologically disruptive water projects that have dominated water-planning agendas for decades.

4

Managing Rangelands

Edward C. Wolf

Rangelands hold many paradoxes. The world's vast plains, prairies, steppes, and savannas seem somehow on the periphery of modern life, and tending livestock, an anachronism in the twentieth century. Though rangelands occupy far more territory than croplands, they contribute a dwindling share of the world's wealth. But the 3 billion domestic ruminants—cattle, sheep, goats, buffalo, and camels—that can turn indigestible cellulose into protein-rich meat and milk form the largest herd ever, and the high-quality protein they supply is widely considered a key to improving human diets.[1]

Colonial empires in Latin America were established on the wealth of grazing herds, and the cattle boom on the U.S. Great Plains earned that region a reputation as the Wall Street of the late nineteenth century. But in recent years, mounting grain surpluses in Europe and North America, along with government subsidies for the production and export of grain-fed beef, pork, and poultry, have narrowed the market for range-fed animals. Affluent consumers concerned about their health have begun to turn their backs on beef as well, and even wool from the world's sheep has been steadily replaced by cheaper, synthetic fibers.

Where grazing animals form the basis of subsistence economies, as in much of Africa, the Middle East, and parts of India and mainland Asia, other paradoxes emerge. In drought-ravaged Africa, starvation and involuntary settlement are narrowing the ranks of livestock-dependent pastoral people and making their share of the continent's population ever smaller. But although overgrazing by their herds has often been blamed for pastoralists' vulnerability to drought and destitution, many analysts now argue that poorly designed development assistance undermined sound traditional practices and hastened environmental deterioration. Perhaps most ironic, some of the innovative methods of grazing management designed to make commercial ranching more profitable and less damaging to rangelands are based on herding strategies similar to those developed by pastoral societies over millennia.

More than other natural systems, rangelands force people who depend on them to cooperate with ecological patterns and recognize limits on what the land will sustain. Examples from around the world show that sound management can reclaim degraded land, raise range productivity severalfold, and increase the land's contribution to human welfare. Unfortunately, vast expanses of wasteland and unproductive range testify that such management remains the exception.

LESSONS OF A MARGINAL RESOURCE

The sheer vastness of the earth's rangelands belies their reputation as marginal lands with limited economic potential. The 3.1 billion hectares of permanent pasture and grazing land constitute more than twice the area of the world's cropland. (See Table 4–1.) While arable lands account for 11 percent of the continental area, lands used for grazing make up nearly a quarter. When grazing lands in forests and woodlands are included, the U.S.-based Society for Range Management is correct in proclaiming "there is more rangeland on earth than any other kind of land."[2]

Rangelands carpet the spaces between well-watered forests and barren deserts. The Arabic word "Sahel" literally means "shore": a coast of seasonal green south of the Sahara's ocean of sand. Where water falls intermittently in a short, intense rainy season, range grasses flourish in a brief burst of growth, flowering and setting seed. In parts of the world where long, cold winters prevail, the short summer sustains a riot of prolific growth on the range. Rangelands mediate between ecological sufficiency and scarcity—whether the critical resource is measured in millimeters of rainfall or in frost-free weeks.

Taken as a whole, the earth's rangeland ecosystems are biologically vigorous. In a 1972 survey of the productivity of plant communities, Russian ecologist L.E. Rodin and colleagues from the Dokuchaev Soil Institute calculated that grasslands—the predominant range ecosystem—represent just 3 percent of the world's total plant matter. Yet their annual growth produces 24.4 billion tons of new biomass, over 14 percent of the accumulation of all ecosystems each year.[3]

This abundant yearly growth represents a substantial resource of solar energy fixed by living plants, but it is not in a form useful to people. Animals that eat grasses or the foliage of range trees create an essential link between rangelands and human needs. Although humans cannot digest cellulose, cattle, sheep, and goats have four-chambered stomachs that break cellulose into its component carbohydrates, sustaining the animals that eventually supply high-quality protein to people.

Grasslands on every continent once

Table 4-1. World Land Resources, by Region, 1983

Region	Crop-land	Range-land	Forest and Woodland
	(million hectares)		
North America	236	265	591
Latin America	175	550	999
Western Europe	95	71	126
E. Eur. and Sov. Union	278	388	949
Oceania	47	459	116
Africa	183	778	688
Asia and Mideast	456	645	561
World	1,470	3,156	4,030

SOURCE: U.N. Food and Agriculture Organization, *Production Yearbook* (Rome: 1984).

sustained vast arrays of wild grazing animals. Only in a few places do intact communities of such mammals remain. Few match the diversity found on East Africa's Serengeti, where 91 species consume the grass and browse on the Plain. "The great diversity of wildlife in the savannas of East Africa is possible due to differences in their dietary requirements," points out a report from Winrock International, a U.S.-based center for livestock research. "For example, elands and Grant's gazelles are predominantly browsers, Thomson's gazelles and wildebeests prefer short grass, and zebras seem to prefer intermediate grass, including stems. Giraffes select leaves and new growth from woody plants while elephants consume large quantities of coarse material." Such selective consumption of many different plants maximizes the land's protein yield. According to a National Academy of Sciences study, while savanna grasslands in the Sahel support 20–28 kilograms of cattle per hectare, they can sustain 65–158 kilograms of wild grazing animals per hectare.[4]

On most rangelands, the availability of nutritious forage depends on the sequence and intensity of grazing. Wild herds, along with periodic natural fires, maintained the productivity of grasslands and savannas for eons before humans domesticated animals. Well-managed grazing by domestic livestock can keep rangelands not only more productive, but biologically more diverse as well.

Attempts to harvest this productivity face inescapable biological trade-offs involving the distribution of water and nutrients. Forage quantity and nutritional quality are seldom at their maximums in the same places. In the northern Sahel, for instance, water is scarce but the available forage is high in both protein and digestibility because the soil has sufficient nitrogen and phosphorus. In the better-watered south, soil mineral deficiencies mean that the forage, though more abundant, is less nutritious. Cattle cannot offset the lack of nutrients in the plants they eat simply by eating more, so herders in the region are forced in normal years to choose between high-quality forage and access to drinking water.[5]

Forage quality varies over the course of the growing season as well. Plants are at their most nutritious and palatable as young, tender shoots—but they are also most likely then to be grazed beyond their ability to regenerate. Preserving the productivity of range vegetation can mean abstaining from grazing during months when animals would be able to gain weight most rapidly. Grazing during the dry season, when plants are dormant, has much less effect on the robustness of forage plants, yet the plants are far less nutritious as well. At this time of year, the foliage of palatable shrubs and trees can be an important forage supplement.

A Winrock International report on arid and semiarid lands sums up the dilemmas of range users: "Grazing management . . . is faced with an apparent contradiction of needing to use the available forage during the time of optimum quality, and at the same time avoid such heavy grazing as to reduce productivity or change the vegetative composition in unfavorable ways."[6] The biology of rangelands forces users to forgo some kinds of production if they want to maintain or enhance other kinds. When these trade-offs are ignored, or when poverty limits peoples' choices, self-reinforcing declines in range productivity and carrying capacity can be set in motion.

RANCHERS AND PASTORALISTS

Domestic livestock dominate the economic activities sustained by rangelands.

Cattle, sheep, goats, and camels are the ubiquitous companions of humans in these areas. Whether they supply meat and milk in market-oriented ranching and mixed farming enterprises or provide the cornerstone of family wealth and community for nomadic pastoralists, livestock remain the focus of most rangeland livelihoods.

Livestock numbers have grown steadily over the past generation, though not quite apace with the human population. The world's cattle herd grew from some 770 million in 1950 to 1.3 billion in 1984, increasing 1.5 percent each year. Sheep and goat herds grew by half, from just over 1 billion at mid-century to 1.6 billion in 1984.[7] (See Table 4-2.)

Three quarters of the world's 3 billion domestic ruminants are raised in conjunction with farming and are fed on hay, sown forages such as alfalfa, and crop residues. Range grazing supports a dwindling share of livestock in industrial and developing countries alike. As intensive livestock production has expanded and range grazing has declined in im-

portance, rangelands everywhere have been converted to more lucrative land uses. Millions of hectares of natural grasslands, often the most fertile of the world's grazing lands, have been plowed and planted to crops in the last century, in tandem with the accelerating growth of the world's population.[8]

Range grazing supports a dwindling share of livestock in industrial and developing countries alike.

The 103 million hectares of fertilized pastures and forage crops like alfalfa in the United States provide 84 percent of all roughage consumed by livestock there. The diminishing role of rangelands is as apparent in much of the Third World. India's livestock get 91 percent of their feed requirements from forage crops and crop residues, and only about 4 percent from rangelands. Though lit-

Table 4-2. World Domestic Ruminant Resources, by Region, 1984

Region	Cattle	Sheep and Goats	Buffalo	Total
		(million head)		
North America	126	14	—	140
Latin America	312	148	—	460
Western Europe	101	115	—	216
E. Eur. and Soviet Union	153	195	—	348
Oceania	30	210	—	240
Africa	176	340	2	518
Asia and Mideast	374	578	122	1,074
World	1,272	1,600	124	2,996

SOURCE: U.N. Food and Agriculture Organization, *Production Yearbook* (Rome: 1984).

tle of India's grain can be spared to feed animals, many of the country's cattle graze crop residues and stubble after the harvest. Their manure fertilizes the fields for the next planting, one of the advantages of integrating farming with livestock production.[9]

The commercial production of beef, hides, and wool remains the most important range-based economic activity in industrial countries. Ranched livestock tend to disperse over large areas, protected from predators by fences and cowboys. They are often trucked to distant pastures when the seasons change. Ranching has been described as "a child of the Industrial Revolution."[10]

With the exception of efforts in the past two decades to promote ranching as an alternative to pastoralism in Africa, the system has been restricted to regions settled by Europeans. The Great Plains of North America, Venezuela's llanos, the Brazilian sertão, and the pampas of Uruguay and Argentina are important ranching areas in the western hemisphere. In Africa, only South Africa's Karroo has a long history of ranching.

The interior of Australia and the high country of South Island, New Zealand, have also been major suppliers of ranched wool.

In the United States, ranching today plays a small but still integral role in cattle and sheep production. U.S. rangeland, an area more than twice as large as the country's cropland base, supplies just 16 percent of the roughage in livestock diets. (See Table 4–3.) Two thirds of this range, 215 million hectares, is private land. The remaining 104 million hectares is publicly owned land, most of it managed by the Bureau of Land Management (BLM) and the U.S. Forest Service.[11]

In 1984, the BLM issued permits allowing private ranchers to graze their herds on 69 million hectares of public land. The 2 million cattle and 2.3 million sheep for which permits were issued accounted for less than 4 percent of the U.S. herds of these animals, indicating how marginal range grazing has become in the American livestock economy.[12]

The seemingly inconsequential contribution of rangeland is due to the

Table 4-3. United States: Sources of Livestock Forage, 1976

Source	Land Area		Feed Value	
	Million Hectares	Percent of Area	Million AUMs[1]	Percent of Roughage
Range Grazing	319	75	213	16
Nonrange Grazing				
All Pasture[2]	79	19	687	51
Crop Residues	n.a.	n.a.	14	1
Forage Crops	24	6	444	32
Total	422	100	1,358	100

[1]Animal Unit Month (AUM) is the quantity of forage needed to sustain a 1,000-pound cow for one month.   [2]Includes nonrange permanent pasture and pasture in rotation with cultivated crops.
SOURCES: U.S. Department of Agriculture, *An Assessment of the Forest and Rangeland Situation in the United States,* Forest Resource Report No. 22 (Washington, D.C.: U.S. Government Printing Office, 1981); and U.S. Department of Agriculture, *Agricultural Statistics 1983* (Washington, D.C.: U.S. Government Printing Office, 1983).

highly stratified system by which beef is produced in the United States today. Calves are commonly raised to maturity on pasture or western rangeland, then shipped to feedlots where they are fed large amounts of grain and protein-rich feeds to fatten them for slaughter. The open range supplies only a small part of these animals' life-cycle food supply.

Advanced technology in livestock production, surplus feed grains, and new ways to manipulate the physiology of ruminants have all increased the efficiency of meat production while reducing the importance of access to grazing land. Once an autonomous system for producing meat and hides, ranching has now become an appendage of more complex, technically sophisticated ways of supplying livestock products. According to Roy Van Arsdall of the U.S. Department of Agriculture, "The concentration of livestock production into ever larger and more highly specialized operations requires direct use of land for little more than a building site."[13]

In much of Africa, the Middle East, parts of India, and parts of Latin America, livestock are herded over vast areas of natural rangeland as they have been for millennia. Pastoralism, as such migratory systems are known, takes many forms—from pure nomadism to virtually settled farming. Pastoralists rely on cattle, goats, sheep, and camels primarily for subsistence and survival, rather than for the production of meat or hides for the marketplace. Pastoralists' economies are based on the natural productivity of the land, and these people are often among the first victims of ecological deterioration.

Sub-Saharan Africa has the most pastoralists, with common estimates of between 15 million and 25 million people. In the Middle East, pastoralists today may number less than 2.5 million, though they were once far more numerous. Other livestock-dependent popula-

tions include approximately 10 million people in Asia, 5 million in North and South America, and less than 500,000 in Australia. The Third World countries with the largest pastoral groups—arranged in order of decreasing numbers —are Sudan, Somalia, Chad, Ethiopia, Kenya, Mali, Mauritania, India, and China. True pastoralists probably account for less than 1 percent of the world's population.[14]

True pastoralists probably account for less than 1 percent of the world's population.

In most pastoral societies, people are sustained primarily by milk. Levels of milk production from pastoralists' animals help them judge the condition of forage supplies. According to the International Livestock Center for Africa (ILCA), emphasizing the production and consumption of milk allows pastoralists to take the best advantage of marginal, semiarid rangeland in two ways: They can maximize both the food output and the number of people that each hectare of land will sustain.[15]

African pastoral systems compare favorably with the market-oriented ranching systems of the United States and Australia as efficient users of rangeland. (See Table 4–4.) Transhumant pastoralism, a system in which herders and their families move with their animals during part of the year and stay in one place for the remainder, can be up to 10 times as productive per hectare as ranching in supplying protein for human diets. Per worker-hour, on the other hand, conventional ranching is vastly more productive. Ranching originally flourished in areas like Australia and the western United States where land was abundant and labor was scarce, whereas pastoralism tends to be practiced where populations are growing and few employment alternatives exist.

In most pastoral communities, the ratio of people to livestock is quite high. This allows pastoralists to supervise their herds and to exploit the subtle variations in vegetation, reflecting rainfall patterns, that determine the nutritional quality of forage. Constantly moving and managing their herds to fully exploit the land's productivity, pastoral societies developed exemplary range management methods. Sadly, few of these practices have survived a generation of contact with the modern world.

Since independence, most African governments have attempted to settle pastoralists, perceiving nomadic people as obstacles to national integration and even as security risks. Misunderstanding pastoralists' priorities, governments have interrupted annual migrations and converted subsistence livelihoods to commercial schemes that produce meat for urban consumers and for export. A review of various attempts to restructure

Table 4-4. Livestock Protein Production in Various Semiarid Regions and Under Several Pastoralist Systems in the Sahel[1]

Region	Per Hectare	Per Worker-Hour
	(grams per year)	
U.S. Southwest	300–500	900–1,400
Australia	400	1,900
African Sahel		
Nomadism	400	10
Trans-humance	600–3,200	10–70
Sedentary	300	40

[1]Each zone receives less than 500 millimeters of rainfall annually.
SOURCE: H. Bremen and C.T. de Wit, "Rangeland Productivity and Exploitation in the Sahel," *Science*, September 30, 1983.

pastoralism led British journalist Lloyd Timberlake to conclude in *Africa in Crisis:* "Africa is littered with examples of arrogant and failed attempts to 'rationalise' pastoralism, which have often caused desertification and bloodshed, as well as wasted considerable amounts of money."[16]

Pastoralists are nowhere free from the influence of modern life. Political authorities curtail their migrations and tax their meager material wealth. Cultivators clear fields in traditional dry-season pastures. Traders encourage dependence on a commercial economy over which pastoralists exercise little control. As populations grow, the rangelands that remain for them can no longer sustain herds or families. No economic margin protects them from the vicissitudes of drought.

In the Sahel countries of West Africa, the breakdown of pastoralism is especially desperate. Droughts there have always taken a high toll of pastoralists' animals; herds were commonly expanded in good years in order to be prepared for the inevitable bad ones. Over the past 18 years, however, sustained drought has been coupled with steady human population growth and the loss of dry-season pastures to cultivators. Herds rebuilt after episodes of drought have proved insufficient to support the families that depend on them.

Writing of the herd losses and pastoralists' response to drought a decade ago, Dutch ecologists H. Bremen and C.T. de Wit observed, "Total herd size has returned to the 1970 level, but livestock density is still only 3.5 tropical animal units per person because of the population growth of 2.5 percent per year."[17] Four to five animals per person is considered the minimum needed to sustain pastoralists' families. Birth rates outpaced the ability of herds to feed pastoralists adequately, a problem that has become more acute with the catastrophic herd losses reported in the early eighties.

When drought strikes, pastoralists respond as a last resort by selling their animals to purchase grain. The ratio of livestock prices to grain prices thus provides an index of pastoralists' access to sufficient food supplies. When grain prices rise due to region-wide food shortages, livestock prices may actually decline as large numbers of animals, many in poor health, are offered for sale. In the Ethiopian famine of 1973–74, starvation's victims included a disproportionately large share of pastoralists. Indian economist Amartya Sen explained their tragic vulnerability: "The characteristics of exchange relations between the pastoral and the agricultural economies thus contributed to the starvation of the herdsmen by making price movements reinforce—rather than counteract—the decline in livestock quantity. The pastoralist, hit by the drought, was decimated by the market mechanism."[18]

Rangelands made barren through misuse look much the same in West Texas and Sudan.

Though worlds apart, pastoralists and commercial ranchers share a common fate. The extraordinary success of modern agriculture and capital-intensive animal husbandry in industrial countries, and the need to feed growing populations in the Third World, have appropriated the best grazing lands for crop production, leaving range-based livelihoods more vulnerable and less viable. Throughout the world, raising livestock on rangeland is an increasingly marginal activity practiced on land of low productivity—land that is often further degraded by current grazing practices.

Rangelands made barren through misuse look much the same in West Texas and Sudan. They can be restored only if new ways to manage the land are integrated with the social and economic needs of people who depend on it. Unfortunately, in many regions today livestock herds and the biological productivity of grazing lands are on a collision course, a path that diminishes both human and ecological welfare.

TURNING FORESTS INTO GRASS

A century ago, North America's vast plains surrendered to the relentless advance of ranchers and their herds. The cattle boom came at a steep price: degraded land that has resisted a half-century of efforts at rehabilitation. In recent years, ranching has been embraced as the key to subduing another "frontier" —the tropical forests of Central and South America. Vast areas of rain forest were cleared during the seventies and planted to exotic grasses, often with the generous support of Latin American governments. The beef raised on these pastures was destined for export markets in North America, Europe, and the oil-rich nations of the Middle East.

Yet scarcely a decade after the expansion began, hopes of sustaining Latin America's cattle boom have been stymied by a combination of ecological and economic factors. Unfortunately, the ecological consequences of this failed revival may prove as lasting as the Badlands created in temperate latitudes.

Cattle and sheep came to Latin America with Spanish and Portuguese colonists in the sixteenth century, and the region's first ranches were established on natural grasslands in Brazil and Venezuela. Year-round grazing on the fertile pampas of Argentina and Uruguay encouraged a steady growth in the size of herds.[19]

Despite the pace of this early development, abundant natural pasture and the physical difficulty of clearing forests precluded the incursion of ranching into forested areas. Though cattle spread with settlers to the farthest reaches of the Amazon Basin, and although ranching has always been a favored way of bringing Brazil's frontier into the national economic sphere, the limits of that region's natural grasslands established the limits of the industry. As geographer Susanna Hecht has noted, "The existence for close to 300 years of successful cattle ranching on Amazonian natural grasslands, with animal populations roughly constant for the last 200 years, may well have acted as a 'blinder' for policy makers to many of the real environmental constraints in the region."[20]

During the seventies, a dramatic increase in deforestation occurred in Central and South America. A simultaneous growth in beef exports to international markets was publicized by British conservationist Norman Myers, who documented this "hamburger connection." The cattle raised on tropical pastures, never fattened in feedlots, supplied beef most suitable for fast-food outlets in North America and other industrial regions, the food industry's most dynamic market. Latin America's rush to create grazing lands and the rapid growth of its cattle herds rivaled the boom years of the cattle drives on the U.S. Great Plains a century ago.[21]

Between 1961 and 1978, Central American forests declined from 29.1 million to 17.8 million hectares. The region's cattle herd increased from 7 million in the early sixties to nearly 12 million in 1978; although cattle ranches were not the sole cause of deforestation, most analysts agree that new pastures were the primary culprit. In the Amazon Basin, an additional 11 million hectares

of land had been cleared by 1980, the greatest part of it for pasture.

Agricultural censuses revealed that cattle numbers in the Amazon doubled, to 2.1 million head, between 1950 and 1975. In the eastern Amazon, herds were expanding at 12 percent each year during the early seventies. The basin accounted for a growing share of Brazil's 90 million cattle.[22]

Central America's beef exports

Table 4-5. Central America: Beef Production and Exports, 1961–85[1]

Year	Production	Net Exports	Exports as Share of Production
	(thousand metric tons)		(percent)
1961	145	20	14
1965	170	34	20
1970	252	95	38
1975	297	118	40
1977	350	126	36
1978	391	155	40
1979	400	162	40
1980	355	110	31
1981	355	101	28
1982	360	91	25
1983	321	81	25
1984	316	65	21
1985[2]	318	61	19

[1]Costa Rica, El Salvador, Guatemala, Honduras, Nicaragua, and Panama. [2]Preliminary.
SOURCES: Data for 1961–78 from Douglas R. Shane, "Hoofprints on the Forest: An Inquiry into the Beef Cattle Industry in the Tropical Forest Areas of Latin America," U.S. Department of State, Washington, D.C., March 1980; data for 1979–84 from U.S. Department of Agriculture (USDA), Foreign Agricultural Service (FAS), *World Livestock and Poultry Situation* (FL&P-1), Washington, D.C., April 1985; estimate for 1985 from Robert Curtis, USDA, FAS, Washington, D.C., private communication, August 22, 1985.

peaked in 1979, when 40 percent of the region's production was sent to overseas markets, principally in the United States. (See Table 4–5.) The "hamburger connection" in that year was unquestionable. Since then, however, beef production has declined by 82,000 metric tons, and exports by over 100,000 tons, making them in 1985 the smallest share of the region's production in 20 years.

The single most important factor in this decline was a substantial, and largely unexpected, drop in beef consumption in the United States, and a resulting 330,000-ton decline in beef imports. (See Figure 4–1.) Annual per capita consumption of beef has declined from its high of 92 pounds in 1977 to an estimated 77 pounds in 1985. The imported share of that consumption has fallen as well. Imports have not supplied this small a share of U.S. beef consumption, now just 6 percent, since the mid-sixties. True, escalating warfare in El Salvador and Nicaragua, and a U.S. trade embargo against the latter country, are contributing to the decline in imports—and in ways that further undermine the region's environmental stability. Nonetheless, liquidation of forests in Central America can no longer be blamed on the "hamburger connection."[23]

In Brazil, pressures on forests have not yet been fully relieved. The size of the country's cattle herd has remained relatively stable since the late seventies, at about 93 million head. Beef production as a whole is stable as well, at a level below the 1977 peak of 2.45 million tons. But faced with a massive foreign debt, Brazil has gone from exporting

Table 4-6. Brazil: Beef Production and Exports, 1961–85

Year	Production	Net Exports	Exports as Share of Production
	(thousand metric tons)		(percent)
1961	1,369	36	3
1965	1,495	63	4
1970	1,845	123	7
1975	2,150	73	3
1977	2,450	156	6
1978	2,200	12	<1
1979	2,100	(−4)[1]	—
1980	2,150	104	5
1981	2,250	224	10
1982	2,400	336	14
1983	2,400	380	16
1984	2,200	470	21
1985[2]	2,300	470	20

[1]Net imports. [2]Preliminary.
SOURCES: Data for 1961–78 from Douglas R. Shane, "Hoofprints on the Forest: An Inquiry into the Beef Cattle Industry in the Tropical Forest Areas of Latin America," U.S. Department of State, Washington, D.C., March 1980; data for 1979–84 from U.S. Department of Agriculture (USDA), Foreign Agricultural Service (FAS), *World Livestock and Poultry Situation* (FL&P-1), Washington, D.C., April 1985; estimate for 1985 from Robert Curtis, USDA, FAS, Washington, D.C., private communication, August 22, 1985.

Thousand
Metric Tons

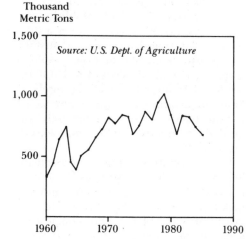

Figure 4-1. U.S. Net Beef Imports, 1960-85

relatively insignificant quantities of beef to being the largest beef exporter in Latin America. (See Table 4–6.) By 1985, Brazil accounted for more than half the beef exports of the entire continent. The country has more than quadrupled its exports since 1980, mostly at the expense of its own citizens. Per capita consumption within Brazil has declined by 25 percent.

Much of Brazil's beef production is being sustained on forest pastures cleared in the last decade, land that many ecologists warn will quickly lose its productivity. The government has recently withdrawn the special subsidies and tax advantages that encouraged pasture clearing during the seventies, making it more difficult for ranchers simply to move on to new forest sites when the productivity of their land declines. Although Brazil's current export boom may only be temporary, the degradation of its intricate tropical forests will prove irreversible.[24]

The Fabric Unravels

When rangelands deteriorate, the fabric of ecological relationships frays. Vegetation disappears from the landscape, leaving soils exposed to wind and water. When it rains, topsoil washes away. Watercourses are scoured by silt, which fills reservoirs or rushes to the sea; the eroded landscape loses its capacity to absorb and store the next rainfall. Depleted soils sustain less robust forage when the next growing season arrives. When degradation and drought coincide, livestock dependent on the range can perish in large numbers. In Inner Mongolia, a drought in the late sixties cut herd numbers from 26 million to only 6 million. Eighteen years of inadequate and declining rainfall have deci-

mated herds throughout Africa, and millions of pastoralists have lost their animals and become ecological refugees.[25]

Desertification—the watchword of rangeland deterioration—has received widespread currency in the last decade. The term refers to a decline in the biological productivity and diversity of the land to levels below the potential of the climate, soil, plant, and animal communities characteristic of a particular location. Economic activities based on the land's natural productivity can precipitate the decline and are diminished as it progresses.

Despite international conferences, the drafting of action plans, and the mustering of task forces in many parts of the world, certainty about desertification's extent and remedies remains elusive. According to Dr. Harold Dregne of Texas Tech University: "There's very little of a scientific nature that is available anywhere in the world to evaluate the status of desertification. We're all going on estimates, guesses, and common knowledge. Nobody has done anything about improving our monitoring and our data base. It's very unsatisfactory."[26]

The most recent global assessment of desertification was assembled by Australian geographer Jack Mabbutt. According to his 1984 survey, over a third of the earth's land surface, land sustaining an estimated 850 million people, is threatened with desertification. Of the world's 3.1 billion hectares of rangeland, Mabbutt estimated that as many as 1.3 billion hectares may be severely degraded: Productivity losses may exceed 50 percent.[27]

Inappropriate grazing can hasten the loss of productivity. Animals are not indiscriminate in their grazing, and domestic as well as wild herbivores tend to favor particular plants. Perennial grasses provide the most nutritious and palatable forage on many kinds of range-lands, and if herds are poorly managed, grazing may eliminate perennials from the landscape. They tend to be replaced by annual grasses and other invading species that may be both less nutritious and far less likely to sprout when rainfall is short. Writing of the Sahel region, World Bank forester Jean Gorse notes that "annual grasses now predominate, having replaced the more valuable, but less resistant perennials. Annuals may not appear for years in an area for lack of adequate moisture, and then produce a flush of good forage when the rains strike again."[28]

This gradual biological simplification of the land can heighten the competition of domestic livestock and wild grazing animals for available forage. Normally, most wild animals and domestic rumi-nants do not interfere with one another because their forage preferences differ. Grazing by domestic livestock can even change plant communities in ways that favor wildlife on the same land. But when the composition of range plants has been altered enough to reduce over-all productivity, competition may inten-sify. According to Winrock Interna-tional: "When ranges are overgrazed, or choices are otherwise severely limited, diets of wild and domestic animals are practically the same. Under such condi-tions competition between and among wild and domestic animals can be se-vere."[29]

It has often been argued that the per-vasive deterioration of pastoralists' range areas simply reflects a "tragedy of the commons," in which the private ben-efits herders enjoy by acquiring more livestock exceed the common costs that they confront as range is overgrazed. This belief has led to suggestions that pastoralists' common grazing lands should be redistributed as private prop-erty, that pastoralists should be settled in ranch-style units in which herd sizes could be restricted, and that a commer-cial, market-oriented economy would generate less degradation of rangelands. Although group ranches have proved successful in parts of Kenya and else-where in Africa, they have not provided a panacea for deteriorating range-lands.[30]

Development assistance to pastoral-ists has sometimes fostered the deterio-ration and vulnerability it was intended to reverse. Since cattle need water every day, and can graze only where they are within a day's walk of it, much develop-ment aid has been used to establish per-manent water sources in dry-season grazing areas. The concentration of herds around wells in the dry season cre-ates a circle of trampled, barren land called a "sacrifice area" that may be as much as several kilometers in diameter. The original scarcity of water, along with traditional grazing restrictions, kept herds within the carrying capacity of their pastures. The newly abundant water supplies attract herds that forage supplies are unable to support. When the resulting range deterioration is com-pounded by drought, the main cause of livestock deaths is starvation, not thirst.[31]

Development assistance to pastor-alists has sometimes fostered the deterioration and vulnerability it was intended to reverse.

In countries where commercial ranch-ing is the rule, rangelands fare no better. ILCA's Stephen Sandford argues that "overstocking and environmental deterioration appear to be just as com-mon and serious in areas of rangeland where, as in parts of the USA and Aus-tralia, both land and livestock are individually owned." In the United States, the privilege of grazing on public lands is rationed by a permit system administered by the Bureau of Land Management, in effect a means of regulating the use of common land. The BLM, responsible for administering 69 million hectares of land primarily in the western states, has assessed the condition of public rangeland four times over the past half-century. These assessments show that despite 50 years of management, the share of public rangelands in "fair" or "poor" condition has never fallen below 60 percent.[32]

In 1983, U.S. ranchers paid a fee of $1.40 per animal to graze on public land. By contrast, private landowners who allowed grazing on comparable land charged $8.85 for the privilege. The low permit prices make grazing on federal land relatively attractive, even where forage is of poor quality. Inexpensive access to federal rangeland actually enhances the value of adjacent private land, leading ranchers to advocate grazing allotments as high as the Bureau of Land Management will allow. Aside from encouraging high stocking levels on the nation's most vulnerable rangeland, the current grazing fee structure constitutes a public subsidy similar to the below-cost rates for water from federal irrigation projects in the West.[33]

Ranchers defend the low permit price by citing the poor quality of forage on federal land. But the low price, and the consequent political pressure on federal authorities to allow as much grazing as possible, maintains the grazing at levels that prevent forage from recovering. Unfortunately, the profit margin has vanished for much of the range-fed livestock production in the United States today, and the prospects of changing grazing regulation in ways that increase ranchers' costs are dim.

In South Africa, where commercial ranching has been practiced by white farmers for generations, similar deterioration of the rangeland is reported. In a speech announcing a National Grazing Strategy before the South African House of Assembly in May 1985, the Minister of Agriculture and Water Supply said: "Approximately three million hectares of [rangeland] area have been invaded to such an extent by [woody] species that they are useless for normal stock farming . . . .Approximately two million hectares of veld in the North-western Cape have deteriorated to such an extent that it cannot be restored to productive grazing using normal control measures. Moreover, veld conditions in half of the 1.4 million hectares of Drakensberg grazing area of the South-eastern Transvaal subregion are so poor that stock ought to be withdrawn from the area for a considerable length of time." According to the Minister, only 10 percent of the natural rangelands of South Africa remain in good condition, and 60 percent are in poor condition.[34]

REGENERATING THE RANGE

As ranchers and pastoralists are squeezed ever more tightly between land claimed by farmers and land too arid to sustain grazing, the effort to regenerate rangelands becomes more challenging. Whatever technical measures are proposed to restore rangelands, their success will depend on whether the people whose livelihoods are affected support them. As range scientist Chris Maser observes in a report from the U.S. Office of Technology Assessment: "We like to think that we manage vegetation, animals, land, water, etc., but we really only manipulate these components of the ecosystem. What we manage is people's attitudes and desires."[35]

In the Third World's rangelands, and especially in Africa, livestock-dependent people remain threatened primarily by the spread of rain-fed farming onto grazing lands. Here, efforts to raise agricultural productivity must be a cornerstone of range management. Researchers at the International Livestock Center for Africa believe that improved animal husbandry on small parcels of land can raise cropland fertility and help reduce tensions between herders and farmers.

In West Africa, ILCA's researchers have developed "fodder banks" to provide adequate livestock feed during the dry season, when animals' milk yields, body weight, and reproductive rates all decline. When the annual rains begin, herds are crowded onto a 2–4 hectare field, where their hooves break the ground surface and their dung fertilizes the soil. The area is then sown with a nitrogen-fixing crop that can be harvested to provide periodic rations of nutritious fodder during the dry season, supplementing range grazing when natural pastures are least productive. Farmers' land is improved and pastoralists' animals are better-fed.[36]

Livestock can also be a key to providing farmers with the financial security that permits them to improve farming practices. According to ILCA's research with small-scale farmers in the central Ethiopian highlands, livestock constitute farmers' main income-earning asset. The sale of animal products and trade in animals themselves generated 83 percent of farmers' cash income in the 42 farms studied, while sales of crops supplied only 17 percent. Enhancing the productivity of livestock raised by farmers helps boost the income farmers need to purchase fertilizer and other inputs that raise crop yields. Only when these yields rise will farmers have a secure alternative to clearing new fields to expand their harvests.[37]

Where commercial ranching is practiced on natural rangelands, grazing management can be patterned more closely on the behavior of the wild herbivores that once flourished on such lands. Most ranchers allow their herds to disperse evenly over available pastures, but dispersed grazing even by small herds can selectively overgraze key forage plants and disrupt the land's natural pattern of ecological succession. When animals are closely herded, their impact on the ecosystem approximates more closely the natural impact of wild herbivores. Concentrated trampling by hoofed animals breaks up the soil surface and improves seeding, while short intervals of close grazing on a small area subjects all plants to equal pressure and fosters complete regeneration of the plant community.[38]

One key to the success of innovative grazing strategies is closer attention to the timing of grazing on natural rangeland. Although most range management has emphasized the importance of animal numbers, other factors influence the adequacy of forage and the condition of the land. A grazing strategy first developed in France by André Voisin is based on the premise that the timing of grazing and rest intervals is more important than the size of herds. The Voisin system seeks to allocate grazing over the course of the year to match the seasonal changes in the productivity of forage plants. This ensures that livestock graze plants at their most nutritious, favors plant regeneration, and protects the perennial grasses that bind the topsoil and increase the land's ability to absorb rainfall.[39]

As in forestry, farming, and many other development efforts in the Third World, strategies to improve the condition of common lands will succeed only if the people who use them benefit from the improvements. In India, the state of Gujarat has led in introducing innovative programs to restore the forage-producing potential of common grazing lands. The state's Forest Department has encouraged villagers to establish forage and fuelwood plantations on these lands, partly to provide dry-season forage for animals owned by landless farmers.[40]

Gujarat and three other Indian states have initiated programs to rehabilitate wastelands and degraded forests by providing one-hectare parcels to the landless. Each family receives technical assistance, tree and fodder seedlings, and a cross-bred cow at the outset of the project. Food-for-work payments free family labor to tend the plots. After three years, the Forest Department takes over management of the land planted to trees, while families retain rights to the forage plots. The sale of dairy products made possible by the new fodder supplies raises family incomes.[41]

Sustainable use of the range has only proved possible where insight into the dynamics of range ecosystems has shaped the economic activities they are expected to support.

Among true pastoralists, traditional grazing practices provide a logical starting point for efforts to restore common lands. In Syria, revival of the "Hema" system of cooperative range management has enabled revegetation of 7 million hectares of rangeland. Herders relinquish their autonomy over grazing decisions in order to join cooperatives whose members are guaranteed exclusive access to particular pastures. The Hema system provides a means for adjudicating disputes that inevitably arise over access to particular pastures, and it maintains the integrity of traditional migration routes. Its successful modern revival is a hopeful sign that other pastoral strategies may provide a culturally acceptable foundation for land restoration.[42]

China has adopted a national grassland law establishing state ownership of common pastures that are then allocated to individual households on long leases. The amount of land provided to each household is determined by a formula that includes the size of the family and the number of livestock owned—a rough estimate of the land's carrying capacity. The recently introduced responsibility system is encouraging families to expand their herds, however; whether rising incomes will encourage herders to invest in improvements on their designated pastures remains to be seen. Revegetation of grasslands has only occurred on a small percentage of the country's land. According to the *China Daily*, the country's English-language daily newspaper, 1.8 million hectares were planted in 1984, and a total of 4.8 million hectares have received such treatment—just over 1 percent of China's grasslands.[43]

Range-based livelihoods have been hardly touched by the technological and social changes that have transformed most other spheres of human activity in the past generation. Advances in other fields have done little to boost the efficiency of economic activities on rangelands, whose inhabitants remain economically and politically isolated from modern society as a result. The discipline of range science has typically emphasized the production of protein rather than the management of the various ecosystem components that sustain that production; the ubiquitous consequences include vegetation declines and disruptions of the hydrological cycle. As grazing and herding have been restricted to lands more susceptible to this deterioration, sustainable use of the range has only proved possible where insight into the dynamics of range ecosystems has shaped the economic activities they are expected to support.

On a semiarid plain north of Nairobi, Kenya, Dr. David Hopcraft is proving that imaginative, ecologically sophisticated management of the African savanna has environmental and economic advantages over conventional ranching. At Hopcraft's 8,000-hectare game ranch at Athi River, 15 native wild-animal species coexist with cattle. Since 1981, the herds have been culled for both beef and venison. Animals and forage have flourished despite the drought that crippled conventional ranches nearby. Hopcraft reports: "From a commercial perspective, the selective harvesting of game animals has been a notable success. Net returns per acre are ten times the average cattle ranch in the area, yet the stocking of wildlife is still one sixth that of normal cattle numbers."[44]

The glimmer of ecological and economic success on the Athi River in Kenya demonstrates that sound use of rangeland, based on the interdependencies of functioning ecosystems, is possible. It exemplifies a pattern of range use that might be a reasonable standard against which other grazing practices are evaluated. Humanity's origins can be traced to bands of hunters that once followed wild grazing herds across Africa's plains. A final paradox: The basis for sustainable rangeland livelihoods in the years ahead may lie in learning and heeding the ecological lessons of the wild herds that remain.

5

Moving Beyond Oil

Christopher Flavin

The world oil outlook is brighter now than it has been for some time. In the two years since Worldwatch assessed the situation in *State of the World-1984*, many aspects of the oil picture have continued to improve. The average price of a barrel has declined from its peak of over $35 in early 1981 to just $27 in 1985. Consumption has fallen a remarkable 9 percent from its high point in 1979. The share of the world oil market controlled by the Organization of Petroleum Exporting Countries (OPEC) has fallen from about half in 1979 to less than 30 percent in 1985.[1]

Although this picture is one of nearly uniform progress, below the surface lie numerous hidden problems. The strength of the U.S. dollar throughout much of the world has kept oil prices high in many countries, which has thwarted Europe's attempted economic recovery. Some of the world's poorest nations, including most of those in Africa, are now virtually priced out of the oil market. Unable to pay for oil or for the investments needed to create non-oil-based economies, many Third World

An expanded version of this chapter appeared as Worldwatch Paper 66, *World Oil: Coping With the Dangers of Success*.

nations are in danger of becoming trapped in an economic underclass. In addition, several governments that have chosen coal as their chief replacement for oil are now facing public health and environmental problems that may make a coal-based economy unsustainable.

Perhaps the key challenge facing world energy planners is that petroleum remains a dwindling resource. While OPEC members are husbanding their oil reserves in an effort to maintain prices, non-OPEC producers such as the United States, the United Kingdom, and the Soviet Union are depleting their reserves at a record pace. The Middle East currently contains nearly six tenths of the world's proven oil reserves. When non-OPEC petroleum production declines in the nineties, Middle Eastern OPEC members will be back in the driver's seat.

The patterns of world energy use, if they continue on their present course, will sow the seeds of another energy crisis. Reduced oil dependence in recent years was made possible by impressive gains in energy efficiency around the world and by the development of alternative energy sources. If oil prices continue to drop, they will soon begin to undermine investments in energy alternatives. Declining prices have already led many countries to cut successful energy programs that would have provided substitutes for oil in the nineties.

The world faces a far different energy challenge today than it confronted in the seventies. We essentially know how long oil reserves will last and what policies work. Thanks to new technologies, the opportunity to develop energy alternatives is greater than ever. Blind faith in monolithic solutions such as synthetic fuels or breeder reactors has fortunately faded. The hard part is continuing the move beyond oil at a time when it is easy to be complacent.

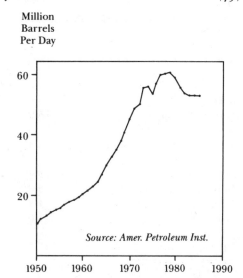

Million
Barrels
Per Day

Source: Amer. Petroleum Inst.

Figure 5-1. World Oil Production, 1950-85

A Reduced Dependence on Oil

1979 probably marked the historic peak in worldwide oil dependence—over 10 years sooner than petroleum geologists in the mid-seventies predicted. Oil production in that year reached almost 66 million barrels per day, before plummeting 14 percent to less than 57 million barrels a day in 1983. The economic recovery of 1984 boosted production slightly, but in 1985 it again fell to less than 57 million barrels daily. (See Figure 5–1.) For the first time in postwar history, world oil production fell during a year of substantial worldwide economic growth.[2]

Western Europe, North America, and Japan together account for two thirds of world petroleum use; oil prices of $35 per barrel in 1981 (five times the level in 1973) led to a historic lowering of oil dependence in industrial countries. Between 1979 and 1984, consumption declined 18 percent in Western Europe and 16 percent in both North America and Japan. (See Table 5–1.) Oil con-

sumption per unit of gross national product (GNP)—a good measure of dependence on petroleum—fell 36 percent in the Western industrial countries and Japan between 1973 and 1984.[3]

In the rest of the world, oil consumption rose 7 percent between 1979 and 1984, despite the intervening economic recession. Most developing countries started at low levels of usage, have inefficient industrial and transportation systems, and have been unable to afford the investments needed to develop alternative energy sources. Countries with centrally planned economies have also been relatively slow to move away from oil, in part because their economic systems protect industries and consumers from the full brunt of higher prices. But even where petroleum use is rising, it is doing so at a much slower rate than during the seventies.

Between 1979 and 1984, oil imports fell 34 percent in Western Europe, 40 percent in the United States, and 26 percent in Japan. Together, these account for over four fifths of the 31 percent decline in world petroleum trade during

Table 5-1. World Oil Consumption, by Region, 1973, 1979, and 1984

Region	1973	1979	1984	Change (1979–84)
	(million barrels per day)			(percent)
North America	18.6	19.8	16.6	−16
Western Europe	15.2	15.0	12.3	−18
Japan	5.5	5.5	4.6	−16
Europe and Soviet Union	8.4	11.1	11.4	+ 3
Latin America	3.4	4.2	4.5	+ 7
Other Asia/Oceania	3.9	5.6	5.8	+ 4
Middle East	1.2	1.5	1.9	+27
Africa	1.0	1.4	1.7	+21
Total[1]	57.1	64.1	58.9	− 8

[1]Numbers may not add to totals due to rounding.
SOURCE: British Petroleum Company, *BP Statistical Review of World Energy* (London: 1985).

this period. In 1984, the two largest exporters of oil to the United States were its neighbors—Canada and Mexico. The Middle East as a whole supplied just 4 percent of the oil used in the United States, down from 20 percent in 1979. Japan, on the other hand, still gets two thirds of its oil from the Middle East.[4]

Adding to competition in world petroleum markets is an increase in non-OPEC oil production of more than 5 million barrels per day since 1979. Over half came from two areas—Mexico and the North Sea. Mexican production has almost doubled since 1979, adding 1.4 million barrels per day to world oil supplies. British and Norwegian production went from near zero in the early seventies to 3.3 million barrels per day in 1984. These countries have become major oil exporters and important counterweights to OPEC in international markets.

Other nations that have significantly boosted production in recent years include Brazil, Colombia, Egypt, Malaysia, and Pakistan. The new oil has provided welcome domestic energy supplies and has improved national trade balances. The Third World has added only 1.3 million barrels per day to the world supply of petroleum, and much of that is used internally. Emerging Third World oil producers have so far had little effect on international oil markets.[5]

The two largest players in the world oil market—the Soviet Union and the United States—have so far staved off anticipated declines in production. Record levels of exploration and drilling caused U.S. petroleum production to rise by 300,000 barrels per day in the early eighties after falling 1.5 million barrels per day in the seventies. Soviet production rose by 500,000 barrels per day between 1979 and 1983, defying Western analysts' predictions of a 15 percent decline. Together, the two superpowers are daily producing about 3 million barrels more than was expected as recently as 1979.

As oil consumption declined and production in non-OPEC countries increased, far-reaching changes occurred in world oil markets. Once controlled by a cartel of multinational corporations and then by OPEC itself, petroleum markets today are increasingly competitive, shaped more by market forces than by governmental and corporate decisions. Whereas 95 percent of the oil traded internationally in the seventies was under long-term contract, today 50–60 percent is sold on competitive markets at prevailing prices.[6]

Petroleum markets today are shaped more by market forces than by governmental and corporate decisions.

Only a small fraction of OPEC oil is now sold at the cartel's official prices. Referring to the practice of discounting official prices, Nigeria's oil minister Tam David West said at a mid-1985 OPEC meeting, "Every one of us is guilty of one thing or another; there is not one country that is exempt." Today, developments in the oil fields of Kuwait or Siberia soon affect producers in the North Sea or Texas. This brave new world of competition generally appears to be a healthy development, providing flexibility and a cushion for future swings in supply and demand.[7]

OPEC's share of world oil output has fallen from about half in 1979 to less than 30 percent in 1985. The major Middle Eastern producers, with the bulk of world reserves, have cut production the most. (See Table 5–2.) By early 1985, Kuwait's production had declined 60 percent and Libya's was down 50 per-

Table 5-2. Oil Production and Revenues in OPEC and Mexico, 1973, 1980, and 1984

Country	Daily Oil Production			Annual Oil Revenues		
	1973	1980	1984	1973	1980	1984
	(million barrels)			(billion dollars)		
Middle East						
Saudi Arabia	7.6	10.0	4.7	4.3	102.2	44.6
Iran	5.9	1.5	2.2	4.4	13.5	19.1
United Arab Emirates	1.5	1.7	1.2	0.9	19.5	10.8
Iraq	2.0	2.6	1.2	1.8	26.1	9.4
Libya	2.2	1.8	1.1	2.2	22.6	10.9
Kuwait	3.0	1.4	1.0	1.8	17.9	10.3
Other OPEC Members						
Venezuela	3.5	2.2	1.9	3.0	16.3	13.3
Nigeria	2.0	2.1	1.4	2.1	23.4	10.8
Indonesia	1.3	1.6	1.4	0.2	12.9	9.7
Algeria	1.1	1.1	1.0	1.0	12.5	5.6
Ecuador, Gabon, and Qatar	0.9	0.8	0.8	0.6	8.0	5.7
OPEC Total[1]	30.8	26.9	17.9	22.5	274.9	150.2
Mexico[2]	0.6	2.2	3.0	n.a.	n.a.	n.a.

[1]Numbers may not add to totals due to rounding.   [2]Mexico is an ex-officio member.
SOURCES: *Petroleum Intelligence Weekly,* various issues; British Petroleum Company, *BP Statistical Review of World Energy* (London: 1985).

cent. The Iran-Iraq war has halved oil production in those two countries. Saudi Arabia remains the dominant "swing producer," however, since it has propped up petroleum prices by removing as much as 7 million barrels a day from the world oil market. Saudi Arabia's daily production fell from 10 million barrels in 1980 to 4.7 million barrels in 1984, and to just 2.5 million barrels in mid-1985—the lowest level in 18 years. By 1985, tension between OPEC members had reached record levels, and Saudi Arabia appeared to be moving toward increased production and the competitive pricing of its oil. If other members respond by raising production and lowering prices, the cartel may well dissolve entirely.[8]

OPEC's efforts to maintain a floor on oil prices have already cost it dearly. From a peak of $275 billion in 1980, OPEC petroleum revenues fell to about $150 billion in 1984, and to even less in 1985. A study by the Oxford Institute for Energy Studies in Great Britain shows that, due to a decline in demand and price, Middle Eastern producers lost close to $200 billion in oil revenues between 1982 and 1984. This is a serious economic crisis for countries that get 95–100 percent of their foreign exchange from these revenues and that have based government spending on overly optimistic projections of such funds.[9]

Many oil exporters—such as Mexico, an ex-officio OPEC member with a $96-billion foreign debt—face a rising tide of economic troubles as prices fall. Venezuela cut a planned $2.4-billion public works program by 75 percent; Nigeria expelled 2 million guest workers. Even wealthy Persian Gulf oil producers have suffered economic problems, including, in the case of Kuwait, a 50 percent decline in land prices and a 30 percent fall in office construction. Saudi Arabia's oil revenues have fallen

from $113 billion in 1981 to a projected $31 billion in 1985. The nation's foreign-exchange holdings dropped from $150 billion to less than $100 billion in 1985, and public spending was cut 23 percent to stem the hemorrhage of capital.[10]

The biggest winner from the shift in oil markets is the United States. The U.S. oil import bill fell from $61 billion in 1981 to an estimated $32 billion in 1985. Petroleum accounted for less than 15 percent of American imports in 1985, down from 34 percent in 1980. Falling prices have helped cut U.S. inflation to a 4 percent annual rate, its lowest level in more than a decade. Economists believe that lower oil prices contributed to the record-breaking economic recovery that culminated in a GNP growth rate of 6.8 percent in 1984. Lower oil prices have caused problems for U.S. oil companies however. During the early eighties, billions of dollars were invested in petroleum exploration and development on the assumption that oil prices would continue upward. Since then, many small companies have retrenched or actually gone out of business, threatening some banks with large oil portfolios.[11]

Other economies have not benefited as much as the United States from the stimulative effect of falling prices. This is because most oil is traded internationally in U.S. dollars, and the value of the dollar in relation to most other currencies rose steadily in the early eighties. While the price of petroleum has declined 23 percent in U.S. dollars since 1981, its cost in Japan dropped just 11 percent. In West Germany, the real cost of oil has risen 7 percent, in India it has gone up 11 percent, and in France it has risen 38 percent.[12]

The average price of petroleum products in Europe has continued to rise since 1981. These high prices have hindered economic recovery and made it more difficult to bring down inflation.

Since OPEC members import large quantities of goods and services from Europe, they have benefited from the strong dollar, which boosts the real value of their oil sales. Consistently high oil prices also account for the continued weakness of petroleum markets in Europe. The World Bank estimates that oil imports in Western Europe would be 1.7 million barrels per day higher if exchange rates had remained at the 1979 level.[13]

After falling 20 percent between 1979 and 1983, European oil consumption leveled off in 1984 and declined again in 1985. The current price of oil serves as ample incentive for investments in improved efficiency and, where possible, conversion to other sources of energy. The high value of the dollar also adds uncertainty to European energy forecasts, which now generally include caveats about future exchange rates. A sudden decline in the value of the dollar would tend to slow Europe's move away from imported oil.

The Soviet Union, with a total output of 12.5 million barrels per day (three quarters as much as recent OPEC production), is the world's largest oil producer and a major player in global energy markets. Rising petroleum prices in the seventies boosted the Soviet economy significantly, providing 60–75 percent of its Western "hard currency" earnings. The Soviet Union exports 1.5 million barrels of oil to the West each day, at competitive international prices, so the Soviet economy has been hit hard by recent declines in the world price of this resource.[14]

Eastern Europe, with the exception of Romania, has little domestic oil and depends on the Soviet Union for 90 percent of its supplies—close to 2 million barrels per day. Soviet oil sales to its East European allies are based on a pricing formula tied to a five-year sliding average of world prices. This system pro-tected Eastern Europe from the full brunt of increases in the early eighties, but prices are now equal to or slightly above the world market level. The burden of spending about $20 billion a year on Soviet oil is a major strain on the struggling economies of Eastern Europe.[15]

Developing countries with struggling economies have in effect been forced out of the world oil market.

Even more than Europe, Third World countries have failed to reap the benefits of lower oil prices. Accumulating debts and deliberate government policies have accelerated the decline of Third World currencies relative to the dollar. Steady erosion in the markets for commodities such as copper and sugar are an additional burden, since export of these goods often finances oil imports. Overall, petroleum imports absorb a large share of the foreign exchange available to most developing countries—as high as 80 percent in some nations.

Third World nations that have extensive indigenous energy sources or that have rapidly industrializing economies have fared the best. Hydropower, alcohol fuels, and oil exploration programs have helped lower Brazil's still-staggering oil import bill, and South Korea's expanding supplies of coal and nuclear power have done the same. But these investments have themselves created large debts. (In Brazil, one fifth of the country's foreign debt can be attributed to power plant construction.) The World Bank projects that Third World energy investments will absorb about 4 percent of GNP in the years ahead and will act as a constraint on other industrial investments.[16]

Developing countries with struggling

economies have in effect been forced out of the world oil market. According to the World Bank, Africa (with the exception of Nigeria) has barely enough petroleum to cover essential needs. Some governments must take extraordinary measures to pay for oil imports. Cuba reportedly sells sugar to the Soviet Union at 10 times the world price and uses the proceeds to buy Soviet petroleum, part of which it resells on the world market to earn hard currency.[17]

In some parts of the Third World, transportation systems, factories, and power plants are occasionally shut down when oil supplies run out. Many nations have begun to cut back on their traditionally heavy subsidies for kerosene and diesel fuel, often at the insistence of the International Monetary Fund. The price of petroleum fuels has risen three- to fourfold in many developing countries since 1981. Rising kerosene prices have led to riots in some cases. Nonetheless, the World Bank projects that the use of petroleum in Third World countries will rise 50 percent between 1980 and 1995, making these nations central in the world oil outlook.[18]

AN EFFICIENCY SUCCESS STORY

Energy efficiency has been far and away the largest contributor to the improved world oil situation during the past decade. Indeed, statistics show that greater efficiency accounts for over half the 36 percent decline in the energy/GNP ratio of industrial countries since 1973.[19] These improvements over the last 12 years have outstripped even the more optimistic forecasts and continue to exceed annually revised official projections. Yet there remains an enormous

potential to improve further the energy efficiency of the world's economies (see *State of the World-1985*).

The United States, starting with one of the world's most energy-intensive economies, has achieved one of the most dramatic turnarounds. Between 1973 and 1984, U.S. energy efficiency rose 23 percent, allowing national energy use to average about the 1973 level despite substantial economic growth. Without this increased efficiency, the nation's use of energy in 1984 would have been higher by the equivalent of 10 million barrels of oil per day—about double the oil imports that year. Annual U.S. energy expenditures would have been at least $100 billion higher. Coal, by comparison, has provided the equivalent of an additional 2 million barrels of oil per day, and nuclear power has accounted for just over 1 million barrels a day.[20]

Western Europe, starting with substantially more efficient economies, realized a 16 percent decline in its energy intensity between 1973 and 1984. Japan led the world with a remarkable 29 percent decline in its energy/GNP ratio, reflecting concerted efforts by industry and government to reduce oil dependence. In Greece and Australia, on the other hand, energy intensity actually rose during the past decade. Data compiled by the International Energy Agency show GNP in the Organisation for Economic Co-operation and Development (OECD) countries rising 24 percent between 1973 and 1984, while total energy use was unchanged. This indicates a 19 percent drop in the energy/GNP ratio. (See Table 5–3.)

Efficiency improvements stem in part from simple housekeeping measures (turning down thermostats and driving slower), in part from structural changes such as the development of less-energy-intensive service economies or communities where cars are not needed as often, and in part from technological im-

Table 5-3. Energy Intensity of Economic Activity in Selected Countries, 1973, 1979, and 1984, With Projections to 2000[1]

Country or Region	1973	1979	1984	2000	Change, 1973–84
	(metric tons of oil equivalent per $1,000 of gross domestic product)				(percent)
Australia	0.68	0.73	0.70	0.63	+ 3
Canada	1.14	1.16	1.09	1.02	− 4
West Germany	0.64	0.59	0.52	0.34	−19
Greece	0.59	0.63	0.64	0.77	+ 8
Italy	0.69	0.64	0.57	0.53	−17
Japan	0.70	0.61	0.50	0.38	−29
Sweden	0.69	0.67	0.64	0.48	− 7
Turkey	0.84	0.76	0.76	0.80	−10
United Kingdom	0.93	0.85	0.73	0.66	−22
United States	1.14	1.05	0.90	0.72	−21
All OECD Countries	0.90	0.84	0.73	0.59	−19

[1]Figures are standardized to show total primary energy use per $1,000 of gross domestic product at 1975 prices and exchange rates.
SOURCE: International Energy Agency, *Energy Policies and Programmes of IEA Countries, 1983 Review* (Paris: Organisation for Economic Co-operation and Development, 1985).

provements such as more efficiently designed homes, automobiles, and appliances. The first wave of increased energy efficiency in the seventies was dominated by housekeeping measures, but these became less important once the easy steps had been taken and energy price increases slowed.[21]

Structural and technological energy efficiency improvements are accelerating, however. The movement away from energy-intensive, heavy-industry-dominated economic systems is driven by major social and economic forces as well as by high energy costs and so has not been greatly affected by the recent decline in oil prices. In practice, the structural economic changes that lower oil use are hard to distinguish from the technological changes that occur purely in response to energy prices. Most analysts believe that the latter are more important in explaining recent energy trends, but precise percentages cannot be assigned.[22]

Many energy-efficient technologies took years to develop and are just now coming on the market. Economic recovery has caused a surge in the purchase of automobiles, appliances, and industrial equipment. As the older equipment is replaced, energy efficiency generally improves. Although lower energy prices cause consumers to be less discriminating when they shop for cars or appliances, even the less-energy-efficient equipment being sold today is usually a big improvement over the equipment being replaced. And efficiency improvements still offer large economic rewards.[23] Electricity prices continue to rise in most countries (see Chapter 6), natural gas prices have remained steady or risen slightly, and, except in the United States, the real price of oil has barely declined.

Anticipating the future pace of energy efficiency improvements is difficult. On the one hand, some of the easiest changes have already occurred. The growth of the service sector is slowing, millions of houses have already been weatherized, and cars are unlikely to get much smaller. On the other hand, a profusion of new, more energy-efficient technologies are just becoming available. New automotive technologies could raise new-car fuel economy from the current average of 25–30 miles per gallon to over 50. Pulse combustion gas furnaces now use 28 percent less fuel than traditional furnaces. The most advanced steel plants using virgin ore are over 25 percent more efficient than the world's average steel plant. And new "minimills" that use recycled steel are even more efficient.[24]

Although energy-efficient technologies continue to emerge from the laboratories, their future popularity remains one of the largest uncertainties in the global energy future. Gains have been slowed by a shortage of good information and investment capital, particularly for consumers, who are in the best position to make many of the improvements. Efficiency ranks higher on national energy planning agendas than it once did, but most policymakers still give lower priority (and far lower investments) to efficiency than to oil exploration or power plant construction.

Even without more government attention and reform of policies that discourage greater energy efficiency, substantial gains are likely during the next decade. But new efforts will be needed to extend these improvements beyond the early nineties, and they will have to begin soon. The efficiency of new homes and automobiles has leveled off since the early eighties in Europe and North America, which could portend a slowdown in improving the efficiency of the

total housing stock and automobile fleet.[25]

Automobiles and other forms of transportation are particularly critical to the world energy future since they are generally run on liquid fuels derived from oil. By the year 2000, transportation will claim a larger share of petroleum—up to 51 percent in industrial countries, and perhaps almost as high in the Third World, where use of energy by this sector is growing fastest. Since affordable alternatives to petroleum for transportation have yet to be found except in a few isolated countries (such as Brazil, where alcohol fuel is increasingly important), the energy efficiency of automobiles, trucks, and planes is a key factor in the world energy future.[26]

In developing a global end-use-oriented energy strategy, the Princeton Center for Energy and Environmental Studies concluded that if available resources were used as efficiently as is now possible, the world could in the year 2020 support a population of 7 billion people with a much higher standard of living on about the current energy budget.[27] Such a scenario is only possible if major energy efficiency improvements are made in developing as well as in industrial countries. Even with these improvements, the Third World would use two thirds of the world's energy, up from one third in 1985.

Developing countries face enormous obstacles in attempting to improve energy efficiency. Third World factories often consume two to five times as much fuel for a given process due to decades-old industrial equipment and a frequent shortage of trained personnel to perform simple maintenance and retrofits. Because factories there are often required to produce a fixed quota of goods at a fixed price, there is little incentive to lower energy costs. Third World buildings and transportation systems are also inefficient. Success in improving Third World energy efficiency—one of the world's most difficult and important challenges—will greatly influence both the development process and the future of the world oil market.

THE CHANGING MIX

Although improved energy efficiency accounts for over half the drop in world oil consumption since 1973, a range of other energy sources have helped reduce oil dependence, chief among them coal, natural gas, renewable sources of energy, and nuclear power. Missing from this list are the two major sources that government planners once counted on to provide energy in the future: synthetic fuels and nuclear breeder reactors. Neither shows any sign of being a major commercial energy source in the foreseeable future. Meanwhile, oil's share of world energy use has fallen from 41 to 35 percent, and continues to decline. (See Table 5–4.)

Coal is the world's second most im-portant energy source. Its 27 percent share of the global energy budget is up from 25 percent in 1978. The coal industry has made impressive strides during this period, but there are clouds on coal's horizon. Markets are now glutted in Europe and North America, and the use of coal in industry and for electricity generation appears likely to stagnate in the years ahead. Not only is electricity use growing much more slowly than in the past, but emerging small-scale generating technologies are beginning to compete with large coal-fired power plants. Coal use is growing rapidly in parts of the Third World, however, particularly in China, where consumption rose 50 percent in the past decade.[28]

The largest cloud hanging over coal is environmental. Acid rain, caused at least in part by the sulfur dioxide and nitrogen oxides emitted by power plants, is believed to be damaging lakes, streams, and forests in many parts of the world. Eastern Europe in particular has been forced for economic reasons to rely on high-sulfur coal rather than oil, and now faces a potential ecological catastrophe; 86 percent of East Germany's forests show air pollution damage. Growing evi-

Table 5-4. World Energy Use by Source, 1973, 1978, and 1984

Source	1973 Amount	1973 Share	1978 Amount	1978 Share	1984 Amount	1984 Share
	(mbd[1])	(percent)	(mbd[1])	(percent)	(mbd[1])	(percent)
Oil	56.0	41	61.6	41	57.1	35
Natural Gas	21.3	16	24.1	16	28.3	17
Coal	33.4	25	37.3	25	43.8	27
Renewables	23.5	17	25.8	17	28.7	18
Nuclear	1.0	1	3.0	2	5.7	3
Total[2]	135.2	100	151.8	100	163.6	100

[1]In terms of million barrels per day of oil equivalent.   [2]Percentage totals do not add to 100 due to rounding.
SOURCE: British Petroleum Company, *BP Statistical Review of World Energy* (London: 1985); Keith Openshaw, "Woodfuel—A Time for Reassessment," *Natural Resources Forum*, Vol. 3, 1978, pp. 35–51.

dence of acid rain damage, combined with concern over future regulations and the cost of pollution control technologies, has contributed to a slowdown in the construction of coal plants. And many researchers are concerned that massive amounts of carbon dioxide, released when coal is burned, may eventually alter the world's climate.[29]

Natural gas has also contributed to declines in world oil consumption—the equivalent of some 28 million barrels of oil each day. Outside the United States, natural gas consumption rose 80 percent during the past decade, led by the Soviet Union, which has 43 percent of the world's gas reserves. Natural gas reserves are now about equal to oil reserves worldwide, but are being consumed only half as fast. World Bank energy planners believe that in much of the Third World natural gas will in the long run be a more important energy source than oil. Increased Third World exploration, advanced exploration and extraction technologies, and more-efficient use are likely to give natural gas a larger role in the world energy system in the years ahead.[30]

Nuclear power generation has grown rapidly during the last 10 years, but not nearly so rapidly as most government energy planners had predicted. In 1985 nuclear power supplied little more than 3 percent of the world's energy, and its contribution is unlikely to exceed 6–8 percent in the year 2000. Only in Europe and parts of the Far East has nuclear power contributed significantly to declining oil dependence. Slowing the development of this energy source are continuing technical difficulties, cost overruns, and political opposition in many countries.[31]

Renewable energy sources now supply the world with the equivalent of 29 million barrels of oil each day, about five times the nuclear contribution. Of this total, hydropower provides the equivalent of about 9 million barrels of oil, and woodfuel and various waste materials provide about 20 million. Renewable energy consists of myriad different resources and technologies and has enjoyed fairly steady growth during the past decade. Renewable sources provide 18 percent of the world's energy, and the way they are managed is one of the most important links in the world's energy future.[32]

Fuelwood is still the predominant energy source in much of the Third World, and it has made a notable comeback in many industrial countries since the early seventies, particularly as a household and industrial heating source. Hydropower is growing rapidly as well, particularly in developing countries, where scores of large projects have been completed in the past decade. So far, other sources of renewable energy (such as wind, solar, geothermal, and advanced bio-energy systems) have contributed only slightly to the global energy budget, but their share is now growing rapidly. Several of these new energy technologies are moving quickly toward commercial development, despite the recent weakness in oil prices.[33]

THE LIMITS TO WORLD OIL

Amid these substantial shifts in world energy trends in recent years, one has remained consistent: World oil reserves are being depleted. This simple fact has been effectively obscured by euphoria over rising petroleum production outside of OPEC. These increases have come largely at the cost of accelerated depletion of some of the world's most limited and strategically important oil reserves, and they cannot continue much longer.

The standard but slightly misleading

measure of world oil resources is proven reserves. Included in this category is petroleum found in known reservoirs but not yet produced. The oil discovered each year is added to proven reserves, while the oil "produced" is subtracted. Global proven reserves increased rapidly throughout the postwar period—rising from 76 billion barrels in 1950 to 664 billion barrels in 1973. But since the mid-seventies, these reserves have increased only 5 percent, even though higher oil prices have encouraged exploration and annual extraction of petroleum has declined.[34]

Additions to world oil reserves after mid-century came principally from the Middle East, where reservoirs vastly larger than those found elsewhere were discovered. Between 1970 and 1977, global reserve figures were sustained by more modest discoveries in the Middle East and by other discoveries in Alaska, the North Sea, and Mexico. But since the late seventies, annual additions to proven reserves have sometimes not even been sufficient to replace the oil extracted. Recent increments have resulted mainly from continued exploration of already established reservoirs in major oil-producing regions.

Estimating the ultimate size of global oil resources is obviously far more difficult than determining proven reserves. However, the ability to predict oil availability has improved enormously in the past few decades, due to advances in petroleum geology as well as extensive drilling throughout the world. A range of 1,600 billion to 2,400 billion barrels encompasses all but the most extreme oil resource estimates of the mid-eighties. Of this total, 554 billion barrels have already been used up; 700 billion barrels of additional proven reserves have been discovered. This leaves a range of between 350 billion and 1,150 billion barrels of oil remaining to be found. About 21 billion barrels are being extracted each year. At the 1985 rate of consumption, the ultimate depletion of global oil resources is between 50 and 88 years away. Little of the world's petroleum is likely to remain by the bicentennial of the world's first oil well in the year 2059.[35]

More than three quarters of the world's sedimentary areas have been explored, and results confirm a key hypothesis on which oil resource estimates are based: Almost 90 percent of all the oil is found in just 25 of the world's 600 identified sedimentary "provinces" or regions. Given their geology, such provinces are easy to target as potential producers, and within them petroleum is concentrated in large fields that are found quickly. Over two thirds of the oil discovered so far is in just 7 "giant provinces." And almost half is in the world's only "mega-province"—located in the Middle East. Once the large early finds are made, discoveries tend to drop off quickly. Richard Nehring of the Rand Corporation believes that only about 10 percent of the world's petroleum lies in small or very small fields.[36]

Little of the world's petroleum is likely to remain by the bicentennial of the world's first oil well in the year 2059.

The largest oil discoveries of the seventies—in Alaska, the North Sea, and Mexico—have added significantly to the world's inventory of proven reserves. By historical standards, however, these are modest in size and so have added little to estimates of ultimately recoverable reserves. Even before this oil was discovered, analysts assumed that such quantities would be found, although they were not sure exactly where.

Some analysts justify higher estimates of ultimate resources by noting that higher prices will encourage greater exploration and more thorough recovery of known deposits. But the estimates just cited—1,600 billion to 2,400 billion barrels—include assumptions that prices will rise and technologies will improve. Enhanced oil recovery using water, steam, and gas injection has begun in some areas, stimulated by the high price of oil in the early eighties. Even the lower resource estimates assume that enhanced recovery will become standard practice in the decades ahead.

A 1983 study by scientists at the U.S. Geological Survey (USGS) reaches similar conclusions, including a mid-range estimate of ultimate reserves of just 1,700 billion barrels. The USGS scientists note that "demonstrated reserves of crude oil have declined over the past 10 years consistent with discoveries lagging production over the same period . . . . Rates of discovery have continued to decline over the past 20 years even though exploration activity has increased in recent years. Prudence dictates, therefore, that the low side of the assessment of undiscovered resources be responsibly considered."[37]

As important as the ultimate size of world resources is their location. Here, too, the concentration in large provinces is key. About 56 percent of the world's proven oil reserves and 23 percent of estimated undiscovered reserves are in the Middle East. Overall, 95 percent of proven reserves are in just 20 countries. Oil remains one of the world's most unequally distributed resources.[38]

The United States is the world's second largest petroleum producer and the most intensively explored country, with 80 percent of the world's oil wells. Oil production in the continental United States peaked in 1970 at over 9 million barrels per day and fell to 7 million barrels per day in 1980. When higher prices and the lifting of price controls caused a surge in U.S. petroleum exploration and secondary recovery, the decline in production was halted temporarily. However, the reserve/production ratio, a key measure of oil resources, has continued to fall, and in 1985 U.S. proven reserves reached their lowest level since 1951. John Lichtblau of the Petroleum Industry Research Foundation writes, "In effect, most of these activities [accelerated drilling and enhanced recovery] have been a form of current production maximization by borrowing from the future."[39]

In recent years, the U.S. oil industry has increasingly turned to offshore oil, which was given a big boost by the Reagan administration's program of accelerated leasing of offshore oil tracts. Unsuccessful exploratory drilling, however, has already dashed some of the more grandiose hopes; in early 1985 the U.S. Geological Survey reduced its estimate of undiscovered offshore oil by 55 percent. This lowered estimated undiscovered U.S. oil resources by 18 percent —or five years of production at current rates. Notably, a six-year, $3-billion exploration of the Atlantic continental shelf yielded mainly dry wells and no exploitable oil. USGS estimates for that region have been lowered 87 percent. In Alaska, the $1.5-billion Mukluk offshore project turned out to be the most expensive dry hole in history. Production from Alaska's North Slope fields, which once offset declines in the lower 48 states, has leveled off at 1.7 million barrels per day. State officials project that North Slope oil production will fall beginning in 1990.[40]

The mid-eighties has already witnessed a substantial decline in U.S. oil exploration and development. In the face of falling prices, many American companies are finding oil on Wall Street (through mergers and acquisitions) rather than in the fields. Substantial further price declines could have an even greater impact. An executive at a major U.S. oil company stated in 1985 that if oil prices fall to $20 per barrel, "we would finish up what we are doing in Alaska and do no more." A precipitous decline in U.S. oil production is now a real possibility in the years ahead.[41]

The world's largest oil producer—the Soviet Union—is also one of the largest question marks. The oil industry is a high priority of the Soviet government, and, as in the West, investments in petroleum rose during the early eighties. Oil drilling increased from 50 million feet of wells in 1979 to 90 million feet in 1984, and production rose by more than a half million barrels per day. Reserve additions have come relatively slowly in recent years, however, and in 1984 and 1985 Soviet oil production declined for the first time since World War II.[42]

The Soviet Union is heavily dependent on relatively old and declining oil fields and is plagued by difficulties in opening new production frontiers. The key producing area of Tyumen in West Siberia, which provides 63 percent of Soviet oil, has fallen below official targets for the past three years, and many fields are producing as much water as petroleum. Since the Soviet Union now produces more than one fifth of the world's total, any significant decline in Soviet production will have an impact on oil markets worldwide.[43]

North Sea oil is one of the largest and most welcome additions to world supplies in recent years. Oil production by the major North Sea producers, Norway and the United Kingdom, reached 3.3 million barrels per day in 1984, greatly easing Europe's dependence on imported petroleum. Exploration and development efforts are continuing in the North Sea, but reserve additions have been modest in recent years as companies turn to fields that are much smaller than those developed initially. Even

without further price decreases, North Sea oil production is projected to peak before 1990 and decline steadily during the nineties. Some North Sea fields have exploration and development costs as high as $20 per barrel, among the highest in the world. Industry officials believe that an additional $2 decline in the world price of oil could make a number of North Sea projects uneconomical.[44]

Mexico has also added to world oil supplies. Production grew steadily in the late seventies, reached 3 million barrels per day in 1982, and has stayed at about that level due to weak demand and a government decision to produce at less than capacity. Mexico's oil resources were developed relatively recently, and its proven reserves of 48 billion barrels are 40 percent higher than those of the United States. Worldwide, only Saudi Arabia, Kuwait, and the Soviet Union have more oil than Mexico does. Some analysts believe that Mexican oil production will rise from the current 3 million barrels per day to 4 million barrels before production peaks in the mid-nineties. However, rapid growth in Mexico's internal oil requirements will probably keep the country from ever exporting much more than the current 1.5 million barrels per day. Unless the Mexican government takes action to restrict oil use, the country could easily become a net importer by the year 2000.[45]

China is another key country in the world oil equation. Production there grew significantly during the fifties and sixties, but then leveled off at about 2 million barrels per day in the late seventies. Major efforts were then launched to open new oil fields, particularly offshore in the South China Sea and the Bohai Gulf. No sizable reserves have been found so far, but many promising areas remain to be drilled and the government has redoubled its efforts. Oil is important to China's ambitious modernization program, and major finds will be necessary simply to maintain the current production level. China's remaining petroleum reserves of 19 billion barrels equal only 19 barrels per person. At the U.S. rate of per capita oil consumption, China's oil reserves would be gone in 10 months. Incredibly, in order to earn precious foreign exchange China has managed to remain an exporter of about 1 million barrels of oil per day. This leaves just one third of a barrel of oil per capita to be used each year domestically.[46]

Petroleum exploration was started or stepped up in at least 30 additional countries during the past five years. Many of these efforts involve Third World governments, multinational corporations, and financial assistance from Western banks or multilateral organizations such as the World Bank. The biggest success stories are in Colombia, where oil production is expected to reach 400,000 barrels per day by 1987, and Brazil, which has similar potential.

Other countries with smaller discoveries include Angola, Argentina, Australia, Cameroon, Egypt, India, Malaysia, Pakistan, Peru, Syria, and Zaire. Thanks to exploration efforts stimulated by the oil price increases of the seventies, these countries have the potential to one day become self-sufficient in oil.[47]

Together, these discoveries have increased global oil reserves less than 1 percent, however, and at their peak they will provide only an additional 1–2 million barrels per day of oil. John Lichtblau concludes: "Production increases can of course be expected from a number of other non-OPEC countries, such as Egypt, Brazil, Colombia, India, and West African countries. But there is nothing in sight which would compare even remotely with the developments of the 1970's."[48] Most developing countries remain desperately short of oil.

As noted earlier, rising production of non-OPEC oil has added 5 million barrels per day to world supplies. Despite

Table 5-5. Oil Production, Reserves, and Reserves/Production Ratios, Major Oil-Producing Nations, 1984

Country	Annual Production	Reserves	Reserves/Production
	(billion barrels)		(ratio)
Kuwait	0.36	90.0	250
Iraq	0.43	44.5	104
Saudi Arabia	1.71	169.0	99
United Arab Emirates	0.44	31.9	73
Iran	0.80	48.5	61
Libya	0.40	21.1	52
Mexico	1.10	48.6	45
Venezuela	0.68	25.8	38
Nigeria	0.51	16.7	33
United Kingdom	0.94	13.6	14
Soviet Union	4.53	63.0	14
United States	3.79	34.5	9
World Total	21.10	707.2	34

SOURCE: British Petroleum Company, *BP Statistical Review of World Energy* (London: 1985).

this recent boost, the long-term outlook remains dominated by Middle Eastern members of OPEC, which have 56 percent of the world's known petroleum reserves. In fact, recent shifts in world oil markets have some rather disturbing long-term implications: The rate of depletion of the world's most abundant oil resources has slowed, while depletion of some of the scarcest and most strategically important reserves has accelerated. At the 1984 extraction rate, U.S. proven reserves will last only about nine years. (See Table 5–5.)

Recent independence from Middle Eastern petroleum has occurred largely at the expense of greater long-term dependence.

Saudi Arabia's oil reserves, on the other hand, would last almost 100 years at the 1984 rate of extraction. Many Middle Eastern oil fields have production costs of less than $2 per barrel, whereas some Alaskan and North Sea oil fields yield oil at a cost of $20 per barrel. Charles Ebinger, an energy analyst at Georgetown University's Center for Strategic and International Studies, believes that as non-OPEC oil production declines, OPEC's share of the world oil market will reach 55 percent in the nineties, above the record levels reached in the late seventies.[49]

Several OPEC members with limited reserves are now producing at near maximum capacity in order to sustain their economies, while Persian Gulf countries with the largest reserves are restricting production in order to support OPEC prices. During the nineties, oil production is almost certain to decline in such OPEC nations as Algeria, Ecuador, Gabon, Indonesia, and Nigeria. None is likely to remain an oil exporter past the mid-nineties. During the next 10 years, OPEC may well become a smaller, more geographically concentrated organization—and a more powerful one.

Non-Middle Eastern oil production is approaching its peak. By 1990, at the latest, declining oil production in the United States, the Soviet Union, and the United Kingdom will greatly outweigh increases in such countries as Brazil, Colombia, and Mexico.[50] These trends should raise warning flags for anyone tempted to celebrate the demise of the Persian Gulf oil producers. Recent independence from Middle Eastern petroleum provides a false sense of security since it has occurred largely at the expense of greater long-term dependence. The lower the current Middle Eastern share of the market, the greater its share at the end of the century, when many countries will be running out of oil. The danger is that the Persian Gulf may again hold all the cards just when world oil resources are more limited than at any time in recent history.

LESSONS OF THE PAST DECADE

It is time to recognize that the oil glut is real and likely to be protracted, although by no means permanent. Fundamental changes mean that declining prices and falling demand for OPEC oil may be key features of the world energy scene for several years. Energy problems have not disappeared, but they have shifted, and new strategies are needed. The challenge is to sustain the positive momentum away from oil that has developed in recent years and, amid conditions that make complacency all too easy, to prepare for a time when oil will be far more expensive.

Downward pressure on petroleum

prices is virtually inevitable during the next several years, and a fall in prices to under $20 per barrel is a real possibility. The momentum behind greater energy efficiency and the development of other energy sources will undermine efforts to stop the erosion of prices. Although lower oil prices benefit the world economy in the short run, they also threaten to establish a "crisis and glut" cycle that makes it difficult for companies, governments, and individual consumers to make sound long-term decisions about energy investments.

Without reinvigorated efforts, recent improvements in the global energy situation will run out of steam by the early nineties. By then the world economy will be substantially more energy-efficient than it is today. Oil will have been largely eliminated as a fuel for power plants and many industries. Natural gas will play a much more central role in the world economy, and the use of coal, renewable energy sources, and nuclear power will also have expanded. But even with these accomplishments, declining domestic production could cause U.S. oil imports to double, reaching 7–9 million barrels per day in the early nineties. Similar problems face Western Europe and the Soviet Union.[51] The world faces a tightening race between successful but vulnerable efforts to develop energy alternatives and the steady depletion of world petroleum resources.

Oil is still likely to provide about 30 percent of the world's energy in the nineties, and its use will be increasingly concentrated in transportation and petrochemicals, two areas where substitution by other energy sources has so far shown little success. Growth in petroleum use during the nineties is likely to be propelled largely by increasing Third World consumption, particularly in the rapidly expanding economies of Asia and Latin America. Developing countries still use a disproportionately small share of the world's oil, and their consumption is bound to increase in the years ahead.[52] Rapid growth in oil use threatens to resume in the early nineties, when the physical limits of non-Middle Eastern oil production will have been reached, causing production to decline steadily.

The events of 1985 demonstrate the dangers of even modest reliance on Middle Eastern oil. Hijackings, terrorism, and the increasingly successful efforts of Iraq and Iran to knock out each other's petroleum facilities make the Middle East an unreliable oil supplier. The seventies showed the impossibility of making accurate predictions about an oil market heavily affected by wars and international politics—a lesson that is likely to be even more true in the late eighties and the nineties. When oil price rises do arrive, they may well be sudden and precipitous. Policymakers should recognize the uncertainty of future trends and the need to reduce the risk of future crises.

The policy guidelines for the next 10 years must start with the past decade's most important lesson: Given the right incentives, energy markets work. Crash government programs to develop major new energy sources have generally failed, and similar efforts to deal with future crises show no signs of being any more successful. But smaller efforts, taken by companies and individuals in response to higher prices, have an excellent record.

The transition from an oil market dominated by the pricing decisions of a few multinational corporations and OPEC members to one driven by the competitive interplay of thousands of buyers and sellers has generally been positive. Price fluctuations have been less severe, and the economic signals for consumers have been more constant. Analysts believe that more competitive oil markets are likely to ease the effect of future disruptions, though it is uncertain whether competition will continue to be effective as Middle Eastern oil-producing countries regain a greater share of the market in the nineties.[53]

The easing of energy market restrictions has helped propel the recent energy advances of most industrial countries. It is now clear that price controls on natural gas, both in Europe and North America, caused artificial shortages during the seventies. At the same time, large government subsidies produced many uneconomical and unnecessary power plants. Decontrol of oil and natural gas prices in the United States helped lead to greater production and more efficient use of these energy sources. Higher energy prices have caused a virtual revolution in the development of energy-efficient technologies. The research thus stimulated continues to yield dozens of promising new technologies each year.

The world's energy markets are still impeded by inefficient or counterproductive government policies. Many national tax systems provide subsidies to a variety of energy industries, often encouraging investments that would otherwise not be economical. In the United States, oil companies can deduct "intangible drilling expenses" to compensate for exploration risks and a "percentage depletion allowance" as compensation for the loss of future revenues as oil reserves are drawn down. In most countries, power plant construction receives special tax credits and low-interest loans. More recently, many nations have encouraged investments in energy efficiency and renewable energy sources by enacting tax credits, grants, and subsidized loans.[54]

Although the motivations for such subsidies are often worthy, they generally do more harm than good, favoring one energy source over another on political rather than on sound economic or environmental grounds. In Europe, the largest subsidies went to nuclear construction programs financed directly through government treasuries or through special financial concessions. The United States provided about $46 billion in energy subsidies in 1984, mainly directed to oil and gas and to power plant construction.[55] Tax loopholes for the U.S. oil industry, aptly dubbed the "drain America first" policy, have depleted U.S. oil reserves at a far faster pace than in other countries. The Netherlands made the opposite error, artificially pricing natural gas on a par with imported oil, which discouraged industries from using gas and caused greater dependence on electricity and imported oil.

Many counterproductive tax credits and subsidies have been removed in recent years, but others remain and continue to impede progress toward an economical and sustainable energy future. The first draft of the Reagan administration's 1985 tax reform proposal called for elimination of virtually all the special energy tax credits in the U.S. tax code. After an intense round of lobbying by oil and utility industry lobbyists, however, the second draft restored most of the credits.[56] Oil and utilities are two of the world's largest industries, exerting considerable influence on policy deliberations in which they have a stake. Reform of this irrational scheme of subsidies will require an enormous political effort by citizens and by the many other industries that pay the price of such policies.

Government energy subsidies are often justified on broad economic and national security grounds. Power shortages and heavier reliance on imported oil are predicted if the subsidies are eliminated. But domestic energy sources compete against one another as much as they compete against imported oil, and so special subsidies for coal or nuclear power often have the unfortunate effect of discouraging the development of less expensive and cleaner energy sources. Energy efficiency investments are particularly discouraged by the subsidies provided to energy industries. In some cases, energy subsidies may actually encourage greater reliance on foreign petroleum by discouraging the development of more energy-efficient technologies that otherwise would be ready the next time energy prices begin to climb.

The centrally planned economies of Eastern Europe and the Soviet Union face some of the most difficult challenges in reforming energy markets. There, energy efficiency has not improved significantly in the past decade, largely because artificially low prices have insulated consumers and industrial managers from rising world energy prices. The Soviet Union has the world's second least energy-efficient steel industry, lagging far behind the efficiency of most Western facilities. Centrally planned economies tend to favor large-scale projects over changes that require thousands of smaller efforts. The energy inefficiency of the Soviet economy undermines its efforts to compete in world markets, but recent economic reforms appear intended in part to address these problems.[57]

Many developing countries have also failed to harness market forces effectively. Energy price subsidies and complex price support systems for various industries leave Third World consumers with little sense of the real cost of different energy options. As a result, countries that can ill afford to waste energy often have the least efficient homes and factories. Simply raising energy prices can cause riots and will not in any case solve these problems. First, improved management and less rigidly structured industries are needed so that market signals can be properly used. The poor must also be provided with affordable options. Many opportunities exist for the exchange of technologies and information on energy efficiency with industrial countries. If even a fraction of the effort devoted to marketing nuclear power in the Third World were turned to industry reforms and efficient technologies, enormous progress could be made.[58]

Countries that can ill afford to waste energy often have the least efficient homes and factories.

Although freer energy markets are central to any effective energy strategy, they will require fine-tuning to meet the challenges of the next decade. The main challenge is that oil prices are likely to continue falling in the years ahead, sending consumers a message that could eventually lead to higher oil consumption and a future crisis. As in the early seventies, oil's price may drop below its long-term replacement value in most countries. This would undermine energy efficiency investments and the development of indigenous energy sources. In the next few years, energy investments in many countries may be unable to compete in cost with Middle Eastern oil, which still comes out of the ground for only a few dollars a barrel.

The current period of falling oil prices is a logical time for governments to step in with higher taxes on oil. Ideally, such a tax would be levied on oil consumption so as to keep real oil prices at a fixed level or cause them to rise slowly over time. However, policymakers so far have focused mainly on the possibility of taxing imported oil, which would insulate domestic energy markets from international competitors but not interfere with the choices between indigenous energy sources.[59]

Oil import taxes obviously present

enormous political difficulties, both within and between countries. Periodic efforts to levy such a tax have failed in several countries in recent years. The time may now be right, however, given the difficulties lower oil prices are beginning to cause for domestic energy producers in many countries. The International Energy Agency (IEA) considered recommending such a tax, but instead has opted for a free trade approach. However, IEA has encouraged more realistic pricing of oil, including increases in consumption taxes.[60] The World Bank and the International Monetary Fund have strongly urged, and in some cases insisted upon, more "realistic" energy pricing in developing countries.

Energy efficiency standards are also needed to supplement market forces in the next few years. The purchase of an automobile or a major appliance such as a refrigerator effectively commits a person to a particular level of energy consumption for 5–20 years, during which time the cost of energy may shift repeatedly. Consumers often have no way of knowing what those charges will be, and they cannot always afford the up-front costs of making sound, long-term investments.

In several countries, most notably Japan, governments have required that manufacturers of automobiles and major appliances meet efficiency standards. Many of these are now outdated; others are about to expire or have been relaxed under industry pressure. Efficiency standards should either be extended and toughened or replaced with financial incentives that encourage sound energy investments. Sales taxes based on the energy requirements of particular appliances would provide manufacturers and consumers more flexibility and might in the long run stimulate development of more-efficient technologies. The key to optimizing energy efficiency is to provide an economic signal but allow manufacturers and consumers to make the final decisions about what is produced and bought.[61]

The enormous strides away from oil dependence in the past decade provide much reason for optimism. Opportunities to increase energy self-sufficiency and even to eliminate the need for imported oil in some countries are far greater than at any time in modern history. But dangers lie behind the recent successes. The momentum achieved can only be sustained by continuing innovation in energy policies in the years ahead. The key test is whether the political will for such change can be mobilized in the absence of an immediate crisis.

6

Reforming the Electric Power Industry

Christopher Flavin

The world's electric power industries may be on the verge of a transformation, one propelled more by new technologies and changing economic circumstances than by internal reforms. Saddled with over $100 billion of debt and implicated in environmental damage costing billions of dollars, the electric power industry has become sluggish and defensive. Many industry executives are preoccupied with the need for "regulatory reforms" and new construction programs, convinced that their salvation lies in business as usual, lubricated with even more generous government subsidies.

But this sixties' approach will not solve the electricity problems of the eighties. It risks burdening utilities with ever greater debts, consumers with still higher bills, and the environment with more pollution. Rather, electricity's future lies in more efficient and more selective use of power, the development of a range of small-scale generating technologies, and a more diverse and competitive electric power industry.

Today, electricity provides a record one third of the world's primary energy, and the industry faces its most serious crisis since Thomas Edison opened the world's first commercial power plant in Manhattan in 1882.[1] Facing reduced growth in power demand and deteriorating balance sheets, utilities have greatly slowed the ordering of new coal and nuclear plants. In the United States, plant cancellations have outweighed new orders since the late seventies; in Europe, nuclear construction has slowed to a crawl.

Already, the push of disgruntled consumers and the pull of new economic opportunities have begun to redirect the power business. The development of industrial equipment and household appliances that are considerably more energy-efficient makes it possible to in effect build power plants in homes and factories at less than one third the cost of power from newly constructed plants. Electric utilities may provide the expertise and investment capital needed to develop the energy-equivalent of hundreds of nuclear and coal plants in the form of improved efficiency.

Small-scale power generation, a seemingly utopian dream in 1980, has become a major business in 1985. In the United States, 1,297 small-scale power projects, with a generating capacity of 24,965 megawatts, had been planned by October 1985.[2] The new sources—including a mix of cogeneration, biomass, small hydropower, wind power, and geothermal energy—will provide enough electricity for 6 million homes. Development of these technologies has also begun in other parts of the world, though at a slower pace.

The electricity business needs a structural overhaul. Utility monopoly of power generation hinders research on new technologies and robs utilities of the spirit of innovation that drove Thomas Edison and his competitors. Advances in energy efficiency have been slowed because efficiency investments rarely get the subsidies and tax breaks that many countries give to power plants. Gradually, mainly so far in the United States, market discipline and limited forms of utility deregulation are being tested. These experiments are being observed with interest by planners in many countries, and modified versions are being adopted in some. But electric utilities, whether publicly or privately owned, are huge and politically powerful institutions, and fundamental change will require years of concerted efforts.

ELECTRICITY IN TRANSITION

The drive to electrification was one of the chief engines of postwar economic growth. Throughout the world, electricity generation rode a seemingly endless curve, doubling every decade. Refrigerators and television sets came to hundreds of small towns and rural areas. Consumers and industries found ever more ingenious uses for electricity. The powerful pull of electrification was demonstrated at the fiftieth anniversary of the U.S. Rural Electrification Administration in 1985, when farmers in Appalachia recalled with tears in their eyes that day in the thirties when the lights went on. Electricity has become central not only to the world energy situation, but to the overall health of the world's economies and environment.[3]

The oil price increases of the seventies began to change things. The first reaction was to assume that electricity would be an affordable alternative to costly oil. Many government and utility planners consequently accelerated their nuclear and coal plant construction programs—most notably in France, which began building six nuclear plants each year. But rising oil prices also pulled up the cost of generating power. In the United States, for example, the cost of fuel oil to utilities rose sixfold in the decade after 1973, and this was echoed by a quadrupling in the cost of coal and a tenfold increase for natural gas. The impact was even greater in Japan, in much of Europe, and in the Third World. In addition, the average thermal efficiency of fossil-fuel-fired plants leveled off for the first time, and economies of scale became more elusive. Many large, complex coal and nuclear plants wound up costing more per megawatt than the smaller facilities they replaced.[4]

Environmental standards have added further to the cost of power plants. In the United States, coal-fired power plants release 64 percent of the sulfur dioxide and 30 percent of the nitrogen oxides emitted by all sources nationwide, contributing to respiratory illnesses as well as the destruction of buildings, forests, crops, and fisheries. Since the late seventies, extensive pollution controls have been required on all new U.S. power plants and on many of those built in other countries. The U.S. Environmental Protection Agency estimates that flue gas desulfurization, the most common technology, adds 1–1.7¢ per kilowatt-hour to the cost of coal-fired power generation, a 20–40 percent boost for a typical new plant. In 1983, U.S. utilities spent $2.2 billion on pollution control equipment.[5]

Most European countries were slower to restrict emissions, but this changed dramatically in the early eighties. Acid rain, caused in part by sulfur dioxide and nitrogen oxide emissions, was found to be severely damaging Europe's lakes, forests, and cropland. Several countries have already implemented strict controls that will increase the cost of power generation significantly, and continent-wide

emission reductions under the auspices of the European Economic Community are being considered. Both in Europe and North America, pressure is growing to retrofit older power plants with pollution controls.[6]

Nuclear power is also under growing pressure. In 1970 the Organisation for Economic Co-operation and Development (OECD) projected that its members would have 568,000 megawatts of nuclear capacity by 1985. The actual total was only about 180,000 megawatts. Plans for nuclear plant construction worldwide leveled off in the mid-seventies and the expected capacity has dropped by more than 100,000 megawatts since 1978. This is due largely to the cancellation of 111 plants in the United States (see Table 6–1), but orders have also slowed in Europe, the So-

Table 6-1. United States: Coal and Nuclear Plant Orders and Cancellations, 1970–84

Year	Orders				Cancellations			
	Coal		Nuclear		Coal		Nuclear	
	(plants)	(mega-watts)	(plants)	(mega-watts)	(plants)	(mega-watts)	(plants)	(mega-watts)
1970	25	12,442	14	14,275	0	0	0	0
1971	18	7,811	21	20,876	0	0	0	0
1972	27	12,682	38	41,526		0	6	5,738
1973	40	22,615	41	46,827	0	0	0	0
1974	71	34,183	26	30,931	0	0	8	8,290
1975	20	11,389	4	4,180	0	0	11	12,291
1976	13	5,938	3	3,790	2	800	2	2,328
1977	24	12,172	4	5,040	11	4,859	9	9,862
1978	28	14,634	2	2,240	5	3,125	13	13,333
1979	20	8,159	0	0	8	4,903	8	9,476
1980	6	2,688	0	0	9	4,348	16	18,085
1981	13	8,135	0	0	1	640	6	4,811
1982	1	600	0	0	0	0	18	22,019
1983	0	0	0	0	21	6,554	6	6,038
1984	1	572	0	0	18	7,923	8	9,040

SOURCES: Atomic Industrial Forum, "Historical Profile of U.S. Nuclear Power Development," Bethesda, Md., January 1984, and private communication; coal data from U.S. Department of Energy, Washington, D.C., and Kidder, Peabody, and Co., New York, private communications.

viet Union, and the several Third World nations with nuclear programs.[7]

The 30 or so U.S. nuclear plants now being completed will have an average cost of close to $3 billion—$3,000 per kilowatt. The bill for the power they produce will be approximately three times the average wholesale cost of electricity in the United States today. And even in France and Japan, where nuclear costs are perhaps half those in the United States, nuclear power has become a large economic burden. With a debt of $30 billion and a glut of generating capacity, the French state utility has slowed its nuclear orders from six per year in the seventies to one in 1985. The financial viability of the vaunted French nuclear industry is now in doubt.[8]

Nuclear power has brought unprecedented citizen participation to the previously closed business of electricity planning. Swedish voters decided in 1980 to shut all of the country's nuclear plants by the year 2010, and Denmark's parliament voted in 1985 to forgo commercial nuclear power entirely. Many privately owned U.S. utilities have been financially damaged and now face protracted hearings before state regulators who must decide how much of the multibillion-dollar cost overruns can be charged to consumers.[9]

Proposed price increases of 50–100 percent are no longer rare, causing cities such as Chicago and New Orleans to consider breaking away to form their own municipal utilities; 23 industrial companies on Long Island have announced plans to leave the area if the Shoreham nuclear plant comes on-line. The old rule that consumers must carry the risk of power plant construction has been broken, and most U.S. regulators will scrutinize construction plans more carefully in the future.[10]

Rising costs have naturally led to higher electricity prices. In the United States, the average residential price of electricity rose from 2.5¢ per kilowatt-hour in 1973 to 7.6¢ in 1985. This is a real annual rate of increase of 5.5 percent, slower than price increases for gasoline or natural gas, but substantial nonetheless. Electricity prices are similar in Europe and even higher in Japan, where dependence on oil-fired generation has pushed them to 12–15¢ per kilowatt-hour. Overall, electricity prices in the OECD kept even with inflation through the mid-seventies, but have risen about 25 percent in real terms since 1979.[11]

> ## The financial viability of the vaunted French nuclear industry is now in doubt.

The use of electricity has grown at less than half the rate projected in the early seventies, confounding planners who expected a massive switch from fossil fuels to electricity. In the United States, usage grew at an annual rate of 7.5 percent between 1963 and 1973, but at just 2.1 percent a year between 1980 and 1985. The ratio of electricity use to gross national product—the best measure of overall electrification—rose 50 percent between 1960 and 1976, but it peaked in 1976 and is now at the lowest level since 1971.[12] (See Figure 6–1.)

In France, electricity growth averaged 3.9 percent during the past decade; in Japan, 2.5 percent; and in West Germany, 2.4 percent. In the United Kingdom, electricity use in 1983 was slightly lower than in 1973. At the same time, growth in per capita use of electricity has also slowed greatly, and the surge of growth caused by the economic recovery of the mid-eighties appears to have been short-lived.[13] (See Table 6–2.)

Forecasters have been struggling for a decade to catch up with the unpredicted

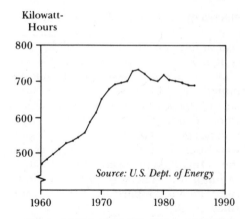

Figure 6-1. U.S. Electricity Use Per $1,000 of GNP, 1960-85

slowdown in the growth in electricity use. The annual forecasts of the North American Electric Reliability Council, used by planners throughout the United States and Canada, have been lowered for 10 consecutive years, invalidating the previous year's efforts almost before the ink had dried. In 1985, summer peak demand in the United States was 40 percent lower than projected a decade earlier. This equals the output of 300 large nuclear plants that would cost $900 billion at current prices—five times the

U.S. government's annual budget deficit.[14]

Utilities, particularly in the United States, have responded to the lowered horizons by canceling dozens of unneeded power plants, but not quickly enough. Most now have "reserve margins" of 30–50 percent, compared with the 15–20 percent that is usually considered adequate. Similar levels of surplus capacity are found in Europe, though not in Japan. This excess capacity will last at least until the early nineties, given the many power plants begun in the mid-seventies that are nearing completion. The construction of unnecessary plants has cost consumers billions of dollars, and U.S. regulators in some states have refused to allow utilities to earn a profit on facilities the regulators believe utility planners should have known were unnecessary.[15]

Although the rules of the game have changed, some are still playing by the old ones. In 1983, for example, the U.S. Department of Energy completed a study that concluded the country would need an additional 438,000 megawatts of generating capacity by the end of the century, about two thirds of current ca-

Table 6-2. Electricity Use Per Capita and Average Annual Rate of Change in Selected Countries, 1962–82

Year	France (kilowatt-hours)	(percent)	West Germany (kilowatt-hours)	(percent)	United Kingdom (kilowatt-hours)	(percent)	United States (kilowatt-hours)	(percent)
1962	1,598	—	2,180	—	2,577	—	4,187	—
1967	2,118	+5.8	2,800	+5.1	3,257	+4.8	5,565	+5.9
1972	2,838	+6.0	4,095	+7.9	4,044	+4.4	7,621	+6.5
1977	3,615	+5.0	4,969	+3.9	4,320	+1.3	8,863	+3.1
1982	4,480	+4.4	5,424	+1.8	4,173	−0.7	9,011	+3.0

SOURCE: United Nations, *Annual Review of Electric Energy Statistics for Europe* (New York: various years).

pacity. The report called for a $1-trillion nuclear and coal construction program as the only way of preventing a power crisis. On a similar note, the International Energy Agency (IEA) continues to urge accelerated construction of large thermal power plants as a way of reducing oil dependence (despite the fact that most IEA countries now burn very little oil in power plants).[16]

For many utilities, forecasting is still as much a political exercise as a technical one. High-demand forecasts are needed to justify plants being planned and even many of those under construction. Apocalyptic visions of blackouts and stagnating economies are called inevitable if there is even a slight pause in the move to electrification. Harvard economist Peter Navarro, author of *The Dimming of America*, argues that "the bulk of energy-saving and productivity enhancing systems, and word-processing equipment . . . are electricity intensive." These systems do use electricity, but the amount is minuscule, particularly compared with the potential for improved efficiency. Some personal computers use only as much electricity as a 100-watt light bulb, and each year new models have even lower power requirements.[17]

Indeed, most of the growth in power demand in recent years has gone to something less exciting than microelectronics—the heating and cooling of buildings. Using very high temperature heat to excite electrons and convey them hundreds of miles to a house where they are simply used to create low-grade heat is inherently inefficient. Even after the natural gas price increases of recent years, electricity has a BTU cost three times higher. Although electricity can be used more efficiently in heat pumps, even these cannot compete economically in most climates with efficient gas heating systems now coming on the market. Yet electric heating is specially subsidized in France and Sweden and is in-

stalled in over half the new homes in the United States and much of Europe.[18]

Wasteful use of electricity is not confined to capitalist or industrial countries. Electrification is promoted with equal fervor in Moscow and Brasilia. It was chosen by many developing countries as the best route away from oil dependence in the aftermath of the price hikes of the seventies, and recent years have witnessed record levels of power plant construction. Electricity has also enjoyed an almost mythical role in economic development efforts, and such projects are the third largest investment of developing-country governments, after agriculture and transportation.

The World Bank reports that less than a quarter of Third World households (excluding China) have a regular supply of electricity, which means that—including China—more than 1 billion people worldwide live without power. In Africa, per capita electricity use is typically one twentieth the level in Europe, and the bulk of the power is used in large urban buildings and inefficient factories.[19]

Third World electricity systems are notoriously inefficient and unreliable. Typically, 15 percent of the power generated is "lost," about twice the normal rate in industrial countries. In India, for example, peasants often make their own patchwork links into nearby power lines, at the cost of occasional electrocutions as well as planning chaos and a loss of revenues for Indian utilities. Blackouts are increasingly common on the thinly stretched electricity systems of these nations.[20]

Developing countries spend some $40 billion a year and the World Bank loans $2–3 billion annually for electricity projects—an average of 17 percent of its total lending. Brazil and China are now in the midst of two of the largest electrification programs in history. Brazil has just built a hydro project as large as 12 nuclear plants, and China is considering an even bigger one. Overall, Third World electricity generation is scheduled to more than double by the end of the century. How effectively these funds are spent will affect Third World industrialization, living standards, and the international financial system.[21]

China's electrification program is at a particularly important crossroads. The nation's 1983 generating capacity of 76,000 megawatts was less than twice California's, though its population was 40 times the size. This capacity provides China with only 75 watts of power per person, compared with 3,000 watts per person in the United States. Approximately 300 million Chinese—30 percent of the population—are still without electricity. The nation plans to triple generating capacity by the year 2000, relying on the construction of large hydro projects and on coal and nuclear plants. China needs additional electricity for its modernization programs. This scheme carries serious economic and environmental risks, however, and there are indications that the cost of the nuclear portion of the program has prompted a reassessment.[22]

Brazil and China are now in the midst of two of the largest electrification programs in history.

The Third World clearly needs additional electricity, and some construction programs make sense. But many countries appear to be unaware of the problems encountered in industrial nations, and they do not have sufficient financial reserves to be able to afford many wrong turns. In developing as well as industrial countries, new opportunities beckon in the electricity business—opportunities that may appear unconventional, but

that are far less risky than continuing along the traditional path.

MANAGING ELECTRICITY'S GROWTH

The notion that a penny saved is a penny earned may be a cliché, but it seems to be a foreign concept to most utility planners. Yet for utilities, saving should be exceedingly attractive, as it is now possible with modern technologies to save a kilowatt-hour of electricity at less than half the cost of producing a kilowatt-hour at a new plant. Using electricity more efficiently is the key to a sustainable power system. And investing in increased efficiency may be the key to a profitable power supply industry.

The average efficiency of new household appliances in the United States has already risen 20–30 percent in the past five years, and in Japan it has increased by half. Socket-type fluorescent light bulbs are now available that use one quarter as much electricity as conventional bulbs. Though they are expensive, they last 13 times as long, repaying a consumer's investment three times over. New industrial motors that include adjustable speed drives are 30–50 percent more efficient.[23]

The cumulative effect of these improvements is mounting. Whenever a company replaces an electric motor, the new one tends to use less electricity. When contractors build new houses, residential electricity use rises more slowly than the rate of housing completion. The remaining uncertainty is the pace of these improvements. Some states have attempted to set the pace by implementing minimum appliance efficiency standards, and the U.S. Court of Appeals decided in 1985 that the federal government must implement similar standards.[24]

The notion that productivity can improve over time has slowly permeated the world of electricity planning. Most forecasts are now at least somewhat disaggregated by sector, and many planners use what are dubbed "end-use models" that include data on the electricity requirements of all major uses of electricity. (Such a model can easily predict the effect on supply requirements of customers buying more-efficient refrigerators or insulating their homes.) Although originally opposed by most planners, the concept of end-use planning is now endorsed by several mainstream organizations, such as the Electric Power Research Institute in the United States and the International Energy Agency. Unfortunately, most utilities have been slow to develop the data base needed to use the most sophisticated and accurate end-use planning models now available. The numbers plugged into the models often reflect efficiencies that are not only far from what is now feasible, but that represent poor economic choices for the consumer.[25]

While the average efficiency of new household appliances has improved gradually in recent years, studies by Howard Geller of the American Council for an Energy-Efficient Economy show that manufacturers have developed much more energy-efficient devices that have not yet found their way into most homes or utility planning scenarios. If gradually introduced, these technologies could free up power supplies for under 2¢ per kilowatt-hour—less than one fifth the generating cost of new power plants today. Studies indicate that even gradual introduction of more-efficient technologies as old ones wear out could lower electricity growth rates from 2–3 percent to less than 1 percent annually.[26]

It is time that utilities became active in enhancing the productivity of electricity —managing demand in a way that is beneficial for all. Amory Lovins of the Rocky Mountain Institute, who has pioneered this concept, writes that "demand for electricity is not fate but choice. Demand is not a predetermined outcome to be prophesied by reading the entrails of forecasters, but rather a variable to be influenced in accordance with policy goals." Indeed, one of the advantages of an efficiency program is that it reduces uncertainty. Planners will have a better idea of the rate at which customers will improve efficiency, allowing construction programs to better match need and reducing the risk of unwarranted construction.[27]

Since the mid-seventies, many U.S. utilities have adopted conservation programs, mostly in response to pressure from state regulators. The federal Residential Conservation Service created by Congress in the late seventies requires utilities to offer energy audits to residential customers, and many states mandate more extensive efforts. A 1983 study by the Investor Responsibility Research Center found that 72 percent of the nation's utilities have formal energy conservation programs and that two thirds have load management programs that redirect power use to off-peak hours. (See Table 6–3.) The 120 utilities surveyed said that their peak load can be reduced by 30,000 megawatts during the next decade, saving $19 billion in avoided construction at a cost of only $6 billion. The programs include energy audits, home weatherization loans, and cash rebates for the purchase of energy-efficient appliances.[28]

One of the more comprehensive energy management efforts, mounted by the Florida Power and Light Company, has a goal of reducing the utility's projected peak power demand by 2,100 megawatts between 1982 and 1992—16 percent of the company's current gener-

Table 6-3. United States: Largest Utility Efficiency and Load Management Programs, 1982

Company	1982 Generating Capacity	Planned Savings by 1992	Savings as Percent of 1982 Capacity	Projected Annual Increase in Demand Through 1992[1]
	(megawatts)		(percent)	
Florida Power	5,899	1,500	25	1.0
Penn Electric	2,736	671	25	2.0
Jersey Central	3,371	800	24	1.5
Duke Power	14,526	2,994	21	3.9
Carolina P&L	8,805	1,750	20	3.0
Florida P&L	12,865	2,100	16	3.5
Houston L&P	12,966	1,700	13	2.6
TVA	32,076	4,000	12	2.4
Pacific G&E	16,319	1,871	11	0.9
Oklahoma G&E	5,359	600	11	n.a.
Public Srv. E&G	9,023	956	11	1.3
So. Calif. Edison	15,345	1,500	10	2.0
Los Angeles DWP	6,749	601	9	1.7
Alabama Power	9,194	800	9	2.6
Bonneville Power	0	802	n.a.	n.a.

[1]Including efficiency programs.
SOURCE: Douglas Cogan and Susan Williams, *Generating Energy Alternatives* (Washington, D.C.: Investor Responsibility Research Center, 1983).

ating capacity. So far the company has performed energy audits on almost 300,-000 homes and encouraged the replacement of 50,000 inefficient central air conditioners and heating systems. And in northern California, the Pacific Gas and Electric Company (PG&E) has provided $168 million worth of zero-interest loans for customers who install specific conservation measures, along with cash rebates for the purchase of energy-efficient appliances. The utility expects to spend $1 billion on these programs over the next decade, while saving at least $3 billion worth of plant construction by reducing projected peak power use by 1,900 megawatts. In Austin, Texas, the city's municipal utility is now building a 553-megawatt "conservation power plant," composed of a variety of household and commercial efficiency in-

vestments that will cost $600 million less than an equivalent coal-fired plant. At least 25 other municipal utilities have rebate programs for the purchase of efficient appliances.[29]

Although these efficiency programs are a good start, many are token efforts; only a handful have the scale and scope to constitute realistic alternatives to power plant construction. Most utilities do little more than make programs available; energy audits are often superficial, revealing only a small part of the conservation potential. Rental units and apartment buildings have been left out of many programs.

Many utility executives still consider efficiency programs inimical to their interests, particularly when faced with temporary excess capacity. In large bureaucratic organizations, programs do not go far without the enthusiastic endorsement of top executives. Some have again started promoting electricity sales—for things like greenhouse heating during off-peak periods—a practice that is euphemistically called "valley filling" but that in the long run is likely to result in the need for more power plant construction and higher electric bills.[30]

To be effective, utility efficiency programs will have to be more extensive and include incentives so that the utility has a real stake in them. Only when a company can realistically expect to earn a profit on efficiency improvements will it invest heavily in them. One approach is for the utility to give the customer a loan for weatherization or the purchase of an energy-efficient appliance at slightly above its own cost of borrowing money (at least 25 percent below the rate for home improvement loans). The loan can then be repaid over several years—entirely out of the savings realized from lower electric bills.[31]

Such programs can in effect provide a community with electricity far less expensively than can a new plant, leaving sufficient margin to give the utility a profit on its loan and providing even greater savings to the consumer once the loan is repaid. Variations on this approach have been tried by utilities in the states of California and Washington, but in most areas they will be possible only with new rules from regulators and new initiatives on the part of utility executives. Energy management firms have sprung up that will now sign contracts to provide a guaranteed level of electricity savings in commercial buildings for a fixed price.

A model effort to promote residential energy efficiency began in Hood River, Oregon, in 1983, sponsored by PacifiCorp (formerly Pacific Power and Light) and the Bonneville Power Administration. Contractors are installing about $4,300 worth of conservation measures —such as efficient water heaters, triple-glazed windows, and extra-thick insulation—in each of 3,000 homes. Preliminary results show that the local utility has spent about 50¢ for each kilowatt-hour saved annually, allowing both for customer savings and a return to the utility during the life of the building. And power use has been cut in half at most houses.[32]

The Hood River project is part of the Northwest Conservation and Electric Power Plan, established under congressional mandate in 1983 in response to cost overruns and the eventual suspension of four nuclear projects in Washington State. Conservation is specifically required where it is the more cost-effective approach. By reducing projected load from 27,000 megawatts to 22,000 megawatts by the year 2000, the plan will allow the region to avoid any new plant construction at least until 1998.[33]

Congress considered legislation in 1985, based on the Northwest Plan, that would establish a least-cost model and a data base allowing utilities to compare investment options—including improved efficiency as well as various kinds of new power plants. This legislation would go far toward institutionalizing energy efficiency investments and would enable states to require that utilities compare strategies fairly.[34]

Utilities in other countries have been even slower to adopt programs to invest actively in energy efficiency. As in the United States, most utilities in industrial nations now have temporary excess capacity (above the normal 15–20 percent reserve margin), ranging from 7.1 percent in Norway to 9.7 percent in the United Kingdom and 30.4 percent in Switzerland. Utilities in many of these countries are promoting electricity use in order to justify the dozens of nuclear and coal plants scheduled to come online in the next few years.[35]

Active promotion of the most wasteful use of electricity—for home heating—is now prevalent in Europe, particularly in France and Sweden. Sweden, despite a national commitment to shut down all of the country's nuclear power plants by 2010, is building mainly electrically heated buildings, which already claim 20 percent of the country's electricity.[36]

Most utilities around the world still have no financial incentive to invest in efficiency, or in many cases do not even have the legal right to do so. Governments in Japan, West Germany, and Sweden have fairly extensive efficiency programs, but these are independent of the utilities, and they are not integral to electricity planning. Japan's Tokyo Electric Company has made a modest effort to encourage greater efficiency by structuring electric prices so that they rise if consumption goes above levels considered adequate to meet basic needs efficiently. But many European utilities actually lower prices as consumption increases.[37]

Even more than in the United States, major institutional changes are required to move utilities beyond a preoccupation with power plant construction. This is particularly true in the Third World, where subsidized electricity prices and the lack of strong institutions have tended to slow efficiency improvements. Utilities' impressive technical and financial capabilities must be harnessed if efficiency's potential is to be realized. Unless they are actively involved, utilities will tend to view improved efficiency as an unwanted competitor and will thwart conservation programs.[38]

THE COGENERATION BOOM

Of all the energy laws passed during the seventies, the U.S. Public Utility Regulatory Policies Act (PURPA) may have the most far-reaching consequences. One part of PURPA, which caused little stir when enacted in 1978, is now eroding the traditional utility monopoly over power generation. The law directs utilities to connect up with small-scale independent power producers (also known as "qualifying facilities") and to pay a fair market price for the electricity. Although based on free-market principles endorsed by corporate executives and conservative governments around the world, PURPA has had a revolutionary—some might say subversive—impact on the utility business.[39]

Cogeneration—the combined production of heat and electricity—is the largest new power source developed so far.

Prompted by PURPA and by the availability of generous tax subsidies for some forms of power generation, several hundred U.S. companies have entered the independent power business since 1980, bringing a spirit of entrepreneurship to electricity that was last seen in the early part of the century. With the knowledge that the risks they take may be well rewarded, independent power producers have experimented with a much wider range of technologies than utilities have, with many facilities less than 1 percent the size of a modern nuclear plant. By harnessing recent advances in microelectronics, materials science, semiconductor physics, and even aerodynamics and biotechnology to generate electricity for the first time, researchers have rapidly raised the efficiency and lowered the cost of many technologies.

Cogeneration—the combined production of heat and electricity—is the largest new power source developed so far. Although industrial cogeneration supplied half of U.S. electricity at the turn of this century, its share had fallen to a meager 7 percent in the early eighties. Cogeneration is somewhat more common in Europe, thanks partly to the prevalence of district heating plants that employ the technology. West Germany and Finland each get about one quarter of their electricity from cogeneration; France and Italy, about 18 percent.[40]

Interest in this technology has revived in the United States, and cogeneration now provides over 15,000 megawatts of capacity. Additional projects, with a generating capacity of 16,000-18,000 megawatts, are planned or under construction. The International Cogeneration Society expects that 3,500 megawatts' worth of cogeneration capacity will have been completed in the United States in 1985 alone.[41]

Electricity generation and transmission capture only one third of a fuel's energy value, making electricity an expensive form of energy. With cogeneration, an industry can raise the total efficiency of its plant from 50–70 percent to 80–90 percent. In most systems, the low-pressure boiler used to generate process steam is replaced by a high-pressure boiler that powers a steam turbine and electric generator. The low-pressure steam exhausted from the turbine is used for industrial heat, space heating and cooling, and water heating. The system is most effective in a facility that has a relatively large and continuous need for heat. The pulp and paper, primary metals, chemicals, petroleum refining, and food processing industries all have large heat requirements and have become major users of this technology.[42] (See Table 6–4.)

Cogeneration is a rapidly growing industry. Frank DiNoto of Hawker Siddely Power Engineering notes, "Right now

Table 6-4. United States: Industrial Cogeneration Capacity, 1982

Industrial Sector	Plants	Capacity	Share of Capacity
	(number)	(mega-watts)	(percent)
Pulp and Paper	136	4,246	29
Primary Metals	39	3,589	24
Chemicals	62	3,438	23
Petroleum Refining	24	1,244	8
Food Processing	42	398	3
Other	68	1,943	13
Total	371	14,858	100

SOURCE: Office of Technology Assessment, U.S. Congress, *Industrial and Commercial Cogeneration* (Washington, D.C.: U.S. Government Printing Office, 1983).

it's the only business of any consequence in power equipment." One of the most aggressive participants is the giant General Electric Company, which is financing as well as building large cogeneration plants worth $600 million. In addition, dozens of smaller companies have joined the industry. Each tends to specialize in a certain size and type of project. Some manufacture equipment; others supervise the design, arrange the financing, and contract out the actual construction work. Most cogenerators rely on natural-gas-driven diesel engines and gas turbines. Others are developing small fluidized-bed plants that burn a variety of solid fuels.[43]

The large petrochemical industry in Houston has thousands of megawatts of cogeneration potential, and several companies are rapidly developing it. One of the largest projects to date provides 1,300 megawatts of power for the Dow Chemical Company in Freeport, Texas. It uses the heat to process chemicals and sells some of the electricity to Houston Lighting and Power. A relatively new use for cogeneration is enhanced recovery of oil at fields where the petroleum is viscous and hard to extract. Cogeneration plants built in these areas can produce steam to be injected into the fields and power to be sold to the utility. Interest in this concept has mushroomed in Kern County, California, where several hundred megawatts of gas-fired cogeneration projects are under way. Several thousand megawatts of additional capacity have been proposed and are awaiting approval by state agencies concerned about air quality and long-range gas supplies.[44]

Most cogeneration projects begun so far range in size from 10 megawatts to 300 and are custom-designed, but much smaller systems may soon be economical. Several companies are building small, modular cogeneration systems that can be mass-produced. About 40 were sold in 1983 and some 200 in 1984, according to the Frost and Sullivan market research company. One promising system is a 65-kilowatt plant fueled by natural gas and designed by Hawthorne Energy Systems of California for McDonald's, the restaurant company. It produces electricity as well as heat to run a restaurant's hot water and air-conditioning systems. A microelectronic chip programmed with climatic and economic data continuously adjusts the system in response to the weather, energy requirements, and the utility's price for cogenerated power.[45]

Engineers believe that similar systems installed in quantity would have a payback period of four years or less in areas where electricity prices are high. If installed in fast-food restaurants, shopping malls, hospitals, and schools, small-scale cogeneration systems would find a market worth billions of dollars and could add significantly to energy supplies.

Cogeneration's potential is immense. Although the U.S. Department of Energy is on record as expecting only an additional 25,000 megawatts from this source by the year 2000, it now appears that this figure will be surpassed in the late eighties. Development accelerated greatly during 1985, with 8,236 megawatts' worth of projects registered with the Federal Energy Regulatory Commission in fiscal year 1985 (through September), exceeding the amount in the two previous years combined. The U.S. Office of Technology Assessment (OTA) estimates a "technical potential" for cogeneration by the year 2000 of 200,000 megawatts—more than one third of current U.S. generating capacity. The International Energy Agency projects that cogeneration in Europe will rise 75 percent by the early nineties, mainly at district heating rather than industrial plants.[46]

Manufacturers have geared up to serve the cogeneration market, now valued at $2–3 billion per year. Investors and regulators have warmed to the economics of cogeneration, which are better than those of virtually any other new generating technology. Installed costs range from $500 to $1,000 per kilowatt, depending on the technology and fuel. Total generating costs are 50 percent lower than for nuclear plants being built and 20 percent less than for coal plants. Whereas most early cogeneration projects were financed by the company actually using the steam, a growing number are now backed by third-party investors, bringing a welcome flow of capital to the business.[47]

RENEWABLE ELECTRICITY

The emergence of the independent power industry has also given new life to many renewable energy technologies. Since 1981, some 7,000 megawatts' worth of power projects driven by renewable energy sources have been launched in the United States, with particularly rapid growth in biomass and wind power. The small hydro, geothermal, and solar industries may not be far behind.[48]

Biological fuels such as wood and agricultural wastes are relatively clean-burning and inexpensive. Although they sometimes have high transportation and handling costs, they need fewer pollution controls than does coal combustion, and in many areas biomass is more readily available than coal. Scores of small plants run on biomass and wastes are now being built, mainly in North America and Scandinavia.

In Burlington, Vermont, the municipal utility completed in 1984 a 50-megawatt wood-fired power plant, the world's largest. It was cheaper to build than an equivalent coal-fired plant. Following the Burlington model, perhaps a dozen wood-fired power plants that can generate 10–20 megawatts are currently being built, mainly in California and New England, for less than $2,000 per kilowatt. In areas with abundant wood supplies, these plants have generating costs of under 7¢ per kilowatt-hour. Wood- and waste-fired power presents few technical or economic obstacles. Much of the challenge comes in ferreting out the abundant but dispersed waste products that can serve as feedstock. The biomass power industry plays a useful role in locating these materials and putting together the technology and financing.[49]

About 90 plants fueled by agricultural or municipal wastes are currently planned or being built in the United States. Garbage can either be burned directly or methane can be extracted from a landfill and used to run a generator. Sludge and methane from sewage treatment plants are also being used as utility fuels in several countries. The incentive for these projects comes mainly from the mounting waste-disposal problems facing many cities. Burning wastes greatly reduces their volume, which will extend the lives of landfills. The revenues from power generation are an extra bonus. In 1985, the waste-to-energy business blossomed, and the number of projects tripled.[50]

The environmental problems associated with burning wastes that contain plastics and heavy metals have put a hold on some projects, including several in New York State. It is hoped that effective pollution control equipment will soon be developed, and fluidized-bed combustion shows promise of controlling some pollutants.[51]

It is difficult to assess the potential for biomass-based electricity generation, but waste products ranging from forest residues to walnut shells are widely available. In the United States, development so far has been concentrated in the Southeast, the West Coast, and New England. The country currently has about 1,400 megawatts of such capacity and another 2,000 megawatts planned or under construction. Close to half the total comes from wood wastes, mainly burned at wood industry plants that generate their own power and sell the excess to a utility company.[52]

Sweden leads in harnessing wood-fired energy, mostly for district heating plants. The pulp and paper industry in that country is already almost energy self-sufficient. Denmark is burning straw in several cogeneration plants that provide district heating. The Philippines has built several wood-fired power plants since the late seventies and has purchased equipment for a total of 17. Each has a capacity of 3.3 megawatts and is fueled by a plantation of fast-growing trees. Together the plants will be a substantial component of that country's power system in the nineties.[53]

Small-scale hydroelectric generators, once major electricity sources, have been neglected in recent decades. In the past few years renovation schemes and newly built facilities have increased small-scale hydropower supplies in the United States by almost 300 megawatts. Several hundred megawatts' worth of additional capacity are currently being built. The cost of a new facility typically ranges from $2,000 to $3,000 per kilowatt, but retrofitting an old dam is considerably less expensive. Rapid development of small-scale hydropower is occurring, but it will likely be slowed by environmental concerns. Growth of this power source will probably be most rapid in the Third World, where power is lacking in many rural areas. China has long relied on small-scale hydro in rural areas and is now exporting its technology.[54]

Geothermal energy is another growing source of electricity. Where high-pressure steam is near the surface, geothermal power generation is already a bargain. Generating costs are reported as low as 5¢ per kilowatt-hour. At The Geysers in northern California, over 20 separate power plants have been installed in the past decade and together provide 1,400 megawatts of power, with another 600 megawatts under development. The Philippines has developed four geothermal fields and is working on several more, hoping to have 1,700 megawatts of capacity by the end of 1985. Mexico has developed three major geothermal fields and now has a capacity of 645 megawatts, with 2,440 megawatts planned by 2000.[55]

Central America, parts of Southeast Asia, and the western United States have the potential for major reliance on geothermal energy. Prime sites also exist in parts of southern Europe and East Africa. Ronald DiPippo of Southeastern

Massachusetts University estimates that 10,000 megawatts' worth of geothermal power plants will be in place by 1990. And the U.S. Geological Survey concluded in 1985 that the country may have a geothermal potential of 100,000 megawatts—including both electricity generation and process heat.[56]

Wind power is the most rapidly growing new electricity source. Starting from near zero in 1981, nearly 13,000 wind machines, with a generating capacity of over 1,000 megawatts, were in place in California by the end of 1985. (See Table 6–5.) Virtually all are installed at wind farms, clusters of 10- to 17-meter-diameter machines located in mountain passes and connected to utility lines. Wind farm development has been spearheaded by independent power producers who lease land in windy areas and manufacture or buy the turbines. Most of the financing is provided by third-party investors, lured in part by state and federal tax credits. A 100-kilowatt wind machine might cost $180,000 and produce $12,000 worth of electricity to be sold to the utility each year. However, with the tax write-offs available, the investment has a payback of less than three years.[57]

Wind power is the most rapidly growing new electricity source.

The tax incentives have resulted in a number of shoddy projects, but the economics of most California wind farms is increasingly sound. Sales to utilities in 1985 reached an estimated 600 million kilowatt-hours or $40 million—about double that of all previous years combined. California wind farms now generate enough electricity for 180,000 homes during the five-month summer windy season. Many wind machines gen-

Table 6-5. California: Wind Farms, 1981–85

Year	Machines Installed	Capacity Installed	Average Capacity	Average Cost	Power Generated[1]
					(million kilowatt hours)
				(dollars/ kilowatt)	
	(number)	(megawatts)	(kilowatts)		
1981	144	7	49	3,100	1
1982	1,145	64	56	2,175	6
1983	2,493	172	69	1,900	49
1984	4,687	366	78	1,860	195
1985[2]	4,500	405	90	1,800	600
Total	12,969	1,014	78	—	851

[1]Most wind machines are installed in the second half of a given year and do not produce substantial power until the next year. [2]Preliminary estimate.
SOURCE: *Alternative Sources of Energy*, September/October 1985.

erate electricity 90–95 percent of the time there is sufficient wind, matching the reliability of coal plants and exceeding that of nuclear plants.[58]

The cost of wind power to an investor has fallen relatively slowly, to $1,800 per kilowatt, but costs are likely to fall substantially in the next few years. Pacific Gas and Electric, which has had its engineers closely studying the wind machines hooked up to its lines, believes that the cost will fall to less than $1,000 per kilowatt and that wind power will be the least expensive new source of electricity available to the utility in the nineties. Continuing deliberations about federal and state tax credits for wind power will have a major impact on how rapidly this energy source is developed.[59]

California so far has about three quarters of the wind capacity hooked up to the world's utility lines. Substantial development has now begun in Hawaii, where the small Hawaii Electric Company plans to be 20 percent reliant on wind power by 1990. Denmark is the second largest national user of wind power, with over 2,000 machines installed mainly on agricultural farms and the world's first offshore wind farm. As in

California, Danish citizens are permitted to sell power to a utility and receive a small subsidy from the government. Wind power will almost certainly one day make a large contribution to the world's electricity systems—perhaps as much as the 13 percent share that nuclear power now provides.[60]

The economic viability of several renewable energy technologies is now proven, and most will be able to stand without tax credits in a few years. Reports by the California Energy Commission show that in 1990, cogeneration, wind power, geothermal energy, and many biomass projects will be less expensive than a coal plant that meets California pollution standards. Small-scale power projects have the added advantage of short lead times and limited investment requirements, allowing planners to follow demand needs closely and to avoid open-ended capital commitments and excessive interest charges. This may well make a small-power project preferable to a large one that is projected to be up to 20 percent cheaper.[61]

Planners have also become increasingly optimistic that dispersed, fluctuating power sources such as wind can be successfully integrated into large power systems. Care must be taken, however, to ensure that sufficient baseload power is provided and that flexible energy sources such as cogeneration are given financial incentives to ensure their availability at times of peak demand. More pumped-storage hydropower may be needed to provide reliability in some areas. The Hawaii Electric Company hopes to meet 57 percent of its peak demand with renewable energy sources within a few years, a formidable technical challenge.[62]

There are a number of other energy sources that are not as well developed as those just described, but that have potential to add to the mix feeding into utility lines in the more distant future. A 1985 study by the Office of Technology Assessment concluded that several major new power sources were likely by the early twenty-first century. OTA expects the development of relatively large gasified coal and fluidized-bed plants and also dispersed and renewable technologies such as photovoltaic cells, fuel cells, and solar thermal power plants. Technology development and cost reduction are essential for all of these.[63]

Solar cells can be installed at generat-ing plants in rural areas or on rooftops, and they will allow a much greater decentralization of electricity supplies than virtually any other technology. Costs must fall to about one fifth their current level to be competitive with utility power, but projections indicate that this may occur by the nineties if research funding is kept high. Fuel cells that run on natural gas, hydrogen, or some other fuel are now projected to be a practical household or industry energy technology. Installed in a basement, they could heat and cool a home as well as produce electricity.[64]

Small-scale power generation is taking hold far more rapidly than projected a few years ago. Half of all U.S. utilities now obtain some of their power from independent producers. Figures from the U.S. Federal Energy Regulatory Commission show that 24,965 megawatts of such projects have been registered since 1980. (See Table 6–6.) The average power output of each facility is under 30 megawatts, less than 3 percent as much as a large conventional plant. Although it is impossible to know how many of these projects will actually be completed, early indications are that it will be a high percentage. Many develop-

Table 6-6. United States: Independent Power Projects Planned, 1980–85[1]

Power Source	1980	1981	1982	1983	1984	1985	Total
				(megawatts)			
Cogeneration	319	844	2,818	3,211	2,531	8,236	17,959
Biomass[2]	0	235	534	401	616	1,029	2,815
Wind	76	24	32	340	384	578	1,434
Hydro	59	45	63	380	382	273	1,202
Geothermal	76	80	76	65	203	151	651
Waste	1	0	0	124	171	470	766
Solar	0	0	0	87	16	35	138
Total	531	1,228	3,523	4,608	4,303	10,772	24,965

[1]Figures listed by fiscal year. Includes projects for which applications have been filed with the Federal Energy Regulatory Commission through September 1985.   [2]Includes wood, agricultural, and municipal wastes.
SOURCES: *Cogeneration & Small Power Monthly*, all issues.

ers do not register their projects until they are ready to break ground; most are scheduled for completion within a few years.

If small-scale power projects continue to be launched at the recent pace, the United States alone could obtain 100,000 megawatts from them by the end of the century, or about as much as nuclear power now provides. There has been a major surge in cogeneration projects in the past year, with indications that as more states begin to open the market for electricity, development is accelerating. Other countries that have not yet pursued small-scale power generation are likely to have similar potential, but they are impeded by institutional barriers. In Europe, for example, independent power production is illegal in many countries.

Several governments are now actively studying the implementation of PURPA in the United States and considering ending the utility monopoly in their own nations. Greece has passed its own PURPA law, hoping to stimulate wind and solar development; Pakistan, with U.S. assistance, is thinking of doing the same. In the United Kingdom, the Conservative government is considering breaking the national utility's monopoly on power generation as part of a general move to put government-owned companies back into private hands. In developing countries, where people are more dispersed and electric grids incomplete, many of these technologies are likely to be useful. Conditions are ripe for a rapid increase in reliance on small-scale power sources.[65]

ELECTRICITY'S FUTURE

California is where fundamental changes in the electricity industry first took hold,

and that state has demonstrated important successes and pitfalls that other states and countries would do well to examine. After protracted political battles, California's consumers and the government under Jerry Brown gradually pushed the state's utilities in a new direction. The centerpiece is efficiency programs: building codes, weatherization for low-income tenants and homeowners, and appliance efficiency standards, as well as the utilities' own efforts. A study by Arthur Rosenfeld of the Lawrence Berkeley Laboratory found that electricity use is growing half as fast in California as in Texas, despite nearly identical rates of building and economic growth.[66]

California utilities that once had to be penalized by state regulators for failing to implement efficiency programs effectively are now actively investing in them. The California Energy Commission estimates that efficiency programs now in place will save between 12,400 and 19,600 megawatts of peak power demand by 1996, worth $2 billion per year in the mid-nineties in avoided power plant construction. Meanwhile, no large conventional power plants are currently planned.[67]

The surge in independent power generation in California has also been remarkable. By mid-1985 the state had 1,921 megawatts hooked up to utility lines, and producers had signed contracts with the state's utilities for another 12,995 megawatts. (See Table 6–7.) What began as a modest effort has led in four years to sufficent proposed capacity to meet 39 percent of the state's peak power needs. New energy sources are being developed at a pace that will not only meet projected growth in electricity needs but allow much of the state's fossil-fuel-fired power generation to be shut down.

What separates California's small-power program from that of most other

Table 6-7. California: Small-Scale Power Technologies Planned by Major Utilities in 1984 and 1985[1]

Utility	Operating		Under Contract		Planned 1985 Sources as Proportion of 1983 Peak Load
	1984	1985	1984	1985	
	(megawatts)				(percent)
Pacific Gas and Electric	684	1,066	2,198	6,855	52
Southern California Edison	552	775	1,718	5,715	48
San Diego Gas & Electric	77	80	50	425	25
Total	1,313	1,921	3,966	12,995	39[2]

[1]Figures for mid-year.   [2]Includes several municipal utilities that have not signed many small-power contracts.
SOURCE: "Alternative Energy Projects," a statistical compilation by Independent Energy Producers Association, Sacramento, Calif., September 1985.

states is its aggressive implementation of the federal PURPA law. Utilities in the state are required to offer standard long-term power sales contracts to independent producers that meet certain technical and legal requirements. Those contracts are currently based on the utilities' "avoided cost" of generating power using natural gas. State regulators plan to base avoided cost in the future on new centralized power plants.[68]

California has in effect deregulated the power generation portion of the utility business, and the result so far is that small-power producers are building all of the new plants in the state. Other states have hardly implemented PURPA, offering only short-term contracts, low rates, or, in some cases, no contract until the plant is complete. Such procedures make it impossible for independent producers to raise capital.

The 1985 *Electricity Report* of the California Energy Commission sums up the changes in recent years: "This *Electricity Report* marks the final stages of a transition from an era of scarcity to an era of abundance. Our concerns have shifted

from . . . what appeared at the time to be the impossible task of acceptably meeting an anticipated seven percent annual growth rate in electricity demand . . . to how can we best choose from an abundance of supply options during an era of unprecedented low growth in demand. While distinctly more desirable than the problems of 'scarcity,' the complications associated with the new problems of 'abundance' are equally difficult."[69]

Indeed, California has run across a number of unanticipated problems. Small-power projects threaten to exceed transmission capacity in some areas. Environmental battles are being waged over many wind, hydro, and biomass projects. Cogeneration could potentially be a large drain on the state's natural gas supplies. In mid-1985, the California Public Utilities Commission decided to suspend for one year the standard long-term contract offers while officials study the apparent glut of nearly 15,000 megawatts of proposed projects and figure out a way to structure future contract offers that is fair to consumers, utilities, and independent producers.[70]

Utilities claim that so many projects were signed up because the avoided-cost rate was too high, but this has not yet been proved. So little was required in the way of environmental permits or a financial commitment that there was not much risk in signing contracts. Many developers wanted to assure themselves a place in the power sales line, particularly as rumors spread that contract signing might soon be suspended.

Although incomplete, the California model provides a useful example to other states and countries wishing to reform the electric power industry. The avoided-cost concept is a good one, but it needs to be widened to include all possible options for meeting electricity needs in a given area, including improved efficiency and renewable-energy-based power generation as well as conventional plants. There should essentially be an electricity-needs auction on a regular basis, allowing the various methods to compete head to head. If the given power need can be met more cost-effectively with a mix of weatherization (provided by an independent energy services company) and wind power than with geothermal power and coal, then the market should rule. All proposed projects would have to obtain the needed environmental permits expeditiously in order to retain a contract.

Addressing the fundamental issues facing the power industry will take more than the tinkering with traditional electricity policies that has occurred so far. With utilities investing in efficiency and entrepreneurs building generating plants, the traditional boundaries of the power business are rapidly breaking down. The energy services industry expands yearly and is finding vast potential for improved efficiency. It is time planners considered seriously the possibility of slowly reduced power use, something that would undermine many economic assumptions on which this industry currently depends. Many utilities may, for example, be overstaffed for the new era, and many of their employees may need retraining.

The traditional boundaries of the power business are rapidly breaking down.

Power generation is no longer a natural monopoly. Although transmission and distribution of power are best done by a large government-owned or government-regulated company, smaller competitive firms can more effectively develop new technologies and build new generating plants. The small-scale power phenomenon has already resulted in de facto deregulation of power generation in some areas of the United States.

Taken a step further, utilities could be excluded from plant construction, opening up competition among private companies in building plants and selling power to customers. Many utilities now hope the PURPA requirement that excludes them from owning more than half of a qualifying independent power plant will be lifted, so they can compete for power sales contracts. But this raises thorny problems, as utilities that compete for such contracts would be unable to serve as evenhanded brokers.

Eventually, even existing central power plants could be operated independently of utilities. Earnings would be based on performance, rather than a guaranteed rate of return to the utility stockholder. California may take a step in this direction: The state Public Utilities Commission is considering allowing PG&E to earn only the avoided-cost rate on its recently completed Diablo Canyon nuclear plants, basing the utility's profits on how the plants are run and how competitive they are with other generating sources in the region.[71]

Electric utilities might one day become "common carriers" similar to pipelines or railroads that link producers and customers. A power producer in one region would be permitted to sign sales contracts with users hundreds or thousands of miles away. The electricity would be "wheeled" across connecting transmission lines for a reasonable charge. The utilities would still be responsible for maintaining power lines and for billing customers, and, in countries where they are privately owned, the regulated utility would earn a profit in return for this service.[72]

Utilities would also help forecast and plan, and would channel funds to customers for improved efficiency. Governments would set rates as well as effi-

ciency and environmental standards. But the business of building new generating plants and tapping the efficiency potential would go to independent entrepreneurial companies.

Once these major institutional changes are made, the possibilities are enormous. Eventually it may be possible to make many farms and homes into power generators, relying on photovoltaic panels on the rooftop and fuel cells in the basement. People would have the option of becoming totally independent of the wider electricity system or of being linked with thousands of other consumers and producers of various sizes. It will be decades before the world moves fully in this direction, but the intervening years are likely to see much more diverse, decentralized, and ecologically sound electricity systems.

7

Decommissioning Nuclear Power Plants

Cynthia Pollock

Nearly four decades and 350 power plants into the nuclear age, the question of how to safely and economically dispose of nuclear reactors and their wastes is still largely unanswered. Unlike other electric generating technologies, nuclear plants cannot simply be abandoned at the end of their operating lives or demolished with a wrecking ball. Radioactivity builds up each year the plant operates, and all of the contaminated parts and equipment must be securely isolated from people and the environment. Some radioactive elements decay quickly, but others remain hazardous for millennia.

No one knows how much it will cost to decommission the hundreds of units in service or under construction around the world. Estimates range from $50 million to $3 billion per plant.[1] The enormous rush to build nuclear power plants before 1980 means that much of the nuclear decommissioning bill may fall due in a single decade—from 2000 to 2010. Although engineers still debate about the life expectancy of a reactor, economical operation may not be feasible for

longer than 30 years. Numerous technical difficulties, including the constraints radiation buildup places on routine maintenance and the inevitable embrittlement of the reactor pressure vessel, are likely to limit opportunities to extend plant life.

At the turn of the century, when growth in the demand for power is likely to be slow (see Chapter 6), nuclear decommissioning could be the largest expense facing the utility industry, outstripping plant construction. Given current policies, most of this bill will be paid by a generation that did not take part in the decision to build the first round of nuclear power plants—and that did not use much of the power generated.

Although nuclear power supplied 13 percent of the world's electricity in 1984, not a single large commercial unit has ever been dismantled.[2] Nuclear engineers have been attracted to the exciting challenge of developing and improving a new technology, not in figuring out how to manage its rubbish. But as a growing number of plants approach retirement age, the problem of dealing with reactors that are no longer usable will demand attention. Not one of the countries currently relying on nuclear power is adequately prepared for this challenge.

The oldest commercial nuclear reactors are already nearing the end of their useful lives, and some plants have closed prematurely because of accidents or faulty designs. In the United States, dozens of tiny research and military reactors are no longer used, four small commercial units are shut down and awaiting decommissioning, and the Nuclear Regulatory Commission estimates that another 67 large commercial units will cease operations before the year 2010. Worldwide, more than 20 power reactors are already shut down, 63 more are likely to retire by the turn of the century, and another 162 between 2000 and 2010.[3] Countries with advanced nuclear programs will soon start to feel the pressure associated with managing the new and broadened "back end" of the nuclear fuel cycle.

The formidable issue of decommissioning will probably continue to get less attention than it deserves. Utility companies and ratepayers balk at yet another large expense associated with using nuclear power. And politicians are reluctant to make waves about an issue that will not come to the forefront until after their political careers are over. In many parts of the world, the nuclear power industry is strapped for cash and no longer commands the attention of scientists, business leaders, or policymakers.

Developing new technologies and formulating complicated regulatory guidelines for safely transporting, storing, and disposing of radioactive wastes will be difficult to accomplish in such a milieu. But there can be little argument that public health and safety and the financial solvency of utilities demand accelerated research on and financial planning for decommissioning.

DECONTAMINATION AND DISMANTLEMENT

Decommissioning is waste management on a new scale, in terms of both complexity and cost. Following plant closure, the company or agency responsible must first decide which of three courses to follow: decontaminate and dismantle the facility immediately after shutdown, put it in "storage" for 50–100 years to undergo radioactive decay prior to dismantlement, or simply erect a "permanent" tomb. Each option involves shutting down the plant, removing the spent fuel from the reactor core, draining all liquids, and flushing the pipes. Elaborate safeguards to protect public and worker health must be provided every step of the way.[4]

Under the immediate dismantlement scenario, irradiated structures would be partially decontaminated, radioactive steel and concrete disassembled using advanced scoring and cutting techniques, and all radioactive debris shipped to a waste burial facility. The site would then theoretically be available for "unrestricted" use.

Plants to be mothballed, on the other hand, would undergo preliminary cleanup but the structure would remain intact and be placed under constant guard to prevent public access. After 50 years in storage, most of the short-lived radioisotopes would have decayed, further safety gains would be negligible, and the facility would be dismantled. Entombment, the third option, would involve covering the reactor with reinforced concrete and erecting barriers to keep out intruders. Although once viewed as the cheap and easy way out, entombment is no longer considered a realistic option because of the longevity of several radioisotopes.[5]

A survey of 30 electric utilities in the United States revealed that 73 percent planned to promptly dismantle and remove their reactors following shutdown. Yet utilities in Canada, France, and West Germany are planning to mothball most of their reactors for several decades prior to dismantlement.[6]

Regardless of the method chosen, decommissioning a large nuclear power plant is a complex engineering task, without precedent. The high levels of radioactivity present at recently closed reactors place numerous constraints on the decommissioning crew. Workers must take elaborate precautions, including wearing protective clothing and breathing apparatus and limiting their time in contaminated environments. Radiation exposure must be carefully monitored, and adhering to regulations can greatly reduce shift length. Productivity is unavoidably low, less than half of what it could be in a nonradioactive environment.[7]

Many activities are so dangerous that workers cannot perform them directly. Remote-control technologies, often used behind protective barriers, are thus a focus of industry research. At the damaged Three Mile Island nuclear plant, reconnaissance vehicles sent in after the accident scanned the general level of radioactivity and pinpointed spots of concentrated contaminants. Small detectors investigated inaccessible sites. A glorified jackhammer and vacuum cleaner unit is decontaminating concrete floors. Advances in robotics will also help reduce the danger during decontamination and dismantlement.

Much of the radioactivity in a retired nuclear plant is bound to the surface of structural components. The type of material and its exterior surface determines the depth of penetration—the range is typically from as little as several millimeters to as much as 15 centimeters for unsealed concrete. Although some surface contamination can be washed off using high-pressure water jets and chemical decontaminants, only a fraction of the material becomes clean enough to recycle or dispose of in commercial landfills.[8]

The volume of solvents used must be carefully regulated because the effluent also becomes radioactive. Spills during either operation or cleanup can result in contamination of the surrounding soil. Keeping waste volumes to a minimum is an elusive goal: Each piece of machinery and every tool that comes into direct contact with a contaminated surface must be decontaminated or added to the radioactive waste pile.

The other source of radiation that confronts decommissioning crews is "activation" products. When nuclear fuel undergoes fission—the splitting of uranium atoms—stray neutrons and other particles escape and enter the surrounding structures. These neutrons bombard the nuclei of many atoms, and the resulting change in composition causes some elements in the steel and concrete that encircle the reactor core to become radioactive.[9]

For the first several decades following plant shutdown, the most problematic elements are those that decay the fastest. Measured in curies, or disintegrations per second, cobalt and cesium are the dominant short-lived radioisotopes in contaminated materials. Other elements with longer half-lives (the time it takes radioisotopes to decay to half their original levels) are present in smaller quantities and will dominate radiation levels in the future. Significant amounts of long-lived nickel and niobium radioisotopes are present in neutron-activated wastes and will likely render them unsuitable for traditional shallow-land disposal.

The longest-lived hazardous element detected to date, nickel 59, has a half-life of 80,000 years. Overall, activated components contain over 1,000 times the radioactivity of contaminated components.[10]

Practical decommissioning experience is limited to very small reactors.

Following preliminary decontamination, the reactor and surrounding structures must be dismantled into smaller pieces for transportation and burial. The pressure vessel containing a 1,000-megawatt reactor is typically over 12 meters high and 4 meters in diameter and may not be able to be shipped intact. But cutting it into pieces is hazardous and expensive. Each cut causes more airborne contamination and greater worker exposure. Remote operations and the need to keep dust formation to a minimum complicate the dismantlement. One technique that has been used successfully is underwater cutting with plasma arc torches. Other methods being evaluated are laser beams, better mechanical cutting tools such as diamond-tipped saws, and explosives to break up concrete shields.[11]

New, larger waste containers will minimize the extent of dismantling required, and volume reduction techniques now being developed may substantially reduce the number of waste disposal shipments. One of the most obvious and simplest approaches is to melt the steel. Other strategies include nesting the components and compacting them under high pressure.

Practical decommissioning experience is limited to very small reactors. The 22-megawatt Elk River plant in Minnesota is the largest that has been fully decontaminated and dismantled. The U.S. Department of Energy (DOE) completed the three-year project in 1974 at a cost of $6.15 million. Underwater plasma arc torches cut apart the reactor, and 2,600 cubic meters of radioactive waste were disposed of at government burial sites.[12] Today's reactors can produce 50 times more power and will have operated for over seven times as long as Elk River. Since radioactivity builds up in proportion to plant size and operating life, a 1,000-megawatt reactor used for 30 years would be considerably more contaminated.

Twenty-five miles outside of Pittsburgh, Pennsylvania, the small 72-megawatt Shippingport reactor is currently being decommissioned by DOE. Opened in 1957 as the first commercial power reactor in the United States, the plant has had three different cores and already undergone one round of decontamination. Despite unique operating experience, Shippingport could be used as a valuable and badly needed decommissioning prototype. Instead, DOE plans to encase the 10-meter-high steel reactor vessel in concrete, lift the 770-ton behemoth intact, and send it by barge down the Ohio and Mississippi rivers, through the Gulf of Mexico and the Panama Canal, and up the Pacific Coast and Columbia River. It will be buried in an earthen trench on the government-run Hanford nuclear reservation.[13]

Keeping the Shippingport reactor pressure vessel in one piece is estimated to lop at least $7 million, or 7 percent, off the total price tag, but this action is shortsighted. Larger reactors may be too big to ship in one piece, and the most difficult task decommissioning crews will face is dismantling the pressure vessel and its contents. Tackling that problem now at Shippingport could provide valuable knowledge and experience.[14]

In Europe, dismantlement of several

commercial reactors is currently being planned. The first three projects are the 100-megawatt Niederaichbach unit in West Germany, the 33-megawatt Windscale advanced gas reactor in the United Kingdom, and the 45-megawatt French G-2 gas reactor at Marcoule. Although the French and U.K. plants are small, each operated for about 20 years—long enough to become well contaminated. The larger, German reactor was in service for only two years before technical difficulties resulted in its closure. Each unit has a different design, and problems unique to specific technologies are likely to be discovered.[15]

Experience gained at the damaged reactor at Three Mile Island—the site of the most serious mishap in the history of nuclear power—will also aid future decommissioning work. The industry's knowledge of robotics, chemical decontaminants, and remote cutting techniques has greatly expanded as a result of the cleanup effort. International information sharing and on-site observations by foreign experts have helped ensure that these lessons will be widely applied. The level of contamination at Three Mile Island is many times higher than will be encountered at most power reactors; cleanup costs are projected to pass $1 billion before decommissioning itself is contemplated.[16]

The overriding consideration in selecting a decommissioning schedule and the appropriate decontamination and dismantlement methods must be worker and public safety. Although radioactivity declines more than tenfold during the first 50 years after plant closure, thereby reducing worker exposure, the reactor is a potential hazard during the cool-down period. The retired Humboldt Bay reactor on the northern California coast is a good example. It lies in a seismically active zone and is not structurally equipped to handle tremors—which is why it was permanently taken out of operation in 1976. Immediate dismantlement would make the site available for other uses and would limit potential public exposure to radiation. Yet efforts to dismantle the plant are not expected until after the turn of the century.[17]

WASTE DISPOSAL

Considering the volume of radioactive waste being accumulated around the world, the lack of progress in its management is disturbing. Few nations have commercial disposal facilities for low-level radioactive wastes. And not a single country has developed a permanent repository for the most dangerous, high-level, wastes—spent fuel and the by-products of fuel reprocessing. Dismantlement and burial of nonoperating and dangerous commercial nuclear facilities will not be possible until there are safe places to put the radioactive remains.

Few nations have commercial disposal facilities for low-level radioactive wastes.

Some 12,000 metric tons of commercial high-level wastes are already in storage in the United States alone and the volume will quadruple in the next 15 years. The toxicity of such wastes requires that they be kept out of the biosphere for at least 10,000 years, longer than recorded history. Most countries plan to bury the waste in geologic repositories between 300 and 1,200 meters deep. One of the strongest reasons for pursuing burial is that it eliminates the need for institutional enforcement.[18]

Where to put these disposal sites is a contentious issue in each of the 26 countries that produce nuclear power. The lack of high-level waste repositories is an omission that will limit the decommissioning of commercial facilities until at least the turn of the century. It is impossible to fully dismantle a reactor if there is nowhere to put the spent fuel cooling in utility storage ponds.

The fuel for most nuclear power plants consists of small pellets of uranium oxide—the size of pencil erasers—that are sealed in 12-foot-long metal tubes and bundled into fuel assemblies. Fission products that result from the splitting of uranium atoms gradually build up to a point that inhibits the chain reaction. One fourth to one third of the fuel in a typical reactor must be replaced each year. The spent fuel is highly radioactive and consequently very warm. Remote handling conducted behind heavy shielding is essential.

Potential host states and environmental groups have filed lawsuits challenging the adequacy of the siting guidelines.

Exposure to the spontaneous decay process can result in radiation sickness, and sometimes death. Long-term effects, intensified if radioisotopes themselves are ingested or inhaled, include cancer, birth defects, and genetic mutations. Radioisotopes are so dangerous because they mimic essential nutrients, concentrate in vulnerable organs, and then decay inside the body. Strontium, for example, accumulates in bones; iodine builds up in the thyroid gland. And unlike many toxic chemicals, radioactive waste cannot readily be detoxified or destroyed. Unreprocessed spent fuel will remain more toxic than the original uranium ore for about 3 million years.[19] High-level wastes must be kept out of

the food chain and water supplies until they have decayed to harmless levels.

Reprocessing of spent fuel, once viewed as essential to the long-term viability of nuclear power and as a way of eliminating the need to dispose of uranium and plutonium, is now practiced commercially in only two countries—France and the United Kingdom. Reprocessing stretches uranium supplies by recovering the unused uranium and plutonium, but the process costs several times more than mining and enriching uranium ore. The British plant at Sellafield and the French Marcoule and La Hague facilities each accept domestic and foreign spent fuels. The recovered uranium and plutonium, and the vitrified high-level wastes (converted by heat into glass cylinders), are to be returned to the countries of origin.[20]

Although reprocessing gets spent fuel away from the reactor, it does not eliminate the waste disposal problem. Indeed, reprocessing compounds this problem because it increases the number of times the fuel is handled and transported. Mobility increases the risk of an accident and the chance that plutonium could be used in weapons production or stolen by terrorist groups.

Several high-level waste repositories have been proposed and tested over the years, most extensively in the United States, but none has yet proved acceptable for receiving commercial spent fuel. Political opposition may be a more difficult obstacle than finding a geologically appropriate site. Waste disposal is likely to be particularly tough where population densities are high, such as in Japan and many European nations. Some countries—the Netherlands, for example, where there is strong public opposition to domestic waste disposal—are hoping that international sites will become available, perhaps operated by reactor suppliers. Yet the likelihood that any nation would want to accept large volumes of waste not generated internally is small. China has reportedly offered to store West German spent fuel in the Gobi Desert, but discussions are still at an early stage. The Soviet Union is the only country that takes back the high-level wastes generated by the reactors it sells, most of them to Eastern European nations.[21]

The geologic medium chosen for a permanent repository is thus likely to be limited by the options available domestically. Sweden plans to dispose of its high-level wastes in granite, West Germany is examining the use of salt mines, and Belgium hopes to place its waste in clay. (See Table 7–1.) At this time, no single disposal medium is considered substantially superior. Problems have been found with each, though in most cases they are not viewed as insurmountable.

Nations must also decide if they want a repository for spent fuel, reprocessing wastes, or both. Spent fuel is solid and contained in metal rods, while reprocessing wastes are in a liquid state and must be solidified before disposal. France has developed a vitrification system that several nations, including Japan, the United Kingdom, and West Germany, intend to adopt. Plans are to keep the glass cylinders in above-ground storage vaults for several decades to cool and then to place them in permanent geologic repositories.[22]

In the United States, spent fuel is currently stored at reactor sites in water-filled basins. Storage space is running out at many older plants. In 1982 the U.S. Congress passed the Nuclear Waste Policy Act (NWPA), requiring the federal government to develop two permanent mined geologic repositories and have the first ready for business by 1998. The Environmental Protection Agency has issued standards limiting radioactivity releases from the 300- to 1,200-meter-deep burial sites for 10,000 years. The location of the first repository has been tentatively narrowed to three sites: Hanford, Washington; Yucca Mountain, Nevada; or Deaf Smith County, Texas.[23]

Final site selection has already become a political hot potato. Potential host states and environmental groups have filed lawsuits challenging the adequacy of the siting guidelines. According

Table 7-1. Geologic Media Selected for Further Study as High-Level Waste or Spent Fuel Repository in Various Countries

Country	Granite	Clay	Salt	Basalt	Tuff	Shale	Diabase
Belgium		X					
Canada	X						
France	X	X	X				
Japan	X				X	X	X
Spain	X		X				
Sweden	X						
Switzerland	X						
United Kingdom	X						
United States	X		X	X	X		
West Germany			X				

SOURCE: K.M. Harmon, "Survey of Foreign Terminal Radioactive Waste Storage Programs," in *Proceedings of the 1983 Civilian Radioactive Waste Management Information Meeting*, Washington, D.C., December 12–15, 1983 (Springfield, Va.: National Technical Information Service, 1984).

to James Martin, a staff attorney with the Environmental Defense Fund: "First, there are concerns that, in its haste to site a repository, [the Department of Energy] has relied on pre-NWPA studies of dubious quality and is delaying analysis of waste transportation risks that cannot be deferred. Second, there is evidence that politics are creeping into and tainting the decision-making process. These factors pose grave threats to the integrity and public acceptance of the siting process."[24]

Each of the proposed sites has drawbacks. There is much concern, for example, that disposal at Hanford could lead to contamination of the nearby Columbia River. And farmers in Texas fear contamination of the aquifer they use to irrigate their crops. Making optimal site selections will be difficult, but the only way to be confident about the final choice is to conduct extensive testing at each proposed location and make the results available for scientific review.

Several nations are examining intermediate storage of spent fuel at centralized locations away from reactor sites. Sweden has the most advanced program: Its CLAB facility, adjacent to the Oskarshamn power station, will hold spent fuel from all Swedish reactors for several decades prior to geologic disposal. In the United States, three sites in Tennessee, including the abandoned Clinch River breeder reactor, are being considered for a monitored retrievable storage program. If adopted, the storage plan would allow the U.S. Department of Energy to fulfill its obligation to take possession of commercial spent fuel in 1998 even if a permanent geologic repository is not yet available. Storing the fuel would result in further cooling, thereby facilitating disposal, but it would also increase fuel shipments, and should not be allowed to slow the development of a permanent disposal site.[25]

In 1976, the California legislature was

the first to enact a bill forbidding further nuclear power plant construction until "the federal government has approved, and there exists, a demonstrated technology or means for the disposal of high-level nuclear wastes." Not a single new nuclear reactor has been ordered in the United States since 1978, but the deteriorating economics of nuclear power, slower than projected electricity-demand growth, and tightened regulation after the accident at Three Mile Island are the principal causes.[26]

Following the California example, Finland, Sweden, Switzerland, and West Germany have enacted "stipulation" laws making continued use or construction of nuclear power facilities contingent upon the development of satisfactory plans for managing the spent fuel and reactor wastes. Japan has similar regulations in place, and one commentator likens its lack of high-level waste disposal facilities to "living in a house without a toilet." According to the International Atomic Energy Agency in Geneva, the present inability to dispose of high-level wastes is impeding the development of nuclear power in developing countries.[27]

Lack of adequate low-level waste disposal facilities may prove to be an equally difficult impediment to decommissioning. Although this waste is considerably less toxic, it is produced in far greater volumes. At the end of a 30-year operating life, dismantling a typical large reactor will produce some 18,000 cubic meters of low-level radioactive waste—enough to dump four meters' worth atop a football field. (See Table 7–2.)

Decommissioning just one large reactor would yield a volume of contaminated concrete and steel equal to one sixth of the low-level radioactive wastes now produced in the United States each year. Decommissioning all U.S. operating reactors would yield well

Table 7-2. Estimated Low-Level Radioactive Wastes from Dismantlement of a Typical 1,100-Megawatt Pressurized Water Reactor

Material	Burial Volume	Truckloads
	(cubic meters)	(number)
Activated		216
Metal	484	
Concrete	707	
Contaminated		967
Metal	5,465	
Concrete	10,613	
Radioactive	618	180
Total	17,887	1,363

SOURCE: R.I. Smith, G.J. Konzek, and W.E. Kennedy, Jr., *Technology, Safety and Costs of Decommissioning a Reference Pressurized Water Reactor Power Station* (Washington, D.C.: U.S. Nuclear Regulatory Commission, 1978).

over 1 million cubic meters of low-level waste, enough to build a radioactive wall three meters high and one meter wide from Washington, D.C., to New York City. All the contaminated and activated components of the reactor require special handling and disposal, and some of the wastes are considered too radioactive for shallow land burial. The staff of the U.S. Nuclear Regulatory Commission have identified "several kinds of decommissioning wastes for which disposal capacity is presently either not available or not assured under the current statutory and/or regulatory framework."[28]

Until the sixties, the United States and many other nations discarded low-level wastes by dumping them at sea. Belgium, the Netherlands, Switzerland, and the United Kingdom were still dumping much of their low-level waste until 1983, when the London Dumping Convention declared a moratorium pending a scientific study of the effect on the marine environment. The reprocessing operation at Sellafield, however, still pumps 1.2 million gallons of slightly radioactive wastewater into the ocean daily.[29]

In the case of on-land disposal, standard procedure is to pack the waste, which includes everything from concrete to workclothes, in barrels, and store them either at the reactor site or in specially designated warehouses. In only a half-dozen countries are the drums transported to land-based commercial low-level waste depositories and buried in earthen or concrete trenches.

Although sometimes regarded as the leader in the waste disposal field, the United States is still far from having a workable, long-term program. In the late seventies only half of the country's low-level waste sites were still operating —one each in Nevada, South Carolina, and Washington. Objecting to their role as the nation's dumping ground, the three state governments closed or restricted access to their facilities for a short time in 1979.[30]

This prompted Congress to pass the Low-Level Radioactive Waste Policy Act in 1980. The law, designed to encourage states to form regional agreements to establish and operate disposal facilities cooperatively, is being complied with only sluggishly. Without last-minute congressional intervention, over half the low-level waste produced in the United States, accounting for nearly three quarters of the radioactivity, would have been barred from the nation's three commercial dump sites as of January 1986. A seven-year extension of the deadline has given states some breathing room. The first seven "regional compacts," involving 37 states, have also been approved. In anticipation of a shutdown, about a dozen utilities recently built on-site storage facilities. These temporary dumps are designed to hold six or seven years' worth of low-level waste.[31]

Even if current waste sites remain

open, they are too small to accommodate the volume of waste expected from decommissioning. At Barnwell, South Carolina, a proposed federal ceiling will limit annual waste shipments to 34,000 cubic meters. Barnwell's 32 trenches could therefore accept the decommissioning wastes from only two reactors each year, assuming all existing disposal contracts were cancelled.[32]

Sweden plans to store its low-level radioactive waste in numerous galleries and chambers sunk into granite rock 50 meters below the seabed. Some nations, including West Germany, are temporarily storing such wastes in above-ground warehouses, waiting for a time when permanent burial sites become available. At least one future German repository is planned at a former iron ore mine. Japanese nuclear plants store the accumulated low-level wastes on-site. Incineration and compression facilities keep waste volumes manageable while research is conducted on both land and sea disposal.[33]

Moving both high- and low-level wastes to their final resting ground is an integral step in the disposal process. Various transport modes are envisioned. In the United States, trains and trucks will carry most of the load. In Sweden all of the waste will be moved by ship; in other countries, a combination of trucks, trains, and boats will be used. The comparatively small volume of wastes currently removed from operating plants is often transported on routes planned to bypass population centers. When this is unavoidable, high-level wastes have sometimes been moved in the middle of the night with armed escorts. In 1976, New York City banned radioactive waste shipments within its borders. Other communities across the country soon followed suit. After a protracted legal battle, the U.S. Department of Transportation ruled these restrictions illegal.[34]

Many countries still have not developed comprehensive regulations governing the packaging, transportation, and disposal of radioactive wastes. Research and development activities are progressing, albeit slowly, and concerned citizens around the world are trying to draw attention to the issue.

Implicit in the decision to develop nuclear power should be acceptance of the responsibility to safely manage radioactive wastes. At present, decommissioning policy is held hostage to the lack of disposal sites. Few electric utilities are likely to proceed with reactor dismantlement until they can be assured that all of the waste will have someplace to go and that the site will then become available for other purposes.

COST ESTIMATION

The cost of decommissioning nuclear power plants is highly speculative: As noted earlier, the figures put forward run from $50 million to $3 billion per reactor. The majority of estimates cluster at the low end of the range. Some cost projections were adopted from generic estimates, others used a rule-of-thumb based on a fixed percentage of construction costs, and a few were arrived at using detailed, site-specific engineering studies. In effect, all the figures put forward are guesses based on numerous uncertain assumptions and varying degrees of wishful thinking.

In 1978 the U.S. Nuclear Regulatory Commission asked the Battelle Pacific Northwest Laboratory to estimate the cost of decommissioning generic 1,100-megawatt pressurized and boiling water reactors (PWRs & BWRs). (These are the most common designs worldwide, accounting for 72 percent of all operating reactors—165 PWRs and 77 BWRs.) Battelle's figures ranged from $61.5 million to $86 million, depending on the plant-specific technology and the number of years after shutdown that dismantlement would be deferred. Immediate dismantlement of a PWR was estimated to be the least expensive, while waiting 30 years to dismantle a BWR was considered to be the most costly. In general, it is more expensive to dismantle a boiling water reactor, all other factors being equal, because a greater volume of contaminated wastes is produced.[35]

For many years, the lack of detailed plant-specific cost estimates led regulatory agencies and utilities to apply the Battelle figures to a great variety of facilities. Little notice was paid to differences in plant size and design, future availability of and distance from waste disposal facilities, and unique site characteristics such as space limitations or difficult topography. But as individual utilities began to conduct their own site-specific cost estimates and as various component costs, such as waste disposal, rose much faster than anticipated, it became obvious that the initial estimates were too low.

In 1984, Battelle updated its estimates, for the Electric Power Research Institute, and costs had indeed risen much faster than inflation over the preceding six years. Waste disposal costs rose the fastest. Assumptions were also modified to reflect current regulations and market conditions. The price tag for immediate dismantlement rose 69 percent for a PWR and 108 percent for a BWR. Comparative site-specific, rather than generic, estimates for the same size plants resulted in estimates of $140.5 million for a PWR (35 percent higher than the updated Battelle estimate) and $133.6 million for a BWR, excluding the costs of removing nonradioactive structures.[36]

Cost estimating guidelines recently developed by the Atomic Industrial Forum, an industry trade group, led members to project a decommissioning cost of $170 million per plant. This is more than a sixfold increase in 10 years. A report issued by the group in 1976 estimated that a 1,100-megawatt pressurized water reactor could be decommissioned for $27 million. And in Switzerland, a detailed three-year study of decommissioning costs concluded that retiring a nuclear plant would cost one fifth as much as the facility originally cost to build. This translates into several hundred million dollars for recently completed plants.[37]

In effect, all the figures put forward are guesses based on varying degrees of wishful thinking.

Economist Duane Chapman at Cornell University, an independent analyst, predicts that decommissioning will cost as much as the original construction, in constant dollars. In the United States, this amounts to an average of about $3 billion for a new 1,000-megawatt unit. Chapman points to the complex procedures and technologies involved, the large volumes of radioactive wastes, and chronically understated nuclear construction costs. Research done at the Rand Corporation introduces another element of uncertainty. Analysts there have concluded that large-scale engineering projects that depend on newly developed technologies cost on average four times more than predicted at the outset. Recent U.S. nuclear power plant construction costs have amounted to 5–10 times the original estimate, even after accounting for inflation. Cost overruns of several hundred percent have become the norm rather than the exception.[38]

Because of gross cost overruns, approximately $20 billion worth of partially constructed nuclear plants have been abandoned in the United States. In the early seventies, reactors were projected to come into service at less than $1 million per megawatt, but none have done so in recent years. Costs for just-completed units have averaged closer to $3 million per megawatt, and at the not-yet-operating Shoreham plant on Long Island, the figure has already surpassed $5 million per megawatt.[39] Decommissioning cost estimates put forward by the nuclear industry presumably count on a learning curve of experience causing costs to fall over time. But U.S. nuclear construction experience appears to defy the learning curve—costs accelerated over the years.

Decommissioning cost estimates for two of the first generation of retired reactors amount to more than $1 million per megawatt. (See Table 7–3.) The Shippingport facility, despite being able to take advantage of a unique transportation arrangement and federally subsidized waste disposal, is expected to cost $98 million to decommission—$1.36 million per megawatt. This figure excludes the cost of dismantling noncontaminated buildings.

It is unlikely that these estimates can be directly scaled on a per megawatt basis, but the proposition may not be farfetched. Although there will be economies of scale involved, the amount of radioactivity that builds up in a plant is proportional to the plant's capacity multiplied by the number of years it operates. Thus the larger the plant, the more radioactive it will be, and the greater the cleanup and disposal effort it

Table 7-3. Estimated Decommissioning Costs for Nuclear Power Plants No Longer in Operation

Owner/Site	Capacity	Estimated Decommissioning Costs	Cost Per Megawatt	Years Operated
	(megawatts)	(million 1985 dollars)		
U.S. Atomic Energy Commission, Elk River	24	14[1]	0.58	1962–68
UK Atomic Energy Authority, Sellafield/Windscale	33	64	1.94	1963–81
Pacific Gas & Electric, Humboldt Bay-Unit 3	65	55	0.85	1963–76
U.S. Department of Energy, Shippingport	72	98	1.36	1957–82
Commonwealth Edison Co., Dresden-1	210	95	0.45	1960–78

[1]Decommissioning of Elk River was completed in 1974.
SOURCES: R. Mark Pocta, "Report on the Decommissioning Costs of Pacific, Gas and Electric Company for Humboldt Bay Power Plant Unit No. 3," California Public Utilities Commission, June 1985; OECD Nuclear Energy Agency, "Compendium on Decommissioning Activities in NEA Member Countries," Paris, January 1985; "DOE Says Decommissioning Costs on Target Despite Shippingport Increase," *Nucleonics Week*, April 25, 1985; Public Citizen/Environmental Action, "Dismantling the Myths About Nuclear Decommissioning," Washington, D.C., April 1985.

will require. If costs can be scaled based on reactor size, then—despite the short-sighted savings being realized by keeping the reactor pressure vessel intact during transport—the Shippingport experience indicates that decommissioning one of today's large reactors could cost over $1 billion.

André Cregut of the French Atomic Energy Commission estimates that utilities will not decommission plants until the cost can be brought down to about 15 percent of initial investment, compared with the 40 percent it is likely to cost using currently available techniques. At 40 percent of investment, decommissioning costs would approach $1 billion for the plants that have recently gone into operation. Whether the expense can be lowered is the crucial, but unanswered, question.[40]

Because reactor designs have changed so much over the years, very few countries—perhaps only France and Canada—will be able to design a uniform decommissioning system. Not only have different countries adopted different reactor technologies, but within some nations the nuclear industry has dabbled in most of the systems available. Nine different designs are represented among the 20 power reactors that have been shut down. (See Table 7–4.) Just as nuclear construction costs continued to multiply in the United States because each utility wanted a custom-built plant, decommissioning cost estimates and experience gained may not be transferable among utilities.

One of the largest components of decommissioning costs will be waste disposal, up to 40 percent of the total according to some industry analysts. In the last decade, the cost of shallow-land burial of a 55-gallon drum of low-level wastes has increased more than tenfold in the United States. Waste disposal costs have tripled in just the past five years and are likely to increase steadily.

Current facilities will continue to raise their rates, and the start-up costs of new sites for both low- and high-level wastes are likely to be high.[41]

Additional expenditures may be required to entice communities to accept radioactive wastes. The United Kingdom is seriously reevaluating its disposal-facility siting policies following vehement local opposition to a plan for using an abandoned salt mine at Billingham in northeast England. Lewis Roberts, director of the Atomic Energy Research Establishment at Harwell, recently acknowledged that the agency may have to adopt the French and Japanese practice of compensating communities for hosting repositories.[42]

Labor expenses may also rise as efforts are made to minimize the radiation doses that personnel receive. Replacement of steam generators at the Surry reactor in Virginia, for example, required more than three times as many worker-hours as expected. Current regulations limit exposure of nuclear industry workers to five rems per year, 10 times as much as permitted for an average person. Many health experts would like the ceiling to be lowered, a move that would significantly increase labor costs during decommissioning.[43]

The number of years a reactor remains in storage prior to dismantlement is a variable that is frequently overlooked when formulating decommissioning cost estimates. Providing on-site surveillance for several decades is expensive. The bill will include salaries for a skeleton staff, radiation monitoring equipment, and, if a high-level waste repository is not available, maintenance of fuel storage facilities. Postponement of decommissioning will also result in the loss of staff most familiar with the plant and require excellent recordkeeping to inform the future crew of the reactor's intricacies and its operating history.

Only seven of the reactors listed in Table 7–4 are scheduled to be dismantled prior to 1995.

As experience is gained in decommissioning and waste handling, regulations are likely to become more strict. If worker radiation exposure limits are lowered, if residual radioactivity standards are set at levels more stringent than predicted, or if transportation and disposal rules are tightened, costs could rise substantially.

Although hundreds of nuclear power plants have been erected around the world, the cost of decommissioning them is highly uncertain. The bill for all the plants now in service could total several hundred billion dollars. The experience necessary to clarify these cost estimates is sadly lacking and urgently required. In order to be manageable, expenses of this magnitude must be budgeted for; they cannot be allowed to come as a surprise.

Table 7-4. Nuclear Power Reactors No Longer in Operation, 1985

Reactor	Location	Year Plant Entered Service	Number of Years Plant Operated	Capacity	Reactor Type[1]
				(megawatts)	
Shippingport	Pennsylvania	1957	25	72	PWR
G-2, Marcoule	France	1958	22	45	GCR
G-3, Marcoule	France	1959	24	45	GCR
Dounreay	United Kingdom	1959	18	14	FBR
Dresden-1	Illinois	1960	18	210	BWR
Indian Point-1	New York	1962	12	257	PWR
Windscale	United Kingdom	1962	19	33	AGR
Chinon-Al	France	1963	10	70	GCR
Humboldt Bay	California	1963	13	65	BWR
JPDR, Tokai	Japan	1963	13	12	BWR
Agesta	Sweden	1963	11	12	PHWR
Garigliano	Italy	1964	14	160	BWR
Karlsruhe	West Germany	1965	19	58	PWR
Gundremmingen	West Germany	1966	11	250	BWR
Lucens	Switzerland	1967	2	7	HWGCR
Peach Bottom	Pennsylvania	1967	7	40	HTGR
Lingen	West Germany	1968	9	256	BWR
Gentilly-1	Canada	1970	9	250	CANDU
NPP-A1	Czechoslovakia	1972	7	110	HWGCR
Niederaichbach	West Germany	1972	2	100	HWGCR

[1]Reactor types, listed in order they appear in table: Pressurized Water; Gas Cooled; Fast Breeder; Boiling Water; Advanced Gas; Pressurized Heavy Water; Heavy Water Moderated GCR; High Temperature Gas Cooled, Graphite Moderated; and Heavy Water Moderated BWR.
SOURCES: OECD Nuclear Energy Agency, "Compendium on Decommissioning Activities in NEA Member Countries," Paris, January 1985; International Atomic Energy Agency, "The Methodology and Technology of Decommissioning Nuclear Facilities" (draft), Annex 2, Vienna, May 1985.

AFFORDING THE FUTURE

The lack of reliable cost estimates makes financial planning for decommissioning extremely difficult. But some mechanism needs to be put in place to assure that there will be enough money available, at the right time, to do the job. When a reactor stops producing power, it also stops earning money for its owner. To ensure that the company can pay for decommissioning, funds need to be set aside during the years that the reactor is operating.

A variety of mechanisms have been proposed and, just like an insurance policy, the plans providing the greatest assurance are the most expensive. One way of guaranteeing that funds will be available in the future is to deposit money in an interest-bearing savings account before the reactor enters service. Interest payments will increase the yearly balance and if the initial cost estimate is correct, or if additional deposits are made when estimates are updated, sufficient funds will be available. This strategy is the most expensive and requires utility customers to pay up front for an expense the company will not incur for several decades.[44]

Making periodic deposits into a decommissioning fund is another way of accruing the money. Customers can be charged a fee, based on the amount of electricity they use, that is collected monthly and put into a decommissioning account. Utilities prefer to keep track of this amount on paper but to use the funds for general purposes, including the construction of more nuclear plants, instead of putting them aside for future decommissioning. This allows the utility to bypass capital markets and keep debt payments low, but the method has been termed "phantom funding" by some observers because the money only exists on paper and is not readily available to the utility.[45]

When the time comes to decontaminate and dismantle the plant, the company will probably need to sell "decommissioning bonds" to raise the required cash. Borrowing capital for unproductive purposes promises to be expensive, as investors will require a high return to cover the perceived risks. A retired and highly radioactive nuclear plant is not likely to be regarded as secure collateral, particularly if the owner is already experiencing financial difficulties. The market value of several U.S. utility company stocks and bonds, those with heavy nuclear commitments, is already less than 50 percent of book value, reflecting lack of investor confidence.[46]

A retired and highly radioactive nuclear power plant is not likely to be regarded as secure collateral.

Bond purchasers will undoubtedly be found if the rate is attractive enough, but ultimately the risk may have to be assumed by the federal government or by pools of electric utilities. The $2.25-billion bond default by the Washington Public Power Supply System in 1983 has made investors especially wary. Municipal and cooperative utilities wholly financed by tax-exempt bonds will be particularly vulnerable because there is no equity cushion provided by shareholders, as there is in private utilities.[47]

If, on the other hand, money is provided by deposits begun when the plant enters service, if the account is managed by professional investors, and if the fund is allowed to grow until it is needed, the utility's financial situation will not be so precarious at plant retirement. This is especially true if the utility has conducted detailed evaluations of the cost of decommissioning at regular intervals during the plant's life. Periodic adjustments of annual deposit amounts will undoubtedly be necessary as more is learned about the costs and techniques of the procedure.

In a study conducted for the U.S. Nuclear Regulatory Commission, University of Pennsylvania economist J.J. Siegel concluded: "The greatest assurance of the availability of decommissioning funding would be attained with an external reserve specifically marked and held by a trustee for the ratepayers and the utility. In this circumstance, it would be virtually impossible for the utility to divert these assets for other uses and funds would be assured no matter what events, legal or financial, occur." Internal funding with no segregated account was ranked last on the list of funding alternatives in terms of assurance.[48]

Even dedicated decommissioning accounts would be inadequate, however, if a plant closes earlier than expected. If this occurs, particularly as the result of a costly accident not fully covered by insurance, the utility would find itself with insufficient funds. A policy to protect against premature closure is a frequently proposed remedy. This is a sound strategy if there are companies willing to provide such coverage.

Yet insurance companies are unlikely to offer premature closure policies at affordable rates unless the industry's operational record improves. Of the reactors that are currently retired and awaiting decommissioning, none operated for the full 30 years used in utility calculations. Nuclear plants are more complicated than other electric generating plants, are subject to more design regulations, and have up to 10 times as many pipes, valves, and pumps.[49] More parts and a harsher operating environment mean a greater number of potential breakdowns. Two thirds of the commercial reactors retired to date produced power for less than 15 years, as Table 7–4 documents.

The least secure method of providing decommissioning funds is to collect them from customers or shareholders at the time they are needed. This strategy puts off until the last possible moment the acquisition of debt that could total billions of dollars and provides no assurance that the money will be available. Such last-ditch efforts are also extremely unfair to customers who will be required to pay for a project they did not benefit from.

In countries where the electric generating system is government-owned, such as France, the "when-needed" principle of funding has been adopted. Utility managers assume they will be able to request funds from the national treasury when the time comes to decommission their reactors. In this case, the burden is placed on future taxpayers instead of utility ratepayers. The French utility debt is now $30 billion because of the accelerated nuclear construction program, and decommissioning costs may result in large government budget deficits.[50] Third World governments already on the edge of insolvency will be particularly hard-pressed to foot the decommissioning bill.

Of the four retired commercial reactors in the United States, only one unit had begun collecting decommissioning funds before it shut down. The Pacific Gas and Electric Company, owner of the Humboldt Bay reactor, collected $500,000 in decommissioning funds during the four years prior to plant shutdown. This lack of financial planning in three instances, and the late and inadequate implementation in the fourth, has led to mandatory periodic deposits into external accounts in eight states: California, Colorado, Maine, Massachusetts, Mississippi, New Hampshire, Pennsylvania, and Vermont.[51]

Similar plans have been adopted elsewhere. In Sweden, each reactor operator pays an annual fee to the government.

The funds are invested in separate accounts from which the utilities can borrow money to pay for decommissioning. Less formal arrangements exist in West Germany and Switzerland.[52]

Although many nations do not set aside money for decommissioning, funds for high-level waste disposal are collected in a dozen North American and European countries. In all cases, the money is paid to the government agency responsible for establishing geologic waste repositories. The fee typically ranges from $1 to $3 per 1,000 kilowatt-hours of nuclear electricity produced.[53]

Setting aside funds for decommissioning is essential in every country that has built nuclear reactors. Regardless of nuclear power's role in a nation's energy plans, existing plants must eventually be scrapped. Decommissioning bills will first fall due in those countries that pio-neered the development of this energy source. And their skill at managing the expense will be closely watched. Nations with newer reactors will learn valuable lessons, and countries that have not yet built such plants will be better able to assess the true lifetime costs of nuclear energy.

The United States has built the most nuclear reactors to date, with the Soviet Union a distant second. (See Table 7–5.) Most utilities throughout the world are financially unprepared for decommissioning. A recent survey of 30 U.S. utilities with nuclear plants revealed that 40 percent of the companies had not conducted site-specific studies of decommissioning costs, two thirds were using the funds they had collected for other activities, and 29 percent did not expect their current funding method to provide enough money to cover the expenses.[54]

Table 7-5. Nuclear Power Reactors in Operation, 10 Leading Countries, 1984

Country	Number of Reactors	Total Nuclear Capacity	Share of Total Domestic Capacity	Share of World Nuclear Capacity
		(megawatts)	(percent)	
United States	84	68,536	13	33
Soviet Union[1]	44	22,706	8	11
France	36	28,015	39	14
United Kingdom	32	6,569	10	3
Japan	28	19,025	12	9
West Germany	19	16,127	18	8
Canada	15	8,617	9	4
Sweden	10	7,355	24	4
Spain	7	4,865	12	2
Belgium	6	3,467	28	2
Total	281	185,282		89

[1]Data are for 1983.
SOURCES: Atomic Industrial Forum (AIF), "International Survey," Bethesda, Md., April 17, 1985; AIF, "Midyear Report," Bethesda, Md., July 10, 1985; Eric Sorenson, International Energy Agency, Paris, private communication, November 8, 1985; Department of Energy, Mines, and Resources, "Electric Power in Canada 1984," Ottawa, 1985; "Electric Power Sector in Spain in 1984," *Boletin Informativo Mensual de Unesa* (Madrid), January/February 1985.

Yet paid over a period of 30 years by all the customers of a utility, decommissioning bills are affordable. The average residential electricity consumer in the United States, if served by an all-nuclear electric utility, would have been charged some $55 for decommissioning in 1984. (This assumes a total decommissioning bill of $1 million per megawatt of plant capacity.) Customers with inefficient electric heating and air conditioning systems might have to pay well over $100 a year, but those using electricity efficiently would pay far less than the average. And the actual charges would be even lower, because no U.S. electric utility relies exclusively on nuclear power.[55]

Commonwealth Edison, an Illinois utility, owns the most nuclear plants. Its nine operating reactors provide 55 percent of the company's generating capacity, and three more units are under construction. Thus an average residential customer of the utility would have paid less than $25 in 1984 toward decommissioning. This charge may be acceptable in affluent societies if fee collection starts when the plant enters service and if the reactor operates for a full 30 years, but the amount needs to be explicitly included in cost projections, starting at the earliest planning stages.[56]

A Long-Term Strategy

More than 30 years after the first nuclear reactor started producing electricity, a viable decommissioning strategy has yet to be formulated. Even if reactor ordering ground to a halt tomorrow, the international nuclear community will eventually have to dispose of more than 500 plants, including those currently under construction. If it cost $1 billion to decommission each unit, the total bill would amount to a staggering $500 bil-

lion. Mountains of radioactive waste will be created, and dozens of waste disposal sites will be required. Aggressive, well-funded research and development programs are needed at both the national and international levels.

No country currently has the capability to permanently dispose of the high-level wastes now stored at a single reactor.

During the next three decades, over 300 nuclear power reactors will be shut down. (See Table 7–6.) Some of the reactors that have already been retired are large enough and operated long enough to yield valuable lessons for future decommissioning projects. One of the largest or most problematic of these should become an international test case, with the owner covering half the costs and governments and research institutes from around the world making additional contributions in exchange for access to the knowledge and experience gained. An ad hoc arrangement like this is now in effect at the damaged Three Mile Island unit, with various U.S. utilities, the U.S. Department of Energy, and international participants sharing the costs with the principal owner in order to learn firsthand about the latest in decontamination and dismantlement techniques.

Decommissioning planning has lagged far behind reactor development. The International Atomic Energy Agency (the United Nations research and watchdog arm of the nuclear industry) did not hold its first meeting on decommissioning until 1973, some 19 years after the first power reactor was built. The initial technical meeting sponsored by the agency was not convened until two years later. Yet by this time,

Table 7-6. Nuclear Power Reactors in Operation Worldwide, 1950–84, and Year of Expected Retirement

Entered Service	Reactors	Capacity	Planned Retirement After 30 Years of Operation
	(number)	(megawatts)	
1950–54	1	5	1980–84
1955–59	10	600	1985–89
1960–64	18	1,971	1990–94
1965–69	34	8,692	1995–99
1970–74	75	43,821	2000–04
1975–79	87	65,002	2005–09
1980–84	103	88,566	2010–14
Cumulative Total	328	208,657	

SOURCE: Atomic Industrial Forum (AIF), "International Survey," Bethesda, Md., April 17, 1985; AIF, "Midyear Report," Bethesda, Md., July 10, 1985.

hundreds of nuclear power plants were being planned by utilities and governments throughout the world. This blatant neglect of the back end of the nuclear fuel cycle has been replicated by national atomic energy authorities everywhere.

The biggest stumbling block for all nations with nuclear plants is the lack of permanent disposal facilities for radioactive wastes. Although many reactor operators around the world agree that plants should be dismantled as quickly as practicable after shutdown, that option has been foreclosed until at least the turn of the century. No country currently has the capability to permanently dispose of the high-level wastes now stored at a single reactor. Just as today's cities would not be habitable without large fleets of garbage trucks and extensive landfills, the international nuclear industry is not viable without a sound decommissioning strategy.

The issuance of detailed technical guidelines should be expedited so utilities can plan for the future. Some nuclear construction programs were begun with designs only 20 percent complete,

rather than the 40 percent considered minimal, only to discover that with regulatory changes they were not even that far along. The consequences of similar inadequate technical planning for decommissioning would be not only costly but dangerous.

Early knowledge of decommissioning requirements would also allow engineers to incorporate design changes that would facilitate later decontamination and dismantlement efforts. A simple concept that eluded manufacturers of the first nuclear plants was the value of putting a protective coating on all surfaces that would be exposed to radiation. Even a thick layer of removable paint reduces the surface contamination of structural components. Limited experience with neutron-activated wastes has also demonstrated the need to minimize the amount of neutron-absorbing impurities used in reactor steel and concrete.[57]

Large, detailed savings programs to provide decommissioning funds are required. Dedicated decommissioning accounts to accumulate the amount of money necessary to safely dismantle and dispose of all operating reactors should be established. And government tax codes that would deplete these funds as they are set aside need to be amended. Revenue deposited in trust funds and interest earned on that money will compound far more rapidly if tax liabilities are deferred until the money is spent. Allowing rapid growth of decommissioning accounts is in everybody's best interest.

Knowledge of what can be done to make the decommissioning process safer and less costly is slowly accumulating, but efforts to expand that information base need to be strengthened. The temptation to use cost-cutting measures in the first projects should be resisted. Saving millions of dollars now could mean spending billions of extra dollars later.

8

Banishing Tobacco

William U. Chandler

Tobacco causes more death and suffering among adults than any other toxic material in the environment. This has long been known, but now it is feared that involuntary exposure to cigarette smoke causes more cancer deaths than any other pollutant. Protecting nonsmokers from cigarette smoke will require a marked change in society's treatment of tobacco, one that could also help eliminate its direct threat to users themselves.

No country is yet taking action against tobacco commensurate with the cost it imposes. The global use of tobacco has grown nearly 75 percent over the past two decades. In China, use has doubled. In only four countries are fewer cigarettes smoked now than in 1964. In the United States, the percentage of adults who smoke has fallen from 43 to 32 percent, but even there 20 percent more tobacco is used than when an antismoking campaign began in 1964, and the country still ranks third in the world in per capita cigarette use.[1] The direct health costs, the health risks to passive smokers, and the economic costs have grown proportionally.

The worldwide cost in lives now approaches 2.5 million per year, almost 5 percent of all deaths. Tobacco kills 13 times as many Americans as hard drugs do, and 8 times as many as automobile accidents. Passive smokers (those who must inhale the smoke of others' cigarettes) are perhaps three times likelier to die of lung cancer than they would be otherwise. The smoking of mothers diminishes the physical and mental capabilities of their children, and in many countries more than one fifth of children are exposed to smoke in this way.[2] These statistics add up to a cost that is increasingly viewed—in countries where the information is available, at least—not only as unnecessary, but as intolerable.

Though the health consequences of tobacco are now well known, policies to avoid them lag far behind. Most efforts to control tobacco are merely attempts to control or color information about the product. Governments sometimes warn people that tobacco is unhealthy, forbid its advertisement, or restrict its use in theaters or buses, though often the effort is no stronger than the Japanese cigarette package warning: "For your health, let's be careful not to smoke too

This chapter appeared as Worldwatch Paper 68, *Banishing Tobacco.*

much."[3] No national tobacco control effort has been launched with the vigor of antidrug campaigns, or even of campaigns against toxic chemicals, though hard drugs and chemicals claim far fewer victims than tobacco.

Health leaders in government, international organizations, and public interest groups have also failed in this fight—partly because tobacco is tenaciously addictive, partly because both governments and industry promote tobacco, but partly because the leadership of health and environmental authorities has been weak. This conclusion is borne out not only by the continued high levels of tobacco use in industrial countries, but by the explosive growth of cigarette smoking in Eastern bloc countries and in China. Yet the informational campaigns of concerned health leaders have at least succeeded in getting many analysts to recognize that tobacco is a high-priority, worldwide public health problem. And one that needs stronger medicine.[4]

THE EPIDEMIC SPREADS

Smoking is an epidemic growing at 2.1 percent per year, faster than world population. (See Figure 8–1.) Growth in tobacco use slowed briefly in the early eighties, primarily for economic reasons, but is resuming its rapid increase. Over a billion people now smoke, consuming almost 5 trillion cigarettes per year, an average of more than half a pack a day. Even in the United States, where smoking prevalence—the portion of a population who smoke—has declined, the 20 percent increase in tobacco use since 1964 indicates that those who smoke now smoke more heavily.[5]

Greece leads the world in per capita cigarette consumption. (See Table 8–1.) Japanese, Americans, Canadians, Yugoslavs, and Poles follow close behind.

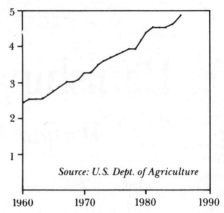

Trillion Cigarettes

Source: U.S. Dept. of Agriculture

Figure 8-1. Cigarette Consumption Worldwide, 1960-85

People in industrial countries smoke twice as much as people in the Third World. Although Chinese men smoke almost as much as Western men do, the negligible amount of smoking by Chinese women means that country does not rank very high in overall per capita consumption. Nevertheless, China uses a quarter of the world's tobacco.[6]

Tobacco is increasingly grown near where it is consumed. China is the world's leading producer, using all it grows. The United States, India, the Soviet Union, and Brazil rank second through fifth, with all but the Soviet Union being major exporters. Other major Third World exporters include Zimbabwe and Malawi.[7]

Change in tobacco use can be measured in two ways: changes in the use of tobacco products, in absolute or per capita terms, and changes in smoking prevalence. Measuring the latter is often preferred by health educators as a sign of progress toward their primary goal, which is to get smokers to quit and nonsmokers not to start. Prevalence also provides an index of a key goal of tobacco control policy—to make smoking socially unacceptable.

Table 8-1. Cigarette Use in Selected Countries, 1984

Country	Cigarette Use Per Capita	Change in Total Consumption Since 1975[1]
	(percent of world average)	(percent)
Greece	237	+ 25
Japan	232	+ 6
United States	227	0
Poland	216	+ 3
Australia	203	+ 9
South Korea	186	+ 45
East Germany	167	+ 23
Italy	162	+ 17
United Kingdom	152	− 27
Soviet Union	150	+ 8
France	145	+ 6
Philippines	130	+ 24
Finland	128	+ 8
Sweden	124	− 3
Egypt	119	+138
Brazil	104	+ 17
China	102	+ 85
Mexico	77	+ 10
India	56	+ 33
Kenya	37	+ 48
Zimbabwe	35	− 35
Bangladesh	19	+ 29

[1]End points are three-year averages.
SOURCE: Worldwatch Institute, derived from U.S. Department of Agriculture data, from United Nations, *World Population and Its Age-Sex Composition by Country* (New York: 1980), and from Population Reference Bureau, *1984 World Population Data Sheet* (Washington, D.C.: 1984).

But the absolute quantity of tobacco used provides an essential measure of total health costs that a society must bear. Indeed, the total number of cigarettes smoked over a lifetime is a more important health index than cigarettes used per day at any given time. Health risks increase in proportion to total amount of tobacco used.[8] Moreover, the quantity of cigarettes smoked, when considered along with smoker-non-smoker interaction and room ventilation rates, provides a measure of passive smoking.

In 63 countries, total cigarette use increased between 1975 and 1985. Half the global increase in tobacco use in the last decade has occurred in China, though the Chinese represent only one fifth of the world's people. The rest of the Third World, 54 percent of all humans, accounted for a little less than a third of the increase. Consumption in the West and in Eastern bloc nations increased in rough proportion to their shares of the world population.[9]

In the second measure of change in use—smoking prevalence—Western nations have seen encouraging reductions during the last decade. In the United Kingdom, the percentage of males who smoke dropped by more than 25 percent. In the Netherlands and the United States, the equivalent reductions were more than a third. And in Norway, a nation often cited as having a model tobacco policy because it completely bans advertising, a one-fifth reduction in smoking among men with some higher education has been reported, though 42 percent of men still smoke.[10] (See Table 8–2.)

In fact, rates of smoking remain quite high among men all around the world. In Bangladesh, two thirds of men smoke, spending on average 5 percent of their household income on tobacco. In Czechoslovakia, the prevalence figure is 57 percent; in south-central European Russia, two thirds of adult males smoke. Smoking among women, on the other hand, remains very low in many countries, including China, Bangladesh, and most of the Third World. Teenage girls in the United States, however, now smoke more than boys do.[11]

One ironic result of campaigns to re-

Table 8-2. Prevalence of Smoking Among Men and Women in Selected Countries, Circa 1980

Country	Men	Women	All Adults
		(percent)	
Poland	70	30	50
Brazil	63	33	48
Ireland	54	36	45
Canada	44	36	40
Japan	66	14	40
Bangladesh	67	1	37
Netherlands	41	33	37
France	49	25	37
Australia	40	31	36
Norway	42	30	36
United Kingdom	38	33	36
Italy	54	17	35
East Germany	53	17	33
Soviet Union	65	11	33
United States	35	30	32
China	56	1	29
Sweden	31	26	28
India	46	<1	24
Greece	41	2	21
Egypt	40	1	21

SOURCE: Worldwatch Institute, based on studies of prevalence in each country as reported in various medical journals and governmental publications.

duce smoking in the absence of a more general effort to control tobacco has been the marked increase in the use of "smokeless" tobacco. The use of "chew" or "snuff" in the United States has increased by over 40 percent in the last two decades. Much of the new interest in these forms of tobacco comes from teenage boys who like the stimulus of the nicotine, perhaps feel "grown-up" when they try it, and believe that it is safer than smoking. Surveys in some localities show that 20–40 percent of high school boys chew tobacco or use snuff. Unfortunately, these forms of tobacco are strongly linked to oral cancer, an effect

seen in India, where chewing—and oral cancer—is common.[12]

Smoking prevalence among young people is changing, sometimes for the better, other times not. Although American, British, Norwegian, and Swedish children appear to be starting this habit later in life as well as being less likely to smoke, this is not the case elsewhere. More young people than adults smoke in Eastern bloc countries, Canada, and Egypt. In some schools surveyed in Santiago, Chile, two thirds of the students smoked. Even in developing societies—among Polynesians, for example—smoking rates reach levels exceeding 50 percent in children. Ironically, in the United Kingdom, a quarter of the children surveyed in one study reported being given their first cigarette by their parents, or at least smoking it in their presence, before age 12.[13]

Measuring smoking by educational level also reveals trends with important implications for policymaking. There is an inverse relationship between educational level and smoking in the United

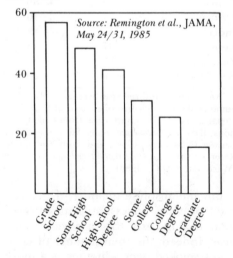

Figure 8-2. Smoking Among U.S. Males, by Education Level, 1982

States (see Figure 8–2), the Soviet Union, and elsewhere. Over 60 percent of U.S. adult males with only a primary education smoke, while less than 20 percent of men with an advanced degree are smokers. This relationship appears to hold in most of Western and Eastern Europe. It is true for women as well, at least in the United States, with the exception that women who have only a grade-school education seldom smoke.[14] In these countries, at least, smoking thus no longer symbolizes fashion, status, and upward mobility, but the opposite.

The Direct Cost of Addiction

No avoidable condition claims more adult lives than tobacco addiction. Between 2 million and 2.5 million smokers die worldwide each year from heart disease, lung cancer, and emphysema—smokers' disease, as it is called—caused by their addiction. Additional thousands die as a result of fires caused by cigarettes and from cancers caused by tobacco consumed as snuff or chew. Almost one fifth of all U.S. deaths can be traced to cigarette smoke.[15] (See Table 8–3.)

No avoidable condition claims more adult lives than tobacco addiction.

Spanish settlers discovered 450 years ago that tobacco was "impossible to give up," even when they were reproached for "a disgusting habit." Despite common knowledge that smokers have "nic-

Table 8-3. United States: Mortality Due to Tobacco and Selected Other Causes, 1984

Cause of Death	Annual Deaths	Share of Total Deaths
	(number)	(percent)
Tobacco Use	375,000	18.8
Alcohol Use	100,000	4.7
Automobile Accidents	50,000	2.3
Use of Hard Drugs	30,000	1.4
Suicide	27,500	1.3
Homicide	19,000	.9

SOURCES: Worldwatch Institute, based on National Center for Health Statistics, *Health, United States, 1984* (Washington, D.C.: U.S. Government Printing Office, 1984), and on R.T. Ravenholt, "Addiction Mortality in the United States, 1980: Tobacco, Alcohol, and Other Substances," *Population and Development Review*, December 1984.

otine fits," scientific understanding of the addictive power of tobacco has progressed slowly. Much more remains to be known, but it seems certain that nicotine is the addictive agent in tobacco, although oral stimulation and the physical manipulation of smoking materials are also habituating to some degree.[16]

The addictiveness of tobacco, in any case, is beyond question. British scientists A.C. McKennell and R.K. Thomas found in 1967 that only 15 percent of teenagers who experimented with tobacco were later able to quit. Others, notably W.A. Hunt and J.D. Matarazzo, have found that 75 percent who do quit smoking start again within six months. Quitters very often "crave" tobacco, probably nicotine, even several years after quitting. There is a withdrawal period of about two weeks, however, during which unpleasant physical symptoms arise as a result, it seems, of the brain's chemical dependence on nicotine.[17]

Withdrawal from tobacco differs from that of heroin only quantitatively, and it is satisfaction of the addiction itself that leads some smokers to believe that tobacco makes them more alert and clearer thinkers. It is more immediately rewarding than caffeine, for example, which takes almost 30 minutes to reach the brain when ingested as coffee. A "hit" of tobacco reaches the brain in 30 seconds.[18]

Cigarette smoke contains, in addition to addictive nicotine, hundreds of mutagens, carcinogens, and cocarcinogens, some 4,000 other chemical compounds, and simple carbon monoxide. These chemicals, including radioactive polonium, not only attack the lungs but reach the bloodstream—where they circulate, causing or accelerating atherosclerosis (clogging of the arteries) and cancer in internal organs.

Heavy smoking can precipitate heart attacks when inhaled carbon monoxide displaces oxygen in the blood. Concentrations of up to 10 percent carbon monoxide in blood hemoglobin can, when coupled with reduced blood flow in heart arteries as a result of atherosclerosis, starve heart muscle of oxygen and damage or destroy the heart muscle —that is, cause a heart attack. The risk is serious at any age, but it is so clearly responsible for most heart attacks in young men that some scientists have called it a disease of smokers. The risk of heart attack among young men who smoke more than two packs per day is over seven times higher than for nonsmokers. (See Figure 8–3.) Fortunately, the risk diminishes rapidly in ex-smokers, approaching that of nonsmokers within one year after they quit.[19]

Fifteen to 30 percent of all heart attacks in the United States and perhaps a third in the United Kingdom are caused by smoking. Smoking is also the leading cause of death from cardiovascular disease for those middle-aged or younger in West Germany, Scandinavian coun-

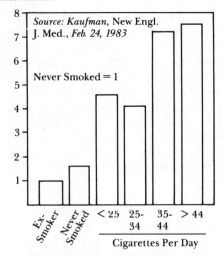

Relative-Risk Estimate of a Heart Attack

Source: Kaufman, New Engl. J. Med., Feb. 24, 1983

Never Smoked = 1

Cigarettes Per Day

Figure 8-3. Additional Risk of Heart Attack Due to Smoking, U.S. Males Aged 30-44

tries, and Australia. An estimate of such deaths worldwide due to smoking cannot be reliably made, however, because of the complicating factors of diet and life-style.[20] This constraint may lead to an underestimate of overall mortality due to tobacco use.

A related cardiovascular disease caused by smoking is arteriosclerosis of the peripheral arteries. As in heart attack and stroke, smoking accelerates or precipitates blockage of arteries. Blockages in the limbs reduce blood supply to muscles and can cause gangrene, sometimes necessitating amputation of victims' legs. Peripheral vascular disease is also an important cause of death due to blood clots moving to the heart.[21]

Smoking carries special risks for young women. One study of women under age 50 found the risk of heart attack to be 10 times greater in women who smoked two packs per day. The authors attributed two thirds of the heart attacks in the group to smoking. A Canadian study found that females who smoked heavily were 7 to 34 times more likely to have a heart attack. Significantly, it also found that women who both smoked heavily and took birth control pills were 8 to 39 times more likely than nonsmokers to have heart attacks. The authors concluded that women under 35 could safely take the pill without additional risk of heart attack, but only if they did not smoke. A review of the epidemiology of heart attacks in women found that female heart attack victims die on average 19 years earlier than other women.[22] Unfortunately, young women are the group in industrial nations whose rate of smoking is increasing fastest.

Some observers have suggested that because carbon monoxide seems to play a role both in the development of atherosclerosis and in the precipitation of heart attacks, safer cigarettes can be developed by reducing their carbon monoxide production. Studies have demonstrated, however, that most cigarettes deliver similar levels of carbon monoxide, even when advertised (as required in a few European countries) as lower in carbon monoxide. Worse still, low tar and nicotine cigarettes may cause many people to smoke more cigarettes to satisfy their addiction, leading to even greater carbon monoxide inhalation.[23]

Lung cancer is predominantly a disease of smoking. Active smoking habits account for an estimated 85 percent of lung cancer. The claims of the tobacco industry that some types of people are predisposed to lung cancer and that some unknown mechanism unrelated to smoking habits causes this condition are unlikely to prove true, because different rates of smoking in men and women over different periods of time produce different rates of lung cancer. When women in the United States did not smoke, for example, they rarely developed lung cancer. But as they took up the habit, lung cancer increased in proportion, after the lag of 20 years that it takes for cancer to develop following exposure to mutagens. In fact, in 1981 lung cancer was as prevalent as breast cancer in American women over age 55 for the first time.[24]

International comparisons of lung cancer rates and earlier smoking habits show a strong correlation.[25] (See Figure 8–4.) Nonindustrial societies with high smoking rates have high lung cancer rates; Polynesians and New Zealanders have little industry, smoke heavily, and have high rates of lung cancer. Trends such as these across varied sections of the world population also tend to implicate smoking over industrial air pollutants as the cause of lung cancer. Smoking may even explain much of the lung cancer in nonsmokers. It should be noted, however, that lung cancer is a function of lifetime smoking habits, not just the use of cigarettes at one given point in time.[26]

Cancer of the bladder, pancreas, lip, mouth, esophagus, and pharynx can also be traced to the use of tobacco, though alcohol plays a strong role in the last two types. The use of tobacco may be linked with cervical cancer and stomach cancer as well, although these connections are less clear.[27]

Smoking causes two other serious lung diseases—bronchitis and emphysema, referred to together as Chronic Obstructive Lung Disease. Bronchitis is a condition of secretions in the large air passages of the lung system that reduces the lungs' ability to expel germs and can lead to infection. In emphysema, the air sacs in the lungs coalesce and become less efficient in absorbing oxygen and releasing carbon dioxide. Smoking kills 52,000 Americans each year through Chronic Obstructive Lung Disease.[28]

The link between tobacco and other

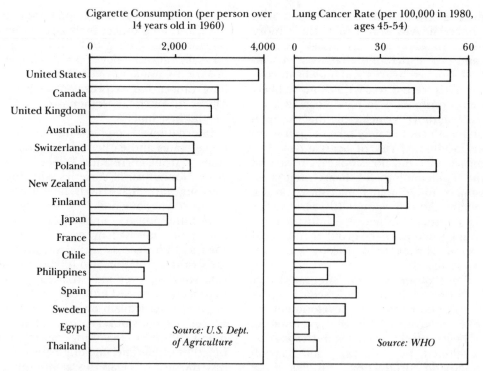

Figure 8-4. International Correlation Between Cigarette Consumption and Lung Cancer Deaths After 20 Years of Smoking

causes of death must not be overlooked. Fires caused by cigarettes kill between 2,000 and 4,000 Americans each year. And passive smoking may cause 5,000 lung cancer deaths each year in the United States alone.[29] Altogether, smoking causes 10–20 percent of deaths in Europe and the United States. (See Table 8–4.)

Several nations have attempted to estimate the direct economic cost of smoking. A major item, naturally, is health care. In the United States, smoking's toll amounts to $12–35 billion per year—3–9 percent of all health care costs. Smoking claims a similar proportion of the total health care expenditures in Australia, Canada, Switzerland, and the United Kingdom.[30]

But the cost of smoking extends be-

yond health care expenditures. Lost income due to death and lost work due to illness cost the United States $27–61 billion a year. Thus, health expenditures plus economic losses in that country range from $38–95 billion, or $1.25–3.15 per pack.[31] These totals do not include the cost of tobacco itself—about $30 billion per year. Nor do they include the suffering borne by victims and their families.

The economic costs of smoking have generated considerable attention and controversy. Policymakers concerned with budget deficits sometimes view the billions of dollars spent on publicly funded health care for dying smokers as an unnecessary expense. Some economists argue that these are merely financial costs that would be incurred anyway

Table 8-4. Tobacco's Toll in Lives, Selected Countries, Circa 1982

Country	Annual Deaths	Share of Total Deaths
	(number)	(percent)
West Germany	140,000	21
United States	375,000	19
United Kingdom	100,000	18
Canada	30,000	17
Italy	97,600	17
New Zealand	4,000	15
France	77,000	14
Australia	11,000	10
Denmark	5,000	9
Sweden	3,200	4

SOURCE: Derived by Worldwatch Institute from various medical journal and governmental reports.

if smokers lived longer, became infirm, and needed medical care. This may be true financially, but from a benefit/cost point of view, smoking imposes unnecessary costs.

If smokers did not smoke, they would live longer and probably enjoy a better quality of life. These are the benefits of policies that reduce and prevent smoking. The improvements in health are benefits in their own right, even if they do not lead to reduced health care costs. Some economists also argue that the jobs and incomes created by the tobacco business must be counted as benefits. Even if other uses of land were not available, tobacco's economic costs alone would exceed its "benefits" by more than two to one.[32]

These costs, moreover, do not include the environmental and agricultural costs of tobacco production. Tobacco curing consumes 1–2 percent of all wood burned each year in Kenya and Tanzania, and one third of all wood harvested in Malawi, where harvesting far exceeds sustainable yields. Many agricultural countries, including Brazil, China, India, Pakistan, and Zimbabwe, dedicate the equivalent of between 0.5 percent and 7 percent of cropland to tobacco, with the United States and China using slightly less than 1 percent in this way. Though these percentages are small relative to global resources of land and firewood, in some countries they become significant. If planted in grain, the land would be sufficient to feed 10–20 million people—assuming, of course, that production and marketing conditions could be created to encourage food production on tobacco land.[33]

Tragically, the cost in lives and money can only be expected to grow. Seventy-three percent more tobacco is consumed now than 20 years ago, so without a sudden drop in smoking, lung cancer deaths, for example, will almost certainly increase by 50 percent by the turn of the century. Many such losses will occur in nations totally unprepared to deal with the new epidemic. But even in the West, where billions of dollars are spent in a fight to control lung cancer, fewer than 10 percent of such patients are cured of their disease. The prospects of surviving for even one year are dismal. Fortunately, the relative risk of lung cancer for ex-smokers, compared with people who never smoked, diminishes to below detectable levels 10–30 years after a smoker quits. Thus, if tobacco use could be halted, this projection would not materialize.[34]

Without a sudden drop in smoking, lung cancer deaths will almost certainly increase by 50 percent by the turn of the century.

It follows, too, that the incidence of bronchitis and emphysema will grow as tobacco use grows. At the current rate, the next 20 years would also witness an increase of 50 percent in these diseases. Heart disease is far more complicated to predict, for it is tied to hypertension, diet, and other factors.

Assuming current trends, the already devastating cost of tobacco is certain to increase over the next few decades. Ironically, it may take the growing realization of this habit's high costs for passive smokers to actually bring about effective action. For no matter how convincing the direct costs may be to rational thinkers, smokers—being addicted—may not be able to act rationally to solve the problem of smoking.

VICTIMS OF OTHERS' SMOKE

Sidestream smoke—which wafts from a smoker's cigarette to an involuntary smoker—puts into the surrounding air 50 times the amount of carcinogens inhaled by the user. It contains several thousand other compounds, many of which cause irritation and allergic reactions in the eyes and nose. Cigarette contamination of indoor air has been linked to increased risk of lung cancer in nonsmoking spouses and to respiratory disease in infants. The scale of these effects has only recently attracted attention, and much more work is urgently needed to define their total impact.[35]

Passive smoking has been correlated with lung cancer in nonsmoking spouses of smokers in more than 10 studies. One particularly important study was derived from other research designed to track lung cancer in smokers in Japan. This work lent itself to a consideration of passive smoking because careful records were kept of spousal smoking habits. Wives who did not smoke but who lived with heavy smokers were found to be al-most twice as likely to die of lung cancer as wives of men who did not smoke.[36] (See Figure 8–5.)

A parallel study in Greece yielded similar results. Lung cancer occurred over twice as often as expected among nonsmoking wives of Greek smokers. Several U.S. studies have now also shown such increased risk of lung cancer for nonsmokers whose spouses smoke. And in West Germany, a report on passive smoking risks showed that nonsmoking women with lung cancer were three times more likely than average to have husbands who smoke. Moreover, a careful examination of their workplaces showed they had not been exposed to carcinogens on the job.[37]

Ambient tobacco smoke clearly carries a risk of cancer in nonsmokers. One recent effort to quantify this risk estimated that passive smoking in the United States

Lung Cancer Deaths
Per 100,000 Population

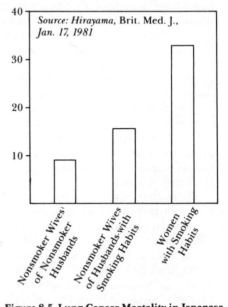

Figure 8-5. Lung Cancer Mortality in Japanese Women Whose Husbands Smoked

causes more cancer deaths than all regulated industrial air pollutants combined. The cost in lives may be as high as 5,000 nonsmokers per year, or one third the cases of lung cancer not already directly attributable to smoking.[38]

Passive smoking in the United States causes more cancer deaths than all regulated industrial air pollutants combined.

Nonsmokers are quite likely to have no choice about breathing tobacco smoke. In the United States, people typically spend 90 percent of their time indoors. On the job, some 63 percent of U.S. workers are exposed to tobacco smoke, while at home over 60 percent of all households have at least one smoker. Altogether, only 14 percent of Americans escape being exposed to tobacco smoke in the home or at the workplace. The rest involuntarily "smoke" on average the equivalent of almost 1 cigarette per day. Some people—a musician, for example, who plays in smoky bars and lives with a chain-smoker—passively smoke the equivalent of 14 cigarettes a day.[39]

Protecting the public from the carcinogens in passive cigarette smoke requires urgent action. Increasing the ventilation in a building appears to be impractical because it is prohibitively expensive. Reducing the risk of cancer due to cigarette smoke would require replacing the volume of air in the living space about 250 times more often than is currently the norm—and use, therefore, 250 times the heating, cooling, and pumping.[40] The only certain way to make indoor air safe from cigarettes is to eliminate the source.

EFFECTS ON CHILDREN

Tobacco's effects on children—beginning with exposure before they are born—deserve special attention. Passive smoking places unborn children at serious risk. Nicotine, numerous toxic chemicals, and radioactive polonium may all interfere with fetal development, and the fetus can receive these substances through the mother's blood whether she smokes or chews tobacco. Furthermore, studies in both industrial and developing countries show that smoking by pregnant women reduces infants' weight at birth by roughly one tenth.[41]

In one U.S. survey, smokers gave birth to underweight babies twice as often as other women did. Research has found a strong, inverse relationship between birth weight and levels of cigarette residue (thiocyanate) in infants' umbilical cords. Low birth weight has also been associated with tobacco chewing in India. (Thirty-nine percent of women in India chew tobacco.) Because birth weight is a key factor in infant mortality, tobacco use seriously endangers infants' lives.[42]

Nicotine also may be the culprit in spontaneous abortions among women who smoke. Epidemiologist R.T. Ravenholt estimates that smoking causes 50,000 miscarriages in the United States each year. This connection has been observed in Italy as well, where women who smoke miscarry in the first month of pregnancy at a rate of 2.4 percent, compared with 0.9 percent for nonsmokers. Smoking can also cause premature delivery. Nineteen percent of the firstborn infants of Italian women who smoke were premature, twice the rate for nonsmokers. The rate of premature delivery in the Italian study declined by almost 25 percent for the secondborn children of nonsmokers, but it increased slightly for smokers.[43]

Unfortunately, women in many countries are smoking in record numbers, even while pregnant. Surveys in the United Kingdom suggest that about 40 percent of pregnant women smoke. A compilation by Ravenholt of surveys showed that in nations as disparate as Sweden and Chile, over a quarter of pregnant women smoked. (See Table

Table 8-5. Smoking During Pregnancy, Selected Countries, Circa 1980

Country	Share of Pregnant Women Who Smoke	Infants Exposed
	(percent)	(number)
Ireland	36	26,000
Sweden	34	33,800
West Germany	32	211,700
Canada	26	104,400
Chile	25	31,600
Belgium	25	31,600
Venezuela	24	125,200
Brazil	20	715,800
Yugoslavia	20	73,900
United States	19	706,800
Colombia	19	150,600
Austria	18	15,700
Hungary	13	21,500
Mexico	9	227,300
Japan	8	130,800
Philippines	6	91,600
Bangladesh	3	135,400
Egypt	1	17,700
India[1]	1	96,900

[1]The percentage of women in India who chew tobacco may be high, however.
SOURCES: R.T. Ravenholt, "Addiction Mortality in the United States, 1980: Tobacco, Alcohol, and Other Substances," *Population and Development Review*, December 1984, and World Bank, *World Development Report, 1982* (New York: Oxford University Press, 1982).

8–5.) Each year, at least 3 million newborn—the estimated number of live births to women who smoke—are thus potentially handicapped by their mothers.[44]

Children with parents who smoke experience much higher rates of respiratory illness, including colds, influenza, bronchitis, asthma, and pneumonia. One British study published almost 10 years ago showed that children under age one whose mothers smoke more than one pack a day are twice as likely to get bronchitis and pneumonia. This finding has since been repeatedly corroborated.[45]

In addition, the evidence indicates that parental smoking retards child development. One study found that lung capacity in boys was reduced by 7 percent by their mothers' smoking. If the teenage boys also smoked, their lung capacity was reduced by 25 percent. The effect of passive smoking in children can last a lifetime because it delays physical and intellectual development, and because the longer people are exposed to carcinogens, the more likely they are to develop lung cancer.[46]

Parents who smoke may also reduce the intellectual development of their children. One study in Italy found that children whose mothers smoked learned to read more slowly than children of nonsmokers. In the United States, the learning ability of 11-year-olds whose mothers smoke has been shown to lag by six months.[47]

ANTISMOKING EFFORTS TO DATE

When a recent medical journal editorial writer rhetorically asked "What if smoking killed baby seals?" he was making the point that environmental and health activists do not accord tobacco the priority it deserves. He suggested that "perhaps the entire antismoking campaign be turned over to Greenpeace."[48] Health and environmental organizations have not moved to protect their constituents' well-being with the same vigor that the tobacco industry protects its pecuniary interests.

Nor have governments assumed their traditional role in protecting public health by acting decisively to reduce tobacco's threat. They move swiftly to remove from the market unsafe medicines. They conduct paramilitary operations to destroy fields of marijuana or opium, but not tobacco, a far deadlier crop. They pay for expensive cleanup operations to remove toxic chemicals from the human environment. But not only do they fail to take these actions for tobacco, which is often more deadly to both users and innocent—or passive—victims, they even support efforts to stabilize the tobacco industry. This sad state of affairs is possible both because the tobacco industry itself is so strong and because the opposition to tobacco is so weak. Health advocates in general have not insisted that governments take appropriate action. They have relied instead on informational programs alone to solve the problem.

Equating smokers with baby seals—as victims rather than willing participants—helps clarify some confusion that contributes to inaction on tobacco. Many people assume it is enough to warn tobacco users, through the media and with labels on tobacco products, of the risks they take and then leave to them the responsibility for their own health. They argue that if users choose to take tobacco's risk, in return for the pleasure or stimulation that it provides, that is their prerogative.[49] To some extent this is true. But the independence and voluntary nature of this choice can be called into question on three counts.

First, tobacco is strongly addictive. Studies have shown that only about one quarter of the people who try more than one cigarette ever succeed in quitting. Young people begin to smoke because of social pressure, curiosity, or a desire to feel "grown-up." But pharmacologically, tobacco acts like heroin in hooking its victims. They rapidly become dependent on nicotine, and then smoke to satisfy their addiction.

Second, smoke harms more than just the smoker. As indicated earlier, children of smokers get sick with respiratory illness twice as often as those of nonsmokers. Their growth and intellectual development as well as lung capacity can be stunted. Exposed for decades to others' smoke, their risk of lung cancer is at least tripled. Similarly, spouses and coworkers of smokers are at higher risk of lung cancer because of smokers' addictions.

Third, when governments act inconsistently in their management of tobacco with respect to other dangerous products that they ban, they confuse tobacco users. Asbestos, heroin, and DDT are banned to protect public health; tobacco is not. This implicitly signals that those responsible for health consider tobacco to be different, and as normal to use. Thus, teenagers can be forgiven for not taking seriously a tiny health warning on shiny new packs of cigarettes. The problem is, of course, made worse when governments actively encourage the production of tobacco.

The point at which society decides to take action on dangerous products is sometimes arbitrary, but it can be based consistently on estimates of risk. It is the overall risk carried by addictive products rather than their capacity to cause addiction per se that—along with economic interest, attitudes, and chance—decides society's treatment of them. Coffee, for example, is addictive but the evidence that it causes cancer or heart disease is mixed. Some studies have estimated that coffee can double the risk of pancreatic cancer; others have found no increased risk at all.

Alcohol is addictive and carries heavy costs for society, though these are at most half as costly as tobacco. Having one drink a day can be tolerated without instilling dependency in most people, so society permits its use. Alcohol, at least, does not quickly addict the majority of those who experiment with it, as do heroin and tobacco. Similarly, nonaddictive products that are carcinogens may be sufficiently low in overall risk to be permitted. Some artificial sweeteners, for example, fall above the level of acceptable risk, while others do not. They may both be carcinogenic, however.[50]

Absolute cigarette consumption has fallen over the last 10 years in only a dozen countries.

Most U.S. federal regulatory agencies draw this arbitrary line at a level of risk of 1 death in 100,000 or, alternatively, 1 in 1 million people over a lifetime of exposure. The risks from passive smoking probably exceed this by a factor of 250. Active smoking, of course, exceeds the lower level by 100,000 because it causes cancer in 1 in 10—some would say 1 in 5—users. Thus, forbidding the sale of tobacco would be consistent with the prohibition of the sale of addictive drugs that harm the user and others. Banning tobacco would also be consistent with the control of strong carcinogens with very high risk factors.

Some people argue that individuals should be able to do whatever they want in the privacy of their own homes. This is an acceptable, even admirable attitude that favors civil liberties. But the limit to one person's pursuit of happiness begins at the point where it clearly harms oth-

ers. If smokers are to be permitted to harm themselves but forbidden to harm their children, spouses, and coworkers, they will have to smoke in their backyards. Because control of tobacco use in private homes is both politically and practically infeasible, the only realistic way to protect children—if parents fail to do so—is to control the product itself.

Societies urgently need to examine how to better control tobacco use, for the current strategy of informational campaigns is not working well. The basis of antitobacco action since the mid-sixties has been information aimed at educating smokers about their health risks and discouraging nonsmokers from starting. The campaign seeks through media coverage of scientific studies to persuade smokers to quit and children never to start. It tries to change society's attitude from a view of smoking as glamorous to one that sees the habit as socially unacceptable. This approach has been tested in a few countries such as Finland, Norway, Sweden, and, to lesser extents, the Netherlands, the United States, and the United Kingdom. It has been practiced de facto in many Eastern bloc countries and in China.[51] The results are decidedly mixed. (See Table 8–6.)

Absolute cigarette consumption has fallen over the last 10 years in only a dozen countries. Of these, only four had moderate to strong antismoking policies, while eight had weak ones. Reduction in countries with weak policies can be attributed to economic decline, specifically to higher costs of imported cigarettes and reduced per capita income.

A dozen countries have had strong antismoking measures—by today's standards—but have experienced strong growth in tobacco use. Tobacco advertising is prohibited in Poland and restrictions are placed on smoking in public, yet that nation ranks among the highest in per capita cigarette consumption in

Table 8-6. Cigarette Use and Antismoking Policies, Selected Countries, 1974–84

Country	Annual Change in Use of Cigarettes (percent)	Package Warning Label	Advertising Ban Total	Advertising Ban Partial	Bans in Public Places Strong	Bans in Public Places Weak
Argentina	+0.1					
Australia	+0.9	X		X		
Brazil	+1.6	X				
Bulgaria	−0.2	X	X		X[1]	
China	+6.2		X			X
Egypt	+8.7	X		X		X
Finland	+0.8	X	X		X	
France	+0.6	X		X	X	
Hungary	+0.4	X	X		X	
India	+2.9	X				
Italy	+1.6		X		X	
Japan	+0.6	X				X
Kenya	+3.9					X
Mexico	+1.0	X		X		
Netherlands	−3.3	X		X		
Norway	−1.6	X	X			
Poland	+0.3		X		X[1]	
Soviet Union	+0.8	X	X		X	
Spain	+1.6			X		
Sweden	−0.3	X		X		
United Kingdom	−3.1	X		X		
United States	0	X		X		X

[1]Includes restrictions on smoking in the workplace.

SOURCE: Worldwatch Institute, based on Ruth Roemer, *Legislative Action to Combat the World Smoking Epidemic* (Geneva: World Health Organization, 1983), on U.S. Department of Agriculture (USDA), Foreign Agricultural Service, "Tariff and Nontariff Measures on Tobacco," *Foreign Agricultural Circular,* Supplement 1–84, Washington, D.C., January 1984, and on USDA, Economic Research Service, *World Indices of Agricultural and Food Production, 1950–84* (unpublished printout) (Washington, D.C.: 1985).

the world. Advertising bans and other antismoking policies exist in China, East Germany, and the Soviet Union, but smoking nevertheless continues at very high levels, at least among men.

Finland, Norway, and Sweden, in contrast, have imposed advertising bans and required strong warnings on tobacco labels, and they have experienced better results. Norway's antismoking policy is exceeded in strength by only four other countries, and tobacco consumption has declined by 15 percent since the imposition of that policy. (This decline takes into account the large use of roll-your-own tobacco in that country.) Sweden's policy has been somewhat weaker than those of other Scandinavian countries, but consumption is down some 3 percent since 1974, about the time its policy was initiated.

Bulgaria, Hungary, and the Soviet

Union have the strongest policies in the world. Bulgarians now smoke 2 percent fewer cigarettes than 10 years ago, while the Soviets and the Hungarians use 8 and 4 percent more, respectively.

Countries with weaker policies but better results include Belgium, the Netherlands, and the United Kingdom. These governments permit advertising in print but forbid it on electronic media. They have negotiated voluntary warnings on tobacco products with the tobacco industry. Perhaps most importantly, they have conducted vigorous antismoking educational campaigns. Cigarette consumption has declined 20 percent or more over the last 10 years in these nations. The per capita consumption level in each is below the average for industrial countries, though well above the mean for the world. Only in the United Kingdom, however, is consumption lower than 20 years ago.

Some countries have had dramatic declines in cigarette consumption without even trying. Drops in consumption of 7 to 32 percent in Bolivia, Chile, and Zaire can be attributed to their economic difficulties: Their antismoking policies are among the weakest in the world.

Changes in income affect tobacco consumption, though the strength of the income effect depends on a country's stage of development. A statistical analysis of 29 industrial and developing countries suggested that, overall, cigarette consumption increases about 3 percent for every 10 percent rise in income.[52] This relation does not apparently hold for industrial countries, however. Consumption seems more related to price and social attractiveness in countries such as the United States, where price increases of 10 percent appear to reduce consumption by 3 to 4 percent. The largest decline ever in U.S. cigarette use occurred, in fact, in 1983, when the government imposed a tax of about 8 percent of the retail price.

This analysis also reveals that the strength of a nation's tobacco information policy does not appear to reduce consumption, if income and price are taken into account. The result suggests that the stronger the antitobacco policy, the greater the consumption and the higher the rate of increase in consumption. This "nonsense" result, of course, can be explained simply. Countries that have had a problem with cigarette consumption are more likely to have taken steps that they believe will reduce that problem. Unfortunately, the steps taken to date have been too weak to achieve the desired results. Lack of time to take effect could also be a factor, although most policies have been in place for almost a decade.

STRONGER MEDICINE

Health advocates have generally dismissed stronger medicine for dealing with smoking and tobacco. The U.K. Royal College of Physicians, for example, the first governmental body in the world to launch a campaign to save the health of smokers, has conceded that banning tobacco is impractical. The physicians compared such a move to prohibition, and expressed fear that it not only would be unenforceable, but would lead to criminality.[53] Yet, there are a few effective ways to strengthen tobacco control policies without an outright ban.

The policy questions are how to prevent the young and the naive from beginning to smoke, how to persuade smokers to quit, and how to protect the health of passive or involuntary smokers in the interim. When naive smokers first light up without understanding the life-threatening implications of their careless experimentation, they can become addicted and, in effect, "involuntary" smokers themselves. Psychology and medicine currently do not know much about how to help these addicts, other than to recommend that they quit cold turkey.[54]

This dilemma may be unique in medicine: A dangerous drug clearly should—but cannot—be banned. The economic strength of the tobacco industry is so great that it can exploit for its own purposes the safeguards built into democracies to protect legitimate minorities. In nondemocracies, governments may lack the credibility—and the motivation—to tackle so insidious and pernicious a habit. And under both systems the social conditioning and chemical habituation characteristic of tobacco make banning the product a formidable task, one that would take a long time. Yet the current "informational" campaign to control tobacco is falling behind as worldwide use increases faster than population.

An alternative approach is inherent in a new movement to protect passive smokers: banishing tobacco. This campaign, which stops short of an outright ban of tobacco sales, includes either the prohibition of smoking in the workplace and in public buildings or the strict limitation of smoking to specified areas. The movement may be the single greatest success of the informational campaign against tobacco. Its leaders insist that despite the continued sale, advertising, and use of tobacco, nonsmokers—the majority in most societies—have every right not to be exposed to the carcinogens, carbon monoxide, and irritants in tobacco smoke.[55] Such a campaign can make three important contributions.

First, by banishing tobacco use from places where innocent people will be exposed and placed at risk, thousands of lives may be saved. Second, forcing smokers to give up their habit while in the presence of nonsmokers will provide

them with an added impetus to quit. If smokers must get through working days without smoking, then they are more likely to be able to quit completely. This has been the result of bans in Minnesota and California.[56] In any case, their total dosage of carcinogens and carbon monoxide should decline. And third, by stigmatizing tobacco use as dangerous and antisocial, the passive smokers' rights movement can accomplish a goal of all antismoking informational campaigns: to make smoking socially unattractive.

By banishing tobacco use from places where innocent people will be exposed and placed at risk, thousands of lives may be saved.

The passive smokers' rights campaign focuses on the workplace, public gathering places, and public transportation. Many countries now prohibit smoking on public transportation and in theaters and auditoriums, though the impetus for these restrictions has usually been conventional safety concerns. In a few areas, such as the state of Minnesota and the cities of San Francisco and Los Angeles, smoking is now prohibited in public buildings (except in restricted areas) and nonsmokers must be protected in restaurants and on the job.[57]

Interestingly, nonsmokers have an important ally in the workplace: employers. Companies, at least in the United States, are rapidly realizing two things. First, most of their employees do not smoke and do not like to breathe the smoke of others. Second, smokers cost employers money. Surveys indicate that the combination of inefficiency and ill health as a result of smoking wastes about 7 percent of a smoker's working time. They also suggest that smokers cost employers at least $650 each per year.[58] Smokers add to insurance and cleanup costs, and they reduce nonsmoker employee morale.

American industry is responding rapidly to the nonsmoker movement. A number of well-known industries have prohibited smoking on the job for most employees. (See Table 8–7.) A few even refuse to hire smokers. The predominant trend, however, is toward banishing the practice from the workplace. In 1984, the rate of increase in adoption of policies against smoking for the publishing, insurance, finance, pharmaceuticals, and scientific equipment industries in

the United States was between 10 and 25 percent. That is, one tenth to one quarter of the top 1,000 businesses in this group of five industries implemented new policies that year to banish smoking.[59]

A particular difficulty in banishing tobacco is the role of government in promoting tobacco use. This schizophrenic state of affairs persists not just in the market-oriented West, but also in centralized economies. Governments most often own the tobacco industries in these areas. China, the Soviet Union, and India, for example, grow their own tobacco—they are not victims of some

Table 8-7. Selected U.S. Corporations with Policies Concerning Smoking in the Workplace, 1985

Policy/Companies	Employees	Date Implemented, If Known
	(number)	
Smoke-Free Areas, Including Work Stations		
CIGNA Insurance (Philadelphia, Pa.)	12,000	
Control Data Corp. (Minneapolis, Minn., and elsewhere)	28,000	January 1984
Grumman Corp.	27,000	November 1984
IBM	200,000	
Pacific Mutual Life Insurance Co. (Newport Beach, Calif.)	1,200	January 1984
Pratt & Whitney Aircraft, Government Products Div. (Palm Beach, Calif.)	7,000	
Smoke-Free Except for Cafeteria, Lounges, and Conference Rooms		
Adolph Coors Co. (Golden, Colo.)	10,000	December 1982
Blue Cross-Blue Shield (Minnesota)	1,600	May 1985
The Boeing Co. (Washington state)	83,000	April 1984
Campbells Soup Co. (Camden, N.J.)	3,300	1869
Merle Norman Cosmetic Co. (Los Angeles, Calif.)	1,300	
Raven Industries (Sioux Falls, S. Dak.)	900	May 1983
Unigard Insurance Group (Seattle, Wash.)	1,600	March 1982
Entirely Smoke-Free		
Johns-Manville (Denver, Colo.)	8,000	July 1978
Pacific Northwest Bell (Seattle, Wash.)	15,000	October 1985
Rodale Press (Emmaus, Pa.)	850	January 1982

SOURCE: Private communications with company representatives, based on list developed by New Jersey Group Against Smoking Pollution, Summit, N.J.

cabal of multinational companies. The state-owned tobacco industry in China is being carefully nurtured and expanded rapidly even as another part of the government is telling the Chinese that smoking is bad for them.[60]

These incompatible policies are also in place in the West. In the United States, the U.S. Department of Agriculture administers a price-support system to protect tobacco producers. West European nations subsidize tobacco farmers with about $660 million in price supports each year. Ironically, the systems protect small, inefficient farmers who earn higher prices than they would obtain without the subsidy. More-efficient producers, who could underprice the small farmers, are not allowed to compete fully. The result is that tobacco costs the user more than it would without the system. As tobacco use varies negatively in response to price increases, smoking is being directly reduced by price supports.[61]

There is an even more subtle effect, however. The tobacco industry, though it loses the right to compete with small-scale farmers for more of the profit of growing tobacco, gains the powerful political support of the small farmer. The added political clout helps counter antismoking forces. Moreover, it retains the appealing appearance of official tolerance and even endorsement of the use of tobacco, which in turn diminishes the effectiveness of the informational campaign in reducing the social acceptability of tobacco. Any child about to start smoking could be inclined to think that the U.S. government sees tobacco use as desirable. This is, of course, the implicit position of any government that promotes tobacco production. Failing to excise this "subsidy," however perverse for the industry, sends a signal both to the young and to other governments that tobacco is not so bad after all.

The overall situation of antismoking efforts, then, is at best a standoff in industrial countries and a rout in developing ones. At the current rate, Western countries will not see a major improvement in the health effects of smoking for many decades, but Eastern and developing countries will see a rapid worsening. It falls to world health leaders to bolster their antismoking efforts. Unfortunately, one lead agency, the World Health Organization, allots less than 1 percent of its budget to this problem, though it calls smoking "the most important preventable health problem in the world." Its current budget for the mid-eighties has no funds for actively reducing tobacco's toll.[62]

Effective policies fall in four categories. The first, continuation of the informational campaign, is worthwhile as a foundation for the others. Now that this exists, at least in some countries, it is time to build on it with more-stringent measures.

The second step is for those countries that have low smoking rates, no indigenous tobacco industry, and a reliance on imported tobacco products to ban tobacco altogether.[63] To do so would completely eliminate the epidemic's threat to them, placing these nations in the forefront of the campaign, much as the industrial world spearheaded the campaign to eradicate smallpox.

These governments have an economic incentive to act—the reduction of foreign-exchange losses for the purchase of a nonproductive product. Only a few people in these societies are now severely addicted, making national withdrawal politically easier. Many African nations fall into this cateqory. Unfortunately, other impoverished nations, such as India, do not, because cigarette consumption is already high.

The third approach is for those nations that must be politically pragmatic to at least act to protect the health of the innocent. Experience in the United

States and in Poland shows that tobacco can be banished from public buildings, from the workplace, and from public eating establishments and meeting places. Banishing cigarette use in the presence of nonsmokers should be considered a minimum level of protection.

All governments can provide national indoor clean air acts for public buildings, workplaces, and entertainment establishments. United Nations organizations could do well to establish no-smoking policies for their employees, especially those who work with children and the poor, for they are unavoidably going to be viewed as symbols of modernity and success, and therefore should not introduce such a clearly harmful product.

The fourth level is to use the power of economic tools to eliminate smoking as much as possible. Estimates of the cost of smoking amount to $1.25–3.15 per pack. A tax of this magnitude in the Western nations would reduce smoking by as much as 40 percent over time. Any tax increase, even of 5–10¢ per pack, would rapidly encourage light smokers to quit in order to avoid the higher cost, would provide additional pressure on the heavily addicted to bring themselves

to the point of enduring withdrawal, and, most importantly, would discourage the young (with low incomes) and poor from ever starting. Additionally, tobacco support systems can be dismantled in order to signal that governments now wish to discourage the use of tobacco. This move would be productive even where such a step would lower the price of cigarettes.

These measures will not be easy, nor will they solve the tobacco problem. They will not, for example, assure that children will be protected in the home against the smoke of their parents. They will not protect the newborn from harm as a result of their mothers' smoking. Parents alone can take this responsibility, though in some cases their addiction makes them risk the health and the intellectual development of their children.

New measures will not assure that smokers themselves will be persuaded to quit. Nor will they guarantee that innocent young people do not become addicted before they realize their new habit eventually kills one out of four users.[64] But without more responsible efforts on the part of the health professions and public interest organizations, even these efforts will be held in abeyance.

9

Investing in Children

William U. Chandler

Child health reflects—and determines—the human condition. It results from and contributes to social development. The growth of societies depends on the quality of its people, and population quality depends on health and education. Child health affects growth, learning, and work. Lowering child mortality reduces parents' economic need to have more children for the work and old-age support they contribute. And when mothers have fewer children, they are more productive in agriculture—the fundamental activity of developing societies and one for which women are often most responsible. When child populations are smaller, any agricultural or economic surplus can be concentrated on improving fewer minds and bodies.[1] When population and natural resources are more in balance, the environmental effects and economic costs of overpopulation, deforestation, desertification, soil erosion, and water and air pollution are reduced.

The notion that economic growth can improve child health and contain popu-

An expanded version of this chapter appeared as Worldwatch Paper 64, *Investing in Children*.

lation growth has been buried under the weight of recent experience. Throughout Africa and in desperate countries such as Bolivia and Bangladesh, food production and economic wealth are falling further behind population growth. Even with optimistically high economic growth rates of 6 percent, half the world would still earn less than $1,000 per capita annually in the year 2010. This realization prompts the search for other solutions to poverty and ill health—a search that begins with the causes of infant and child mortality.

More children die because they are improperly weaned than because of famine. More children die because their parents do not know how to manage diarrhea than because of epidemics. More children die because their mothers have no wells, hoes, or purchasing power than because of war. They die because their mothers are exhausted from excessive childbirth, work, and infection. And when children are stunted and retarded from disease and malnutrition, when overburdened parents cannot generate wealth for education and development, then burgeoning populations inadequately prepared for life add to the degradation of natural systems. These stresses perpetuate drought, disease, and famine.

Warding off death does not ensure a decent life. Primary education is essential for understanding better health and agricultural practices, but as the relatively literate countries of Tanzania and Bolivia have shown, education will not compensate for lack of incentives in agriculture. Agriculture is the basis of rural economies, but as India has shown, the Green Revolution will not compensate for infected bodies unable to make use of food. Clean water, as many failed projects have shown, will not compensate for a lack of understanding of hygiene.

A strategy of integrated development to meet "basic needs" all across the Third World demands not just techniques that prevent death, but also planning for food production, clean water, education, and, ultimately, health. It is a strategy that can incorporate measures to counter the drought through revegetation of desiccated lands. It is a strategy of investing in people, one that could truly revolutionize the prospects for child survival.[2]

Improvements made in child health over the last 20 years stand as an impressive achievement, even in Africa. The notion of a "child survival revolution" has taken root and is spreading. The developing world has cut infant deaths from 20 percent of live births in 1960 to 12 percent today, though averages mask drastic regional variations. (Infant mortality and child mortality are defined, respectively, as death between birth and age 1 and between age 1 and age 5, expressed in percent.) Most developing countries even accelerated their progress during the economically difficult decade of the seventies. The World Health Organization (WHO), however,

projects that the Third World will not reach WHO's infant mortality goal of 5 percent by the end of the century. Industrial countries, by contrast, have achieved rates between 0.7 percent and 2 percent.[3]

The notion of a "child survival revolution" has taken root and is spreading.

Analysts generally agree that about 17 million children die each year from the combined effects of poor nutrition, diarrhea, malaria, pneumonia, measles, whooping cough, and tetanus. Virtually all these deaths occur in the Third World, and half to two thirds could be prevented with relatively simple measures.[4] The cause of death may be ascribed to pneumonia, measles, or malaria, though the "initiating" cause may have been simple diarrhea. To save a child's life from measles may be to lose it to whooping cough. Nevertheless, regional studies and case histories do suggest that the combination of primary education and primary health care has led to rapid progress.

Africa, the continent of crisis, has made great strides toward improving child health. Its nations, however, still dominate the list of countries with the highest rates of infant and child mortality, and in recent years 1.5 million children have starved to death. Only two countries in the western hemisphere, Bolivia and Haiti, have very high infant mortality rates—10 percent—while four fifths of Africa exceeds this level. Africa also compares unfavorably with Asia. Only Afghanistan, Bangladesh, India, Kampuchea, and Pakistan rank as poorly.[5] (Twice as many people live in these five nations, however, as live in the high-infant-mortality African nations.)

China has reduced infant mortality to a rate close to that in some U.S. cities, despite income levels among the lowest in the world. It apparently has already achieved the WHO goal of 5 percent.[6] Malnutrition is an uncommon problem in China, and since the economic reforms that began in 1978, agricultural production has grown 6–8 percent per year, further ensuring nutritional sufficiency. China in the last 15 years achieved the most dramatic, and possibly the most important, reduction in fertility in history.

The situation of the world's children today brings to mind an age-old question—Is the glass half full or half empty? An optimist would answer that the child mortality rate has been halved. A pessimist would answer with statistics on famine. A realist would be buoyed by the statistical improvement in child health, but sobered by the fact that, thanks to explosive population growth, as many children suffer and die today as did 20 years ago. Our progress has only offset the growth of our problems.

BASIC PREVENTIVE HEALTH MEASURES

Malnutrition caused by poor child feeding practices claims over 10 times as many lives as actual famine. Coupled with diarrheal dehydration, malnutrition is the leading killer in the world, taking 5 million children each year—10 percent of all deaths. It is caused by a combination of factors that includes poor sanitation, infectious diseases such as measles, failure to breast-feed, and poor weaning practices, especially the failure to supplement breast milk adequately after five or six months of age.

The most effective strategy for countering diarrhea, malnutrition, and infections includes nutritional education, breast-feeding, oral rehydration (reversing diarrheal dehydration with simple sugar, salt, and water solutions), and immunization. (See Table 9–1.) Progress in this strategy, known as primary health care, can be determined by measuring progress in each of its components.

A major component of a strategy to fight malnutrition is female education, both in primary schools and through ma-

Table 9-1. Potential Reduction in Infant and Child Deaths with Proven Disease-Control Technologies

Disease	Estimated Deaths	Interventions	Effectiveness	Lives Potentially Saved
	(million)		(percent)	(million)
Diarrhea	5	Oral Rehydration	50–75	3
Immunizable Diseases	5	Vaccines	80–95	4
Pneumonia/Lower Respiratory Infection	4	Penicillin	50	2
Low Birth Weight, Malnutrition	3	Maternal Supplements; Treat Infections; Contraception	30	1
Total	17			10

SOURCE: J.E. Rohde, "Why the Other Half Dies," *Assignment Children* (UNICEF/Geneva), No. 61–62, 1983.

ternal education. Progress in this area has perhaps contributed most to improving the health of the world's children. Female education is essential in hygiene, oral rehydration, immunization, breast-feeding, family planning—in short, child health. The strongest relationship observed globally in reducing infant mortality is female literacy. (See Figure 9–1.)

Countries that have attained both lower fertility and lower mortality rates also have high female literacy rates. Fortunately, the Third World has made sig-

nificant progress in female literacy. In 1960, 26 percent of the world's girls did not attend primary school; by 1982, this figure was reduced to 17 percent. The children not in school continue to be found almost exclusively in countries with the highest child mortality rates.[7]

Malnourished children often have well-nourished mothers, who mainly lack good information about the best foods for their children. Dr. Jean Paul Beau demonstrated this in his rehydration and feeding clinic in the slum of Guediawaye, Senegal. He put his fingers

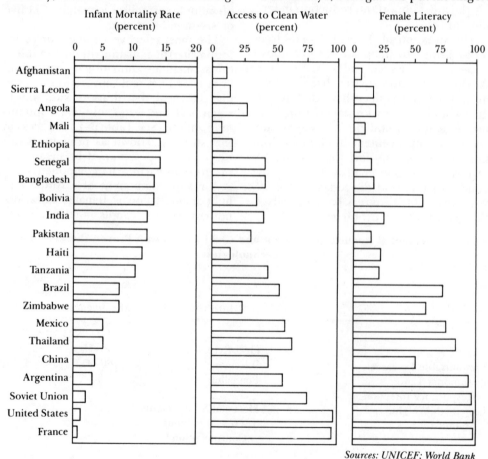

Sources: UNICEF; World Bank

Figure 9-1. Infant Mortality, Female Literacy, and Access to Drinking Water in Selected Countries, Circa 1980

around the skinny legs of a two-year-old so starved he could not walk, or even smile. Then, reaching to the child's mother nearby, he pinched the excess fat on her arm, indicating that she is not only well nourished, but overnourished. The mother appeared sad and explained, "We never learned how to feed a child." Beau suggests not that the mothers are deliberately depriving their children of food for themselves, but that poor weaning practices and infection cause the malnourishment.[8]

Diarrhea, especially repeated infections, reduces appetite and is commonly and mistakenly treated by withholding food. The illness also reduces the body's ability to make use of food. Diarrheal infections cause the body to secrete fluids rapidly, and the combined effects of energy deprivation and dehydration are deadly.

Poor nutrition and infection in Latin America and some parts of Asia increasingly begin with the failure to breast-feed. Bottled milk denies children not only the best nutritional formula, but also antibodies that fight infection. Human milk contains many agents that fight bacteria and viruses. Breast milk has 3,000 times as much lysozyme—an enzyme that destroys *Escherichia coli* bacteria and some *Salmonella*—as cow's milk does. In both urban and rural health centers in the northern Santiago area of Chile, surveys found that half of all infants were fed breast-milk substitutes by the age of two months.[9] Similar rates have been noted in Honduras and Venezuela.

Often children receive unnourishing food—in ignorance—even when adequate supplies are available. Breast milk, for example, should be supplemented with solid foods after 5–7 months. But African women often breast-feed exclusively for 18 months or longer. Late weaning with poor food is the leading child health problem in Africa. When weaned, many children are given adult foods they cannot chew or digest, or that are unnourishing.[10]

WHO and the United Nations Children's Fund (UNICEF) have launched major campaigns to combat the decline of breast-feeding. Beginning with simple education programs through posters and radio broadcasts, efforts now include day-care centers for mothers who work on plantations and in factories. Day care permits mothers to keep a child close enough to be breast-fed, but inflexible work schedules and high costs often undermine such efforts.

Educational campaigns are also under way to improve weaning practices in Africa. A poster produced by UNICEF's Ivory Coast office encourages, "After five months, more than the breast." It urges breast-feeding supplementation with "one food for strength (meat), one for development (fruit), and one for energy (millet/rice)."[11] Some projects now teach mothers to make a dry, sanitary mixture of nourishing food to leave for the child when they must be away.

India's child health problems resemble Africa's. A WHO survey found that over 90 percent of Indian mothers breast-feed their children up to one year, and that 85 percent still do so after 18 months. Solid food supplements often begin too late, only after 12 to 18 months. Again, weaning practices are the main problem.[12]

Dehydration, a common factor in diarrheal malnutrition, is beginning to yield to the elegance of oral rehydration therapy (ORT). ORT consists of a simple sugar and salt solution to correct the ionic imbalance in the small intestine that results from diarrheal infection. The technique averts death in 90 percent of diarrheal dehydration cases. In

countries where ORT has been promoted, hospital admission rates and
mortality from this condition have been
cut in half. Only about 10 percent of the
children who are at serious risk of diarrheal dehydration ever receive ORT,
however. As UNICEF points out, even
this low rate already saves a half-million
young lives each year.[13] ORT is in such
demand in the camps of Ethiopia that
UNICEF has requested bulk packaging
instead of the small, individually packaged sachets: It is simply too time-consuming to tear them open one package
at a time.

Throughout the Third World, health
workers are promoting home preparation of ORT mixtures. In The Gambia,
Julbrew bottles, which hold beer or soft
drinks, are ubiquitous, and health educators have turned them into a tool for
child health. They urge a mother whose
child has diarrhea to mix eight Julbrew
bottle caps full of sugar and one of salt
with three bottles of water, and to have
the child drink the solution. Elsewhere,
posters and radio programs explain how
parents can mix a fistful of sugar and a
pinch of salt with water to save their children from diarrheal dehydration. Constraints on such efforts can be as simple
as a lack of poster-making skills and
equipment, and aid agencies frequently
contribute this expertise to local health
workers.

Controlling infectious childhood diseases has also helped reduce diarrhea-
related mortality. For example, diarrhea
frequently accompanies measles. Theoretically, vaccinating 75 percent of a
child population for measles would reduce diarrheal mortality 10–20 percent.
Only about 40 percent of the world's
children, however, have been vaccinated
against measles, diphtheria, whooping
cough, or tetanus. (See Table 9–2.) Full
coverage against the major childhood infectious diseases would cost only $2–15
per child worldwide. To extend vaccina-

tion coverage to all the world's children
would cost some $600 million to $4 billion per year.[14]

Particularly effective immunization
programs have been conducted by Dr.
Jean-Hubert Thieffry of the Enfant de
Partage organization in the Thiès region
of Senegal. Health care workers, with
logistical support from a central supply
area, visit remote sites in mobile units
that permit quick travel from village to
village. All across Thies one sees long
lines of mothers waiting to have their
children inoculated against polio,
measles, whooping cough, tetanus,
diphtheria, yellow fever, and tuberculosis. The various problems of mobile
units have been solved ingeniously with
methods that may find worldwide application.

A major problem with immunization
campaigns everywhere is the dropout
rate for the second and third in the usual
series of inoculations. Dropouts are due
to the inconvenience of returning for
more shots, as well as fears stimulated by
children's minor fevers and aches after
the first shot. Thieffry reduced his dropout rate by shortening the series of shots
from three to two. Some fear that combining antigens in only two inoculations
reduces their effectiveness. But
Thieffry's detailed analysis discounts

**Table 9-2. Global Immunization Rates
for Infectious Diseases, 1980**

Disease/Inoculation	Children Vaccinated
	(percent)
Diphtheria, Pertussis, Tetanus[1]	41
Measles	37
Polio	43
Tuberculosis	54

[1]Combined inoculation; pertussis is known commonly as whooping cough.
SOURCE: Derived from UNICEF, *State of the World's
Children 1984* (New York: Oxford University Press,
1983).

this concern. Since his teams were created in 1981, they have attained an 80 percent coverage rate for the first shot and almost 60 percent for the second. In 1984, no epidemics of measles or whooping cough occurred in the region served, nor were there any cases of polio or tetanus.[15]

Participation in immunization programs is encouraged by good advance work. The Thiès team visits village leaders six months before the scheduled date of arrival in a village. If the leaders consent to participate, the team arrives again the day before scheduled inoculations to announce their availability. The next morning, mothers and children gather and the workers explain that they have a choice between risking the effects of a "little disease"—the fever and aches that sometimes follow vaccination—or the "big disease"—the all too familiar results of polio, for example. The mothers are put at ease and made to feel comfortable about returning with their children for the second series of shots. The mobile team workers, wielding pneumatic guns in each hand on two buttocks at a time, effectively immunize whole villages of several hundred people in a morning.

Brazil has successfully conducted mass immunization campaigns, declaring the second Saturday in June and the third Saturday in August as "National Vaccination Days." The government promotes the campaign through loudspeakers and thousands of radio advertisements. Eighteen million Brazilian children have been immunized in this campaign, leading to some dramatic results. Polio cases, for example, dropped from over 2,500 in 1979 to 10 in 1983. Colombia also launched a massive campaign based on the National Vaccination Day concept. It includes endorsement by the country's president, and mobilization of the Red Cross, police, military, U.N. agencies, and tens of thousands of

volunteers to supply and deliver vaccines. In a few months, three fourths of the children were vaccinated. El Salvador, during a lull in its civil war, sent out immunization teams in a similar effort to vaccinate 400,000 children. National campaigns are encouraging because in some countries, such as rural areas of Mexico, mobile teams have not achieved high coverage rates.[16]

Full coverage against the major childhood infectious diseases would cost only $2–15 per child worldwide.

India began extended immunizations in 1978, with a goal of vaccinating all two-year-olds by 1990 for six diseases. Progress has been noticeable, with diphtheria-pertussis-tetanus (DPT) inoculations increasing from 6 million in 1981 to 10.3 million in 1983. Polio vaccinations increased over the same period from 1.3 million to 4.4 million. Vaccination against tuberculosis increased from 13 million to 14 million. Unfortunately, the dropout rate between the first and the third doses of DPT and polio is 30 percent. More unhappily, the annual number of newly eligible children totals more than 24 million.[17]

No country can afford to promote ORT, nutrition education, and immunizations simultaneously as separate items. Primary health care must be delivered as a package. The effectiveness of the entire package determines long-run success or failure. Many large-scale primary health care efforts in India, Indonesia, and the Philippines have failed to reduce infant mortality.[18] Most suffered from poor supervision of health workers.

A relatively successful example from West Africa suggests both the potential and the problems with primary health care. In The Gambia, village health workers are trained for six weeks, then provided with simple tools of the trade: oral rehydration salts, antibiotics, bandages, antimalarial drugs, aspirin, and other curative items that villagers want very much. They learn to recognize diarrhea, measles, whooping cough, malaria, or cholera.[19]

Workers teach mothers to administer the ORT salts for episodes of diarrhea, and not to wait until the child is dehydrated. They make a record of any such cases on picture-sheets, usable by illiterates, and then follow up the initial contact with a home visit. Workers ensure that advice is followed and explain how to prevent recurrence of diarrhea or other avoidable problems. Difficult cases are referred to a district health post staffed by more highly trained workers, or to a regional hospital, which the parents can reach within a day by donkey cart and where a doctor is available.

The world has not invested enough in primary care, population planning, or development to reduce the absolute numbers of people suffering.

Supervisors with two years of training monitor the work of five village health workers. They visit each village once weekly to ensure that drugs are available, records are kept, and preventive services are performed. If special problems arise, regional medical professionals are alerted. This system enables the health ministry to respond quickly to any epidemic of measles or cholera, and to dispatch an emergency team to give immunizations or to take other preventive actions, such as securing the water supply. Malaria incidence has also been reduced in children by dispensing chloro-

quine, an effective antimalarial drug, to feverish children during the rainy season, particularly when their resistance is low due to depleted food stocks from the previous harvest.

A vast difference in performance, however, can be seen even within this tiny country. A random inspection of villages in the central region reveals that some village health and maternity workers fail to live up to expectations. Records are not kept. Children with eye infections, measles, or injuries are in evidence. The maternity kits appear poorly maintained or unused. Sterile razor blades are not replaced when the original supply runs out. Here infant mortality approaches 17 percent—the national average—and maternal mortality is over 1 percent. In the nearby Arasemmi district, using almost the same approach, infant mortality is only 5 percent. Better administration, and perhaps more positive tribal attitudes toward hygiene, account for the difference.[20]

Administrative problems have been relatively easy to identify. Poor recordkeeping is due to lack of training. Administrators acknowledge that six to eight weeks is not enough time to convince people who have never kept written information that it can be useful to distant strangers. Inadequate training is blamed on shortages of funds and a rush to meet international goals and guidelines. New workers, health organizers say, would benefit from longer training. For workers already practicing, intensive retraining is attempted each year.

The absence of formal recordkeeping does not guarantee that the system will fail. Weekly visits to each village by health supervisors have created a network that enables the national center to respond quickly to epidemics. In The Gambia, measles and cholera outbreaks have been effectively contained as a result of these word-of-mouth reports. Though primary health care has a long way to go in The Gambia, the absence of epidemics in that country is a powerful indicator that the system is working.[21]

The importance of building a foundation for health care has been shown in China. The Chinese system of "barefoot doctors" is a classic example of what can be done to improve the human condition. Since the fifties, these rural health workers have spent most of their time delivering simple curative care. They also act as preventive technicians, inspecting water and sanitary systems and providing health education. By providing curative services that the villagers badly want, health workers gain leverage in delivering preventive services.[22]

The record in primary health care is mixed. Most developing countries practice some level of primary care, and countries such as China, The Gambia, Thailand, and Zimbabwe have had considerable success. Others, such as Brazil and Colombia, have impressive immunization programs. UNICEF and WHO have spurred the global movement to promote breast-feeding where its practice is decreasing. And oral rehydration, vaccines, antibiotics, and progress in female education have, over the last 20 years, cut the rate of worldwide infant mortality almost in half—an unprecedented achievement. Sadly, the progress has been matched by the growth of natural disasters and human numbers. The world has not invested enough in primary care, population planning, or social and economic development to reduce the absolute numbers of people suffering. Relative improvements are satisfying, if at all, only to the fortunate whose children do not suffer and die.

WOMEN, WATER, AND AGRICULTURE

Peter Bourne, president of Global Water, Inc. (an organization formed to help implement the goals of the U.N.'s International Drinking Water Supply and Sanitation Decade) relates two stories that capture the meaning water carries for human health. The first comes from an African woman asked whether she understood the importance of encouraging her children to wash their hands after defecation, particularly before eating. She replied, "I have to carry our water seven miles every day. If I caught anyone wasting water by washing their hands, I would kill them." The second comes from another African woman asked how having water taps installed in her village had changed village life. Her immediate response: "The babies no longer die."[23]

One quarter of the world's people lack clean drinking water and sanitary human waste disposal. As a result, diarrheal diseases are endemic throughout developing countries and are the world's major cause of infant mortality. Cholera, typhoid fever, guinea worm, schistosomiasis, and intestinal parasites also infect hundreds of millions. Many people who must visit rivers and swampy areas to obtain water risk contracting malaria, river blindness, and sleeping sickness. Experts estimate that a sanitary water supply would eliminate half the diarrhea, including 90 percent of all cholera, 80 percent of sleeping sickness, and 100 percent of guinea worm infestation, as well as small fractions of several other serious tropical diseases.[24]

Some observers have argued that water and sanitation systems should receive higher priority than other investments, including major reservoir projects, because they fundamentally improve the human condition, while some reservoirs have caused serious problems such as the tripling of cases of schistosomiasis. Clean drinking water, unfortunately, has not been a high priority for many countries. Four fifths of the rural populations of 73 African and Asian countries do not have access to clean drinking water. Most have no toilet or latrine. (See Table 9–3.) Worldwide, 1.3 billion people lack clean water and 1.7 billion lack adequate sanitation.[25]

Water plays two important roles in malnutrition: Its shortage reduces not only food production but also the efficiency with which food is used. Contaminated wells, buckets, and pots, along with unclean food, carry diarrheal disease to children. When women walk up to three hours to get minimal water supplies, water becomes too valuable for washing, and an important defense against infection is lost. The association between water and child health, and the direct bearing water wells now have on garden crop production and community development, is second only to that of female education. The strength of this relationship has led UNICEF to dedicate a quarter of its global budget to providing simple water supplies. In Ethiopia, water is the largest item in the UNICEF budget after relief.

Even where available, most wells are open to contamination. Often animals are watered from the same wells from which drinking water is drawn. Without a concrete apron, bacterially contaminated water will seep into the well. Piped and chlorinated water is generally unaffordable in the high-mortality countries, but sealing and protecting wells, even in village settings, can be made affordable.

The water bucket is a major source of contamination. Held in dirty hands or placed on filthy ground, it can easily spoil a well. The bucket and pulley ropes can be sealed to prevent soiling, though this requires some expense and expertise. Well placement also requires expertise. Put in a depression, a well can be easily contaminated. If too shallow, it will dry up near the end of the dry season. Hand-dug wells usually dry out fastest because they are shallow, yet digging

Table 9-3. Availability of Clean Drinking Water and Human Waste Disposal in Selected Countries, Circa 1982

| | | Share of Population with Service | |
Country	Infant Mortality	Clean Drinking Water Supply	Human Waste Disposal
		(percent)	
Burkina Faso	21	31	n.a.
Afghanistan	20	11	n.a.
Angola	15	27	n.a.
Ethiopia	15	16	14
Bolivia	13	37	24
India	12	42	20
Pakistan	12	34	6
Turkey	12	78	8
Indonesia	10	22	15
Tanzania	10	46	10
Honduras	9	44	20
Brazil	8	55	25
Mexico	5	57	28
Philippines	5	51	56
Chile	4.1	85	32
Costa Rica	2.7	72	97
Portugal	2.6	73	n.a.
Soviet Union	2.6	76	n.a.
Cuba	1.9	62	36
United States	1.2	99	99

SOURCES: United Nations Children's Fund, *State of the World's Children 1984* (New York: Oxford University Press, 1983); Ruth Leger Sivard, *World Military and Social Expenditures 1983* (Washington, D.C.: World Priorities, 1983); Pan American Health Organization, *Health Conditions in the Americas* (Washington, D.C.: 1982).

far below the water table requires expensive hydraulic equipment.[26]

Because water contaminated with feces or urine is a major source of disease, toilets are essential. Diarrhea and roundworm each affect more than a half-billion people, and clean water and sanitation could eliminate almost half of these cases. Ninety percent of all cholera cases could be prevented with adequate sanitation systems. Their design and placement can be complicated, however, and costs are sometimes high. Toilets must provide privacy, not contaminate groundwater, and last 10–20 years. Screened vents are required to remove odors that will deter use. Pit latrines meeting these requirements can be installed for less than $10 per person in the Third World.[27]

Many water and sanitation problems are behavioral rather than technical. But the use of these technologies breaks down in the systems themselves. If a pump has many moving parts and is complicated or expensive to fix, the first time it fails will be the last time it is used. Similarly, if toilets do not control flies they will be abandoned.

Zimbabwe has long funded a unique institution to develop solutions to such problems. The Blair Research Laboratory has, since 1939, developed controls for malaria and schistosomiasis, and designed systems for clean water and sanitation. The Blair Toilet—the prototype vented pit latrine—and the Blair Pump have become internationally renowned for their effectiveness and low cost. The latter is a shallow well pump, completely sealed and sanitary, with only three moving parts. It has no handle or lever to break. It consists simply of two pipes, one of which moves inside the other, and two one-way valves. The pipes are plastic and can break, but these can be repaired in five minutes with glue by someone who has an hour of training. Thirty thousand Blair Pumps and 20,000 Blair Toilets have been installed in Zimbabwe since 1981. The laboratory promotes this effort not only with demonstrations, but with simple educational materials.[28]

Although healthy people can make better use of available food, reducing water-borne bacteria alone will not solve malnutrition problems. If food production in southern Africa, for example, grows only at historic rates of 1.4 percent per year while population grows 3.5 percent annually, more trouble lies ahead. Southern Africa has not been self-sufficient in food since the sixties, and only the most optimistic agricultural forecasts foresee self-sufficiency before the year 2000. Cereal imports, in fact, are expected to increase by 800 percent by then and to cost $4 billion per year in foreign exchange. The prospect that southern Africa will be unable to continue food imports to meet future demands is, according to the U.N. Food and Agriculture Organization (FAO), "too grave to contemplate." FAO estimates that Angola, Botswana, Mozambique, Tanzania, Zambia, and Zimbabwe will fall short of the investment capital needed to become food self-sufficient by a total of more than $2 billion per year. In fact, the organization describes the current situation as "a doomsday trend."[29]

East and West Africa face a similar scenario (see Chapter 10), as does much of southern Asia. Twelve of Afghanistan's 28 provinces are threatened by famine, partly as a result of war. A half-million people are at risk of starvation. Three quarters of the children in Bangladesh still suffer severe malnutrition. Food intake per person there has fallen since the early sixties, a fact that can be attributed to falling food production per capita. Grain production has increased at a rate of only 1 percent per year since 1965, compared with a population growth rate of 2.6 percent. Farmers lack seed, irrigation during the dry season, means to control erosion, and access to capital to improve production. Moreover, prices for food products are controlled to protect the urban middle class. Analysts suggest remedies that parallel those for Africa: small wells for hand irrigation, local reforestation projects, loans for farmers without collateral, and better incentives and markets for farmers.[30]

Women must receive much higher priority in water, health, and agriculture development. Women do over half the work involved in food production in non-Muslim parts of India and in Nepal, and up to 80 percent in Africa. (See Table 9–4.) Yet extension services, loans, fertilizer subsidies, and most other productivity improvement projects are aimed at men. But with simple devices that can be produced locally, such as hoes, buckets, fertilizer, and efficient wood stoves, women's work loads can be eased and some buying power generated, particularly if they control the marketing of their products.[31]

Some women have found a way to improve their situation. They persuade their husbands to dig several open wells, to erect a fence, and to prepare the soil,

Table 9-4. Share of Work in Africa Performed by Women

Task	Share
Growing Food	70
Storing Food	50
Grinding, Processing Food	100
Caring for Animals	50
Selling, Exchanging Produce	60
Fetching Water	90
Fetching Fuel	80
Child Care	100
Cooking	100
Cleaning	100
House Building	30
House Repair	50
Community Projects	70

SOURCE: U.N. Economic Commission for Africa, New York, private communication, April 1985.

and then they do the rest. They plant tomatoes, lettuce, beans, bananas, and other fruits. The gardeners usually keep half the money from their individual plots and give half to a community fund. Some groups have built new maternities and schools, and, with some help, have equipped and operated them.[32]

Communal garden projects are an ideal target for development assistance. They provide women with not only food but also increased economic power, which usually means increased status and decision-making authority. Improved agriculture also means a better environment and a long-term reduction of the deforestation that worsens drought. One African leader, whether facing the reality of women's work or continuing the bias against men doing such jobs, uses the slogan "one woman, one tree." Though the original Chinese version, "one person, one tree," may be preferable, it is a start.[33]

Particularly troublesome in improving the productivity of peasants—in agriculture, water supply, or household crafts— is access to financing. Peasants often have no direct ownership of communal land or land of sufficient value as collateral for loans. Women have even less access, for they usually do not hold title to land that their families might own. One development group, the International Fund for Agricultural Development, provides loans to such persons by offering a simple incentive: Failure to repay means further loans are denied. Often the loans are given to a group, so peer pressure is placed on individuals whose failure to repay would jeopardize everyone. The fund has a 99 percent repayment rate, but only $1 billion in loan funds. And even that may be lost due to donor-country budget-cutting.[34]

Integrated development on a scale sufficient to arrest declining living conditions will be relatively expensive. Water and sanitation projects to supply safe water within 10 years to the third of the world's population who lack it would cost about $50 billion per year. Extending loans of $500 to some 150 million Third World peasant families for farm improvements would require an initial loan fund of $75 billion. Interest costs, however, would total only about $7.5 billion annually, and most of this could be recovered. Most of these funds will have to come from the developing countries themselves, but development assistance, appropriately designed, can provide a large boost.[35]

Supporting small farmers to increase agricultural productivity and reduce environmental damage is a good investment in its own right. Productivity improvements are usually large and provide rapid payback. Loans to peasants without collateral can be made relatively risk-free to the lender. And when the funds for investment come from bilateral or multilateral sources, they can be tied to agricultural policy reform. But most important, investment in agriculture is also a good investment in children. For without a sound agricultural base, societies will be unable to grapple with overpopulation and economic decline. Malnutrition, poverty, and even famine will spread.

POPULATION PLANNING

Poor families are caught in a trap: They need many children to help with the work and provide security to parents in old age. But by having more children, families share fewer hectares of land, fewer liters of water, and less income per person. The only escape from this trap is having fewer—but more productive—children. Family planning improves the lives of children two ways: by increasing the health care and educational services

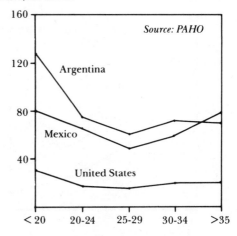

Infant Deaths Per 1,000 Births

Source: PAHO

Argentina

Mexico

United States

< 20   20-24   25-29   30-34   >35

Figure 9-2. Infant Mortality and Age of Mother

available per child and by making the survival of each child more likely.

Family planning has the greatest impact on infant mortality when it is used to prevent the highest-risk pregnancies. These include pregnancies to mothers under age 20 or over 35, pregnancies spaced close together, and pregnancies after a mother has already had several children. (See Figures 9-2, 9-3, and 9-4.) Families that minimize high-risk pregnancies lose fewer children and so do not need one or two extra as "insurance."

The risk of infant death is high for very young mothers, whose bodies may not have matured enough to deliver a healthy child. Princeton researchers James Trussell and Anne Pebley point out that family planning is unlikely to reduce early pregnancy unless girls marry later in life. Age at first marriage varies across Africa, generally being lower in the West and higher in the East. In many African countries, girls may legally marry at age 12. In Guinea and Niger, for example, most women marry before age 17. In Senegal, Mauritania, Mali, Nigeria, and Chad, most females

Infant Deaths
Per 1,000 Births

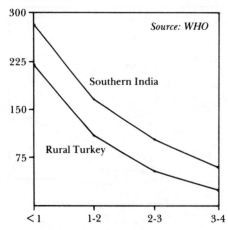

Figure 9-3. Infant Mortality and Years
Between Births

Infant Deaths
Per 1,000 Births

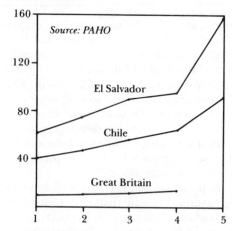

Figure 9-4. Infant Mortality and Birth Order

marry before they turn 18. Age at first marriage in Kenya rose from 18.5 years to over 20 between 1962 and 1979, but birth rates increased anyway. Bangladeshi women, on the average, marry before age 16, though Asians in general marry later than Africans. Most Latin American women now delay marriage until they are 20 or older. Sixteen years is the minimum age for marriage for women in many developing countries.[36]

The length of time between births—child spacing—is crucial at all ages. A child's chances of survival are reduced by pregnancies in rapid succession that deplete a mother's nutritional reserves and overall condition. Children born closely together also compete for maternal care and resources. The older child will be at higher risk because breast-feeding is likely to be withdrawn sooner.

Early cessation of breast-feeding can, at the same time, shorten birth intervals. Breast-feeding stimulates the production of hormones that reduce ovulation and the risk of pregnancy. This evolved as a natural mechanism to protect the health of both mother and child. In the

areas where breast-feeding is declining, in fact, the birth intervals are the shortest. In a survey of 26 countries, 30 percent of births were spaced less than 24 months apart. Africa, because the traditions of breast-feeding and postpartum abstinence—which frequently exceeds one year—continue, has longer intervals. But all of the 26 developing countries surveyed had at least 15 percent of births too close together.[37]

A child's chances of survival also decrease rapidly with the number of children delivered by the mother. Maternal depletion and competition for resources again account for the risk. One study, using World Fertility Survey data, suggests that family planning for mothers between the ages of 20 and 34 would reduce infant mortality by 5 percent. Maintaining a space of two years between births would reduce infant mortality by 11 percent. Avoiding more than four births per mother would reduce infant mortality by about 8 percent. Child and maternal mortality would also be reduced. The cumulative reductions are difficult to estimate, however, because of their complex interplay.[38]

Family planning's contribution to child development is perhaps greatest on the social level, where high fertility gets translated into reduced living standards. Primary education, nutrition, and water and sanitation are essential to child survival and development, but rapid population growth can overload a society's ability to provide classrooms and food. The educational disadvantage of being born in a developing country is large and growing. The World Bank estimates that Western countries spend 50 times more per primary school student than the least-developed countries. Yet, the school-age population of a country such as Kenya will double or triple by the year 2000. If such countries act to reduce population growth rapidly, the cost of educating their children can be cut in half over the next 25 years. Savings can be used to improve the quality of education, reducing the immense gap throughout the world.[39]

The elements of family planning are well understood, but questions remain on how to promote and deliver it. Early marriage and childbearing in the Third World are inextricably tied to the economic and social rewards that societies attach to childbearing. Without improvements in the status of women, increased economic security for families, and food supplies less dependent on child labor, family planning cannot fully succeed. But without effective family planning, efforts to improve the quality of life cannot succeed.

Changes in social attitudes toward family planning in the Third World usually reflect government leadership. Most population policy analysts describe progressive government policy as the biggest factor in rapid fertility decline. African nations have been far more reluctant than the rest of the world to support family planning, and they are paying the price. Nevertheless, Africa's leaders have shown a growing awareness that

population growth plays a serious role in reducing economic growth and living standards. The impetus for family planning efforts in The Gambia, Kenya, and Zimbabwe, for example, has come from ministries of finance, where budget officers projecting future revenue needs become alarmed when they see where current rates of population growth are leading them. According to Nancy Harris, formerly of International Family Planning Assistance, "Africa has made 30 years of progress in family planning in the last five years."[40]

African nations have been far more reluctant than the rest of the world to support family planning, and they are paying the price.

The new awareness of African leaders is typified in a recent speech by President Kountche of Niger: "It is established . . . that our rate of demographic growth is not at all in step with our economic growth rate. In other words, our tendency to create needs is vastly superior to our capacity to produce the corresponding vital resources . . . .How [can we] reconcile demographic growth and economic growth taking into account, of course, the sacrosanct regulations of Islam and the traditional values which we have inherited? How [can we] free our society from the socio-educational sluggishness, from fatalism, apathy and running away from responsibility which are obstacles to its maturity and equilibrium? Is it normal to impose on a woman successive pregnancies which impair the life of the mother and that of the child? Is it normal to inflict on our sisters in the towns and particularly in the country, the almost inevitable obligations to become old before their time, crushed under the weight of daily work and ravaged by almost constant nursing? . . . We should guarantee the future of our children."[41]

Such support is vital for bringing Africa's population growth into harmony with its resources. If Africa had the financial power of Europe or Japan and the agricultural and technical resources of the United States, it could perhaps support a quadrupling of its population. Additional mouths could be fed by increasing grain production per hectare, now at only a quarter of the level in Europe and the United States. But no such miracle is in sight. Africa, realistically, must cope with peasant agriculture and modest incomes for the foreseeable future, as must Bangladesh, India, Pakistan, and most other Third World countries. Government leaders who recognize this fact and incorporate it into their national planning will be crucial to successful family planning in the Third World.

Providing family planning services would not be unduly costly. According to Joseph Speidel of the Washington-based Population Crisis Committee, family planning services to a Third World couple cost about $10 per year. He estimates that family planning programs over the last 15 years have reduced world population by 130 million, entailing a savings of $175 billion in food, shelter, clothing, health care, and education. For about $4 billion per year, the world could provide family planning to all who want it. About $500 million is currently being provided by international donors.[42]

The common goals of improving human nutrition, health, physical well-being, and the status of women all require greater efforts in family planning. The achievements of China, Indonesia, and Thailand demonstrate that these goals can be reached. Though family planning has come under attack recently in the United States, the burden of proof is on critics to show how human needs in Africa and Asia can be satisfied without rapid and permanent declines in population growth rates.

ENDING THE CYCLE OF CRISIS

The African famine has alerted the world to at least some of the people who live on the edge between subsistence and dissolution. But disaster threatens millions more in Bangladesh, India, Pakistan, Turkey, and other parts of Asia and Latin America. In all, almost 1.4 billion people live in countries where children die more often than adults, where 145 million children are malnourished, and where more than two thirds of the people are illiterate. Any assessment of a child survival revolution must also ask: "Survival for what?" The answer is that children need development as well as survival, to help make their lives more than a series of crises.

Failed development efforts, however, litter the landscape like abandoned factories and silted reservoirs. Most development aid assumes that economic growth alone will improve health, nutrition, and education. This approach relies on foreign aid, reduced domestic consumption, and increased savings to stimulate economic growth. Yet a country like Malawi experienced 8 percent annual economic growth throughout the seventies and still ranked fourth worst in the world in child health. Faced with examples like this, it has become obvious that rapid economic growth will not necessarily improve living conditions for the majority of people in developing countries.[43]

An alternative development strategy focuses on improving education and health and resists foreign investment, particularly from the West. Tanzania, for example, worked hard to increase literacy and improve child health. Economically, however, Tanzania and many countries following this model stagnated because they eliminated incentives for agricultural and industrial production and cut themselves off from badly needed foreign capital.

China has recently shown how these two development strategies can be effectively combined. The leaders made necessary investments in population quality, as measured by low infant mortality and high literacy rates, but these alone did not stimulate economic growth. Now that incentives for private agricultural production have been introduced, large gains are being made.

Once the model for developing countries in primary health care and primary education, China has now become the model for economic development as well. And the nation is proving right economists such as Nobel Laureate Theodore Schultz, who argues that investment in people is far more important than investment in machines.[44] China is also proving that market pricing and financial incentives are powerful forces for improving economic conditions. If adopted throughout the Third World, the Chinese triad of primary health care, primary education, and agricultural reform could spur a lasting child survival and development revolution.

Once the model for developing countries in primary health care and education, China has now become the model for economic development as well.

The world's poorest people themselves can hardly increase their savings to provide the funds for development.

Reducing consumption any further would be virtually impossible. Much waste and corruption exists in the Third World, but without outside pressure—which can be exerted with aid—reform is unlikely. Much of the additional funds will have to come from the industrial world. The United States, which in absolute terms is the world's largest aid donor, gives less in terms of percent of gross national product (GNP) than all but 2 of the 17 members of the Development Assistance Committee of the Organisation for Economic Co-operation and Development. Eastern bloc countries give 30 percent less than the United States in terms of donations as a percent of GNP. Much of the world's official emergency aid to African famine victims has simply been reallocated from existing programs.[45]

If such investments—investments in the next generation—make so much sense, why have more not been made? The reasons vary, but they include the fact that the necessary savings have been wasted by both natural disasters and those caused by humans. Investments in children also do not pay off for a long time, and most people have far more immediate needs. People in the Third World are not unwilling to sacrifice for their children, but their margin of existence is so narrow that they often must choose between their children and their own lives. The poor health of women in so much of the Third World reflects just such a choice.

In these cases, industrial countries can siphon off part of their surplus to help out those who have nothing extra. The outpouring of private donations to famine victims suggests that people feel compelled to provide disaster relief. But disasters will only grow unless investments are made in family planning, health care, and education, and so will the costs of disaster relief.

When development relief does more

than just stave off famine, when it is invested to provide benefits for years to come, then savings—in lives and money —will be made. Growth in the Third World means additional prosperity in the industrial world through increased trade. But a moral burden also rests on those who could have done so much to help so many at so little real cost, but did not.

10

Reversing Africa's Decline

Lester R. Brown and Edward C. Wolf

Although essentially agrarian, Africa is losing the ability to feed itself. In 1984, 140 million of its 531 million people were fed entirely with grain from abroad. In 1985, the ranks of those fed with imported grain may have reached 170 million—two thirds as many people as live in North America. In February of 1985, the United Nations reported that some 10 million people had left their villages in search of food, many of them crowded into hastily erected relief camps. Starvation deaths had passed the 1 million mark.[1]

During the two decades after World War II, grain production per person in Africa either remained steady or increased slightly, peaking in 1967 at 180 kilograms. This level, roughly one pound of grain per day, is widely viewed as the subsistence threshold, below which malnutrition begins to erode human development and labor productivity. Since 1967, per capita grain pro-

An expanded version of this chapter appeared as Worldwatch Paper 65, *Reversing Africa's Decline*.

duction has been declining. In 1983 and 1984—years in which low rainfall depressed the harvest—118 and 120 kilograms of grain were produced per person, down more than a third from the peak.[2] (See Figure 10–1.) Few countries have escaped this downward trend. But more serious, there is nothing in prospect on either the agricultural or the family planning side of the food-population equation to reverse the situation.

As per capita grain production has declined in this agrarian society, so has per capita income. The policymakers responsible for economic development and planning are now painfully aware of this development. At a ministerial-level meeting in late April 1985 they drafted a memorandum to the United Nations Economic and Social Council, which was in effect a plea for help. They observed that "as a result of sluggish [economic] growth and a high rate of population growth, per capita income, which was growing at negligible rates during the seventies, has consistently declined since 1980 at an average annual rate of

Kilograms
Per Person

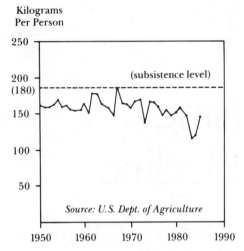

Figure 10-1. Per Capita Grain Production in
Africa, 1950-85

4.1 percent and average per capita income is now between 15 and 25 percent less than 15 years ago."[3]

The crisis has prompted a few laudable initiatives, such as World Bank efforts to raise an additional $1 billion for long-term economic assistance and the appointment of an Emergency Relief Coordinator for Africa by the U.N. Secretary General.[4] But these actions deal largely with the symptoms of Africa's decline, not the causes. An economic assistance strategy dictated by traditional financial criteria—the rate of return on project investments—is destined to fail. Indeed, it is already failing.

Continuing a "business as usual" policy toward Africa amounts to writing off its future. Without a massive mobilization of resources, the prospect of reversing the decline in per capita grain production is poor, suggesting that famine will become chronic, an enduring feature of the African landscape. At issue is whether national governments and international assistance agencies can fashion new, environmentally based development strategies to reverse the ecological deterioration and economic

decline that is inflicting such suffering on the people of Africa.

This raises several questions: Are the political leaders of Africa prepared to make the tough decisions needed to reverse the decline? And is the international community prepared to mobilize to help Africa save itself? Can African governments and the international development community adopt a development strategy based on environmental rather than narrow economic goals, one that restores and preserves natural support systems—forests, grasslands, soils, and the hydrological regime—rather than meeting a specified rate of return on investment in a particular project?

With environmental deterioration undermining economic progress all across the continent, the only successful economic development strategy will be one that restores the natural systems on which the economy depends. Reversing Africa's decline will require carefully orchestrated national efforts to organize millions of people to plant trees, build soil conservation terraces, and plan smaller families. An environmentally oriented effort to change the situation in Africa will, of necessity, be people-based rather than capital-based. To be sure, more capital will be needed—much more. But the heart of the strategy will be the mobilization of people.

BRAKING POPULATION GROWTH

In the late twentieth century, the increase in human numbers has shaped the destiny of Africa far more than it has any other continent. Not only is its population growth the fastest of any continent in history, but in country after country, demands of escalating human numbers are exceeding the sustainable yield of local life-support systems—croplands, grasslands, and forests. Each year Africa's farmers attempt to feed 16 million additional people, roughly 10 times the annual addition in North America or Europe.[5]

According to U.N. projections, Africa's 1980 population of just under 500 million will reach 1.5 billion by 2025—a tripling within just 45 years.[6] Virtually all governments will have to contend with the momentum of growth that results when populations are dominated by people born since 1970. In some African societies, children under age 15 constitute almost half the total, far higher than in most of the world. All of these young people will reach reproductive age by the end of the century.

If African governments take a serious look at future population/resource balances, as China did almost a decade ago, they too may discover that they are forced to choose either a sharp reduction in birth rates or falling living standards and, in some cases, rising death rates.

Over the long term, nature provides no alternative to getting the brakes on population growth. But doing this by reducing birth rates will be extraordinarily difficult for all African governments, especially in those countries where couples still have five to eight children. Yet, the alternative may be an Ethiopian-type situation in which population growth is checked by famine.

Concern about population growth appears to be growing. Over the last 18–24 months, the United Nations Fund for Population Activities and the World Bank have received numerous requests from African governments for family planning assistance. Although these requests will not immediately translate into couples having smaller families, they are a step in the right direction.

As recently as 1974, when the U.N. Conference on World Population was held in Bucharest, only 2 countries in sub-Saharan Africa had policies to reduce population growth—Kenya and Ghana. By mid-1984, 13 had such policies. The additional countries were Botswana, Burundi, The Gambia, Lesotho, Nigeria, Rwanda, Senegal, South Africa, Uganda, Zambia, and Zimbabwe. U.S. demographer Thomas Goliber points out that of this group, 5 had explicit fertility reduction goals. Botswana wanted to increase contraceptive use to 15 percent of all couples of reproductive age by 1985; Ghana wishes to reduce population growth to 2 percent annually by the year 2000; Kenya, to 3.3 percent by 1988; Rwanda, to 3.5 percent by 1986; and Uganda, to 2.6 percent by 1995.[7]

After a long silence on the population issue, key African leaders are now making it a matter of public discussion.

At an early 1984 conference on population convened in Arusha, Tanzania, by the Economic Commission for Africa, the 36 assembled countries observed that "current high levels of fertility and mortality give rise to great concern about the region's ability to maintain even [those] living standards already attained since independence." Conference attendees adopted the Kilimanjaro Program of Action on Population, which called on Commission member-states to "ensure the availability and accessibility of family planning services to all couples or individuals seeking such services freely or at subsidized prices."[8] After a long silence on the population issue, key African leaders are now making it a matter of public discussion.

Among the countries with family planning programs, Zimbabwe's may be the most vigorous. In early 1985 demand for family planning services outstripped projections, forcing the government to request an emergency air shipment of contraceptives from the United States. In a continent where emergency food shipments dominate the news, such a request is a welcome development. According to a recent survey, close to one third of married women of reproductive age in Zimbabwe are using contraception. More important, this figure is growing rapidly.[9]

Discussions with Zimbabwean officials and farmers suggest at least three reasons for the soaring interest in limiting family size. First, since local communities are responsible for educational services beyond primary school, they finance secondary school education largely by assessing student educational fees. For parents who want a good education for their children, the incentive to reduce family size is strong. Second, in rural areas, where most Zimbabweans live, people are increasingly aware that growth in family size will no longer be matched by growth in cropland area. Third, contraceptive services are readily available through community-based distribution centers now operating throughout Zimbabwe. People can now consciously weigh the advantages of planning their families, and do something to have a smaller family if they so choose, whereas in the past they could not. In effect, the supply of family planning services is generating its own demand.[10]

Recent studies by both the Population Institute and the World Bank shed light on the magnitude of the effort needed to halt population growth in Africa. The Population Institute based its assumption on the announced population goals of four countries. Egypt, for example, wants to reduce its population growth rate from 2.7 percent at present to roughly 1 percent by the year 2000. The other three countries considered in the study have established somewhat similar fertility reduction goals.[11]

The cost of providing family planning services to achieve these goals, though substantial, is modest indeed compared with the ecological, economic, and social costs of inaction. The Population Institute notes that funds would come from four sources—individual couples who pay some or all of the expense of the contraceptives they use, private family planning organizations, governments of the countries in question, and international family planning groups.

The World Bank estimates that adoption of a "rapid" fertility decline goal in sub-Saharan Africa would require a twentyfold increase in family planning expenditures by the end of this century —a 16 percent increase per year. Yet these would be more than offset by reduced public spending in other sectors. Savings in education costs alone in the year 2000 would reach $6 or more per capita in a country such as Zimbabwe.[12]

These projected expenditures over the next 15 years are not beyond reach. Yet, they cover only the first gap in family planning—the provision of services. For the typical African country, bridging the second gap—that between desired family size and the much smaller family required to meet stated national population goals—will mean reducing average family size from five or six children today to about two by the year 2000. This may not be possible without substantial financial incentives or disincentives, such as those now being used in China to encourage one-child families. Wherever desired family size exceeds that which is consistent with the goals for social improvement, substantial expenditures or penalties may be required to reconcile the two.

Experience has repeatedly shown that grass-roots programs—those staffed and led by local people—are the most successful ones. The advice locals give is always more acceptable than that of someone brought in specifically to promote a program. Convenience and cost are also important. Surveys show that couples wishing to control their fertility are unlikely to travel more than an hour to reach a family planning service center. If services are too costly, they go unused. One reason for the surge in demand for contraception in Zimbabwe noted earlier was the decision to provide services without cost to those with annual incomes below $150.[13]

Family planning programs that work best offer a full range of contraceptives and sterilization for both men and women. The more methods offered, the more likely couples are to find one that meets their particular needs. For personal or medical reasons, some contraceptives may not be acceptable. When couples are satisfied with a method, continued use is far more likely.

Given the unprecedented numbers of young people who will reach reproductive age in Africa within the next two decades, the adoption of the two-child family as a social goal may be the key to restoring a sustained improvement in living standards. Success in striving for two children per couple will bring problems of its own, including a severe distortion of age-group distribution. But it may be the price many societies will have to pay for neglecting population policy for too long.

REPLANTING FORESTS

The future of the continent's forests lies in farmers' hands. Lacking modern inputs, many Africans working the land can increase harvests to feed growing populations only by clearing new fields, often at the expense of forests. Rising urban demand for fuelwood, which offers a steady source of cash to rural families, increases the pressures on woodlands. As trees disappear, the land steadily becomes less fit for agriculture. The new forests on which Africa's future depends will have to help make farming more secure and productive.

Overall, about 3.6 million hectares of the continent's forests are cleared each year, an annual rate of about half of 1 percent of remaining forests. Shifting cultivation accounts for 70 percent of the clearing of closed-canopy forests and 60 percent of the cutting of savanna forests, according to the U.N. Food and Agriculture Organization (FAO).[14] The continent-wide rates understate the regional pressures on forest resources. In some parts of the continent, permanent forest clearing is accelerating.

More than 5 percent of the moist forests of coastal West Africa (the countries from Guinea through eastern Nigeria) were being cleared by commercial loggers and subsistence farmers each year in the early eighties. At this rate, these forests have a "half-life" of just 13 years. Well over half the outright deforestation in Africa takes place in these coastal states, which contain only 7 percent of the continent's forests and a quarter of its people. (See Table 10–1.) Though small by comparison with the vast remaining forests of the Zaire Basin, this coastal greenbelt of rain forests may play a critical role in recycling the moisture from the Gulf of Guinea that provides summer rains from Senegal to Sudan.

Despite a decade of rapidly increasing international support for reforestation, little progress has been made toward restoring Africa's woodlands and better managing its forests. After sustained drought turned to famine during the early seventies, a partnership of European countries and Sahelian nations created the Club du Sahel to promote drought recovery and long-term development. Forestry and ecological restora-

Table 10-1. Africa: Clearing of Closed Forests, by Major Forested Region, 1985

Region	Area of Closed Forest	Annual Clearing	Change
	(thousand hectares)		(percent)
Coastal W. Africa	13,752	703	−5.1
Zaire Basin	171,540	351	−0.2
East Africa	12,957	105	−0.8
Total	198,249	1,159	−0.6

SOURCE: Worldwatch Institute estimates based on U.N. Food and Agriculture Organization, *Tropical Forest Resources,* Forestry Paper 30 (Rome: 1982).

tion were high on the group's agenda. Starting from a base of only $2.9 million in 1975, international assistance to forestry and reforestation in the Sahel grew more rapidly than any other development sector, reaching $45.3 million in 1980. Over that period, nearly $105 million was spent to restore forests and supply wood for fuel and construction in the region. Yet even with this rapid growth, aid for forests yielded funds that represented just 1.4 percent of the total international assistance to the Sahel in those years.[15]

Much the same pattern was repeated throughout Africa by major international donors. The U.S. Agency for International Development budgeted nearly $220 million to forestry and fuelwood projects in Africa between 1977 and 1984, although the annual amount committed has declined since 1982. The World Bank had spent nearly $93 million on fuelwood projects alone before 1983, and between 1968 and 1984, the Bank invested $426 million in forest management, watershed protection, or agricultural development with a forestry component.[16]

Despite all these expenditures, World Bank forestry advisor John Spears wrote in 1984: "The challenge remains of how to multiply what are in many cases relatively small scale initiatives, particularly in countries like Rwanda and Burundi, into larger scale rural forestry programs that will penetrate throughout the rural areas as quickly as possible. The current rate of tree planting in many Bank member countries is less than one-fifth (in many small African countries one-twentieth) of the rate needed to assure a reasonable supply of fuelwood, fodder, and poles by the year 2000."[17]

A comparison of rates of tree planting with rates of deforestation supports this conclusion. FAO's survey of African forest resources showed that the area cleared each year exceeds that on which trees are deliberately planted by a ratio of 29 to 1, far higher than any other region in the developing world. If degradation and the unsustainable harvest of woodlands are added, the ratio would be higher still.[18]

Most of the international agencies that support forestry have begun a thorough reexamination of their reforestation efforts. New recognition of the complex relationship between forests, farmland, and household fuel supplies is beginning to influence the way money is spent to plant trees. The traditional rationale for forestry programs—that impending wood shortages simply mean the more trees planted the better—is no longer a reasonable guide to setting planting priorities. Without question, more trees must be planted in Africa. But which trees, in which regions, for whom, and by whom are the critical questions that will determine whether the next decade of replanting fares better than the last.

Plantations of fast-growing trees that can supply fuelwood and charcoal to Africa's expanding cities are essential. Plantations now supply less than 5 percent of the continent's fuelwood demands, and perhaps less than one sixth of the wood and charcoal burned in cities and towns. Opportunities for plantations near settlements are far from exhausted, and the technical experience to establish and manage them can be put to best use near cities where a commercial market can justify the steep investment —up to $1,000 per hectare—required.[19]

In rural areas, where most African families still live, trees should be planted not primarily for fuelwood but to restore fertility and productivity to agricultural land. Though household cooking fuels are no less vital for rural families than for city dwellers, dispersed and self-reliant people in the countryside provide no market for plantations, even if trees could be planted on the necessary scale. By emphasizing the role trees play in soil fertility and stable farming systems, reforestation efforts can enlist the help of rural families. Professional foresters working year-round cannot possibly oversee the necessary planting effort. By contrast, Dennis Anderson and Robert Fishwick of the World Bank estimate that providing tree seedlings to families to plant and maintain on their own lands, even assuming that people devote no more than 10 days each year to caring for the trees, would create a work force between 40 and 400 times larger than even the largest national forestry service.[20]

Reintroducing agroforestry in its various forms could rebuild African traditions in which crops, livestock, and trees are integrated as a matter of course. Most research in this area has emphasized reintroducing trees to cultivated land and grazing land. Researchers at the Nairobi-based International Council for Research in Agroforestry argue that farmers and foresters might both benefit from agroforestry in remaining intact forests. National forest reserves in many countries simply cannot be adequately protected from agricultural settlement.

Encouraging the interplanting of trees and crops where forest boundaries have been breached will establish some common interest between farmers and foresters and expand the potential labor force for forest management.[21]

Careful management of the continent's forests can boost wood supplies more cheaply than any fuelwood plantation scheme. Africa still has over a billion hectares of forests and shrubland from which firewood, building materials, medicines, and wild foods are gathered. U.S. Agency for International Development forester Thomas Catterson points out that "even modest gains in productivity could have significant impact on the fuelwood supply."[22] The cost of restoring degraded but intact forests to productivity could be as low as $200 per hectare—one fifth the cost of many intensive plantations. Natural forests maintain hydrologic and nutrient cycles and an important refuge for wild plant and animal species, critical functions that are often excluded from cost-benefit calculations.

Any tree planting in the extensive crescent of savannas from the western Sahel to South Africa will have to consider the impact of livestock. The sale of livestock due to drought, and the migration of pastoralists from grazing lands that can no longer sustain their herds, has tragically disrupted a traditional way of life (as discussed in Chapter 4). But adjustments now may offer opportunities to restore productivity to some of Africa's rangelands. Livestock can be managed to favor the regeneration of woodlands. Controlled grazing helps trees compete with grasses for soil moisture. Young seedlings, however, require several seasons of protection from grazing, so rangeland reforestation requires cooperation from pastoralists if it is to succeed.

Sophisticated tools can sometimes help transform fundamental problems, and scaled-up reforestation programs can take advantage of proven biotechnologies to screen useful tree species and propagate large numbers for planting. Poor genetic quality accounts for part of the failure of past planting efforts. According to international forestry consultant Fred Weber, "in the average nursery, we are still raising genetic garbage."[23] Better screening and selection of trees that survive droughts and perform well in marginal environments is likely to increase success rates markedly.

The 380 million people in the countryside constitute the only labor force large enough to turn Africa's forest decline around.

As important as the trees themselves are their invisible companions—the symbiotic fungi and microorganisms that play a critical role in supplying nutrients and water in harsh environments. Since commercial fertilizers will not likely be used on a large scale in African reforestation efforts, research on nitrogen-fixing microbes and on fungi that improve the uptake of phosphorus (especially lacking in many soils) deserves high priority. Simple techniques for inoculating tree seedlings with the proper bacteria and fungi can dramatically increase plantation survival rates and boost productivity. Research on nitrogen-fixing bacteria and acacia trees is under way at the West African Microbiological Resources Center in Senegal. Involving institutes and universities from other parts of Africa could expand the use of symbiotic microbes in tree-planting programs and help reduce costly losses.[24]

Selecting suitable trees and designing technologies to quickly propagate and establish them will be useless unless trees are made available to the farm families that must plant and maintain them. Michael Dow of the U.S. National Research Council speaks of a "genetic supermarket" offering an array of tree seeds and seedlings that would allow farmers to choose familiar species and those that fit their specific economic and environmental needs. Dennis Anderson and Robert Fishwick of the World Bank argue for a decentralized network of tree nurseries as the key to successful rural tree planting programs, concluding that "ideally, there should be a small tree nursery at every market center in Africa."[25]

Restoring Africa's woodlands and forests is essential to the recovery of agriculture, on which the continent's economic prospects depend. It will require sustained effort and cooperation among governments and an unprecedented willingness by international donors to acknowledge the needs and defer to the judgment of the rural people who will do the bulk of the planting, maintenance, and forest management. These 380 million people in the countryside constitute the only labor force large enough to turn Africa's forest decline around. No simpler rationale for restoring woodlands throughout the continent is needed than an observation by West African foresters recalled by Fred Weber: "Regardless of how well all other rural development efforts may succeed, a Sahel without trees is dead."[26]

RESTORING SOILS

Five years ago, a World Bank report, *Accelerated Development in Sub-Saharan Africa,* announced that "a strategy to stop the accelerating degradation of soils and vegetation is overdue."[27] It is even more overdue today. Restoring the fertility of

African soils, restraining agriculture on unsuitable land, and making farming far more productive on the best land deserve priority attention from African governments and the international community.

Ethiopia illustrates both the potential and the pitfalls of large-scale efforts to conserve soils. In 1977, the government launched a massive program in several provinces to construct soil-conserving terraces and drains. The campaign mobilized subsistence farmers through the country's peasant associations and marshaled international assistance from the United Nations World Food Programme for "food for work" and "cash for work" programs. By 1984, some 590,000 kilometers of contour ditches called "bunds" had been constructed and trees had been planted on 150,000 hectares of erosion-prone slopes. Yet of 500 million tree seedlings distributed from nurseries for planting, only 15 percent survived—as a result of drought, careless planting to fill quotas, and poor choice of tree species.[28]

One promising step taken in Ethiopia was the creation in 1981 of an applied research program to assess the country's conservation efforts, recommend techniques, and monitor erosion in several agricultural areas. With staff from the University of Berne, Switzerland, and support from the United Nations University, the Soil Conservation Research Project has trained Ethiopian technicians and gathered four years of information on erosion rates and conservation work. As programs begin in other African countries, similar sustained research will be essential to evaluate progress and refine techniques.[29]

Kenya, with a long history of soil conservation efforts, offers an example of a promising combination of conservation and new farming practices that increases the land's vegetative cover and reduces the likelihood of severe erosion. In 1974, the Kenyan Ministry of Agriculture began a soil conservation extension program with the assistance of the Swedish International Development Authority. Farmers were encouraged to terrace sloping land by leaving unplowed strips along the contour. To compensate them for the economic penalty of leaving some land out of crop production, the government distributed fruit and fuelwood tree seedlings and cuttings of quality fodder grasses for the unplowed strips. Tree crops diversified the produce farmers could sell, while high-quality fodder enabled them to restrain the destructive free grazing of cattle. Terraces retained water and soil nutrients and visibly raised yields on their upslope side. In the semiarid Machakos district, maize production in some fields actually increased by half after the land was terraced.[30]

Despite their agronomic advantages, terraces have drawbacks. On steep slopes where constructing terraces requires excavation, the labor involved can be prohibitive. Where farmers have reached the limits of the available arable land, as they have in the Ethiopian highlands and in some central African areas, leaving terraces in grass rather than crops reduces the cultivated area, adding to short-term food aid needs. And terraces must be maintained and in some cases rebuilt every year, as experience in Ethiopia has shown. In Rwanda and Burundi, contour ditches introduced by colonial governments to control soil loss have been abandoned since independence because farmers feel the ditches are not worth the maintenance they require.[31]

Although terraces are needed in some places to slow soil loss, particularly where land is likely to remain in continuous production, soil scientist Michael Stocking of the University of East Anglia emphasizes that "the only *real* way of controlling erosion rates is through vegetative protection, whether directly through high-input farming and dense stands of monocrops or indirectly through fertility-enhancing farming systems aimed at the small farmer."[32] Developing and introducing such fertility-enhancing systems has become a major goal of agricultural research in Africa.

One of the more promising approaches in humid areas is to grow crops without plowing at all. Since 1974, Rattan Lal and his colleagues at the International Institute of Tropical Agriculture (IITA) in Ibadan, Nigeria, have been studying low-cost minimum-tillage and no-till systems for humid and subhumid areas in Africa. No-till methods, which involve planting directly into a stubble mulch and using herbicides for weed control, can reduce soil losses to nearly zero, increase the capacity of cropland to absorb and store water, and reduce the energy and labor needed to produce a harvest. Perhaps most important, Lal points out that "no-tillage generally outyields the conventional tillage systems if the crops suffer from moisture, temperature, or nutritional stress."[33]

An IITA report sketches the rationale for farming systems that reduce or eliminate plowing: "Erosion must be prevented by keeping a continuous ground cover, and by avoiding soil compaction from the use of machinery. Organic matter must be maintained by the use of mulch. And leaching must be countered, as it is in the natural forest and in the long-fallow system of shifting cultivation, by deep-rooted trees or plants, which pump nutrients up into the foliage, from which they ultimately fall back into the soil."[34]

Minimum-tillage systems that maintain the productivity of cropland offer an alternative to shifting cultivation and a chance to remove some marginal land from cultivation entirely. Where unplowed land is still available and, therefore, shifting cultivation is unlikely to be abandoned, the fertility of fallow land can sometimes be restored quickly. A research project in Nyabisindu, Rwanda, has developed an "intensive fallow" using deep-rooted legumes when land is taken out of production; World Bank analysts report that "the soil fertility improvement achieved within one year with this type of fallow is remarkable."[35] Where new land remains available for clearing, however, or where livestock are allowed to graze fallow land, farmers may be slow to change their fallow practices.

Minimum-tillage systems offer an alternative to shifting cultivation and a chance to remove some marginal land from cultivation entirely.

On fertile land, as much biological activity occurs in the topsoil itself as in the crops it sustains. The renewed interest in intercropping, minimum tillage, and managed fallows has rekindled investigation of the soil organisms that synthesize and release plant nutrients in the absence of artificial fertilizer. Little is known about the ecology of microbes in the soil. Since fertilizer-intensive farming certainly will not reach most African farmers in the years ahead, research on biological fertility, especially nitrogen fixation, can complement soil conservation work as well as reforestation efforts, as mentioned earlier. In early 1984, the International Union of Biological Sciences proposed a major collaborative research program to "determine the management options for improving tropical soil fertility through biological processes."[36]

Although slowing severe erosion and improving low-input shifting cultivation practices are important, the momentum of population growth and increasing pressure on soils in African countries demands more radical changes in the continent's agriculture. According to Ermond Hartmans, Director of IITA, "in the long run Africa's growing population can be fed only if traditional systems are changed . . . .The solution of Africa's food crisis will not be by a gradual evolution of existing systems only."[37] The revolution in farming systems that conserves soil and permits continuous cultivation will take African agriculture back to its cultural and climatic roots—a savanna agriculture patterned on the natural vegetation that it replaces.

On savannas, trees and grasses grow together. There is no closed forest or unbroken prairie. The new agricultural methods known collectively as agroforestry mimic this natural relationship by combining useful tree crops with cultivated food crops. Agroforestry systems can be tailored to the desiccated Sahel and to the moist farmlands of equatorial and coastal West Africa. Their universal appeal is reduced soil erosion, increased nutrient cycling and biological activity in the topsoil, and resilience to drought. The trees used in agroforestry can help secure terraces on sloping land. A World Bank study of Rwanda, Burundi, and Zaire pointed out that "the existing hundreds of thousands of square kilometers of terraced land should be considered as a huge sunken capital left over from colonial times . . . .The stabilization of these terraces would be a first step for future introduction of agro-forestry farming systems and changes in land use."[38]

For humid areas, IITA and the Nairobi-based International Council for Research in Agroforestry are investigating a technique called alley cropping. Rows of crops are grown between hedgerows of trees or perennial shrubs. Prunings from the trees mulch the crops, returning nutrients to the soil. Fast-growing, nitrogen-fixing trees like leucaena work well in this system, improving the soil and providing the farmer with fuelwood and fodder. Alley cropping recovers soil fertility in the same way that traditional bush-fallow methods do, but it permits continuous cultivation.[39]

In parts of the semiarid Sahel where cash crops have replaced traditional agroforestry methods based on the native acacia trees, seasonal grazing lands have been converted to cropland. Many valuable trees and perennial grasses have disappeared from the landscape. Research in Senegal reveals some of the advantages of reintroducing native nitrogen-fixing trees to agriculture in this area: "Yields of millet and groundnuts grown under *Acacia albida* trees on infertile soils increase from 500 kilograms per hectare to 900 kilograms per hectare. In addition to increased crop yields, there are 50–100 percent increases in soil organic matter, improved soil structure, increased water-holding capacity, and a marked increase in soil microbiological activity beneath the trees."[40] As with alley cropping in wetter lands, agroforestry in the Sahelian countries can shorten fallow intervals, enrich soils, and reduce the pressure to expand farming onto marginal land.

GETTING AGRICULTURE MOVING

By almost any standard, agriculture is not doing well in Africa. Declining per capita food production, abandoned cropland, rising food imports, and famine are among the most visible failures. This dismal record stems in part from the record population growth described earlier and the associated deterioration of the agricultural resource base. Agriculture also suffers from low priority and prestige, national food price policies that discourage investment, and declining rainfall.

Within Africa, agriculture is widely neglected. International aid programs have focused on specific projects rather than overriding issues such as food pricing policy. Too often this assistance has been directed at the symptoms of agricultural stresses rather than the causes. Fortunately, awareness of these shortcomings is slowly spreading. World Bank Senior Vice-President Ernest Stern describes the situation thus: "We, along with other donors, I think it is fair to say, among all our achievements, have failed in Africa. We have not fully understood the problems, we have not identified the priorities, we have not always designed our projects to fit the agroclimatic conditions of Africa and the social, cultural and political frameworks of Africa . . . we, and everybody else, are still unclear about what can be done in agriculture in Africa."[41]

A 1981 report from IITA summarized the dilemma: "In Africa, almost every problem is more acute than elsewhere. Topsoils are more fragile, and more subject to erosion and degradation. Irrigation covers a smaller fraction of the cultivated area . . . leaving agriculture exposed to the vicissitudes of an irregular rainfall pattern. The infrastructure, both physical and institutional, is weaker. The shortage of trained people is more serious. The flight from the land is more precipitate. . . . In one respect, namely the failure to develop farming systems capable of high and sustained rates of production growth, the problems of Africa have reached the stage of crisis."[42]

As the continent's population approaches 600 million, centuries-old agricultural systems of shifting cultivation that were ecologically stable as recently as 1950, when the population was only 219 million, are breaking down. As mentioned in the preceding section, marginal land is being plowed and fallow cycles are being shortened. The new agricultural technologies and inputs needed to offset land productivity losses either have not been developed or are not being applied.

One reason for Africa's agricultural disappointment is the expectation that the dramatic advances in grain production in Asia that began some two decades ago could be duplicated. Unfortunately, differences between the two continents make it impossible to transfer the Asian formula. For example, Asian agriculture is dominated by wet rice cultivation. A single package of successful yield-raising rice technologies could be easily adapted for use throughout the region. Indeed, essentially the same approach was used for Asia's second food staple, wheat, most of which is also irrigated. Africa, in contrast, depends on several staples—corn, wheat, sorghum, millet, barley, and rice among the cereals, plus cassava and yams—and a highly heterogenous collection of farming systems.

Even more important, much of Africa is semiarid, which limits the profitable use of yield-raising inputs such as fertilizer. In Asia and elsewhere, dramatic gains in food production have been achieved in large part because abundant moisture enables crops to respond strongly to chemical fertilizer. In this respect, Africa more nearly resembles semiarid Australia, which despite a technologically advanced farm system has raised grain yields per hectare only 18 percent over the last 30 years. By comparison, African agriculture does not fare too poorly, since grain yield per hectare is up some 38 percent. Yet North America, East Asia, and Western Europe have more than doubled grain yields during that time.[43]

The key to raising cropland productivity in Asia has been the interaction of irrigation, fertilizer, and high-yield dwarf wheats and rices. In Africa, the use of irrigation and fertilizer has been growing, though from a small base. Even though irrigated area has increased—from 5.8 million hectares in 1963 to 8.6 million hectares in 1981 (about 7 percent of cropland)—it still leaves the continent, a region with 11 percent of the world's people, with only 4 percent of its irrigated area.[44]

Within Africa, irrigated area is highly concentrated in a few countries. Egypt, whose agriculture depends on irrigation from the Nile, has 34 percent of the continent's irrigated area. Sudan, also relying on the Nile, has 21 percent. At the southern end, South Africa has invested heavily in irrigation, accounting for 12 percent of the total. Thus these three countries account for two thirds of the continent's irrigated land; the remaining one third is widely scattered throughout the rest of Africa.[45]

The pattern of fertilizer use is similar to that of water. Usage climbed from negligible levels at mid-century to 3.6 million tons in 1982, but this still amounts to only 3 percent of the world total. The patterns parallel irrigation, with South Africa and Egypt accounting for 55 percent of the continent's total.[46] With only a modest amount of fertilizer used outside of Egypt, Sudan, and South Africa, it comes as no surprise that since 1950 Africa has increased output more from plowing new land than from raising land productivity. This contrasts sharply with the rest of the world, where more than four fifths of production gains have come from boosting yields.

Although gains in land productivity for Africa as a whole have not been particularly impressive, those in a few countries have been exceptional. South Africa has nearly tripled yields over the last three decades, matching or exceeding the gains in North America, Western

Europe, and Japan. Tunisia and Zimbabwe have each more than doubled yields. Egypt, starting from a far higher base, has nearly accomplished the same thing. At the other end of the spectrum, a number of countries have lower crop yields today than they did 30 years ago. In Nigeria, for example, grain yields per hectare are 9 percent lower today than they were in the early fifties. They have declined even more in Mozambique, Sudan, Tanzania, and Zambia.[47] In all, more than 40 percent of Africans live in countries where grain yields per hectare are lower today than they were a generation ago.

Yield-raising technologies such as chemical fertilizer and improved varieties have been adopted, at least to some extent, in all countries. But in some these inputs have been more than offset by soil erosion, the addition of low fertility land to the cropland base, shorter fallow periods, and declining rainfall. Indeed, if changes in land use and land degradation are contributing to a long-term decline in rainfall, then efforts to raise Africa's land productivity will face even stiffer odds in the future.

More than 40 percent of Africans live in countries where grain yields per hectare are lower today than they were a generation ago.

Land productivity has declined most in countries where the cultivated area has expanded most, such as Nigeria, Zambia, and Sudan (see Figure 10–2). In addition to lower inherent fertility, the newly cultivated land typically suffers more from soil erosion, either because it is steeply sloping and vulnerable to water erosion, or because it is semiarid and more susceptible to wind erosion.

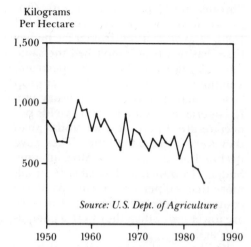

Figure 10-2. Grain Yield in Sudan, 1950-84

Soils on many of Africa's subsistence farms are also suffering from nutrient depletion as firewood shortages lead to the burning of cow dung and crop residues, both traditional fertilizers.

Some segments of the continent's agriculture, such as the irrigated farms of Egypt and South Africa or the rain-fed corn production of Zimbabwe, have been developed largely by technologies from elsewhere in the world. In many situations, however, relatively few specific technologies can be introduced from abroad. Little research has been done, for example, on improving the productivity of transhumant pastoralism, a system of livestock husbandry where some or all of the herding family moves with the herd during part of the year to take advantage of various seasonal forage sources.

Much of African agriculture once consisted of a complex, interactive mixture of crops, livestock, and trees—a system that contrasts sharply with the monocultures on which most world agricultural research is based, which African farmers have been encouraged to adopt in recent years. What is needed in large areas of the continent is a holistic or systems approach to both research and project design. As World Bank forester Jean Gorse has observed, the people with the information and understanding needed to help design strategies to raise the productivity of farmers and pastoralists in these complex systems are the farmers and pastoralists themselves.[48] This suggests that only a more time-consuming approach to project design, one that involves local people in planning, is likely to succeed.

Of all the steps that governments can take to raise agricultural productivity in Africa, a reorientation of food price policies is most important. Too many governments have followed policies designed to placate urban consumers. Ceiling prices for foodstuffs discourage agricultural investment and modernization. A better policy would offer government-backed price supports to provide the assurance that farmers need to invest. In some cases, average prices for farm commodities after the adoption of price supports are little changed from before. But the assurance of guaranteed prices removes market uncertainty, thus encouraging investment at planting time.

In Zimbabwe, one of the few countries with effective price supports, both the farmers on large commercial holdings and those on tribal lands are responding enthusiastically to price incentives. With a return to near normal rainfall for the 1985 crop, Zimbabwe will have a large exportable surplus of corn. Farmers on the tribal lands alone have produced a record marketable surplus of corn estimated at 800,000 tons. Indeed, Zimbabwe indicated in April 1985 that it was providing 25,000 tons of grain to Ethiopia as food aid.[49]

Price supports can partly offset other constraints, such as extensive illiteracy and the lack of effective agricultural extension systems, as they have, for example, in India over the past two decades.

If a yield-enhancing technology is obviously profitable, market forces and the demonstration effect will help spread its use from farm to farm.

Until recently, labor was the principal constraint on the productivity of Africa's traditional agricultural production systems. But as the population/land ratio increases, land is becoming a major constraint. Research to identify means of substituting labor for land in the effort to increase productivity could pay high dividends. Among the labor-intensive activities that might effectively boost the land's carrying capacity are tree planting, stall feeding, and composting. When feasible, feeding animals in stalls permits a more carefully regulated harvest of forage and the concentration of animal manure in a single location. This in turn facilitates the systematic composting of animal manure with crop residues such as straw, leaves, and other organic materials.

In a continent where livestock figure so prominently as a source of food, draft power, and, increasingly, fuel, livestock productivity is a key agricultural indicator. Any successful agricultural strategy will include efforts to increase livestock productivity, either through breeding or better management. In this vein the International Livestock Center for Africa is crossing European dairy cattle with local draft breeds in an effort to develop a breed of hardy dual-purpose animals that can be used for both plowing and milking. Success would enable farmers to produce food and draft power with fewer animals and less feed.[50]

One long-recognized need of African agriculture is millet and sorghum varieties that are more resistant to drought. Closely related is the need for more-drought-resistant, faster-growing varieties of multipurpose trees. FAO has begun to collect seed and coordinate field trials of useful tree varieties in semiarid areas; Senegal and Sudan are already cooperating in this effort, and other countries have been invited to participate.[51]

African governments and the agricultural research community must recognize the need for numerous technological packages for the continent's agriculture. These include technologies developed elsewhere for irrigated agriculture or for dryland farming, as well as new technologies oriented toward bush fallow cultivation, nomadic pastoralism, agroforestry, and integrated crop-livestock farming. Given the enormous diversity in the agricultural systems of the continent, no one package will work for more than a small segment of the continent's farm sector. As a result, the research investment needed to achieve a given advance in farm output in Africa may be far greater than in Asia or in North America.

For some areas, no technologies are available to boost productivity and carrying capacity dramatically. In many cases, none are even in sight. Agricultural science simply does not yet offer the subsistence farmer in semiarid conditions as much as it does the market farmer with an abundance of water.

MORE THAN A MARSHALL PLAN

A mammoth effort is required to avert economic collapse in Africa. In many ways, it is similar in spirit to the Marshall Plan that revitalized Western Europe after World War II, but it will be far more demanding. Africa's population, at over a half billion, is more than double that of Western Europe at the end of the war. The Marshall Plan was designed to rebuild war-devastated economies rather than ecologically devastated ones.

Europe would have recovered without the Marshall Plan, albeit much more slowly.

Africa, on the other hand, is not likely to arrest the ecological deterioration and the economic decline that follows without assistance from abroad. Europe had the basic institutions in place; most of the damage was physical—the destruction of cities and of industrial capacity. Africa does not yet have all the institutions and skills needed to reverse its decline. Europe was geographically compact, with well-developed communication and transport systems. Africa is vast, with only the most rudimentary transportation network. The cost of transporting food from surplus to deficit areas, whether by truck or draft animals, can be prohibitive.

The mobilization of human and capital resources needed to turn Africa around is perhaps more like the emergency mobilization of the Allied Powers in the early forties, which required quick, broad-based action. Had the Allied Powers reacted slowly, events, and even the outcome of World War II, might have been quite different. Faced with an emergency, national governments adopted compulsory military service, imposed rationing, and commandeered industrial facilities and research institutes to achieve wartime goals. Winning the war required a single-mindedness and a unified sense of purpose, including a common appreciation of why sacrifices were needed. A similar effort will be needed to reverse environmental decline in Africa.

Leadership will be needed to coordinate the international effort. In earlier times, the United States provided such leadership. It led the reconstruction of Europe and Japan after World War II. In 1966 and 1967 it shipped a fifth of its wheat crop to India in a highly successful effort to stave off famine after two massive crop failures in that country. But the United States does not now appear to have the leadership, even if it had the will. Nor are any institutions within Africa yet capable of providing this key element.

In the past few years, the United Nations Economic Commission for Africa, directed by a Nigerian, Adebayo Adedeji, has taken the lead among African institutions in assessing long-term economic and development trends. The African Development Bank, the continent's key development institution, recently convened a workshop on desertification, signaling its recognition that environmental deterioration diminishes the effectiveness of its lending programs.[52] Unfortunately, however, the African Bank's neglect of population issues and policy continues.

At the international level, only the World Bank appears to be institutionally strong enough to lead such an effort, but it is not ideally suited for this role. The Bank's experience lies primarily in financing large-scale development projects, not in fostering local mobilization of the kind needed in Africa. But despite the need for a philosophical reorientation, the Bank seems destined to fill the leadership role simply because no other international group has the capability.

As a start, national assessments and long-term projections of environmental, resource, demographic, and economic trends are needed. A similar effort undertaken in China in the late seventies provided the foundation for reorienting that country's population, environmental, and agricultural policies. Without a better understanding of where existing trends are leading, it will be difficult to mobilize support to reverse them, either within or outside Africa. Few countries have even attempted to measure topsoil losses from erosion, much less project the cumulative consequences of continuing losses for land productivity. Assessments are needed of the deterioration of grasslands, the loss of forest cover, changes in the hydrological cycle, soil erosion, and the effect on soil fertility of burning cow dung and crop residues for fuel.

Most important, explicit projections of ecological trends will facilitate the analysis of how changes in natural systems affect economic trends. Trend projections would also help define the thrust and scale of a successful reversal strategy. Such projections can help national political leaders inform themselves, and they can provide the information to help people understand the need for, and accept, dramatic new initiatives.

If the economic decline affecting Africa is to be reversed, each country will need an environmentally based development strategy. The World Bank, given its research capacity and its experience in formulating policies and establishing priorities, is best equipped to assist individual countries in outlining a national development strategy to reverse the broad-based ecological deterioration and set the stage for the resumption of growth in per capita food production and income. If events confirm that land use changes and soil degradation are altering the hydrological cycle and reducing rainfall, a continental strategy will be needed to reverse the drying out of Africa's land. Given the scale of climatic processes, only a coordinated, continent-wide reversal strategy will have much prospect of success.

Once national strategies are outlined, and goals and timetables are established for such things as planting trees and lowering birth rates, it would be up to each national government to mobilize its own people and integrate assistance from abroad into the national strategy. Outside assistance can come from international development agencies such as the World Bank, the International Fund for Agricultural Development, and the African Development Bank; from the spe-

cialized organizations of the United Nations system, such as the U.N. Fund for Population Activities and FAO; from the bilateral aid agencies of the major industrial countries; from private development groups, such as CARE and Church World Service; from private foundations; and from numerous other sources. Without clearly defined national strategies, neither indigenous resources nor those coming from the outside will be efficiently used.

If the economic decline affecting Africa is to be reversed, each country will need an environmentally based development strategy.

To mobilize people to reverse Africa's decline, the World Bank might consider organizing an international youth assistance corps, modeled after the Peace Corps, whose staffing and recruitment would be designed to fill the specific gaps in skills that emerge as national efforts to reverse recent trends get under way. Getting people involved at the local level is more akin to the Peace Corps model than the large-scale, project-oriented approach that has dominated aid to developing countries. This latter approach, most compatible with the industrial world's strengths in administration and management, is a legacy of the colonial era that has proved sadly mismatched to Africa's needs. As *New York Times* columnist Flora Lewis observed: "A way has to be found to reintroduce Western capacity for organization, without old forms of domination, if the cycle of degeneration is to be reversed."[53]

Many of the lessons most relevant to Africa's crisis have been learned not in the industrial world but elsewhere in the Third World. South Korean and Chinese successes in national reforestation, Indian and Nepalese experiences with village woodlots, and community-based family planning programs in Thailand and Indonesia, where population growth has been halved within a decade, suggest potential partnerships that African leaders might pursue.

Africa faces difficult choices. Success in saving the continent hinges on whether political institutions are strong enough to make the course corrections needed to reverse the decline without coming apart. The economic conse- quences of continuing ecological decay are clear. The social costs—the human suffering and loss of life—could eventu- ally approach those of World War II.

The greatest risk is that there will be a loss of hope. However bleak the deteri- orating situation may appear, it is of human origin and can yield to human remedy. How African leaders and the in- ternational community respond to the challenge will reveal much about the human prospect over the remainder of this century and the beginning of the next one.

11

Redefining National Security

Lester R. Brown

Throughout most of the postwar period, an expanding economy permitted the world to have both more guns and more butter. For many countries, however, this age has come to an end. As pressures on natural systems and resources build, as the sustainable yield thresholds of local biological support systems are breached, and as oil reserves are depleted, governments can no longer both boost expenditures on armaments and deal effectively with the forces that are undermining their economies.

The choices are between continued militarization of the economy and restoration of its environmental support systems. Between continued militarization and attempts to halt growth of the U.S. debt. Between continued militarization and new initiatives to deal with the dark cloud of Third World debt that hangs over the world's economic future. The world does not have the financial resources and leadership time and attention to militarize and to deal with these new threats to security.

"National security" has become a commonplace expression, a concept regularly appealed to. It is used to justify the maintenance of armies, the development of new weapon systems, and the manufacture of armaments. A fourth of all the federal taxes in the United States and at least an equivalent amount in the Soviet Union are levied in its name.

Since World War II, the concept of national security has acquired an overwhelmingly military character, rooted in the assumption that the principal threat to security comes from other nations. Commonly veiled in secrecy, considerations of military threats have become so dominant that new threats to the security of nations, threats with which military forces cannot cope, are being ignored.

The new sources of danger arise from oil depletion, soil erosion, land degradation, shrinking forests, deteriorating grasslands, and climate alteration. These developments, affecting the natural resources and systems on which the economy depends, threaten not only national economic and political security, but the stability of the international economy itself.

MILITARIZATION OF THE WORLD ECONOMY

The notion that countries everywhere should be prepared to defend themselves at all times from any conceivable external threat is a relatively modern one. Prior to World War II, countries mobilized troops in times of war instead of relying on a large permanent military establishment. Since then, the military burden on the world economy has grown enormously. Global military expenditures in 1985 of $940 billion exceeded the income of the poorest half of humanity. Stated otherwise, they surpassed the combined gross national products of China, India, and African countries south of the Sahara.[1]

Militarization can be measured nationally as the share of gross national product (GNP) devoted to the production of military goods and services, or as the military share of the federal budget. Globally, it can be judged by the military share of global product and the arms share of international trade. For international comparisons, the share of GNP used for military purposes is the best yardstick, since it can be applied to countries with widely differing economic systems. Militarization can also be gauged in terms of employment—the number of people serving in the armed forces, employed in weapons production, or involved in weapons research.

By all measures, the world economy has a decidedly more military cast today than it did a generation ago. Using 1984 dollars as the yardstick, world military expenditures totaled roughly $400 billion in 1960, some 4.7 percent of eco-

nomic output. (See Figure 11-1.) Expanding faster than the world economy since 1960, the growth in military spending has raised the military share of world economic activity to over 6 percent in 1985. During this quarter-century span, global military expenditures have increased every year, regardless of economic downturns, or of arms control treaties between the two superpowers.[2]

The principal force driving global militarization is the ideological conflict between the Soviet Union, with its socialist allies, and the United States, in alliance with the industrial democracies. In addition, alignment of the Third World states with the two military superpowers has made militarization a global phenomenon, independent of the level of economic development. The continued striving for an advantage has led to enormous growth in military expenditures in both camps. While the United States devoted some 7 percent of its GNP to defense in 1985, the Soviet Union, trying to maintain a competitive military establishment with a much smaller economy, allocated 14 percent.[3]

Although the military efforts of the

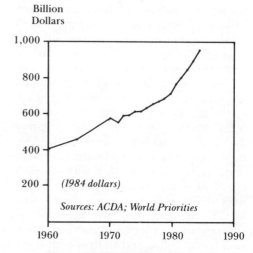

Figure 11-1. World Military Expenditures, 1960-85

United States and the Soviet Union are aimed primarily at each other, the two countries have managed to avoid direct conflict. Not risking the engagement of each other's mutually destructive military capacity, the superpowers have waged their ideological conflict through proxies, including Korea, Vietnam, Afghanistan, and countries in East Africa and Central America. These campaigns have fueled Third World militarization, distorting priorities and postponing development. Mahbub ul Haq, chairman of Pakistan's planning commission, has observed, "Developing countries can't afford the burden imposed on us by the tense geopolitical situation."[4]

Another source of militarization has been the influx of oil wealth into the politically volatile Middle East. Traditional tensions between Arabs and Israelis have generated heavy armaments expenditures by Israel, Egypt, and Syria. More recently, conflicts among various Muslim sects have been a source of stress. Indeed, Muslim factionalism is a major factor in the costly conflict between Iraq and Iran that has already claimed several hundred thousand lives. Sadly, much of the region's windfall gains in oil income are being invested in militarization and in destruction of the region's petroleum infrastructure rather than in restoration of the region's degraded environmental support systems or in economic modernization.

Ideological conflicts worldwide, religious differences in the Middle East, and aggressive arms exporting have contributed to a rate of growth in Third World military expenditures that far exceeds that in the industrial world. Between 1960 and 1981, these outlays grew by some 7 percent per year, compared with 3.7 percent in the industrial world. In 1960, Third World military activities accounted for less than one tenth of the global total; in 1981, they were more than one fifth of a far larger total.[5]

The share of national product devoted to military purposes varies widely among countries. In the industrial world, the Soviet Union and the United States lead the list; their key allies in the Warsaw Pact and NATO, respectively, are not far behind. (See Table 11–1.) Japan, benefiting from U.S. defense of the region and a constitutional limit on its militarization, is spending just under 1 percent of its GNP for military purposes.

Global military expenditures in 1985 of $940 billion exceeded the income of the poorest half of humanity.

Within the Third World, military sectors are largest in the tension-ridden Middle East. Syria, Jordan, Saudi Arabia, and Israel spend between 13 and 29 percent of their economic resources to maintain large military establishments. Most disturbing, militarization is spreading rapidly in Africa, the region that can least afford it. The continent as a whole now spends $16 billion per year in this sector. In Latin America, military expenditures in Brazil and Mexico, the two most populous countries, are surprisingly low—averaging less than 1 percent of GNP. Central America, however, departs from the Latin norm, with El Salvador spending 4 percent and Nicaragua more than 10 percent of GNP for military purposes.[6]

Over the past quarter-century, the international commerce in arms has soared, largely because of the militarization of Third World economies that lack their own arms manufacturing capacity. Expenditures on arms imports have eclipsed those on other goods, including grain. For example, although world grain trade expanded at nearly 12 percent per year from 1970 to 1984, it was

Table 11-1. Military Expenditures as Share of GNP for Selected Countries, 1984

Country	Share
	(percent)
Industrial Countries	
Japan	1.0
Canada	2.1
West Germany	3.3
United Kingdom	5.4
United States	6.9
Soviet Union	14.0
Middle East	
Egypt	8.3
Syria	13.0
Jordan	14.9
Saudi Arabia	24.0
Israel	29.0
Asia	
Sri Lanka	1.5
India	3.5
Pakistan	5.4
China	8.0
Africa	
Nigeria	2.5
South Africa	4.3
Ethiopia	11.0
Libya	17.5
Latin America	
Mexico	0.6
Brazil	0.7
Venezuela	1.3
El Salvador	4.0
Chile	4.5
Nicaragua	10.2

SOURCES: U.S. Arms Control and Disarmament Agency, *World Military Expenditures and Arms Transfers, 1985* (Washington, D.C.: 1985); Stockholm International Peace Research Institute Yearbook, *World Armaments and Disarmament* (London: Taylor and Francis, 1985).

overtaken during the eighties by arms dealings, which grew at over 13 percent annually during the same period. As of 1984, world arms imports totaled $35 billion per year, compared with $33 billion worth of grain, putting guns ahead of bread in world commerce.[7] (See Figure 11–2.)

The United States and the Soviet Union dominate arms exports, together accounting for 53 percent of the world total in recent years. In 1984, U.S. arms exports totaled $7.7 billion, under 4 percent of the nation's total. Soviet arms exports of $9.4 billion accounted for nearly 12 percent of their exports, and earned enough foreign exchange to pay their grain import bill of $6 billion. The other ranking world exporters are U.S. allies France, the United Kingdom, West Germany, and Italy, which rank third through sixth as world arms suppliers.[8]

Arms imports are much more widely dispersed among countries, though the Middle East accounts for over half the total. During the early eighties, 7 of the 10 leading Third World arms importers were in this region—Egypt, Syria, Iraq, Libya, Jordan, Saudi Arabia, and Israel. India, in fourth place, was the only country outside the region in the top 5.[9]

In addition to its economic role, mili-

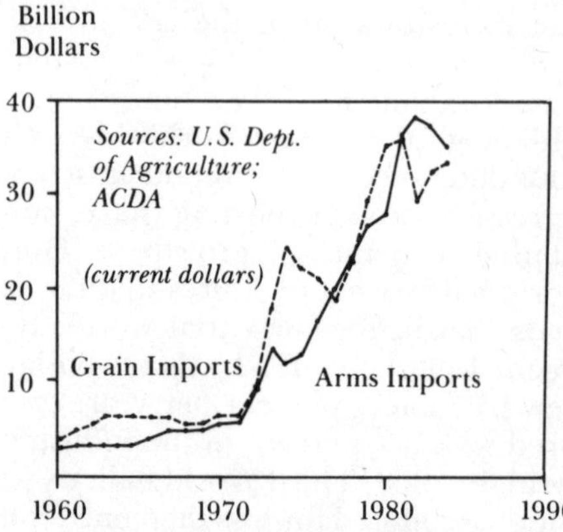

Figure 11-2. Grain Imports and Arms Imports Worldwide, 1960-84

tarization has important political dimensions. As the military establishments gain strength in Third World countries, they often assume power by force. In some instances, military coups d'état are justified by the need to rescue a country from corruption or from economic deterioration as a result of inept leadership. More often, they reflect the ambition of military leaders who are ill equipped to lead, but who have acquired the weapons and the command of troops that allow them to assume leadership positions by force.

When governments are taken over by the military, they often shift priorities toward further militarization of the economy. During the decade since the military coup that overthrew Haile Selassie, for example, Ethiopia has assembled the largest army in sub-Saharan Africa, and now spends 42 percent of its budget for military purposes.[10]

In many Third World countries, internal security forces are flourishing even as economic conditions deteriorate. Ironically, soldiers often use their weapons to become a self-appointed ruling group, terrorizing the people they are theoretically there to protect. Military forces in Africa, used only rarely to defend against attacks by outsiders, are deployed mostly against people within their own borders. *New York Times* reporter Clifford May writes of a new warrior caste that has evolved into a ruling class. Generously supported by the government, soldiers "are issued guns and bullets while farmers lack hoes and seeds." May also notes the technological incongruity of MIG fighter planes soaring above fields plowed by oxen.[11]

Nowhere are the distorting efforts of militarization more evident than in its claims on the world's scientific personnel. Each year the world spends several times as much on research to increase the destructiveness of weapons as on attempts to raise the productivity of agri-

culture. Indeed, expenditures on weapons research, in which a half-million scientists are now employed, exceed the combined spending on developing new energy technologies, improving human health, raising agricultural productivity, and controlling pollution.[12]

Each year the world spends several times as much on research to increase the destructiveness of weapons as on attempts to raise the productivity of agriculture.

The military's dominance of the world's scientific research effort will certainly grow if the U.S. government proceeds with its proposed Strategic Defense Initiative. The largest research project ever launched, the so-called Star Wars project will further divert resources from humanity's most pressing needs. The effect of such distortions was noted by Colin Norman in a 1979 Worldwatch Paper: "The United States has the ability to survey virtually every square meter of the Soviet Union, yet the world's scientists have barely begun to survey the complex ecosystems of fast-disappearing tropical rain forests or the malignant spread of the world's deserts."[13]

Costs to the Two Superpowers

As noted in Chapter 1, the cost of the arms race to the superpowers goes beyond any mere fiscal reckoning. It is draining their treasuries, weakening their economies, and lowering their position in the international economic hierarchy. This long, drawn-out conflict is contributing to a realignment of the leading industrial countries, with Japan assuming a dominant position in the world economy. One of the keys to Japan's emergence as an economic superpower is its negligible level of military expenditures—less than 1 percent of GNP.

The doubling of the U.S. national debt, from $914 billion in 1980 to $1,841 billion in 1985, is due more to the growth in military expenditures than to any other factor. Between 1980 and 1985, U.S. military expenditures climbed from $134 billion to $244 billion (in current dollars). This increase of roughly $110 billion dwarfs growth in all other major economic sectors, including health, which increased $11 billion, and agriculture, which rose $15 billion. While debt was more than doubling between 1980 and 1985, interest payments on the total due, reflecting higher real interest rates, were climbing even more, reaching an estimated $143 billion in 1986.[14] (See Figure 11–3.)

The growing federal debt is mortgaging the U.S. economic future and, consequently, the nation's position in the world economy. Among other things, it

Figure 11-3. Net Interest Paid on U.S. Federal Debt, 1960-86

is leading to record-high real interest rates (the rate of interest after subtracting for inflation) and an overvalued dollar that makes U.S. exports more costly, in turn weakening the country's competitive position.

Industry in the United States has been doubly handicapped by these soaring military expenditures. Averaging over $200 billion per year since 1981, U.S. military expenditures have totaled $1,000 billion during the first half of the eighties, siphoning capital away from investment in industrial plant and equipment and leaving the nation with outdated, inefficient industrial facilities. Even when American corporations have capital to invest, they are reluctant to commit it at home, given their inability to compete in either overseas or domestic markets. One result is declining output in basic industries, such as steel, automobiles, and machine tools. Between 1981 and 1984, a period of moderate economic expansion in the United States and worldwide, 2 million Americans lost jobs in these basic industries.[15]

The overvalued dollar and the lack of investment in new industrial capacity have dramatically altered the U.S. position in world trade. As recently as 1975, the United States had a small trade surplus. In 1980, it registered a trade deficit of $36 billion. (See Table 11–2.) Though large by international standards, this position posed few problems at that time, given the income from heavy U.S. foreign investments and loans, which offset the net trade outflow.

The balance was upset, however, as the trade deficit climbed to $70 billion in 1983, and to a staggering $150 billion in 1985. This ballooning U.S. trade deficit and the associated borrowing abroad to finance the federal debt have cost the country its position as the world's leading international investor. Almost overnight, the United States has become a debtor nation. This is a worrisome shift

Table 11-2. U.S. Balance of Trade, 1950–84 (current dollars)

Year	Exports	Imports	Balance of Trade
	(billion dollars)		
1950	10	10	0
1955	16	13	+ 3
1960	21	16	+ 5
1965	27	23	+ 4
1970	43	43	0
1975	108	106	+ 2
1980	221	257	− 36
1981	234	273	− 39
1982	212	255	− 43
1983	200	270	− 70
1984	218	341	−123
1985	217	367	−150

SOURCES: International Monetary Fund, *International Financial Statistics Yearbook—1984* and Monthly Supplement (Washington, D.C.: 1984 and July 1985); Worldwatch Institute.

for the United States, as its international leadership role since World War II has derived in large part from its economic strength and prestige. The military expenditures that are weakening the United States economically are diminishing both its stature within the international community and its capacity to lead.

The Soviet Union, too, is paying a heavy price for its role in the arms race, retaining second-class economic status despite its wealth of natural resources. Military spending channels roughly one seventh of the nation's resources to nonproductive uses. It also diverts leadership attention from the economic reforms required if the Soviet economy is to remain a world economic power.

From the early fifties through the late seventies, the Soviet economy grew at roughly 5 percent per year, a rate of expansion that brought progress on many fronts. Heavy forced savings and a large, poorly used reservoir of rural labor to draw upon for industrialization spurred growth. Today, the high enforced savings continue, but little additional labor can be shifted from the struggling farm sector into industry.[16]

Soviet industrial growth has slowed to a crawl. In agriculture, less grain is being produced now than in the late seventies. Production of livestock is expanding, but only with record feedgrain imports. Oil extraction peaked in 1983 and has fallen in each of the two years since. With the output of wheat and oil—the two principal commodities in the Soviet economy—either stagnating or declining, the economic prospect is less than bright. Falling production of oil, the source of over half the country's hard currency, will restrict the imports of essential products.[17]

Land degradation is also weakening the economy. Extensive soil erosion, one source of declining land productivity, has long been a concern of Mikhail Gorbachev, predating his rise to leadership. But despite the concern of Gorbachev, other members of the Politburo, and Soviet soil scientists, little progress has been made in arresting this drain on Soviet agricultural productivity.[18]

Growing water scarcity throughout the south central and southwestern parts of the country is another emerging constraint on Soviet economic activity, particularly agriculture. Water is among the factors limiting crop production in these regions, yet the Soviets have made only minimal investments in water efficiency.[19]

Similarly, the efficiency of energy and other resource use in the Soviet Union is among the lowest in the world. In contrast to the western industrial societies and China, which have reduced the oil intensity of their economies by roughly a fifth since the 1973 oil price boost, the Soviets have made little or no progress.[20]

One reason for the Soviet's inefficient use of resources is the lack of broad-based technological innovation. In key industries, such as oil extraction and the manufacture of motor vehicles and computers, the Soviet Union depends heavily on imported Western technology. Future gains in economic efficiency depend on the use of computers, but in this modernizing activity, the Soviets lag far behind, trailing even Third World countries such as Brazil and South Korea. In addition to production shortfalls, the shoddiness of Soviet consumer goods and farm equipment make it virtually impossible for them to compete on the world market.

Ironically, the one sector in which the Soviet economy is competitive in world markets is weapons manufacture. By focusing on arms production to the exclusion of other sectors, the Soviet Union is able to maintain military production schedules and quality standards, but only by circumventing conventional management control mechanisms. To make sure that weapons manufacture proceeds on schedule, this sector can use its special status to reorder priorities in its favor and to commandeer industrial facilities or transport capacity. To maintain quality standards, for example, it can requisition the highest quality steels. Unfortunately, exercising this privileged status can disrupt the rest of the economy.[21]

The one sector in which the Soviet economy is competitive in world markets is weapons manufacture.

A centrally planned, state-controlled economy, such as that of the Soviet Union, can work reasonably well in the early stages of industrial development, when the emphasis is on the production of coal, steel, and hydroelectric power, and when agriculture is a traditional, largely self-contained sector. But the closer such an economy tries to move toward a modern, diversified, consumer-oriented, industrial society, the less well it works. Some economic analysts now believe that, lacking basic reform, specifically a shift to a more market-oriented system, the Soviet economy will do well to expand at 2 percent annually in the years ahead.[22]

Soviet economists and planners regularly acknowledge the need for change, but Soviet leaders have not been able to translate this into reform, because they have been either too weak or simply unable to devote the time and attention that an exhaustive economic reform would require. Unless the Soviet Union decentralizes its cumbersome, state-controlled economy, it will fall even further behind.[23]

While the United States and the Soviet Union have been preoccupied with each other militarily, Japan has been moving to the fore economically. By some economic indicators, it now leads both military superpowers. In a world where the enormous investment in nuclear arsenals has no practical use, the terms denoting leadership and dominance are shifting in Japan's favor.

For many years, the Soviet Union has enjoyed its status as the world's second-largest economy, the base from which it challenged the United States position of world leader. Japan's per capita income, which surpassed that of the Soviet Union during the sixties, is now close to double the Soviet's. (See Figure 11–4.) If recent economic trends continue, Japan will overtake the Soviet Union in total economic output before the century ends, reducing it to third place. The combination of negligible defense expenditures

Thousand
Dollars

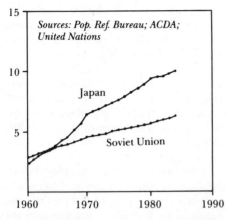

Sources: Pop. Ref. Bureau; ACDA; United Nations

Japan

Soviet Union

Figure 11-4. Per Capita GNP, Japan and the Soviet Union, 1960-84

Table 11-3. Annual Exports, the United States and Japan, 1950–85, With Projections to 1990 (current dollars)

Year	United States	Japan	Ratio
	(billion dollars)		(U.S./Japan)
1950	10	1	10.0
1955	15	2	7.5
1960	21	4	5.2
1965	27	8	3.4
1970	43	19	2.3
1975	108	59	1.8
1980	221	130	1.7
1985	217	174	1.2
1990	217	233	0.9

SOURCES: Historical data from International Monetary Fund, *International Financial Statistics Yearbook—1984* (Washington, D.C.: 1984); projections by Worldwatch Institute.

and high domestic savings have enabled the Japanese to invest heavily in modernizing plant and equipment. This in turn enhances the nation's competitive position, enabling it to run a large foreign trade surplus, even though it imports virtually all its oil and most of its raw materials.[24]

As it narrows the output gap with the Soviet Union, Japan is challenging U.S. dominance of world trade. In 1950, exports from the United States exceeded those from Japan by more than 10 to 1. (See Table 11–3.) Over the years, this gap slowly narrowed, until by 1970 it was little more than 2 to 1. As recently as 1980, it was still near this level, but the U.S. advantage is disappearing during the eighties. By 1985, U.S. exports were only 20 percent greater than those of Japan.

During the eighties, the United States has exported some $217 billion worth of goods per year. If current conditions prevail, exports will remain at this level. Meanwhile, if Japan's exports continue to expand at 6 percent yearly, as they have from 1980 to 1985, they will surpass those of the United States in 1988,

removing that country from the leadership position it has long held.

In concert with the ballooning American trade deficit during the eighties, U.S. net foreign assets have fallen sharply, disappearing within three years. (See Figure 11–5.) By the end of 1985, the United States had become a debtor country. Meanwhile, Japan, with its highly competitive economy and heavily protected domestic market, is moving vigorously to the fore, generating ever greater trade surpluses.[25]

The combination of the surpluses, high domestic savings, and a near negligible level of military expenditures in Japan has generated enormous internal cash surpluses. These, too, are flowing abroad to areas with higher rates of return—including, importantly, U.S. Trea-

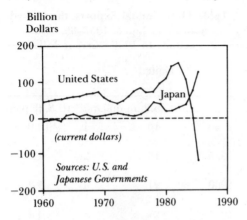

Figure 11-5. Net Foreign Assets, the United States and Japan, 1960-85

sury bonds. In effect, the Japanese are now helping finance the U.S. national fiscal deficit, and collecting hefty interest payments for doing so.

The U.S. economy is still twice as large as Japan's, and the country has a vastly superior indigenous resource base of land, energy fuels, minerals, and forest products. Nonetheless, the United States is in the process of abdicating its role of world leadership. A country that is a net debtor, borrowing heavily from the rest of the world, cannot effectively exercise economic or political leadership.

NEW THREATS TO SECURITY

The extensive deterioration of natural support systems and the declining economic conditions evident in much of the Third World pose threats to national and international security that now rival the traditional military ones. Ecological stresses and resource scarcities eventually translate into economic stresses with social and political dimensions: falling land productivity, falling per capita income, or rising external debt, to cite a few.[26]

The first resource scarcity that dramatically affected the global economy was that of oil. The 1973 price hike sent shock waves throughout the world, the reverberations of which are still being felt more than a decade later. These and other consequences of oil reserve depletion have dominated headlines over the past dozen years, but the depletion of forests, grasslands, and topsoil and the alteration of the hydrological cycle are of greater consequence over the long term.

Unfortunately for economic planners and policymakers, there has been little systematic gathering of data on the condition of these basic resources and support systems. The ecological deterioration outlined in Chapters 2, 3, and 4 indicates the extent to which national economies are adversely affected, particularly in the Third World. The dramatic rise in external debt in recent years is perhaps the most visible manifestation of this ecological and economic deterioration, and the most worrisome new threat to security.

Governments faced with rising external debt appear to pass through certain stages in what is becoming a recognizable syndrome. The initial response of countries experiencing difficulty making payments is to convert short-term debt into long-term debt. This works for some countries for a while, but eventually many find that they can no longer make both principal and interest payments. Mexico, for example, is now in such a situation. Some governments are even capitalizing the interest, converting it into additional principal and thus increasing their debt.[27]

There is a remarkable parallel between countries crossing the sustainable yield threshold of their biological support systems and those crossing the sustainable debt threshold. Once the demand on a biological system exceeds its sustainable yield, further growth in demand is satisfied by consuming the basic resource stock. In such a situation, the deterioration begins to feed on itself.

So it is with external debt: As it grows faster than the economy, eventually a point is reached where servicing the debt, even if limited to interest payments, becomes such a drain on the economy that output is actually reduced, as has occurred, for instance, in Brazil and Mexico. When governments can no longer pay all the interest, then the debt begins to expand, and the growth feeds on itself. Once countries cross these sustainable yield or debt-servicing thresholds, it is difficult for them to reverse the process.

In many Third World countries, the past three years have been a time of enforced austerity and sacrifice. Imports of consumer goods, including food, have been reduced; food subsidies have been eliminated; unemployment has risen. Belt-tightening has allowed Third World countries to maintain access to international credit and it has kept the lending banks solvent, but, because it has led to even greater debt, this approach has diminished the prospect of restoring a sustained improvement in living standards.

By the end of 1985, many Third World countries were delinquent in their debt payments. (See Table 11–4.) Bolivia, for example, described in a U.S. government report as "in economic and political chaos," did not make any payments during 1985. Morocco's external debt is now approaching the size of its annual GNP, making it extremely difficult, if not impossible, to service.

Sudan, on the brink of famine in 1985, illustrates the complex relationship be-

Table 11-4. Selected Countries Delinquent in Servicing External Debt, 1985

Country	External Debt	Financial Situation
	(billion dollars)	
Bolivia	5	Debt service payments remain unpaid over the past year; country is in "economic and political chaos." (USDA)
Guyana	2	"Not likely to continue making its payments." (*Economist*)
Liberia	1	"Could soon be an embarrassment to the IMF." (*Economist*)
Mauritania	2	Debt is "insupportable." (USDA)
Morocco	13	"Financial situation is precarious; total external debt is approaching value of GNP." (USDA)
Nicaragua	5	Could not meet its debt service obligations in 1984; appears that renegotiation of debt will be necessary in 1985.
Peru	14	Refused negotiation with IMF for restructuring debt; debt servicing limited to 10 percent of exports.
Philippines	26	Moratorium on principal payments in effect since late 1983; government denied additional funding by IMF "until it brings itself back in line."
Sudan	9	Far in arrears in debt repayment; IMF and major creditors have halted financial assistance.
Vietnam	7	Has fallen far behind with interest and capital payments; declared ineligible for further loans by IMF.

SOURCES: External debt information for all but Sudan from Morgan Guaranty Trust Company, *World Financial Markets,* New York, September/October 1985, and private communication, and from U.S. Department of Treasury, Washington, D.C., private communication; Sudan's external debt and all quotes attributed to USDA from U.S. Department of Agriculture, Economic Research Service, *World Food Needs and Availabilities* (Washington, D.C.: U.S. Government Printing Office, 1985).

tween ecological deterioration, declining per capita food production, and soaring external debt. As 1 of the 14 countries in which farmland productivity is lower today than it was a generation ago, mainly agrarian Sudan will obviously find it difficult to honor its external financial obligations, however well intentioned its leaders may be.[28]

Peru, also facing a deteriorating domestic resource base, including the collapse of its anchovy fishery a decade ago and a heavy continuing loss of topsoil, has imposed a cap on debt servicing, limiting payments to 10 percent of export earnings. In effect, this is a way of getting the private banks holding the loans to begin writing them off, thus forcing them to participate in the adjustment process. This action means Peru will probably not pay more than half the interest due, making it the largest debtor to refuse to pay all the interest on its debt.[29]

More important, however, major debtor countries such as Mexico and Brazil are beginning to realize that the austerity and associated economic shrinkage that they agreed to in exchange for rescheduled loans are worsening economic and social conditions. Indeed, they are concerned that the belt-tightening may eventually lead to political unrest, thus interfering with the very process of economic expansion required to service and repay the debt. Increasingly, debtor countries talk about lenders as well as borrowers needing to make adjustments.

With this in mind, the United States proposed a modest increase in World Bank lending at the annual Bank/Fund meeting in Seoul, South Korea, in October of 1985. Although intended to be responsive to Third World concerns, this gesture was not large enough to be meaningful. It did, however, open a dialogue on what the lending countries might do to help resolve the debt crisis.[30]

The Third World debt threat is not a trivial issue. Not only are hundreds of billions of dollars at risk, but the political stability of governments—indeed, the future of democracy in some societies—hangs in the balance. Recognizing these broad implications of Third World external debt, Peru's new President, Alan García Pérez, has observed, "We are faced with a dramatic choice: it is either debt or democracy." Similar concerns are voiced in Brazil and Argentina, countries that have recently returned to democratic administrations after years of military rule.[31]

Assessments of Third World debt repayment prospects are grim, but they would be even grimmer if financial analysts understood what is happening to the environmental support systems underpinning most Third World economies. It is not a matter of an occasional country here or there experiencing deforestation, soil erosion, or land degradation. The great majority of Third World countries have crossed the sustainable yield thresholds of their basic biological support systems.

Finally, a bank's existence rests on the confidence of people whose money has been entrusted to it. If this trust erodes, the bank cannot survive. The 1984 collapse of Continental Illinois National Bank and Trust, the seventh largest U.S. bank, and runs on savings and loans institutions in the states of Ohio and Maryland are indicative of what could happen at the national and international levels.[32]

Within the United States, the soaring federal debt is eroding trust in the country's economic future. The farm debt is very much in the news and very much on the minds of Washington political leaders. The Farm Credit System, which holds $74 billion—one third—of farm debt, reports that some $11 billion is uncollectible. If a federal rescue effort is needed, as seems likely, it would dwarf the 1984 bailout of Continental Illinois

Bank, which required an infusion of $4.5 billion.[33]

In these circumstances, inaction poses serious risks. As the stresses on the system build, eventually they will become excessive, and something will start to give. Prudence suggests that action be taken sooner rather than later. Once a large-scale erosion of confidence begins, it may be difficult to contain. To quote Fred Bergsten, President of the Institute for International Economics, "The fire brigade may not have enough water to douse this one, once it ignites."[34]

COUNTRIES REDUCING ARMS OUTLAYS

A few governments have begun to redefine national security, putting more emphasis on economic progress and less on buying arms. At a time when global military expenditures are rising, some countries are actually cutting military outlays. A handful are reducing them sharply, not only as a share of GNP, but in absolute terms as well. Among these are China, Argentina, and Peru.

As recently as 1972, China was spending 14 percent of its GNP for military purposes, one of the highest levels in the world at the time. Beginning in 1975, however, China began to systematically reduce its military expenditures, and, except for 1979, it has reduced them in each of the last eight years. By 1985, military spending had fallen to 7.5 percent of its gross national product. (See Table 11–5.)

Indications are that this trend may continue throughout the eighties. In July 1985, Beijing announced a plan to invest $360 million over two years to retrain 1 million soldiers for return to civilian life. Such a move would cut the armed forces in China from 4.2 million in 1985 to 3.2

Table 11-5. China: Military Expenditures as Share of GNP, 1967–85

Year	Share
	(percent)
1967	13.8
1968	13.8
1969	14.9
1970	13.5
1971	17.4
1972	14.3
1973	13.2
1974	13.5
1975	13.1
1976	12.7
1977	12.3
1978	11.4
1979	12.6
1980	10.4
1981	9.9
1982	9.3
1983	8.6
1984	8.0
1985	7.5

SOURCES: U.S. Arms Control and Disarmament Agency, *World Military Expenditures and Arms Transfers, 1985* (Washington, D.C.: 1985); Chinese Embassy, Washington, D.C., private communication.

million in 1987, a drop of 24 percent. And worldwide, it would reduce the number of men and women under arms by some 4 percent.[35]

In Argentina, the military government that was in office in the late seventies and early eighties increased military expenditures from the historical level of 1.5 percent of GNP to almost 4 percent. One of the first things that Raúl Alfonsín did as newly elected President in late 1983 was to announce a plan to steadily lower this figure. When he took office, there was broad public support for a reduction in arms expenditures, partly because of the ill-fated Falklands War, which undermined the military's credibility throughout Argentina. By 1984, arms outlays had been cut to half the peak level of 1980, earning Alfonsín a well-deserved reputation for reordering priorities, and shifting resources to social programs.[36] (See Figure 11–6.)

More recently, Peru has joined the ranks of those announcing plans to cut military expenditures. One of the first actions of President García on taking office in the summer of 1985 was a call to halt the regional arms race. García is convinced of the need to reduce the 5 percent of Peru's GNP allotted to the military, a sum that consumed one fourth of the federal budget. As an indication of his sincerity, the President announced that he was canceling half of the order for 26 French Mirage fighter planes.[37]

The overriding reason for cutting military expenditures in each of these three countries is economic. In effect, the three political leaders are defining security in much more economic terms. For the Chinese, the military sector was one place harboring the additional resources needed to achieve the desired gains in living standards. Once the goal of rapidly improving living standards was adopted, the reduction of resources devoted to the military was inevitable.

In Argentina, the economic incentive

was burgeoning public debt, inflation, and a huge external debt that threatened to become unmanageable. One source of Argentina's external debt was the taste for modern arms exhibited by Alfonsín's predecessors. In Peru, the challenge was to arrest the decline in living standards. At the time García took office, payments on the international debt were $475 million in arrears, and the government was threatened with a complete cutoff of all new sources of investment capital. García found that internal economic decline was leading to social deterioration and political violence.[38]

García is convinced of the need to reduce the 5 percent of Peru's GNP allotted to the military.

Encouragingly, the reductions in military expenditures undertaken by these three governments were independent of any negotiated reductions in neighboring countries. China lowered its military outlays unilaterally, despite its 3,000-kilometer border with the Soviet Union, which has continued to increase its military might.

Over the next few years, as governments everywhere face difficulties in maintaining or improving living standards, others may also choose to reduce military expenditures. Quite apart from the positive momentum of the international peace movement in recent years, worsening economic conditions may become the key motivation for reversing the militarization of the past generation.

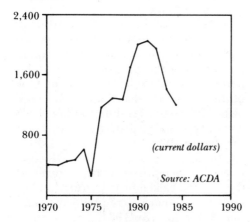

Million
Dollars

(current dollars)

Source: ACDA

Figure 11-6. Military Expenditures in Argentina, 1970-84

THE CHALLENGE

For many Third World countries, the threats to well-being and survival come not from other countries, but from each step that pushes them past the sustainable yield thresholds of their biological systems and the debt-servicing threshold of their economies. The estimated million lives lost to famine in Africa in 1984 and 1985 exceeds that in any conflict since World War II. How many more lives will eventually be lost? No one knows, but the number of people at risk is growing as the disintegration of their life-support systems accelerates.[39]

Reversing these trends requires a shift in development strategy, particularly where economic demands already exceed the sustainable yield of forests, grasslands, and soils. In these circumstances, continuing to rely primarily on narrow economic criteria—such as the time-honored rate of return on project investments—to shape development strategies can lead biological and economic systems to collapse. The only viable development strategy for many Third World countries is one that rests on environmental criteria, one that concentrates on restoring the economy's environmental support systems. Any other is destined to fail.

For national governments and international development agencies, the time has come to rethink development. Policies that once led to a sustained 5 percent global economic growth are no longer doing so. The rising economic tide that once pulled living standards up throughout the world is beginning to recede in many Third World countries. As discussed in Chapter 2, understanding why this is so requires projections of both environmental and economic trends, and, more importantly, of their continuous and complex interaction. For example, food production forecasts are meaningful only if they allow for the effect of soil erosion on land productivity. The only agricultural projections that provide a solid base for policy are those that incorporate agronomic, eco-

logical, and hydrological data as well as the more conventional economic and demographic information.

Once made, these projections could provide the rationale for launching massive tree-planting efforts, accelerating family planning programs, and making many of the other interventions so urgently needed. They are also the key to generating the support of the international community. Without some understanding of the consequences of continuing on the current path, governments will be reluctant to intervene to reverse ecological deterioration and associated economic decline. Unfortunately, the countries that are most affected by environmental deterioration are those least able to undertake these projections, suggesting an important new role for the World Bank and other development assistance groups.

The principal obstacle to Third World progress, one caused in part by ecological degradation, is mounting external debt. International financial institutions have been reluctant to recognize that scores of developing countries have crossed their debt-servicing thresholds. Private banks fear they will have to write off so many bad loans that it will greatly reduce their earnings and even threaten their solvency. Nonetheless, a substantial share of the Third World's $800 billion external debt will never be repaid.[40]

At the moment, institutions such as the World Bank and the International Monetary Fund lack the lending capacity to restore the growth needed in Third World debtor countries. Private banks are unwilling to increase their lending, with the result that developing countries are unable to obtain the capital needed to sustain progress. The only acceptable resolution is one that leaves part of the interest payments in debtor countries, in order to get their economies moving again.

Many strategies have been proposed to resolve the mounting debt problem.

One, put forward by Professor Robert Wesson of Stanford University's Hoover Institution, seems to satisfy at least the basic criteria for success. It involves setting up an investment trust within the countries with unpayable external debts. Under this system, international lending banks could use an agreed-upon portion of their interest repayments to buy shares in the trust. The trust, in turn, would lend to indigenous enterprises, providing the private sector with sorely needed capital. Such an approach would help restore investor confidence in Third World countries, and it would also give the private banks a long-term stake in these economies. For the lending institutions, the alternative may be to write off otherwise bad loans.[41]

A substantial share of the Third World's $800 billion external debt will never be repaid.

Continuing a "business as usual" approach to the Third World debt problem, with the deterioration in living standards that will result, is a recipe for political unrest, at best—and at worst, for social disintegration. Fortunately, more and more Third World leaders and international lenders are coming to this conclusion.

Understanding the new threats to national security and economic progress will challenge the analytical skills of governments. Sadly, the decision-making apparatus in most governments is not organized to balance threats of a traditional military nature with those of ecological and economic origin. Nonmilitary threats are much less clearly defined. They are the result of cumulative processes that ultimately lead to the collapse of biological systems. These processes are seldom given much thought until they pass a critical threshold, and disaster strikes. Thus it is easier in the government councils of developing countries to justify expenditures for the latest-model jet fighters than for family planning to slow the population growth that is destroying the economy's environmental underpinnings.

The new threats to national security are extraordinarily complex. Ecologists understand that the deterioration in the relationship between ourselves, now numbering nearly 5 billion, and the environmental support systems on which we depend cannot continue. But few political leaders have grasped the significance of this unsustainable situation.

National defense establishments are useless against these new threats. Neither bloated military budgets nor highly sophisticated weapons systems can halt deforestation or arrest the soil erosion now affecting so many Third World countries. Blocking external aggression may be relatively simple compared with stopping the deterioration of life-support systems.

The key to demilitarizing the world economy and shifting resources is a defusing of the arms race between the United States and the Soviet Union. Whether this can be achieved in the foreseeable future remains to be seen. But as the costs of maintaining the arms race multiply, both for the superpowers and for the world at large, the likelihood of reducing tensions may be improving.

In East Asia, traditional adversaries China and Japan appear to be in the process of establishing strong economic ties. In contrast to the United States, China appears to be abandoning military competition with the Soviet Union. With Japan showing little interest in becoming a military power, the stage is being set for peace in the region. Both countries have redefined security and reshaped their geopolitical strategies, accordingly setting aside any ideas of political domination in favor of pursuing mutually beneficial economic goals.

In Western Europe, France and Germany have battled each other periodically over the centuries, but armed conflict between these two countries now appears unlikely. It is difficult to imagine, in an economically integrated Europe, how either of these countries could possibly attack the other. Within North America, the United States, Canada, and Mexico have lived peacefully for generations. No armed forces face each other across national borders in this area. Although conflicts exist here, they center around isolated issues such as acid rain, illegal immigration, and trade restrictions, which do not appear likely to threaten their generally amiable relations.

If ideology gives way to pragmatism, as it is doing in China, then the conflicts and insecurities bred by the ideological distinctions between East and West can soften. Indeed, this ideological softening appears to be coloring China's foreign policy, improving its relations with other countries and contributing to its reduction of military expenditures.

If the Soviet Union adopts the reforms needed to get its economy moving ahead again, a similar ideological softening may result. Turning to the market to allocate resources and boost productivity could not only restructure the Soviet economy, but also reorient Soviet politics. Although pragmatism has typically taken a back seat to ideology in the Soviet Union, the leaders have demonstrated that they can be pragmatic when circumstances require, as when they import grain from the United States, their ideological rival.

For the world as a whole, the past generation has seen an overwhelming movement toward militarization. Apart from the heavy claim on public resources, the East-West conflict contributes to a psychological climate of suspicion and distrust that makes the cooperative, international address of new threats to the security of nations next to impossible. China and Argentina, which have already cut the military's share of their GNP in half, and Peru, which promises to do so, may provide the model for the future. If demilitarization could replace militarization, national governments would be free to reorder their priorities, and could return to paths of sustained progress.

Ironically, for the United States and the Soviet Union, maintaining a position of leadership may now depend on reducing military expenditures to strengthen their faltering economies. Acting thus in their own interests, they could set the stage for demilitarizing the world economy. Once it starts, demilitarization—like militarization—could feed on itself.

Notes

Chapter 1. A Generation of Deficits

1. Job loss estimates from Robert B. Reich, "Reagan's Hidden 'Industrial Policy'," *New York Times*, August 4, 1985, and from tables prepared for the Congressional Joint Economic Committee by Bureau of Labor Statistics, Office of Employment and Unemployment Analysis, United States Department of Labor, Washington, D.C., June 7, 1985.

2. Farm debt from U.S. Department of Agriculture (USDA), Economic Research Service (ERS), *Agricultural Finance: Outlook and Situation Report,* Washington, D.C., December 1984; Charles F. McCoy, "Commercial Agriculture Banks' Woes From Failing Farm Economy Intensify," *Wall Street Journal,* September 5, 1985; farm foreclosures from Ronald L. Meekhof, USDA, ERS, Washington, D.C., private communication, November 14, 1985.

3. Export information from U.S. Arms Control and Disarmament Agency (ACDA), *World Military Expenditures and Arms Transfers 1985* (Washington, D.C.: 1985); per capita income from World Bank, *World Development Report 1985* (New York: Oxford University Press, 1985).

4. Japanese net foreign assets derived from Japan Statistical Bureau, *Japan Statistical Yearbook* (Tokyo: 1965), from Bank of Japan, *Balance of Payments Monthly* (Tokyo: April 1973), from Bank of Japan, *External Assets and Liabilities of Japan* (Tokyo: April 1981), and from Laura Knoy, Institute for International Economics, Washington, D.C., private communication, September 1985; U.S. foreign assets from U.S. Department of Commerce, *Historical Statistics of the United States Volume II* (Washington, D.C.: annual).

5. Export information from International Monetary Fund (IMF), *International Financial Statistics Yearbook 1985* (Washington, D.C.: 1985).

6. "Japanese Diplomats Expand Global Role," *Journal of Commerce,* August 9, 1985.

7. Military share of gross national product in China from ACDA, *World Military Expenditures and Arms Transfers.*

8. U.S. federal debt from U.S. Census Bureau, *Statistical Abstract of the United States 1985* (Washington, D.C.: U.S. Government Printing Office, 1985); figures on total external debt of Third World nations from IMF, *World Economic Outlook* (Washington, D.C.: April 1985).

9. U.S. military expenditures from Census Bureau, *Statistical Abstract;* data for 1950–55 and 1985–86 from Office of Management and Budget (OMB), *The Budget of the United States Government* (Washington, D.C.: U.S. Government Printing Office, various years).

10. U.S. budget deficit and gross federal debt from Census Bureau, *Statistical Abstract;* debt for 1985–86 from *Economic Report of the President* (Washington, D.C.: U.S. Government Printing Office, 1985).

11. Quoted in Karin Lissakers, "Dateline Wall Street: Faustian Finance," *Foreign Affairs,* Summer 1983.

12. Ibid.

13. Morgan Guaranty Trust Company, *World Financial Markets*, New York, September/October 1985.

14. For a further discussion of the Third World debt crisis and international banking, see Lissakers, "Dateline Wall Street"; C. Fred Bergsten, William R. Cline, and John Williamson, *Bank Lending to Developing Countries: The Policy Alternatives* (Cambridge, Mass.: MIT Press, 1985); Morgan Guaranty, *World Financial Markets;* World Bank, *World Development Report*.

15. Morgan Guaranty, *World Financial Markets*.

16. USDA, ERS, *World Indices of Agricultural and Food Production 1950–84* (unpublished printout) (Washington, D.C., 1985); cereal import bill figure from U.N. Economic Commission for Africa, "Report of the Sixth Meeting of the Preparatory Committee of the Whole," Addis Ababa, April 24, 1985.

17. Quoted in Elaine Sciolino, "Chinese Official Asks End to Arms Race in Space," *New York Times*, October 1, 1985.

18. Erik Eckholm, *The Dispossessed of the Earth: Land Reform and Sustainable Development* (Washington, D.C.: Worldwatch Institute, June 1979).

19. See Sandra Postel, "Protecting Forests from Air Pollution and Acid Rain," in Lester R. Brown et al., *State of the World–1985* (New York: W.W. Norton & Co., 1985).

20. See Chapter 4 for a full discussion of rangelands.

21. For a discussion of trends in world fish catch, see Lester R. Brown, "Maintaining World Fisheries," in Brown et al., *State of the World–1985*.

22. For a discussion of worldwide soil loss, see Lester R. Brown, "Conserving Soils," in Lester R. Brown et al., *State of the World–1984* (New York: W.W. Norton & Co., 1984).

23. Oil import statistics from British Petroleum Company, *BP Statistical Review of World Energy* (London: 1985).

24. International Energy Agency, *Energy Policies and Programmes of IEA Countries: 1984 Review* (Paris: Organisation for Economic Co-operation and Development, 1985).

25. For more information on Brazil's alcohol fuels program, see Howard S. Geller, "Ethanol from Sugar Cane in Brazil," in Annual Reviews Inc., *Annual Review of Energy, Vol. 10* (Palo Alto, Calif: 1985); South African coal liquefaction from Emil Parente, Fluor Corporation, Anaheim, Calif., private communication, August 17, 1983.

26. Motor Vehicle Manufacturers Association, *World Motor Vehicle Data Book, 1984–85 Edition* (Detroit, Mich.: 1985).

27. For trends in oil-based electricity generation, see Chapters 5 and 6.

28. World coal, oil, and natural gas production figures derived by Worldwatch Institute from American Petroleum Institute, *Basic Petroleum Data Book*, Vol. 5, No. 2 (Washington, D.C.: 1985), from U.S. Department of Energy (DOE), Energy Information Administration (EIA), *Monthly Energy Review* (Washington, D.C.: March 1985), and from DOE, EIA, *Annual Energy Review, 1984* (Washington, D.C.: U.S. Government Printing Office, 1985).

29. "Natural Gas: World Status," *Financial Times Energy Economist*, March 1984.

30. For a discussion of trends in oil production, see Chapter 5.

31. All agricultural productivity and per capita grain consumption trends in this section from USDA, ERS, *World Indices*, unless otherwise noted.

32. Consumption of leguminous crops in India derived from "India's Agricultural Success Story," USDA, ERS, *Agricultural Outlook* Washington, D.C., October 1985, and from United Nations Food and Agriculture Organization, *Production Yearbook* (Rome: 1983).

33. Derived from USDA, *Agricultural Statistics 1984* (Washington, D.C.: U.S. Government Printing Office, 1984), and from Evelyn Blazer, USDA, ERS, Washington, D.C., private communication, July 1985.

34. Gerald M. Boyd, "U.S. Fights Europeans' Wheat Aid," *New York Times,* October 17, 1985.

35. Frederick M. Surls, "Widening Scope of Agricultural Reforms," in USDA, ERS, *China: Outlook and Situation Report,* Washington, D.C., July 1985.

36. Soviet and Chinese grain production data from USDA, ERS, *World Indices.*

37. For information on China's agricultural reform, including changes in procurement prices and shifting terms of trade, see Surls, "Widening Scope of Agricultural Reforms."

38. Ibid.

39. Terry Taylor, "China's Farmers Shift Into High Gear," *Foreign Agriculture,* USDA, Washington, D.C., April 1985.

40. Ibid.

41. Soviet grain production from USDA, ERS, *World Indices;* grain import data from USDA, Foreign Agricultural Service, *Foreign Agriculture Circular,* FG-13-85, Washington, D.C., October 1985.

42. Leslie H. Gelb, " 'Gradual' Changes in Soviet 5-Year Plan," *New York Times,* October 14, 1985.

43. Information on China's military budget comes from ACDA, *World Military Expenditures and Arms Transfers,* and from private communication, Peng Fei Fei, Chinese Embassy, Washington, D.C., September 1985.

44. Data on Sri Lanka from World Bank, *World Development Report.*

45. William U. Chandler, *Investing in Children* (Washington, D.C.: Worldwatch Institute, June 1985).

46. Brazil's debt from Morgan Guaranty, *World Financial Markets;* infant mortality and income distribution data from World Bank, *World Development Report.*

47. Mexico's debt from Morgan Guaranty, *World Financial Markets;* infant mortality and income distribution data from World Bank, *World Development Report.*

48. Per capita grain production trends in India and China derived from USDA, ERS, *World Indices.*

49. For more information on the effects of smoking on life span and health, see Chapter 8; estimate of famine deaths in Africa from U.N. Economic Commission for Africa, "Second Special Memorandum by the ECA Conference of Ministers: International Action for Relaunching the Initiative for Long-Term Development and Economic Growth in Africa," Addis Ababa, April 25–29, 1985.

50. Data on Soviet cigarette use cited in U.S. Department of Health and Human Services, Office of Smoking and Health, translated abstract of A.G. Shevchuk and R.N. Tarasova, "The Organization of Antismoking Education," *Zdravookhraneniye Rossiyskoy Federatsii,* Vol. 5, 1983; for a discussion of declining life expectancy and the role of smoking and alcoholism-related illnesses in the Soviet Union, see Murray Feshbach, "Issues in Soviet Health Problems," in Joint Economic Committee, U.S. Congress, *Soviet Economy in the 1980's: Problems and Prospects* (Washington, D.C.: U.S. Government Printing Office, 1983); information on alcoholism and smoking campaigns from Dr. Galina V. Sdasyuk, Senior Research Associate, Institute of Geography, Academy of Sciences of the USSR, Washington, D.C., private communication, July 23, 1985, and Dr. Sergey M. Rogov, First Secretary, Institute of United States and Canadian Studies of the Academy of Sciences of the USSR, Washington, D.C., private communication, October 15, 1985.

Chapter 2. Assessing Ecological Decline

1. Ken Newcombe, *An Economic Justification for Rural Afforestation: The Case of Ethiopia,* En-

ergy Department Paper No. 16 (Washington, D.C.: World Bank, 1984); F.H. Bormann, "Air Pollution and Forests: An Ecosystem Perspective," *BioScience,* July/August 1985.

2. Newcombe, *An Economic Justification*.

3. United Nations Development Program (UNDP)/World Bank Energy Sector Assessment Program, *Ethiopia: Issues and Options in the Energy Sector* (Washington, D.C.: World Bank, 1984).

4. Kenneth Newcombe, "Household Energy Supply: The Energy Crisis That Is Here To Stay!" presented to the World Bank Senior Policy Seminar-Energy, Gabarone, Botswana, March 18–22, 1985.

5. United Nations Food and Agriculture Organization (FAO), Forestry Resources Division, *Tropical Forest Resources,* Forestry Paper 30 (Rome: 1982); World Bank survey from Gunter Schramm and David Jhirad, "Sub-Saharan Africa Policy Paper-Energy" (draft), World Bank, Washington, D.C., August 20, 1984.

6. Schramm and Jhirad, "Sub-Saharan Africa Policy Paper."

7. Ibid.

8. Bormann, "Air Pollution and Forests."

9. Livestock data from FAO, *Production Yearbook* (Rome: various years); population data from United Nations, Department of International Economic and Social Affairs, *World Population and Its Age-Sex Composition By Country, 1950–2000* (New York: 1980), and Population Reference Bureau, *1983 World Population Data Sheet* (Washington, D.C.: 1983).

10. Livestock data from FAO, *Production Yearbook*.

11. Southern African Development Coordination Conference, *SADCC Agriculture: Toward 2000* (Rome: FAO, 1984).

12. U.S. Department of Agriculture (USDA), Economic Research Service (ERS), *World Indices of Agricultural and Food Production 1950–84* (unpublished printout) (Washington, D.C.: 1985).

13. For waterlogging and soil salinization trends, see Sandra Postel, *Water: Rethinking Management in an Age of Scarcity* (Washington, D.C.: Worldwatch Institute, December 1984); data on grain yields in Iran from USDA, ERS, *World Indices*.

14. UNDP/World Bank, *Ethiopia: Issues and Options*.

15. Centre for Science and Environment (CSE), *The State of India's Environment 1984–85* (New Delhi: 1985).

16. Ibid.; population data on Madhya Pradesh from Alex Von Cube, Population Reference Bureau, Washington, D.C., private communication, November 8, 1985.

17. National Academy of Sciences, *Firewood Crops: Shrubs and Tree Species for Energy Production* (Washington, D.C.: 1980); India's projected population from World Bank, *World Development Report 1985* (New York: Oxford University Press, 1985).

18. Andrew Csepel, "Czechs and the Ecological Balance," *New Scientist,* September 27, 1984.

19. Ibid.

20. Environmental Resources Limited, *Acid Rain: A Review of the Phenomenon in the EEC and Europe* (London: Graham & Trotman Ltd., 1983).

21. Anders Wijkman and Lloyd Timberlake, *Natural Disasters: Acts of God or Acts of Man?* (Washington, D.C.: Earthscan/International Institute for Environment and Development, 1984).

22. "Wound in the World," *Asiaweek,* July 13, 1984.

23. Information on tropical forest fires in Ivory Coast and Ghana from World Bank, "The 1983–84 Drought in Sub-Saharan Africa—Short Term Impact—Desertification and Other Long-Term Issues" (draft), Washington, D.C., May 1984.

24. Ibid.

25. Ibid.

26. Ibid.

27. Land productivity from USDA, ERS, *World Indices;* population data from Population Reference Bureau, *1985 World Population Data Sheet* (Washington, D.C.: 1985); per capita income from World Bank, *World Development Report*.

28. Population data from Population Reference Bureau, *1985 World Population Data Sheet*.

29. George R. Gardner, "Saudia Arabia Drives For Agricultural Self-Sufficiency: A Political Goal With High Economic Costs," in USDA, ERS, *Middle East and North Africa: Outlook and Situation Report*, Washington, D.C., April 1985.

30. William I. Jones and Roberto Egli, *Farming Systems in Africa*, Technical Paper No. 27 (Washington, D.C.: World Bank, 1984).

31. "Food Price Rioting Persists in Sudan," *New York Times*, March 29, 1985; for information on the effects of Sudan's heavy debt burden see USDA, ERS, *Agricultural Outlook*, Washington, D.C., October 1985.

32. Tunisian food riots and debt burden discussed in USDA, ERS, *Middle East and North Africa*.

33. Warren Hoge, "Brazil's Poor Raiding Food Stores in Rio Area," *New York Times*, September 11, 1983; Mac Margolis, "Brazil Dust Bowl Five Times the Size of Italy," *Christian Science Monitor*, August 26, 1983.

34. Assessment of displaced people from United Nations, "Report on the Emergency Situation in Africa," New York, February 22, 1985; information on Ethiopian and Mozambican refugees from United Nations Office of Emergency Operations in Africa, *African Emergency Bulletin*, July 15, 1985, and from U.S. Committee for Refugees, *World Refugee Survey 1984* (New York: American Council for Nationalities Service, 1984).

35. Situation in Nouakchott, Mauritania, from Brian Urquhart, United Nations Undersecretary General for Special Political Affairs, private communication, May 19, 1985; refugee flows reported in U.N. Office of Emergency Operations, *African Emergency Bulletin*.

36. U.N. Office of Emergency Operations, *African Emergency Bulletin;* U.S. Committee for Refugees, *World Refugee Survey*.

37. U.N. Office of Emergency Operations, *African Emergency Bulletin*.

38. Walter Truett Anderson, "The Real Domino Theory in Central America," *Pacific News Service*, August 9–16, 1984.

39. Robert S. Kandel, "Mechanisms Governing the Climate of the Sahel: A Survey of Recent Modelling and Observational Studies," Organisation for Economic Co-operation and Development and Permanent Interstate Committee for Drought Control in the Sahel, Paris, October 1984.

40. Jean Gorse, "Desertification in the Sahelian and Sudanian Zones of West Africa" (draft), World Bank, Washington, D.C., February 1985.

Chapter 3. Increasing Water Efficiency

1. Donald Janson, "Kean Adds Restrictions on Water Use in Jersey," *New York Times*, May 17, 1985; Wayne King, "Severe Drought Hits Southwest," *New York Times*, June 6, 1984; "Managua to Ration Water," *New York Times*, December 20, 1984; Deng Shulin, "Tianjin—the City that Needed Water," *China Reconstructs*, February 1982.

2. Alfred G. Cuzen, "Appropriators Versus Expropriators: The Political Economy of Water in the West," in Terry L. Anderson, ed., *Water Rights: Scarce Resource Allocation, Bureaucracy, and the Environment* (San Francisco: Pacific Institute for Public Policy Research, 1983); number of dams and projects from U.S. Congressional Budget Office, *Efficient Investments in Water Resources: Issues and Options*

(Washington, D.C.: U.S. Government Printing Office, 1983).

3. For a more thorough discussion of emerging water problems, see Sandra Postel, "Managing Freshwater Supplies," in Lester R. Brown et al., *State of the World-1985* (New York: W.W. Norton and Co., 1985).

4. U.S. water use from Wayne B. Solley et al., *Estimated Use of Water in the United States in 1980* (Alexandria, Va.: U.S. Geological Survey, 1983).

5. Irrigated area and efficiency estimates from W.R. Rangeley, "Irrigation and Drainage in the World," paper presented at the International Conference on Food and Water, Texas A.& M. University, College Station, Tex., May 26–30, 1985; see also, Mohamed T. El-Ashry et al., "Salinity Pollution from Irrigated Agriculture," *Journal of Soil and Water Conservation,* January/February 1985.

6. Rangeley, "Irrigation and Drainage."

7. For a good overview of irrigation efficiency, see E.G. Kruse and D.F. Heermann, "Implications of Irrigation System Efficiencies," *Journal of Soil and Water Conservation,* November/December 1977.

8. Wayne Clyma et al., *Land Leveling,* Planning Guide No. 1, Water Management Synthesis Project, prepared in cooperation with U.S. Agency for International Development, Fort Collins, Colo., July 1981; California Department of Water Resources, *Water Conservation in California* (Sacramento, Calif.: California Resources Agency, 1984).

9. For background on sprinkler and other irrigation systems, see Kenneth D. Frederick and James C. Hanson, *Water for Western Agriculture* (Washington, D.C.: Resources for the Future, 1982); conventional sprinkler efficiency from Kruse and Heerman, "Implications of Irrigation System Efficiencies"; for discussion of LEPA, see William M. Lyle, "Water Saving Techniques," in *Hope for the High Plains,* Proceedings of the Twenty-Sev-

enth Annual New Mexico Water Conference, New Mexico Water Resources Research Institute, Las Cruces, N.M., April 1982; Kenneth Carver, Assistant Manager, High Plains Underground Water Conservation District No. 1, Lubbock, Tex., private communication, March 25, 1985; payback from Comer Tuck, Texas Department of Water Resources, Austin, Tex., private communication, July 10, 1985.

10. Background and basic features of drip irrigation from Kobe Shoji, "Drip Irrigation," *Scientific American,* November 1977; see also Sterling Davis and Dale Bucks, "Drip Irrigation," in Claude H. Pair et al., eds., *Irrigation* (Silver Spring, Md.: The Irrigation Association, 1983); estimated water savings from J.S. Abbott, "Micro Irrigation—World Wide Usage," *ICID Bulletin,* January 1984.

11. Current Israeli estimates from Y. Kahana, Israel Ministry of Agriculture, Water Commission, Tel Aviv, Israel, private communication, April 28, 1985.

12. 1983 U.S. drip area from "1983 Irrigation Survey," *Irrigation Journal,* 1983; current area worldwide from Abbott, "Micro Irrigation," plus known increases in the United States from the "1983 Irrigation Survey" and in Israel from Kahana, private communication.

13. National Academy of Sciences, *More Water for Arid Lands: Promising Technologies and Research Opportunities* (Washington, D.C.: 1974); Christiaan Gischler and C. Fernandez Jauregui, "Low-Cost Techniques for Water Conservation and Management in Latin America," *Nature and Resources,* July/September 1984.

14. Investment cost from Rangeley, "Irrigation and Drainage"; World Bank, *World Development Report 1983* (New York: Oxford University Press, 1983).

15. J. Alwis et al., *The Rajangana Irrigation Scheme, Sri Lanka: 1983 Diagnostic Analysis,* prepared in cooperation with the U.S. Agency for International Development,

Water Management Synthesis Project, Report No. 19, Colorado State University, Fort Collins, Colo., December 1983.

16. Robert Chambers, "Food and Water as if People Mattered: A Professional Revolution," paper presented at the International Conference on Food and Water.

17. See California Department of Water Resources, *Water Conservation in California;* for a more technical discussion, see Edward A. Hiler and Terry A. Howell, "Irrigation Options to Avoid Critical Stress: An Overview," in H.M. Taylor et al., *Limitations to Efficient Water Use in Crop Production* (Madison, Wisc.: American Society of Agronomy, 1983); gypsum block test results from Gail Richardson, *Saving Water from the Ground Up* (New York: INFORM, 1985).

18. Gaston Mahave and Jorge Dominguez, "Experiments at Farm Level to Introduce Technology in Irrigation: Its Influence on Production and Water Resources," in Brazilian National Committee, *Transactions of the lst Regional Pan-American Conference*, Vol. 1 (Salvador (Bahia), Brazil: October 1984).

19. Irrigation costs from Rangeley, "Irrigation and Drainage."

20. B.A. Stewart and Earl Burnett, "Water Conservation Technology in Rainfed and Dryland Agriculture," paper presented at the International Conference on Food and Water.

21. Ibid.

22. Robert S. Loomis, "Crop Manipulations for Efficient Use of Water: An Overview," in Taylor et al., *Limitations to Efficient Water Use.*

23. National Academy of Sciences, *More Water for Arid Lands;* United Nations Environment Programme, *Rain and Stormwater Harvesting in Rural Areas* (Dublin: Tycooly International Publishing, 1983).

24. National Academy of Sciences, *More Water for Arid Lands;* see also Chapter 10 in this volume.

25. J. Doorenbos and A.H. Kassam, *Yield Response to Water* (Rome: U.N. Food and Agriculture Organization, 1979).

26. Hiler and Howell, "Irrigation Options."

27. Doorenbos and Kassam, *Yield Response to Water;* M.A. Kahn et al., "Development of Supplies & Sanitation in Saudi Arabia," *African Technical Review,* June 1984.

28. Carl N. Hodges and Wayne L. Collins, "Future Food Production: The Potential is Infinite, the Reality May Not Be," *Proceedings of the American Philosophical Society*, Vol. 128, No. 1, 1984; James W. O'Leary, "The Role of Halophytes in Irrigated Agriculture," in Richard C. Staples, ed., *Salinity Tolerance in Plants: Strategies for Crop Improvement* (New York: John Wiley & Sons, 1984).

29. National Research Council, *Amaranth: Modern Prospects for an Ancient Crop* (Washington, D.C.: National Academy Press, 1984); C.S. Kauffman, *Amaranth Grain Production Guide 1984* (Emmaus, Pa.: Rodale Press, 1984); Wayne W. Applegate, Post Rock Natural Grains, Luray, Kans., private communication, February 19, 1985; Charles D. McNeal, Paradise, Kans., private communication, February 5, 1985; David Pimentel, Ithaca, N.Y., private communication, June 6, 1985.

30. Culp/Wesner/Culp, *Water Reuse and Recycling: Evaluation of Needs and Potential*, Vol. 1 (Washington, D.C.: U.S. Department of the Interior, 1979); Ronald J. Turner, "Examining the Opportunities for Recycle and Reuse of Chemical Industry Wastewaters," in *Proceedings of the Water Reuse Symposium II*, Vol. 1 (Denver, Colo.: AWWA Research Foundation, 1981).

31. Armco example cited in Robert A. Hamilton, "What Will We Do When the Well Runs Dry?" *Harvard Business Review*, November/December 1984; L. Rakosh, "Water Reuse in the American Israeli Paper Mills, Hadera," in *Israqua '78: Proceedings of the International Conference on Water Systems and Applica-*

tions (Tel Aviv: Israel Centre of Waterworks Appliances, 1978); Soviet citation from Yu P. Belichenko and T.L. Dolgopolova, "Creation of Closed Water Management Systems at Industrial Enterprises," *Water Resources,* July 1984, translated from original article in *Vodnye Resursy,* January 1982.

32. Sandra Gay Yulke et al., "Water Reuse in the Pulp and Paper Industry in California," in *Water Reuse Symposium II;* for other examples, see Leonard B. Antosiak and Charles A. Job, "Industrial Water Conservation Within the Great Lakes Region: An Overview," *Journal AWWA,* January 1981.

33. Swedish Preparatory Committee for the U.N. Water Conference, *Water in Sweden* (Stockholm: Ministry of Agriculture, 1977).

34. Saul Arlosoroff, "Water Management Policies Under Scarce Conditions," presented at Water for the 21st Century: Will It Be There? Southern Methodist University, Dallas, Tex., April 1984; see also Nina Selbst, "Water Management in Israel," paper presented at 1 Congreso Nacional de Derecho de Aguas, Murcia, Spain, May 1982.

35. Gastón Mendoza Gamez and Francisco Flores Herrera, "Mexico City's Master Plan for Reuse," in *Water Reuse Symposium II*.

36. Selbst, "Water Management in Israel"; Aaron Meron, "Experience with Israel's Reclamation Systems," in *Future of Water Reuse: Proceedings of the Water Reuse Symposium III,* Vol. 1 (Denver, Colo: AWWA Research Foundation, 1985).

37. Survey data from Culp/Wesner/Culp, *Water Reuse and Recycling*.

38. California figures from James Crook, "Water Reuse in California," and Kenneth W. Willis, "The Future of Water Reclamation in California," in *Future of Water Reuse*.

39. John R. Sheaffer and Leonard A. Stevens, *Future Water* (New York: William Morrow and Company, 1983).

40. Ibid.

41. John F. Donovan and John E. Bates, *Guidelines for Water Reuse* (Cincinnati, Oh.: U.S. Environmental Protection Agency, 1980).

42. Charles P. Gerba et al., "Virus Removal During Land Application of Wastewater: Comparison of Three Projects," in *Future of Water Reuse;* Crook, "Water Reuse in California."

43. D.E. Bourne and G.S. Watermeyer, "Proposed Potable Reuse—An Epidemiological Study in Cape Town," in *Water Reuse Symposium II;* William C. Lauer et al., "Denver's Potable Water Reuse Project: Current Status," in *Future of Water Reuse;* Lee Wilson & Associates, "Water Supply Alternatives for El Paso," prepared for El Paso Water Utilities Public Service Board, Santa Fe, N.M., November 1981; Lee Wilson, Lee Wilson & Associates, Santa Fe, N.M., private communication, June 1985.

44. Carl R. Bartone and Henry J. Salas, "Developing Alternative Approaches to Urban Wastewater Disposal in Latin America and the Caribbean," *Bulletin of the Pan American Health Organization,* Vol. 18, No. 4, 1984.

45. Tucson Water, "Conservation Programs," Tucson, Ariz., undated.

46. Ibid.

47. Ibid.; Tucson Water, "Energy Innovation through Applied Technology," Tucson, Ariz., 1984; Janet Garcia, Tucson Water, Tucson, Ariz., private communication, April 19, 1985.

48. See American Water Works Association, *Water Conservation Management* (Denver, Colo.: 1981).

49. West Germany reference from *World Environment Report,* April 4, 1984; Scandinavia reference from Robert L. Siegrist, "Minimum-Flow Plumbing Fixtures," *Journal AWWA,* July 1983.

50. Donald W. Lystra et al., "Energy Conservation Opportunities in Municipal Water and Wastewater Systems," *Journal AWWA,*

April 1981; California study from Jimmy Koyasako, "Water Conservation and Wastewater Flow Reduction—Is It Worth It?" in Dynamac Corporation, ed., *Proceedings of the National Water Conservation Conference on Publicly Supplied Potable Water* (Washington, D.C.: U.S. Department of Commerce, 1982).

51. Estimate of savings from Brown and Caldwell (Inc.), *Residential Water Conservation Projects* (Washington, D.C.: U.S. Department of Housing and Urban Development, 1984). The report assumes an electricity cost of 7¢ per kilowatt-hour.

52. Case is described in U.S. Geological Survey (USGS), *National Water Summary 1983 —Hydrologic Events and Issues* (Washington, D.C.: U.S. Government Printing Office, 1984) and in Conservation Foundation, *State of the Environment: An Assessment at Mid-Decade* (Washington, D.C.: 1984).

53. "Runaway Water: The Lost Resource," *World Water*, November 1983; Fred Pearce and Mick Hamer, "The Empire's Last Stand," *New Scientist*, May 12, 1983.

54. Austria citation from F. Auzias, "Economie d'Eau et Lutte contre le Gaspillage," *Aqua*, Vol. 5, 1983; Manila program described in "Leak Detectives Boost Manila Supply," *World Water*, November 1983.

55. Latin American usage rates from E. Glenn Wagner, "The Latin American Approach to Improving Water Supplies," *Journal AWWA*, April 1983; Latin American projects from Bartone and Salas, "Developing Alternative Approaches to Urban Wastewater Disposal."

56. African programs from E.J. Schiller, "Water and Health in Africa," *Water International*, June 1984.

57. Laurence J.C. Ma and Liu Changming, "Water Resources Development and Its Environmental Impact in Beijing," *China Geographer*, No. 12, 1985.

58. Share paid by U.S. farmers from Congressional Budget Office, *Efficient Investments;*

David L. Wilson and Harry W. Ayer, "The Cost of Water in Western Agriculture," Economic Research Service, U.S. Department of Agriculture, Washington, D.C., July 1982. For historical background, see Gary Weatherford and Helen Ingram, "Legal-Institutional Limitations on Water Use," in Ernest A. Engelbert and Ann Foley Scheuring, eds., *Water Scarcity: Impacts on Western Agriculture* (Berkeley, Calif.: University of California Press, 1984).

59. Study described in United Nations, *Efficiency and Distributional Equity in the Use and Treatment of Water: Guidelines for Pricing and Regulations* (New York: 1980).

60. Loren D. Mellendorf, "The Water Utility Industry and Its Problems," *Public Utilities Fortnightly*, March 17, 1983. For a good discussion of this issue, see William E. Martin et al., *Saving Water in a Desert City* (Washington, D.C.: Resources for the Future, 1984).

61. W.D. Watson et al., *Water 2000: Agricultural Water Demand and Issues* (Canberra: Australian Government Publishing Service, 1983); U.N. Economic Commission for Europe, *Policies and Strategies for Rational Use of Water in the ECE Region* (New York: United Nations, 1983); Gaylord V. Skogerboe and George E. Radosevich, "Future Water Development Policies," *Water Supply and Management*, Vol. 6, No. 2, 1982. For a discussion of water markets, see Terry L. Anderson, *The Water Crisis: Ending the Policy Drought* (Baltimore, Md.: The Johns Hopkins University Press, 1983).

62. Watson et al., *Water 2000;* California Department of Water Resources, *Water Conservation in California;* "Colorado Rejects 'Use It or Lose It'," *U.S. Water News*, July 1985.

63. California Department of Water Resources, *Water Conservation in California;* Robert Stavins, *Trading Conservation Investments for Water* (Berkeley, Calif.: Environmental Defense Fund, 1983).

64. Stavins, *Trading Conservation Investments*.

65. Tony Profumo, Parsons Corporation, Pasadena, Calif., private communication, July 1985.

66. Sadiqul I. Bhuiyan, "Water Technology for Food Production: Expectations and Realities in the Developing Countries," paper presented at the International Conference on Food and Water; Rangeley, "Irrigation and Drainage." See also Michael Cross, "Irrigation's Role in Solving the Food Crisis," *New Scientist,* May 9, 1985.

67. Yearly groundwater use from Solley et al., *Estimated Use of Water in the United States;* depletion figures from USGS, *National Water Summary 1983.*

68. Projections from Arizona Department of Water Resources, "Proposed Management Plan: First Management Period 1980–1990," Phoenix Active Management Area, 1984, and companion document for Tucson.

69. Arlosoroff, "Water Management Policies."

70. Estimated savings are for common water-efficient fixtures given in Brown and Caldwell, *Residential Water Conservation Projects.* Calculated savings assume that the entire increase in population between 1985 and the year 2000 would be using the more efficient fixtures, as well as 15 percent of the existing population (because of remodeling, or purchases of new homes or new appliances). No attempt was made to discount for states with water-efficient plumbing codes already in effect.

71. Diversion plans described in O.A. Kibal'chich and N.I. Koronkevich, "Some of the Results and Tasks of Geographic Investigations on the Water-Transfer Project," *Soviet Geography,* December 1983; cost estimate from Philip M. Micklin, "Recent Developments in Large-Scale Water Transfers in the USSR," *Soviet Geography,* April 1984.

72. Based on figures and discussion in A.S. Kes' et al., "The Present State and Future Prospects of Using Local Water Resources in Central Asia and Southern Kazakhstan," *Soviet Geography,* June 1982.

73. Ibid.

74. Ibid.

75. Office of Natural Resources, "Water Program for Texas Agriculture," Department of Agriculture, Austin, Tex., December 1984; Rick Piltz, Texas Office of Natural Resources, Austin, Tex., private communication, June 1985.

76. Water use savings from Office of Natural Resources, "Water Program for Texas Agriculture"; Corps findings from High Plains Associates, *Six-State High Plains Ogallala Aquifer Regional Resources Study* (Austin, Tex.: 1982); quote from Jim Hightower, "Incentive is Needed to Stretch Water Supply," *U.S. Water News,* February 1985.

Chapter 4. Managing Rangelands

1. Estimate of ruminant populations from United Nations Food and Agriculture Organization (FAO), *Production Yearbook* (Rome: 1984).

2. Society for Range Management, "Rangelands Can Be Forever" (promotional brochure), Denver, Colo., undated.

3. Based on data from L.E. Rodin, N.I. Bazilevich, and N.N. Rozov, "Productivity of the World's Main Ecosystems," in National Academy of Sciences, *Productivity of World Ecosystems* (Washington, D.C.: 1975).

4. R. Dennis Child et al., *Arid and Semiarid Lands: Sustainable Use and Management in Developing Countries* (Morrilton, Ark.: Winrock International, October 1984); National Research Council, Board on Science and Technology for International Development, *Environmental Change in the West African Sahel* (Washington, D.C.: National Academy Press, 1983).

5. H. Bremen and C.T. de Wit, "Rangeland Productivity and Exploitation in the Sahel," *Science,* September 30, 1983.

6. Child et al., *Arid and Semiarid Lands*.

7. FAO, *Production Yearbook* (Rome: various years).

8. Estimate of share of ruminants raised in conjunction with farming is from Winrock International, *Annual Report 1984* (Morrilton, Ark.: 1984); conversion of grasslands to farming is discussed in John F. Richards, "Global Patterns of Land Conversion," *Environment*, November 1984.

9. Area of pastures and forage crops in United States from U.S. Department of Agriculture (USDA), *Agricultural Statistics 1984* (Washington, D.C.: U.S. Government Printing Office, 1984); share of roughage consumed by livestock from USDA, *An Assessment of the Forest and Rangeland Situation in the United States*, Forest Resource Report No. 22 (Washington, D.C.: U.S. Government Printing Office, 1981); data on India from William Hansel, "Future Agricultural Technology and Resource Conservation: Beef and Dairy Cattle, Sheep, Goats, Swine, and Poultry," in Burton C. English et al., eds., *Future Agricultural Technology and Resource Conservation* (Ames: Iowa State University Press, 1984).

10. D.B. Grigg, *The Agricultural Systems of the World* (New York: Cambridge University Press, 1974).

11. USDA, *Assessment of the Forest and Rangeland Situation*.

12. U.S. Department of the Interior, Bureau of Land Management (BLM), *Managing the Nation's Public Lands Fiscal Year 1984* (Washington, D.C.: 1984).

13. Roy N. Van Arsdall, "Discussion," in English et al., *Future Agricultural Technology*.

14. Child et al., *Arid and Semiarid Lands;* Stephen Sandford, *Management of Pastoral Development in the Third World* (New York: John Wiley & Sons, 1983).

15. International Livestock Center for Africa (ILCA), *ILCA Annual Report 1983* (Addis Ababa: 1984).

16. Lloyd Timberlake, *Africa in Crisis: The Causes, the Cures of Environmental Bankruptcy* (Washington, D.C.: Earthscan/International Institute for Environment and Development, 1985).

17. Bremen and de Wit, "Rangeland Productivity and Exploitation in the Sahel."

18. Amartya Sen, *Poverty and Famines* (New York: Oxford University Press, 1981).

19. For a thorough history of ranching in Latin America, see Grigg, *Agricultural Systems*.

20. Susanna B. Hecht, "Cattle Ranching Development in the Eastern Amazon: Evaluation of a Development Policy," Ph.D dissertation, University of California, Berkeley, 1982.

21. Norman Myers, "The Hamburger Connection: How Central America's Forests Become North America's Hamburgers," *Ambio*, Vol. X, No. 1, 1981; Norman Myers, *Conversion of Tropical Moist Forests* (Washington, D.C.: National Academy of Sciences, 1980).

22. Central America data from Myers, "The Hamburger Connection"; Amazonia data from Hecht, "Cattle Ranching Development."

23. USDA, *Agricultural Statistics* (Washington, D.C.: U.S. Government Printing Office, various years); USDA, Foreign Agricultural Service, *World Livestock and Poultry Situation* (FL&P-1), Washington, D.C., April 1985.

24. For an overview of the ecological effects of forest clearing for pasture, see Susanna Hecht, "Cattle Ranching in the Eastern Amazon: Environmental and Social Implications," in Emilio F. Moran, ed., *The Dilemma of Amazonian Development* (Boulder, Colo.: Westview Press, 1982), and Philip M. Fearnside, "The Effects of Cattle Pasture on Soil Fertility in the Brazilian Amazon: Consequences for Beef Production Sustainability," *Tropical Ecology*, Vol. 21, No. 1, 1980.

25. Estimate of cattle losses in Mongolia from Jacob A. Hoefer and Patricia Jones Tsu-

chitani, *Animal Agriculture in China* (Washington, D.C.: National Academy Press, 1980); losses in Africa during the early seventies discussed in Child et al., *Arid and Semiarid Lands;* for a contemporary example of the social consequences of animal losses, see Michael Asher, "In Sudan's Dying Deserts," *New Scientist,* April 4, 1985.

26. Quoted in Philip M. Boffey, "Spread of Deserts Seen as a Catastrophe Underlying Famine," *New York Times,* January 8, 1985.

27. Jack A. Mabbutt, "A New Global Assessment of the Status and Trends of Desertification," *Environmental Conservation,* Summer 1984.

28. Jean Gorse, "Desertification in the Sahelian and Sudanian Zones of West Africa" (draft), World Bank, Washington, D.C., February 1985.

29. Child et al., *Arid and Semiarid Lands.*

30. Garrett Hardin, "The Tragedy of the Commons," *Science,* December 13, 1968; for a contrary view of the allocation of common resources by pastoral societies, see Sandford, *Management of Pastoral Development,* and Jere Lee Gilles and Keith Jamtgaard, "The Commons Reconsidered," *Rangelands,* April 1982.

31. Sandford, *Management of Pastoral Development.*

32. Ibid.; U.S. Department of the Interior, BLM, *50 Years of Public Land Management* (Washington, D.C.: 1984).

33. For an overview of grazing fees on public rangelands, see USDA and U.S. Department of the Interior, *1985 Grazing Fee Review and Evaluation Draft Report* (Washington, D.C.: 1985); for a critique of the current grazing fee structure, see Katherine Barton, "Wildlife on Bureau of Land Management Lands," in National Audubon Society, *Audubon Wildlife Report 1985* (New York: 1985).

34. Sarel Hayward, Minister of Agriculture and Water Supply, House of Assembly Debates (Johannesburg), South Africa, May 15, 1985.

35. Chris Maser, "Rangelands, Wildlife Technology, and Human Desires," in Office of Technology Assessment (OTA), U.S. Congress, *Technologies to Benefit Agriculture and Wildlife—Workshop Proceedings* (Washington, D.C.: U.S. Government Printing Office, 1985).

36. ILCA, *ILCA Annual Report 1983.*

37. Guido Gryseels and Getachew Asamenew, "Links Between Livestock and Crop Production in the Ethiopian Highlands," *ILCA Newsletter* (Addis Ababa), April 1985.

38. For a discussion of alternative grazing strategies, see OTA, *Impact of Technologies on U.S. Cropland and Rangeland Productivity* (Washington, D.C.: U.S. Government Printing Office, 1982); for a broader discussion of ecologically based grazing practices, see Allan Savory, "Holistic Resource Management," presented to University of Wyoming Conference on Holistic Ranch Management, Laramie, Wyo., May 28–30, 1985.

39. The Voisin method is discussed in William A. Murphy and David T. Dugdale, "The Voisin Pasture Management System," *New England Farmer,* April 1984, and in Savory, "Holistic Resource Management."

40. Kirin N. Shelat, "Protecting the Small-Scale Dairyman," *Ceres,* December 1984.

41. Ibid.

42. The Hema system is discussed in National Research Council, *Environmental Change;* in Douglas L. Johnson, "Desertification and Nomadic Pastoral Development," in E.T. Bartlett and Neville Dyson-Hudson, eds., *The Man and the Biosphere Program in Grazing Lands* (Washington, D.C.: U.S. Department of State, U.S. Man and the Biosphere Program, 1980); and in Child et al., *Arid and Semiarid Lands.*

43. China's livestock economy and the role of grasslands are discussed in Hoefer and Tsuchitani, *Animal Agriculture in China;*

and in Dillard H. Gates, "A Dynamic Ecosystem—Rangelands, Livestock, and People in Northeastern China," in Larry D. White and James A. Tiedeman, eds., *Proceedings of the International Rangelands Resources Development Symposium,* Salt Lake City, Utah, February 13–14, 1985; announcement of China's grassland law from "Press Hails Law to Save Grasslands," *China Daily,* June 21, 1985; data on grassland revegetation from "Grass Planting," *China Daily,* January 23, 1985.

44. David Hopcraft, "Wildlife Land Use at Athi River, Kenya: A Perspective and Update," Wildlife Ranching and Research, Athi River, Kenya, September 1985; for a discussion of game ranching, see OTA, *Water-Related Technologies for Sustainable Agriculture in Arid/Semiarid Lands: Selected Foreign Experience* (Washington, D.C.: U.S. Government Printing Office, 1983); for a dated but useful introduction to the economics of game ranching, see Robert E. McDowell et al., "Game or Cattle for Meat Production on Kenya Rangelands?" Department of Animal Science, Cornell University, Ithaca, N.Y., October 1983.

Chapter 5. Moving Beyond Oil

1. World oil statistics in this chapter, unless otherwise noted, are from British Petroleum Company (BPC), *BP Statistical Review of World Energy* (London: 1985). The average world oil price used here is a composite figure, based on a weighted average of domestic and imported crude oil at the U.S. refinery gate as listed in U.S. Department of Energy (DOE), Energy Information Administration (EIA), *Monthly Energy Review* (Washington, D.C.: August 1985).

2. BPC, *BP Statistical Review of World Energy.* The oil production figures in the text include about 4 million barrels per day of natural gas liquids. The data illustrated in Figure 6–1 are from the American Petroleum Institute (API), *Basic Petroleum Data Book,* Vol. 5, No. 2 (Washington, D.C.: 1985), and do not include gas liquids. Preliminary 1985 oil pro-

duction estimates are based on "First Half Oil Flow Fails to Sustain 1984 Increase," *Oil and Gas Journal,* September 9, 1985.

3. BPC, *BP Statistical Review of World Energy;* oil/GNP figure from International Energy Agency (IEA), *Annual Oil Market Report, 1984* (Paris: Organisation for Economic Cooperation and Development, 1985).

4. BPC, *BP Statistical Review of World Energy.*

5. John H. Lichtblau, "OPEC Oil in a Global Context: The Next 10 Years," presented at seminar on The Future of OPEC, The Centre for OPEC Studies, Caracas, Venezuela, April 25, 1985.

6. Daniel Yergin, *The Reshaping of the Oil Industry* (Cambridge, Mass.: Cambridge Energy Research Associates, 1985).

7. West quoted in William Drozdiak, "OPEC Fails to Reach Agreement," *Washington Post,* July 8, 1985.

8. Peter Behr, "Saudis Said to Boost Oil Output," *Washington Post,* September 18, 1985.

9. OPEC revenues from *Petroleum Intelligence Weekly,* February 23, 1981, and April 23, 1984; Oxford Institute study described in Roger Vielvoye, "OPEC Oil Outlook," *Oil and Gas Journal,* May 27, 1985.

10. Richard J. Meislin, "Mexico Encounters Problem of Growth," *New York Times,* June 10, 1985; "Hard Times Hit OPEC Oil Producers," *Journal of Commerce,* August 20, 1985; Sandra Feustel, "Lower Oil Prices End 'Gold Dust Days' on Persian Gulf," *Washington Post,* January 15, 1984; David B. Ottaway, "Saudi Arabia: The Boom Ends" (a series), *Washington Post,* November 25–27, 1984.

11. DOE, EIA, *Annual Energy Review 1984* (Washington, D.C.: 1985); Edward Boyer, "Winners and Losers from Cheaper Oil," *Fortune,* November 26, 1984.

12. API, *Basic Petroleum Data Book;* International Monetary Fund, *International Financial Statistics* (Washington, D.C.: March 1985).

13. World Bank estimate reported in Philip K. Verleger, Jr., *CRA Petroleum Economics Monthly* (Charles River Associates, Boston, Mass.), May 14, 1985.

14. "Soviets Demand More from East Bloc Allies," *Washington Post*, June 17, 1985.

15. Ed A. Hewett, *Energy, Economics, and Foreign Policy in the Soviet Union* (Washington, D.C.: Brookings Institution, 1984).

16. World Bank, *World Development Report 1984* (New York: Oxford University Press, 1984); Brazil figure from Howard S. Geller, American Council for an Energy-Efficient Economy, Washington, D.C., private communication, June 21, 1985.

17. Clyde H. Farnsworth, "Cuban Report Is Candid On Economic Burdens," *New York Times*, June 5, 1985.

18. World Bank, *The Energy Transition in Developing Countries* (Washington, D.C.: 1983).

19. Efficiency's contribution estimated by comparing the 36 percent decline in the oil/GNP ratio with the 19 percent decline in the energy/GNP ratio between 1973 and 1984.

20. U.S. energy efficiency improvement measured by change in energy/GNP ratio, from figures in DOE, EIA, *Monthly Energy Review*. They show a slightly higher improvement than do the International Energy Agency figures listed in Table 6–3. Dollar saving from increased efficiency is based on a total 1984 energy bill of $603 billion ($8.15 per million BTU), which would have been $790 billion if the energy/GNP ratio had remained at the 1973 level and the country had used 96 quadrillion BTUs of energy instead of the 74 quadrillion BTUs actually used.

21. Eric Hirst et al., "Recent Changes in U.S. Energy Consumption: What Happened and Why," in Annual Reviews Inc., *Annual Review of Energy, Vol. 8* (Palo Alto, Calif.: 1983).

22. DOE, Office of Policy Planning and Analysis, "Energy Use Trends in the United States, 1972–1984," draft, Washington, D.C., May 1985; Marc Ross, "Industrial Energy Conservation," *Natural Resources Forum*, April 1984.

23. William U. Chandler, *Energy Productivity: Key to Environmental Protection and Economic Progress* (Washington, D.C.: Worldwatch Institute, January 1985).

24. Ibid.

25. IEA, *Fuel Efficiency of Passenger Cars* (Paris: Organisation for Economic Co-operation and Development, 1984).

26. IEA, *Energy Policies and Programmes of IEA Countries: 1984 Review* (Paris: Organisation for Economic Co-operation and Development, 1985); World Bank, *Energy Transition in Developing Countries*.

27. Jose Goldemberg et al., *An End-Use Oriented Global Energy Strategy* (Princeton, N.J.: Princeton Center for Energy and Environmental Studies, 1985).

28. IEA, *Coal Information 1984* (Paris: Organisation for Economic Co-operation and Development, 1984).

29. Sandra Postel, "Protecting Forests from Air Pollution and Acid Rain," in Lester R. Brown et al., *State of the World-1985* (New York: W.W. Norton & Co., 1985); figure on East German forests from Susan Tifft, "Europe's Dying Forests," *Time* (International Edition), September 16, 1985.

30. World natural gas production and reserve figures from BPC, *BP Statistical Review of World Energy;* "Natural Gas: World Status," *Financial Times Energy Economist*, March 1984; World Bank estimate from Marcia A. Parker, "Less Developed Countries Push Campaigns to Tap Natural Gas," *Oil and Gas Journal*, June 1985. For information on the long-term potential of natural gas, see Office of Technology Assessment (OTA), U.S. Congress, *U.S. Natural Gas Availability Through the Year 2000* (Washington, D.C.: 1985).

31. Christopher Flavin, *Nuclear Power: The Market Test* (Washington, D.C.: Worldwatch Institute, December 1983); the current outlook is described in IEA, *Energy Policies and Programmes*.

32. Hydropower figures from BPC, *BP Statistical Review of World Energy;* biomass figures are Worldwatch Institute estimates based on Keith Openshaw, "Woodfuel—A Time for Reassessment," *Natural Resources Forum*, Vol. 3, 1978, pp. 35–51; see also Daniel Deudney and Christopher Flavin, *Renewable Energy: The Power to Choose* (New York: W.W. Norton & Co., 1983).

33. Recent commercial developments in renewable energy described in Christopher Flavin, *Renewable Energy at the Crossroads* (Washington, D.C.: Center for Renewable Resources, 1985).

34. API, *Basic Petroleum Data Book*.

35. Richard Nehring, "Prospects for Conventional World Oil Resources," in Annual Reviews Inc., *Annual Review of Energy, Vol. 7* (Palo Alto, Calif.: 1982); Charles D. Masters, "World Petroleum Resources: A Perspective," U.S. Geological Survey, Alexandria, Va., mimeographed, 1985 (unpublished).

36. Nehring, "Prospects for Conventional World Oil Resources."

37. Charles D. Masters, David H. Root, and William D. Dietzman, "Distribution and Quantitative Assessment of World Crude-Oil Reserves and Resources," U.S. Geological Survey, Alexandria, Va., mimeographed, 1983 (unpublished).

38. Ibid.

39. U.S. oil production figures include all crude oil and natural gas liquids outside Alaska and are from DOE, EIA, *Monthly Energy Review;* Lichtblau, "OPEC Oil in a Global Context."

40. OTA, *Oil and Gas Technologies for the Arctic and Deepwater* (Washington, D.C.: U.S. Government Printing Office, 1985); "Alaska Drilling: Disappointments," *Energy Daily,*

March 29, 1985; Bob Williams, "Apparent Mukluk Wildcat Failure Doesn't Dim North Slope Outlook," *Oil and Gas Journal,* January 16, 1984; Mark Potts, "Oil Hopes Dashed in Atlantic," *Washington Post,* December 23, 1984.

41. Yergin, *The Reshaping of the Oil Industry;* John M. Berry, "Oil Price Decline Could Create Winners, Losers," *Washington Post,* July 14, 1985.

42. "Soviet Drilling Program Shy of Target," *Oil and Gas Journal,* April 29, 1985; "Soviet Oil Output Still Below Target," *Journal of Commerce,* June 17, 1985.

43. "Soviets Seek to Stir Up Stagnant Oil Sector," *Journal of Commerce,* March 25, 1985; Leonard Silk, "Soviet Oil Troubles," *New York Times,* June 5, 1985.

44. "Oil Production Up, Activity Levels High Off Northern Europe," *Oil and Gas Journal,* June 10, 1985.

45. William A. Orme, "Mexican Oil Dependence Grows," *Journal of Commerce,* June 14, 1985; William A. Orme, "Reserve Estimate Declines in Mexico," *Journal of Commerce,* March 20, 1985.

46. Peter Hills, "China's Offshore Oil Boom," *New Scientist,* September 8, 1983; Amanda Bennett, "Promise of China's Oil Starts Slowly Changing People and Landscape," *Wall Street Journal,* February 5, 1985; Kim Woodard, China Energy Ventures Inc., "Development of China's Petroleum Industry: An Overview," prepared for the China Energy Workshop, East-West Center, Honolulu, Hawaii, April 25–26, 1985.

47. World Bank, *Energy Transition in Developing Countries;* updated information from Farrokh Najmabadi, World Bank petroleum economist, Washington, D.C., private communication, June 28, 1985.

48. Lichtblau, "OPEC Oil in a Global Context."

49. Charles Ebinger, Georgetown University Center for Strategic and International

Studies, Washington, D.C., private communication, June 13, 1985.

50. Lichtblau, "OPEC Oil in a Global Context"; H. Tahmassebi, "World Energy Outlook Through 1990," Ashland Oil Inc., Ashland, Ky., June 1984.

51. DOE, EIA, *Energy Projections to the Year 2000* (Washington, D.C.: 1983); DOE, EIA, *Annual Energy Outlook 1984* (Washington, D.C.: 1985); IEA, *Energy Policies and Programmes*.

52. World Bank, *Energy Transition in Developing Countries*.

53. Douglas Bohi, *Energy Security in the 1980s: Economic and Political Perspectives* (Washington, D.C.: Brookings Institution, 1984).

54. IEA, *Energy Policies and Programmes*.

55. H. Richard Heede, Richard E. Morgan, and Scott Ridley, *The Hidden Costs of Energy* (Washington, D.C.: Center for Renewable Resources, 1985).

56. U.S. Treasury Department, *Tax Reform for Fairness, Simplicity, and Economic Growth* (Washington, D.C.: 1985).

57. Hewett, *Energy Economics and Foreign Policy in the Soviet Union*.

58. Information on energy efficiency of Third World economies from Alain Streicher, Hagler Bailly & Company, Inc., Washington, D.C., private communication, June 20, 1985; Michael Fisher, "Innovative Approach to Financing Energy Conservation Investments in Developing Countries," *Natural Resources Forum*, May 1985.

59. Gary Hart, "Tax Imported Oil," *New York Times*, August 2, 1985.

60. Energy Advice, *Energy Supplies and Prices in Western Europe to the Year 2000* (Geneva: 1985); World Bank, *Energy Transition in Developing Countries*.

61. IEA, *Energy Policies and Programmes*.

Chapter 6. Reforming the Electric Power Industry

1. Estimate based on data in International Energy Agency (IEA), *Electricity in IEA Countries* (Paris: Organisation for Economic Co-operation and Development, 1985).

2. Figures from *Cogeneration & Small Power Monthly*, all issues through September 1985.

3. Thomas P. Hughes, *Networks of Power: Electrification in Western Society, 1880–1930* (Baltimore, Md.: The Johns Hopkins University Press, 1983).

4. U.S. fuel cost data from U.S. Department of Energy (DOE), Energy Information Administration (EIA), *Monthly Energy Review* (Washington, D.C.: September 1985); data on plant efficiency and production costs from DOE, EIA, *Thermal Electric Plant Construction Cost and Annual Production Expenses, 1980* (Washington, D.C.: 1980).

5. T.A. Burnet et al., "Economic Evaluation of Limestone and Lime Flue Gas Desulfurization Processes," U.S. Environmental Protection Agency, Washington, D.C., March 1984; H.A. Cavanaugh, "Utility Cleanup Spending to Drop 23%," *Electrical World*, July 1984.

6. Carlos Murawczyk and Ken M. Moy, "Environmental Protection from Power Generation: An International Overview," *Public Utilities Fortnightly*, April 28, 1983; Environmental Resources Limited, *Acid Rain: A Review of the Phenomenon in the EEC and Europe* (London: Graham & Trotman Ltd., 1983).

7. "Nuclear: World Status," *Financial Times Energy Economist*, January 1985.

8. Cost estimate based on I.C. Bupp and Charles Komanoff, *Prometheus Bound: Nuclear Power at the Turning Point* (Cambridge, Mass.: Cambridge Energy Research Associates, 1983); French utility debt from Jim Harding, Friends of the Earth, private communication, October 8, 1985.

9. Swedish referendum reported in Elizabeth Taylor and William G. Davey, "Energy

in Western Europe," *Energy Policy,* December 1984; decision of Denmark's parliament from Preben Maegaard, The Danish Centre for Renewable Energy, private communication, August 27, 1985.

10. Bill Richards, "Power Users Seek Relief from Nuclear Costs," *Wall Street Journal,* September 12, 1985; Stuart Diamond, "Sweeping Effects of Shoreham Fine," *New York Times,* June 29, 1985; Lori A. Woehrle, "New Orleans May Go Municipal," *Public Power,* March/April 1985; Bill Rankin, "Chicago Considers Divorce From Its Electric Utility," *Energy Daily,* October 15, 1985.

11. IEA, *Electricity in IEA Countries;* DOE, EIA, *Monthly Energy Review.*

12. DOE, EIA, *Electric Power Monthly* (Washington, D.C.: April 1984); "36th Annual Electric Utility Industry Forecast," *Electrical World,* September 1985.

13. United Nations, *Annual Review of Electric Energy Statistics for Europe* (New York: various years).

14. North American Electric Reliability Council, *Electric Power Supply and Demand* (Princeton, N.J.: 1985).

15. IEA, *Electricity in IEA Countries.*

16. U.S. Department of Energy, *The Future of Electric Power in America: Economic Supply for Economic Growth* (Washington, D.C.: 1983); IEA, *Electricity in IEA Countries.*

17. Peter Navarro, "Our Stake in the Electric Utility's Dilemma," *Harvard Business Review,* May/June 1982; John R. Siegel and John O. Sillin, "Changes in the Real Price of Electricity: Implications for Higher Load Growth," *Public Utilities Fortnightly,* September 15, 1983.

18. "France—Towards an Electric Economy," *European Energy Report,* January 11, 1985; Per Kageson, Swedish energy writer, private communication, September 19, 1985; statistics on electric heating in new homes from "36th Annual Electric Utility Industry

Forecast" and from IEA, *Electricity in IEA Countries.*

19. World Bank, *The Energy Transition in Developing Countries* (Washington, D.C.: 1983).

20. Ibid.

21. Hugh Collier, *Developing Electric Power: Thirty Years of World Bank Experience* (Baltimore, Md.: The Johns Hopkins University Press, 1984); "Record Lending for World Bank," *Energy Daily,* August 1, 1984.

22. World Bank, *China: Long-Term Development Issues and Options* (Washington, D.C.: 1985); information on number of Chinese without electricity from Wang Tingjiong, Director, Institute of Scientific and Technical Information of China, private communication, October 2, 1985; "China's Nuclear Boom May Soon Go Bust," *New Scientist,* February 14, 1985.

23. "Progress and Tradition in Energy Conservation," *Chikyu no Koe* (Tokyo), November 1981; Howard Geller, "Residential Appliances and Space Conditioning Equipment: Current Savings Potential, Cost Effectiveness and Residential Needs," presented at the 1984 Summer Study on Energy Efficiency in Buildings of the American Council for an Energy-Efficient Economy (ACEEE), Santa Cruz, Calif., June 1984; Amory B. Lovins, "Saving Gigabucks with Negawatts," *Public Utilities Fortnightly,* March 21, 1985; "Evolution in Lighting," *EPRI Journal,* June 1984; David B. Goldstein, "Wasted Light: An Economic Rationale for Saving 75% of Lighting Energy in Commercial Buildings," Natural Resources Defense Council, San Francisco, Calif., 1984 (unpublished); "Pacing Plant Motors for Energy Savings," *EPRI Journal,* March 19-21, 1984; Walter J. Martiny, "Making the Choice Between Normal & Hi-Efficiency Motors," presented at 11th Energy Technology Conference, Washington, D.C., March 1984.

24. "California Adopts Efficiency Standards," *Energy Daily,* December 20, 1984; Vic

Reinemer, "Progress—After 10 Years—on Appliance Efficiency Standards," *Public Power*, September/October 1985.

25. Lovins, "Saving Gigabucks with Nega-watts."

26. Howard S. Geller, "Progress in the Energy Efficiency of Residential Appliances and Space Conditioning Equipment," in *Energy Sources: Conservation and Renewables* (New York: American Institute of Physics, 1985); estimates of the economics of improved efficiency and the potential to reduce demand growth are included in Amory B. Lovins, "Least-Cost Electricity Strategies for Wisconsin," prepared testimony before the Wisconsin Public Service Commission, September 24, 1985.

27. Lovins, "Least-Cost Electricity Strategies for Wisconsin."

28. Douglas Cogan and Susan Williams, *Generating Energy Alternatives* (Washington, D.C.: Investor Responsibility Research Center, 1983).

29. M. Centaro, Florida Power and Light Company, private communication, October 11, 1984; Lee Calloway, Pacific Gas and Electric Company, private communication, October 11, 1984; City of Austin Electric Utility Department, *Austin's Conservation Power Plant* (Austin, Tex.: 1984).

30. "Utilities Gear Up for New Marketing Thrust," *Electrical World*, August 1982; "Utilities are Tempting Big Customers to Turn Up the Juice," *Business Week*, October 31, 1983.

31. Lovins, "Least-Cost Electricity Strategies for Wisconsin."

32. Bonneville Power Administration, "BPA Launches the Hood River Conservation Project," Portland, Ore., November 1983; H. Gil Peach, Terry Oliver, and David B. Goldstein, "Cooperation & Diversity in a Large-Scale Conservation Research Project," presented at the ACEEE 1984 Summer Study; update provided by H. Gil Peach, private communication, October 18, 1985.

33. Northwest Power Planning Council, *Northwest Conservation and Electric Power Plan* (Portland, Ore.: 1983).

34. Statement of Arthur Rosenfeld on the Least Cost Utility Planning Initiative before the Subcommittee on Energy Development and Applications of the Committee on Science and Technology, U.S. House of Representatives, September 26, 1985.

35. IEA, *Electricity in IEA Countries*.

36. Information on Sweden from Kageson, private communication.

37. IEA, *Electricity in IEA Countries*.

38. World Bank, *Energy Transition in Developing Countries*.

39. Federal Energy Regulatory Commission (FERC), *Small Power Production and Cogeneration Facilities; Regulations Implementing Section 210 of the Public Utility Regulatory Policies Act of 1978* (Washington, D.C.: 1980).

40. IEA, *Electricity in IEA Countries*.

41. Office of Technology Assessment (OTA), U.S. Congress, *Industrial and Commercial Cogeneration* (Washington, D.C.: 1983); Glenn H. Lovin, "The Resurgence of Cogeneration in the United States," paper presented to the New York Society of Security Analysts, April 4, 1984; International Cogeneration Society estimate from Kirby V. Freeman, "Growing Cogeneration Trend Could be Threat to Coal," *Journal of Commerce*, February 25, 1985.

42. OTA, *Industrial and Commercial Cogeneration*.

43. DiNoto quoted in Joseph A. Glorioso, "Cogeneration: A Technology Reborn," *Industry Week*, January 23, 1984.

44. "HL&P Signs Big Cogeneration Pact With Dow," *Oil & Gas Journal*, February 4, 1985; information on enhanced oil recovery facilities from Jan Hamrin, Independent Energy Producers Association, private communication, August 26, 1985.

45. Ravi K. Sakhuja, "Modular Cogeneration for Commercial Light Industrial Sector," *Cogeneration World,* January/February 1984; Frost and Sullivan study cited in Stuart Diamond, "Cogeneration Jars the Power Industry," *New York Times,* June 10, 1984; The Sievert Group, "Packaged Gas Fired Cogeneration Systems for Fast Food Restaurants," presented at 11th Energy Technology Conference; Paul Johnson, "McDonald's Looks at Cogeneration," *Diesel Progress,* July 1984.

46. DOE, *Industrial Cogeneration Potential: Targeting of Opportunities at the Plant Site* (Washington, D.C.: 1983); figures on FERC registrations from *Cogeneration & Small Power Monthly,* all issues through September 1985; OTA, *Industrial and Commercial Cogeneration;* IEA, *Electricity in IEA Countries.*

47. Goran Weibull, "Squeezing Extra Dollars Out of Cogeneration," *Alternative Sources of Energy,* September/October 1984; dollar value of cogeneration business is author's estimate based on 3,000–4,000 megawatts of cogeneration annually at a cost of $500,000 to $1 million per megawatt.

48. *Cogeneration & Small Power Monthly,* all issues.

49. Thomas Carr, "The Burlington Electric Experience with 50 MW McNeil Municipal Power Plant," and Scott Noll, "Small Wood Fired Power Plants—The Ultrapower Experience," presented at 12th Energy Technology Conference, Washington, D.C., March 25–27, 1985.

50. James L. Easterly and Elizabeth C. Saris, "A Survey of the Use of Biomass as a Fuel to Produce Electric Energy in the United States," paper presented at 11th Energy Technology Conference; Colin Leinster, "The Sweet Smell of Profits from Trash," *Fortune,* April 1, 1985; "Wastewater Plant Pioneers Electric Power from Sludge," *Power,* October 1985.

51. Jeffrey Schmalz, "The Next Decade's Agenda: Garbage," *New York Times,* August 17, 1985; Joseph Bonney, "GE, Pyropower Sign Joint Venture," *Journal of Commerce,* October 10, 1985.

52. Easterly and Saris, "A Survey of the Use of Biomass."

53. Government of Sweden, "Green Power: Biofuels Are a Growing Concern," *Scientific American,* August 1984; information on Denmark's biomass-fueled power plants from Maegaard, private communication; information on Philippines program from Pedro Dumal, Director, National Electrification Administration, Manila, private communication, November 14, 1985.

54. Donald Marier, "Hydropower Begins to Deliver Its Promise," *Alternative Sources of Energy,* January/February 1984; William A. Loeb, "How Small Hydro is Growing Big," *Technology Review,* August/September 1983; U.S. use and cost figures from Raymond J. O'Connor, chairman of the Federal Energy Regulatory Commission, response to inquiry by the Subcommittee on Enegy Conservation and Power, House Committee on Energy and Commerce, February 17, 1984.

55. Pacific Gas and Electric Company, "The Geysers Power Plant Development," internal memorandum, March 26, 1982; Bob Williams, "U.S. Geothermal Retrenching from Period of Vigorous Expansion," *Oil & Gas Journal,* September 30, 1985; Ronald DiPippo, "Development of Geothermal Electric Power Production Overseas," presented at 11th Energy Technology Conference.

56. DiPippo, "Geothermal Electric Power"; Bill Rankin, "DOE and Industry Unite to Boost Geothermal," *Energy Daily,* August 27, 1985.

57. Paul Gipe, "An Overview of the U.S. Wind Industry: The Road to Commercial Development," *Alternative Sources of Energy,* September/October 1985.

58. 600 million kilowatt-hour estimate is based on total of 522 million kilowatt-hours for the first nine months of 1985, according to *Wind Energy Weekly,* October 28, 1985.

59. Donald Marier, "Windfarm Update: Energy Production Improves Dramatically," *Alternative Sources of Energy,* September/October 1985; Robert Lynette, "Wind Turbine Performance—An Industry Overview," *Alternative Sources of Energy,* September/October 1985.

60. Hawaii Electric Company plans described in OTA, *New Electric Power Technologies: Problems and Prospects for the 1990s* (Washington, D.C.: U.S. Government Printing Office, 1985); wind energy developments in Denmark described in *Windpower Monthly* (Knebel, Denmark), July 1985.

61. Economics of various small power sources discussed in California Energy Commission, *Affordable Electricity in an Uncertain World* (Sacramento, Calif.: 1985); advantages of small-scale projects to utility planners discussed in OTA, *New Electric Power Technologies.*

62. OTA, *New Electric Power Technologies.*

63. Ibid.

64. Edgar A. DeMeo and Roger W. Taylor, "Solar Photovoltaic Power Systems: An Electric Utitity R&D Perspective," *Science,* April 20, 1984; "Fuel Cells for the Nineties," *EPRI Journal,* September 1984.

65. IEA, *Electricity in IEA Countries;* "Greek Legislation Frees Electricity Market," *European Energy Report,* July 26, 1985; information on Pakistan from Bob Eichord, U.S. Agency for International Development, private communication, September 12, 1985; information on United Kingdom from Peter James, independent energy analyst, private communication, October 15, 1985.

66. Arthur Rosenfeld remarks before the American Physical Society Short Course on Conservation and Renewables, Washington, D.C., April 27, 1985.

67. California Energy Commission, *Affordable Electricity in an Uncertain World.*

68. N. Richard Friedman, Resource Dynamics Corporation, "State Rulemaking and Utility Pricing for Cogeneration: National Trends in PURPA Implementation," presented at Renewable Energy Technologies Symposium and International Exhibition, Anaheim, Calif., August 29-September 1, 1983; David K. Owens, Edison Electric Institute, "Overview of the States Regulations and Rate Settings Under PURPA Section 210," presented at Renewable Energy Technologies Symposium and International Exhibition, Anaheim, Calif., June 4-9, 1984; Richard Myers, "Cogeneration: After PURPA the Deluge," *Energy Daily,* September 17, 1985.

69. California Energy Commission, *Affordable Electricity in an Uncertain World.*

70. Bill Rankin, "California Regulators Call a Halt to Gold Rush by Cogenerators," *Energy Daily,* July 12, 1985.

71. Bill Paul, "Electricity Pricing Policy That Switches Risks to Investors Planned in California," *Wall Street Journal,* October 11, 1985.

72. David A. Huettner, "Restructuring the Electric Utility Industry: A Modest Proposal," in Howard J. Brown, ed., *Decentralizing Electricity Production* (New Haven, Conn.: Yale University Press, 1983).

Chapter 7. Decommissioning Nuclear Power Plants

1. Public Citizen/Environmental Action, "Dismantling the Myths About Nuclear Decommissioning," Washington, D.C., April 1985.

2. Atomic Industrial Forum (AIF), "International Survey," Bethesda, Md., April 17, 1985.

3. Steve Olson, "Nuclear Undertakers," *Science 84,* September 1984; reactor inventory numbers from AIF, "International Survey," from AIF, "Midyear Report," Bethesda, Md., July 10, 1985, from International Atomic Energy Agency (IAEA), "The Methodology and Technology of Decommissioning Nuclear Facilities" (draft), Annex 2,

Vienna, May 1985, and from Nuclear Energy Agency (NEA), "Compendium on Decommissioning Activities in NEA Member Countries," Organisation for Economic Co-operation and Development, Paris, January 1985; retirement date obtained by adding 30 years to the date the reactor went into commercial operation.

4. U.S. Nuclear Regulatory Commission, "Decommissioning Criteria for Nuclear Facilities," *Federal Register*, February 11, 1985.

5. Taylor Moore, "Decommissioning Nuclear Power Plants," *EPRI Journal*, July/August 1985; Colin Norman, "A Long-Term Problem for the Nuclear Industry," *Science*, January 22, 1982.

6. "Survey on Nuclear Decommissioning Methods/Costs," presented at American Gas Association (AGA) Depreciation Committee and Edison Electric Institute Depreciation Accounting Committee Conference, Dallas, Tex., February 11–13, 1985; NEA, "Compendium on Decommissioning."

7. World Health Organization, *Health Implications of Nuclear Power Production* (Copenhagen: WHO Regional Office for Europe, 1978); Daniel H. Williams and Thomas S. LaGuardia, "Guidelines for Producing Commercial Nuclear Power Plant Decommissioning Cost Estimates," for AIF, Bethesda, Md., March 1985.

8. M. Lasch et al., "Estimation of Radioactive Waste Quantities Arising During Decommissioning," in K.H. Schaller and B. Huber, *Decommissioning of Nuclear Power Plants*, proceedings of a European Communities Conference, Luxembourg, May 22–24, 1984 (London: Graham & Trotman, for Commission of the European Communities, 1984).

9. For a general discussion of the nuclear fuel cycle and various reactor technologies, see Walter C. Patterson, *Nuclear Power* (Middlesex, U.K.: Penguin Books, 1983). For a technical discussion, see R.I. Smith, G.J. Konzek, and W.E. Kennedy, Jr., *Technology,*

Safety and Costs of Decommissioning a Reference Pressurized Water Reactor Power Station (Washington, D.C.: U.S. Nuclear Regulatory Commission, 1978).

10. E.S. Murphy, "Technology, Safety and Costs of Decommissioning a Reference Pressurized Water Reactor Power Station: Classification of Decommissioning Wastes," U.S. Nuclear Regulatory Commission, Washington, D.C., 1984.

11. Smith, Konzek, and Kennedy, *Decommissioning a Reference Pressurized Water Reactor;* Moore, "Decommissioning Nuclear Power Plants"; Commission of the European Communities, "The Community's Research and Development Programme on Decommissioning of Nuclear Power Plants, Third Annual Progress Report," Luxembourg, 1984; Tokai Research Establishment, "Development of Reactor Decommissioning Technology," Japan Atomic Energy Research Institute, Tokyo, 1985.

12. Smith, Konzek, and Kennedy, *Decommissioning a Reference Pressurized Water Reactor;* NEA, "Compendium on Decommissioning."

13. Bill Rankin, "Long Odyssey for a Little Reactor," *Energy Daily*, May 23, 1985.

14. Ibid.; Moore, "Decommissioning Nuclear Power Plants."

15. NEA, "Compendium on Decommissioning."

16. John J. Taylor, "Remote Systems for TMI-2 Surveillance and Characterization," *EPRI Journal*, March 1985; "Utility Starts Extracting Wrecked Core From TMI," *Energy Daily*, October 29, 1985.

17. Annie Stine, "The Short, Sad Life and Long, Slow Death of Humboldt Bay," *Sierra*, September/October 1984.

18. Office of Technology Assessment (OTA), U.S. Congress, *Managing the Nation's Commercial High-Level Radioactive Waste* (Washington, D.C.: U.S. Government Printing Office, 1985).

19. Union of Concerned Scientists, *The Nuclear Fuel Cycle* (Cambridge, Mass.: MIT Press, 1975); OTA, *Managing Commercial High-Level Waste*.

20. For an extensive discussion of international fuel reprocessing plans and activities, see *Fuel Reprocessing and Waste Management*, proceedings of the American Nuclear Society International Topical Meeting, Jackson, Wyo., August 26–29, 1984 (LaGrange Park, Ill.: American Nuclear Society, 1984).

21. Judith Perera, "China and Sudan Want Germany's Nuclear Waste," *New Scientist*, September 5, 1985; Karol Szyndzielorz, chief political commentator, *Zycie Warszawy* (Warsaw), private communication, September 18, 1985.

22. *Fuel Reprocessing and Waste Management*.

23. OTA, *Managing Commercial High-Level Waste;* "EPA Issues 10,000-Year Standard," *Energy Daily*, August 16, 1985; Mark Crawford, "DOE, States Reheat Nuclear Waste Debate," *Science*, October 11, 1985.

24. James B. Martin, Review of "Managing the Nation's Commercial High-Level Radioactive Waste," *Environment*, July/August 1985.

25. "SKB—Swedish Nuclear Fuel and Waste Management Company," information brochure, Stockholm, 1985; Benjamin S. Cooper, "Monitored, Retrievable Storage: Priority Needed," *Nuclear News*, November 1984; Thomas O'Toole, "Clinch River Site Urged for Storing Atomic Waste," *Washington Post*, April 26, 1985.

26. California legislature quote from Fred C. Shapiro, *Radwaste* (New York: Random House, Inc., 1981); Christopher Flavin, *Nuclear Power: The Market Test* (Washington, D.C.: Worldwatch Institute, December 1983).

27. K.M. Harmon, "Survey of Foreign Terminal Radioactive Waste Storage Programs," in *Proceedings of the 1983 Civilian Radioactive Waste Management Information Meeting,*

Washington, D.C., December 12–15, 1983 (Springfield, Va.: National Technical Information Service, 1984); Bob Johnstone, "A Country Without a 'Nuclear Toilet'," *New Scientist*, October 3, 1985; "No One is Emptying the Nuclear Dustbins," *New Scientist*, October 3, 1985.

28. Approximately 113,000 cubic meters of commercial low-level radioactive waste were produced in the United States in 1984; this encompasses wastes from all sources— medical laboratories to nuclear power plants. Lack of disposal sites is outlined in William J. Dircks, "Disposal Capability for Decommissioning Wastes," Nuclear Regulatory Commission, Washington, D.C., memorandum, March 8, 1985.

29. Luther Carter, nuclear waste analyst, Washington, D.C., private communication, October 15, 1985; Richard L. Hudson, "Atomic-Age Dump: A British Nuclear Plant Recycles Much Waste, Stirs a Growing Outcry," *Wall Street Journal*, April 11, 1984.

30. Taylor Moore, "The Great State of Uncertainty in Low-Level Waste Disposal," *EPRI Journal*, March 1985. For a general discussion of nuclear waste problems in America, see Donald L. Barlett and James B. Steele, *Forevermore* (New York: W.W. Norton & Co., 1985).

31. Moore, "Uncertainty in Low-Level Waste Disposal"; "Passage of Waste Bill Ends Threat on Dumps," *New York Times*, December 20, 1985; Bill Paul, "Three States Score Victories in Struggle to Make Others Accept Nuclear Wastes," *Wall Street Journal*, October 8, 1985.

32. U.S. House of Representatives, Committee on Interior and Insular Affairs, "Low-Level Radioactive Waste Policy Amendments Act of 1985," Washington, D.C., October 22, 1985; Gale Warner, "Low-Level Lowdown," *Sierra*, July/August 1985.

33. David Fishlock, "The Swedish Lesson in Nuclear," *Energy Daily*, February 6, 1985;

"Radioactive Waste Management Policies," *IAEA Bulletin*, Vol. 25, No. 4.

34. National Research Council, *Social and Economic Aspects of Radioactive Waste Disposal* (Washington, D.C.: National Academy Press, 1984); Fishlock, "Swedish Lesson"; Michael Oreskes, "U.S. Refuses to Forbid Trucking Atomic Waste Through New York," *New York Times*, September 10, 1985.

35. Share of reactors that are PWRs and BWRs from AIF, "International Survey"; Smith, Konzek, and Kennedy, *Decommissioning a Reference Pressurized Water Reactor*; H.D. Oak et al., *Technology, Safety and Costs of Decommissioning a Reference Boiling Water Reactor Power Station* (Washington, D.C.: U.S. Nuclear Regulatory Commission, 1980).

36. R.I. Smith et al., "Updated Costs for Decommissioning Nuclear Power Facilities," Electric Power Research Institute, Palo Alto, Calif., May 1985; J.T.A. Roberts, R. Shaw, and K. Stahlkopf, "Decommissioning of Commercial Nuclear Power Plants," in Annual Reviews Inc., *Annual Review of Energy, Vol. 10* (Palo Alto, Calif.: 1985).

37. Williams and LaGuardia, "Guidelines for Decommissioning Cost Estimates"; AIF, "An Overview of Decommissioning Nuclear Power Plants," Bethesda, Md., March 1983; "Swiss Estimate Price of Decommissioning as 20% Cost of Building Plant," *Nucleonics Week*, February 26, 1981.

38. Duane Chapman, Cornell University, Ithaca, N.Y., private communication, September 12, 1985; Rand Corporation research from Public Citizen, "Dismantling the Myths"; U.S. Department of Energy (DOE), "Nuclear Power Plant Construction Activity 1984," Washington, D.C., July 1985.

39. Investment in canceled nuclear plants is a Worldwatch Institute estimate based on numerous reports and news articles; DOE, "Nuclear Power Plant Construction Activity."

40. A. Cregut, "Decommissioning Philosophy in France," presented to International Nuclear Reactor Decommissioning Planning Conference, Bethesda, Md., July 16–18, 1985.

41. Roberts, Shaw, and Stahlkopf, "Decommissioning of Commercial Nuclear Power Plants"; Moore, "Uncertainty in Low-Level Waste Disposal."

42. "U.K. Considers Compensation for Those Near Waste Dumps," *Energy Daily*, September 4, 1985.

43. Roberts, Shaw, and Stahlkopf, "Decommissioning of Commercial Nuclear Power Plants"; Public Citizen, "Dismantling the Myths."

44. R.S. Wood, "Assuring the Availability of Funds for Decommissioning Nuclear Facilities," U.S. Nuclear Regulatory Commission, Washington, D.C., 1983; John S. Ferguson, "Influence of Accounting Concepts and Regulatory Rules on the Funding of Power Reactor Decommissioning Costs," presented to International Nuclear Reactor Decommissioning Planning Conference.

45. Public Citizen, "Dismantling the Myths."

46. J.J. Siegel, "Utility Financial Stability and the Availability of Funds for Decommissioning," U.S. Nuclear Regulatory Commission, Washington, D.C., September 1984.

47. Chip Brown, "An Ambitious Nuclear Empire Goes Awry," *Washington Post*, December 2, 1984; Siegel, "Utility Financial Stability."

48. Siegel, "Utility Financial Stability."

49. John Douglas, "Nuclear Power: The Next Generation," *EPRI Journal*, March 1985; "Electricity," *Financial Times Energy Economist*, August 1985.

50. Cregut, "Decommissioning Philosophy in France"; Jim Harding, Friends of the Earth, private communication, October 8, 1985.

51. Public Citizen, "Dismantling the Myths."

52. B. Schultz, "The Back-end of the Swedish Nuclear Fuel Cycle," *IAEA Bulletin*, Vol. 24, No. 2; S. Fareeduddin and J. Hirling, "The Radioactive Waste Management Conference," *IAEA Bulletin*, Vol. 25, No. 4.

53. Harmon, "Survey of Radioactive Waste Programs"; Fareeduddin and Hirling, "Radioactive Waste Management Conference."

54. "Survey of Decommissioning Methods/Costs," AGA Depreciation Committee.

55. The average residential electricity customer in the United States used 8,965 kilowatt-hours of electricity in 1984, according to unpublished statistics compiled by the Edison Electric Institute.

56. Roland Krantz, Commonwealth Edison, private communication, October 17, 1985.

57. E.B. Moore, Jr., "Facilitation of Decommissioning Light Water Reactors," U.S. Nuclear Regulatory Commission, Washington, D.C., December 1979; A. Bittner et al., "Concepts Aimed at Minimizing the Activation and Contamination of Concrete," in Schaller and Huber, *Decommissioning of Nuclear Power Plants*.

Chapter 8. Banishing Tobacco

1. Estimates based on U.S. Department of Agriculture (USDA) computer printout, private communication, August 29, 1985; U.S. prevalence rates from U.S. Department of Health and Human Services (DHHS), National Center for Health Statistics, *Health, United States, 1984* (Washington, D.C.: U.S. Government Printing Office, 1984).

2. Worldwide cost in lives derived from published estimates of heart disease, lung cancer, and emphysema due to cancer; comparisons of the health costs of tobacco based on data from R.T. Ravenholt, "Addiction Mortality in the United States, 1980: Tobacco, Alcohol, and Other Substances," *Population and Development Review*, December 1984, from Royal College of Physicians, *Health or Smoking* (London: Pitman Publishing Ltd, 1983), from Takeshi Hirayama, "Non-Smoking Wives of Heavy Smokers Have A Higher Risk of Lung Cancer: A Study from Japan," *British Medical Journal*, January 17, 1981, from James L. Repace and Alfred H. Lowrey, "A Quantitative Estimate of Nonsmokers' Lung Cancer Risk from Passive Smoking," *Environment International*, Vol. 11, 1985, and from Ira B. Trager et al., "Longitudinal Study of the Effects of Maternal Smoking on Pulmonary Function in Children," *New England Journal of Medicine*, September 22, 1983.

3. Quote in USDA, Foreign Agricultural Service (FAS), "Tariff and Nontariff Measures on Tobacco," *Foreign Agricultural Circular*, Supplement 1–84, Washington, D.C., January 1984. See also Ruth Roemer, *Legislative Action to Combat the World Smoking Epidemic* (Geneva: World Health Organization, 1983).

4. See, for example, special editions of *New York State Journal of Medicine*, July 1985, and *Journal of the American Medical Association*, May 24/31, 1985, both dedicated to the smoking problem.

5. Estimates based on USDA computer printout. For prevalence in the United States, see DHHS, National Center for Health Statistics, *Health, United States, 1984*. Note also that the percent of U.S. male smokers who consumed more than 25 cigarettes per day in 1965 and 1983 was 24.1 and 33.6, respectively. The respective rates for U.S. female smokers in those years were 13.0 and 20.6 percent.

6. USDA computer printout. The Third World, excluding China, has 54 percent of the world's population and uses 25 percent of the world's tobacco; industrial Western nations, 16 percent of the population and 37 percent of the tobacco; Eastern bloc nations, including the Soviet Union, 8.5 percent of the population and 16 percent of the tobacco. USDA, computer printout; Population

Reference Bureau, *1984 World Population Data Sheet* (Washington, D.C.: 1984).

7. USDA, FAS, "Tobacco—World Tobacco Situation," *Foreign Agriculture Circular FT 6–85*, Washington, D.C., June 1985.

8. Richard Doll and Richard Peto, "Quantitative Estimates of Avoidable Risks of Cancer in the United States Today," *Journal of the National Cancer Institute*, November 1981; U.S. Department of Health, Education, and Welfare (DHEW), Public Health Service, *Smoking and Health: A Report of the Surgeon General* (Washington, D.C.: U.S. Government Printing Office: 1979).

9. Estimates based on USDA computer printout.

10. Royal College of Physicians, *Health or Smoking;* DHHS, National Center for Health Statistics, *Health, United States, 1984;* Hans Adriaanse et al., "Physicians, Smoking, and Health in the Netherlands," *New York State Journal of Medicine*, July 1985; K. Bjartveit et al., "Controlling the Epidemic: Legislation and Restrictive Measures," *Canadian Journal of Public Health*, November/December 1981.

11. J. Akbar, N. Cohen, and A.R. Measham, "Smoking and Respiratory Disease Symptoms in Rural Bangladesh," *Public Health*, November 1983; A. Kubik, "The Influence of Smoking and Other Etiopathogenetic Factors on the Incidence of Bronchogenic Carcinoma and Chronic Nonspecific Respiratory Diseases," *Czechoslovak Medicine*, Vol. 7, No. 1, 1984; Soviet data cited in U.S. Office of Smoking and Health translated abstract of A.G. Shevchuk and R.N. Tarasova, "The Organization of Antismoking Education," *Zdravookhraneniye Rossiyskoy Federatsii*, Vol. 5, 1983; Dean T. Jamison et al., *China: The Health Sector* (Washington, D.C.: World Bank, 1984); DHHS, National Center for Health Statistics, *Health, United States, 1984*.

12. Figures for U.S. increase from Verner Grise, USDA, private communication, September 9, 1985; Claudia Wallis, "Into the Mouths of Babes," *Time*, July 15, 1985; L.D. Sanghvi, K. Jayant, and S.S. Pakhale, "Tobacco Use and Cancer in India," *World Smoking and Health*, Winter 1980.

13. DHHS, National Center for Health Statistics, *Health, United States, 1984;* information on British children from "Curry-Eating Teenage Smokers Cough On," *New Scientist*, April 21, 1983; information on Norwegian children from Bjartveit et al., "Controlling the Epidemic: Legislation and Restrictive Measures"; P. Nordgren, "Sweden Launches New Anti-Smoking Offensive: Government-Appointed Commission Presents New Plans for a 25-Year Program," Comprehensive Smoking Prevention Education Act, Hearings before the Subcommittee on Health and the Environment, U.S. House of Representatives Committee on Energy and Commerce, March 5, 11, and 12, 1982; information on Eastern bloc from translated asbtract, D.N. Loranskiy et al., "The Smoking Problem," *Sovetskoye Zdravookhraneniye*, 1983 (in Russian); "18–19-Year-Old Women Are Smoking Up a Storm," *Canadian Family Physician*, August 1983; L.A. Cappiello and E.A. El Maksoud, "A Profile Study of High School Boys Who Smoke Cigarettes in Alexandria, Egypt, and Buffalo, New York," *International Journal of Health Education*, March 1983; I. Salas et al., "Prevalence of Tobacco Smoking in Adolescents in Third Year of Secondary Education," *Revista Medica de Chile*, December 1982 (in Spanish); J. Cohen and M. Solal, "Antismoking Actions in France: Five Year Results," *World Smoking and Health*, Summer 1982; Royal College of Physicians, *Health or Smoking*.

14. Patrick L. Remington et al., "Current Smoking Trends in the United States," *Journal of the American Medical Association*, May 24/31, 1985. The low rate for women with only a grade-school education probably relates to their age. Few women born in the first quarter of this century smoked. These women also were less likely to have had advanced educational opportunities.

15. The estimate of 2 million to 2.5 million annual deaths worldwide includes an ex-

trapolation of lung cancer deaths using an equation derived from death and smoking rates in 20 industrial and developing countries. It also includes the sum of the deaths due to heart disease and emphysema in industrial countries, derived from various published estimates (see notes 20 and 25). For the United States, Ravenholt estimates mortality due to tobacco use at almost 500,000, or 25 percent of all deaths. Ravenholt, "Addiction Mortality in the United States, 1980."

16. Jerome H. Jaffe and Maureen Kanzler, "Smoking as an Addictive Disorder," in Norman A. Krasnegor, ed., *Cigarette Smoking as a Dependence Process* (Rockville, Md.: National Institute on Drug Abuse, 1979).

17. A.C. McKennell and R.K. Thomas, *Adults' and Adolescents' Smoking Habits and Attitudes* (London: Her Majesty's Stationery Office, 1967), as cited in M.A.H. Russell, "Tobacco Dependence: Is Nicotine Rewarding or Aversive?" in Krasnegor, *Cigarette Smoking as a Dependence Process;* W.A. Hunt and J.D. Matarazzo, "Three Years Later: Recent Developments in the Experimental Modification of Smoking Behavior," *Journal of Abnormal Psychology,* Vol. 81, No. 2, 1973, as cited in Saul M. Shiffman, "The Tobacco Withdrawal Syndrome," in ibid.

18. See various chapters in Krasnegor, *Cigarette Smoking as a Dependence Process*.

19. David W. Kaufman et al., "Nicotine and Carbon Monoxide Content of Cigarette Smoke and the Risk of Myocardial Infarction in Young Men," *New England Journal of Medicine,* February 24, 1983; diminished risk discussed in W.P. Castelli, "Cardiovascular Disease and Multifactorial Risk: Challenge of the 1980s," *American Heart Journal,* November 1983.

20. Some prospective studies, including one forthcoming from the American Cancer Society, suggest a higher range of heart attacks are due to smoking, R.T. Ravenholt, private communication, October 28, 1985. See also Castelli, "Cardiovascular Disease and Multifactorial Risk"; DHHS, Public

Health Service, Office on Smoking and Health (OSH), *The Health Consequences of Smoking—Cardiovascular Disease: A Report of the Surgeon General* (Washington, D.C.: U.S. Government Printing Office, 1983), and A. Keys et al., "The Seven Countries Study: 2,289 Deaths in 15 Years," *Preventive Medicine,* March 1984.

21. See Jay D. Coffman, "Diseases of the Peripheral Vessels," in James B. Wyngaarden and Lloyd H. Smith, eds., *Cecil Textbook of Medicine* (Philadelphia: W.B. Saunders Company, 1982); S. Shinonoya, "What is Buerger's Disease?" *World Journal of Surgery,* July 1983.

22. L. Rosenberg et al., "Myocardial Infarction in Women Under 50 Years of Age," *Journal of the American Medical Association,* November 25, 1983; "Oral Contraceptives, Age, Smoking and Circulatory System Disease," *Chronic Diseases in Canada,* June 1983; epidemiology survey cited is S. Johansson, A. Vedin, and C. Wilhelmsson, "Myocardial Infarction in Women," *Epidemiologic Reviews,* Vol. 5, 1983.

23. C. Borland et al., "Carbon Monoxide Yield of Cigarettes and Its Relation to Cardiorespiratory Disease," *British Medical Journal,* November 26, 1983.

24. DHHS, National Center for Health Statistics, *Health, United States, 1984*.

25. A linear regression (correlation coefficient —.796) of lung cancer deaths in 20 countries on cigarette consumption was performed using data on smoking (adjusted for age) obtained from USDA computer printouts for 1960 and data on lung cancer deaths in 1980, from World Health Organization, *World Health Statistics, 1980–1981* (Geneva: 1981). This method of comparing lung cancer with smoking rates 20 years earlier is similar to one proposed in Doll and Peto, "Avoidable Risks of Cancer," and explained in detail in Appendix E there.

26. B.E. Henderson, L.N. Kolonel, and F.H. Foster, "Cancer in Polynesians," Na-

tional Cancer Institute Monograph No. 62, National Institutes of Health, U.S. Department of Health and Human Services, Bethesda, Md., December 1982; Repace and Lowrey, "Nonsmokers' Lung Cancer Risk from Passive Smoking."

27. DHEW, Public Health Service, *Smoking and Health*.

28. Karl Kronebusch, "Smoking Related Deaths and Financial Costs," Office of Technology Assessment, U.S. Congress, Staff Memo, Washington, D.C., September 1985; DHHS, OSH, *The Health Consequences of Smoking—Chronic Obstructive Lung Disease: A Report of the Surgeon General* (Washington, D.C.: U.S. Government Printing Office, 1984).

29. Fire fatalities from Ravenholt, "Addiction Mortality in the United States, 1980"; Repace and Lowrey, "Nonsmokers' Lung Cancer Risk from Passive Smoking."

30. D. Hill, "Tobacco Dependency-Problems and Progress," in National Alcohol and Drug Dependence Multidisciplinary Institute 78, Canberra, Australia, August 27-September 1, 1978 (Canberra: Australian Foundation on Alcohol and Drug Dependence, date unknown); N.E. Collishaw and G. Myers, "Dollar Estimates of the Consequences of Tobacco Use in Canada, 1979," *Canadian Journal of Public Health*, May/June 1984; OSH translated abstract of R.E. Leu et al., "The Political-Economical Costs of Smoking: A Reply" (letters), *Schweizerische Medizinische Wochenschrift*, September 24, 1983 (in German); Royal College of Physicians, *Health or Smoking*.

31. Numbers do not add up to total due to rounding; Kronebusch, "Smoking Related Deaths and Financial Costs." See also Bryan R. Luce and Stuart O. Schweitzer, "Smoking and Alcohol Abuse: A Comparison of Their Economic Consequences," *New England Journal of Medicine*, March 9, 1978; Dorothy P. Rice and Thomas A. Hodgson, "Economic Costs of Smoking: An Analysis of Data for the United States," presented at the Allied Social Science Association Annual Meetings, San Francisco, Calif., December 28, 1983.

32. As cited in translated abstract, K. Gibinski et al., "Morbid Economic Effects of Tobacco Smoking in the District of Katowice," *Polski Tygodnik Lekarski*, May 19, 1980 (in Polish); M.E. Thompson and W.F. Forbes, "Costs and 'Benefits' of Cigarette Smoking in Canada," *Canadian Medical Association Journal*, November 1, 1982.

33. Estimates based on data in USDA, FAS, "Tobacco—World Tobacco Situation," and in USDA, Economic Research Service, *World Indices of Agricultural and Food Production, 1950–84* (unpublished printout) (Washington, D.C.: 1985).

34. The 50 percent increase in lung cancer deaths is based on the equation of deaths as a function of cigarettes consumed, assuming that lung cancer in the year 2000 would be a function of cigarette consumption in 1980; reduced risk for ex-smokers from Doll and Peto, "Avoidable Risks of Cancer."

35. Repace and Lowrey, "Nonsmokers' Lung Cancer Risk from Passive Smoking"; James L. Repace and Alfred H. Lowrey, "Indoor Air Pollution, Tobacco Smoke, and Public Health," *Science*, May 2, 1980; James L. Repace, "The Problem of Passive Smoking," *Bulletin of the New York Academy of Medicine*, Second Series, December 1981; Pelayo Correa et al., "Passive Smoking and Lung Cancer," *Lancet*, September 10, 1983.

36. Hirayama, "Non-Smoking Wives of Heavy Smokers: A Study from Japan." For a brief review of 14 studies of passive smoking, see Repace and Lowrey, "Nonsmokers' Lung Cancer Risk from Passive Smoking."

37. Greek study from D. Trichopoulos et al., "Lung Cancer and Passive Smoking," *International Journal of Cancer*, Vol. 27, 1981, pp. 1–4; Correa et al., "Passive Smoking and Lung Cancer"; German study from translated abstract of A. Knoth, H. Bohn, and F. Schmidt, "Passive Smoking as a Causal

Factor of Bronchial Carcinoma in Female Nonsmokers," *Medizinische Klinik*, February 4, 1983.

38. Repace and Lowrey, "Nonsmokers' Lung Cancer Risk from Passive Smoking"; Repace and Lowrey, "Indoor Air Pollution, Tobacco Smoke, and Public Health"; Vivian E. Thompson et al., "The Air Toxics Problem in the United States: An Analysis of Cancer Risks Posed by Selected Air Pollutants," *Journal of the Air Pollution Control Association*, May 1985.

39. These examples assume 1-milligram tar cigarettes. J.L. Repace, "Effect of Ventilation on Passive Smoking Risk in a Model Workplace," in J.E. Janssen, *Management of Atmospheres in Tightly Enclosed Spaces*, Proceedings of an Engineering Foundation Conference, Santa Barbara, Calif., October 17–21, 1983 (Atlanta: American Society of Heating, Refrigerating, and Air Conditioning Engineers, Inc., 1983).

40. Ibid.

41. I. Batar, R.P. Bernard, and L. Lampe, "Effects of Hypertensive Disorders on the Outcome of Pregnancy: Early Findings of Maternity Care Monitoring (MCM) in Debrecen, Hungary," *Clinical and Experimental Hypertension*, 1982; J.M. Foidart, "Tobacco and Pregnancy," *Revue Medicale de Liege*, September 1, 1983 (in French).

42. S. Wilner et al., "A Comparison of Smoking and Other Maternal Behavior During Pregnancy of Patients in a Health Maintenance Organization and Fee-For-Service Practices," in *Maternity Care in Two Health Care Systems*, Doctoral Dissertation Abstracts, Harvard University, June 1981; M. Chansoriya, K.K. Kaul, and R.C. Verma, "Effect of Tobacco Chewing by Mothers on Fetal Outcome," *Indian Pediatrics*, February 1983.

43. Ravenholt, "Addiction Mortality in the United States, 1980"; E. Menghetti, "Maternal Smoking in Pregnancy: Recent Acquisitions on Its Consequences in Infants," *Rivista Italiana di Pediatria*, March/April 1983 (in Italian); G. Moggian et al., "Statistical Investigation of the Effects of Smoking During Pregnancy," *Giornale Italiano di Ostetricia e Ginecologia*, November 1983 (in Italian).

44. U.K. surveys from N. Nichol and J. Russell, "A Study of the Smoking Habits of Pregnant Women and Their Attitudes to Smoking in Hospital," *Health Bulletin*, September 1983; Ravenholt, "Addiction Mortality in the United States, 1980." The estimate of 3 million is a minimum based on the data in Table 8–5.

45. As cited in Royal College of Physicians, *Health or Smoking*. Recent studies suggesting increased risk of respiratory disease in children as a result of parental smoking include A. Charlton, "Children's Coughs Related to Parental Smoking," *British Medical Journal*, June 2, 1984, and W.J. Morgan and L.M. Taussig, "The Chronic Bronchitis Complex in Children," *Pediatric Clinics of North America*, August 1984.

46. Trager et al., "Longitudinal Study of Maternal Smoking."

47. Ibid.

48. Alan Blum, "If Smoking Killed Baby Seals," *New York State Journal of Medicine*, July 1985.

49. For an example of this argument, see William F. Buckley, Jr., "The Weed," in William R. Finger, *The Tobacco Industry in Transition* (Lexington, Mass.: Lexington Books, 1981).

50. Bryan R. Luce and Stuart O. Schweitzer, "Smoking and Alcohol Abuse: A Comparison of Their Economic Consequences," *New England Journal of Medicine*, March 9, 1978; National Research Council, Committee on Diet, Nutrition, and Cancer, *Diet, Nutrition, and Cancer* (Washington, D.C.: National Academy Press, 1982). For an overview of the relative carcinogenic risk of common items, see B.N. Ames, "Dietary Carcinogens and Anticarcinogens," *Science*, September 23, 1983.

51. Roemer, *Legislative Action;* USDA, FAS, "Tariff and Nontariff Restrictions on Tobacco."

52. A number of multiple linear regressions were performed with data on smoking per capita, cigarette price, per capita income, and policy strength. The strength of policy consistently showed a small but positive association with consumption even when price and income were controlled for. The association between price and consumption was not meaningful, perhaps because prices are controlled in many countries. In one regression of consumption on per capita income and policy strength, the result was Ln Consumption = 4.2 + .31 × Ln Income + .21 × Ln Policy Score (t = 4.15 and 1.77, respectively; R^2 = .63). Policy scores were based on Roemer, *Legislative Action,* and on USDA, FAS, "Tariff and Nontariff Measures on Tobacco." Price elasticity for the United States was estimated to be -.3, using data from Tobacco Institute, *The Tax Burden on Tobacco: Historical Compilation 1983* (Washington, D.C.: 1984). Consumption data in this section are from USDA, computer printout. See also "The Cigarette Excise Tax," Harvard University for the Study of Smoking Behavior and Policy, Cambridge, Mass., April 17, 1985.

53. Royal College of Physicians, *Health or Smoking*.

54. Shiffman, "The Tobacco Withdrawal Syndrome."

55. For a brief overview of specific actions in the nonsmokers' rights movement, see *New York State Journal of Medicine*, July 1985, Phyllis L. Kahn, "The Minnesota Clean Indoor Air Act, A Model for New York and Other States," *New York State Journal of Medicine,* December 1983, and "Effects of 'Passive Smoking' Lead Nonsmokers to Step Up Campaign," *Journal of the American Medical Association,* May 24/31, 1985.

56. American Cancer Society, "Clean Indoor Air Legislation—Update on Division Experience," Washington, D.C., revised, January 1985.

57. Ibid.

58. Jonathan E. Fielding, "Effectiveness of Employee Health Improvement Programs," *Journal of Occupational Medicine,* November 1982; Environmental Improvement Associates, "Improving the Work Environment: A Management Guide to Smoke Free Work Areas," Salem, N.J., January 1983; Marvin M. Kristein, "How Much Can Business Expect to Profit from Smoking Cessation?" *Preventive Medicine,* Vol. 12, 1983, pp. 358–381.

59. Human Resources Policy Corporation, "Smoking Policies in Large Corporations," Los Angeles, 1985.

60. Zhao Jinming, "Tobacco Industry Sets Dual Targets," *China Daily,* May 22, 1985; Bharat Dogra, "Farm Exports from a Hungry Land," *Economic and Political Weekly,* March 23, 1985.

61. "How EEC Subsidises Smoking," *New Scientist,* May 17, 1984; Lawrence Spohn, "Tobacco Dilemma Intensifying in North Carolina," *New York State Journal of Medicine,* July 1985.

62. World Health Organization, *Smoking Control Strategies in Developing Countries,* Technical Report Series 695 (Geneva: 1983).

63. The nations in this category are mainly in Africa. Examples include: Chad, Ethiopia, Niger, Nigeria, Peru, Sudan, Uganda, and Zaire, all of which record annual consumption of fewer than 300 cigarettes per capita (age 15 and older), and in many of which the figure is less than 200.

64. Royal College of Physicians, *Health or Smoking*.

Chapter 9. Investing in Children

1. Kathleen Newland, *Infant Mortality and the Health of Societies* (Washington, D.C.: Worldwatch Institute, March 1981). For an excellent analysis of the effect of population growth on economic development, see World Bank, *World Development Report 1984* (New York: Oxford University Press, 1984).

2. Paul Streeten et al., *First Things First: Meeting Basic Human Needs in the Developing Countries* (New York: Oxford University Press, 1981); Theodore Schultz, *Investing in People* (Berkeley, Calif.: University of California Press, 1981).

3. United Nations Children's Fund (UNICEF), *State of the World's Children 1985* (New York: Oxford University Press, 1984); World Bank, *World Bank Atlas 1985* (Washington, D.C.: 1985); UNICEF, *State of the World's Children 1984* (New York: Oxford University Press, 1983); World Health Organization, *Development of Indicators for Monitoring Progress Towards Health For All by the Year 2000* (Geneva: 1981); "The Major Public Health Killers," *International Health Magazine* (International Drinking Water and Sanitation Decade), No. 10, 1984.

4. For a discussion of this potential, see William U. Chandler, *Improving World Health: A Least Cost Strategy* (Washington, D.C.: Worldwatch Institute, July 1984).

5. United Nations, Department of International Economic and Social Affairs, *Demographic Yearbook* (New York: 1982); Population Reference Bureau, *1985 World Population Data Sheet* (Washington, D.C.: 1985).

6. World Health Organization press releases; UNICEF, *State of the World's Children 1984*.

7. Derived from World Bank, *World Development Report 1984*.

8. "Diarrhoea, Dehydration, and Drugs," *British Medical Journal*, November 10, 1985; UNICEF, *State of the World's Children 1984*; Jean Paul Beau, L'Organisation de Science et Technologie d'Outre Mer, Pikine, Senegal, private communication, March 6, 1985.

9. J. Welsh and J. May, "Anti-infective Properties of Breast Milk," *Journal of Pediatrics*, Vol. 94, No. 1, 1979; I. Bravo et al., "Breast-feeding, Weight Gains, Diarrhea, and Malnutrition in the First Year of Life," *Bulletin of the Pan American Health Organization*, Vol. 18, No. 2, 1984.

10. Margaret Cameron and Yngve Hofvander, *Manual on Feeding Infants and Young Children* (New York: Oxford University Press, 1984).

11. Poster displayed at UNICEF office in Dakar, Senegal, March 1985.

12. "Food Program for Pregnant Women Raises Infant Birth Weight, Gestational Age, Reduces Mortality," *Family Planning Perspectives*, Vol. 17, No. 1, 1985.

13. UNICEF, *State of the World's Children 1985*.

14. R. Feachem and M. Koblinsky, "Interventions for the Control of Diarrhoeal Diseases Among Young Children: Measles Immunization," *Bulletin of the World Health Organization*, Vol. 61, No. 4, 1983; UNICEF, *State of the World's Children 1984*.

15. Jean-Hubert Thieffry, "Un Thesis de Medicine," Université d'Anies, France; Michelle Thieffry, Voluntaire du Cooperation, Thiès, Senegal, private communication, March 1985.

16. "One Way to Get Results," *World Development Forum*, October 15, 1984; "Vaccination Blitz," *China Daily*, February 5, 1985.

17. R. N. Basu, "India's Immunization Programme," *World Health Forum*, Vol. 6, No. 1, 1985; Population Reference Bureau, *1985 World Population Data Sheet*.

18. W. Henry Mosely and Lincoln Chen, eds., *Child Survival: Strategies for Research*, reprinted in *Population and Development Review*, Supplement to Vol. 10, 1984.

19. Hattib N-Jie, Deputy Director, Medical and Health Ministry, The Gambia, private communication, March 12, 1985.

20. Norbert Engel, UNICEF Information Officer, Dakar, Senegal, private communication, March 14, 1985.

21. Curt Fischer, Regional Medical Director, Ministry of Health, The Gambia, private communication, March 16, 1985; Engel, pri-

vate communication; N-Jie, private communication.

22. Dean T. Jamison et al., *China: The Health Sector* (Washington, D.C.: World Bank, 1984).

23. Peter Bourne, President, Global Water, Inc., Washington, D.C., private communication, April 3, 1984.

24. U.S. Agency for International Development (AID), *Safe Water and Waste Disposal for Human Health: A Program Guide* (Washington, D.C.: 1982); Pan American Health Organization, *Health Conditions in the Americas 1977–1980* (Washington, D.C.: 1982); World Bank, *Health Sector Policy Paper* (Washington, D.C.: 1980); World Bank, "Water Supply and Waste Disposal," *Poverty and Basic Needs Series,* Washington, D.C., 1983.

25. John M. Hunter, Luis Rey, and David Scott, "Man-made Lakes—Man-made Disasters," *World Health Forum,* Vol. 3, No. 2, 1983; Paul L. Aspelin and Silvio Coelhodas Santos, *Indian Areas Threatened by Hydro-electric Projects in Brazil* (Copenhagen: International Working Group for Indigenous Affairs, 1981); AID, *Safe Water and Waste Disposal*.

26. AID, *Safe Water and Waste Disposal;* Environmental Sanitation Information Center, *Human Waste Management For Low-Income Settlements* (Bangkok: 1983); World Bank, "Water Supply and Waste Disposal"; John M. Kalbermatten et al., *Appropriate Sanitation Alternatives* (Baltimore, Md.: The Johns Hopkins University Press, 1982).

27. Chandler, *Improving World Health*.

28. Peter Morgan, Blair Research Laboratory, Harare, Zimbabwe, private communication, April 3, 1985; Peter Morgan, "Blair Research Bulletins for Rural Water Supply and Sanitation," Blair Research Laboratory, Harare, Zimbabwe, March 1985.

29. Southern African Development Coordination Conference, *SADCC, Agriculture Toward 2000* (Rome: Food and Agriculture Organization, 1984).

30. Edward Girardet, "Afghanistan: No. 1 Need is Food," *Christian Science Monitor,* December 28, 1984; Institute of Nutrition and Food Science, "Nutrition Survey of Rural Bangladesh," *ADAB News* (Association of Development Agencies in Bangladesh), May/June 1984; Mushtaq Ahmed and D.J. Clements, "Problems Associated with Wheat Production in Bangladesh," and "Food Policy," editorial in *ADAB News,* September/October 1984; Hugh Brammer, "Development Strategies in Famine Prone Areas," *ADAB News,* November/December 1984.

31. See Robert Orr Whyte and Pauline Whyte, *The Women of Rural Asia* (Boulder, Colo.: Westview Press, 1982); Edna G. Bay, ed., *Women and Work in Africa* (Boulder, Colo.: Westview Press, 1982); Catherine Overholt et al., eds., *Gender Roles in Development Projects* (West Hartford, Conn.: Kumarian Press, 1985); Karen Oppenheim Mason, *The Status of Women* (New York: The Rockefeller Foundation, 1984); Natalie Kaufman Hevener, *International Law and the Status of Women* (Boulder, Colo.: Westview Press, 1983); U.S. Bureau of the Census and AID, *Women of the World: Sub-Saharan Africa* (Washington, D.C.: U.S. Department of Commerce, 1984); U.S. Bureau of the Census and AID, *Women of the World: Latin America and the Carribean* (Washington, D.C.: U.S. Department of Commerce, 1984); Sue Ellen M. Charlton, *Women in Third World Development* (Boulder, Colo.: Westview Press, 1984).

32. Engel, private communication.

33. ENDA community worker, Dakar, Senegal, private communication regarding the Senegalese Minister of Agriculture, March 10, 1985.

34. Ann Crittenden, "Shortchanging a Food Program That Works," *Wall Street Journal,* February 28, 1985; International Fund for Agricultural Development (IFAD), *A Fund For the Rural Poor* (Rome: 1984).

35. The cost of providing agricultural productivity loans is a crude extrapolation from

the experience of the International Fund for Agricultural Development (see IFAD, *A Fund for the Rural Poor*) and observations in Zimbabwe. Most estimates include a conservative assumption that the high end of the range of costs will be necessary for delivery of the services.

36. Bureau of the Census and AID, *Women of the World: Sub-Saharan Africa;* U.S. Bureau of the Census and AID, *Women of the World: Latin America and the Carribean;* Whyte and Whyte, *Women of Rural Asia;* James Trussell and Anne R. Pebley, "The Potential Impact of Changes in Fertility on Infant, Child, and Maternal Mortality," *Studies in Family Planning,* November/December 1984; Marilyn Edmonds and John M. Paxman, "Early Pregnancy and Childbearing in Guatemala, Brazil, Nigeria, and Indonesia: Addressing the Consequences," *Pathpapers* (Pathfinder Fund, Boston), September 1984.

37. UNICEF, *State of the World's Children 1984;* Cécile de Sweemer, "The Influence of Child Spacing on Child Survival," *Population Studies,* Vol. 38 (1984), pp. 47–72; M. Potts, B.S. Janowitz, and J.A. Forney, eds., *Childbirth In Developing Countries* (Hingham, Mass.: MTP Press, 1983); Rodolfo A. Bulatao and Ronald D. Lee, *Determinants of Fertility in Developing Countries,* Vols. 1 and 2 (New York: Academic Press, 1983).

38. Trussell and Pebley, "Potential Impact of Changes in Fertility."

39. World Bank, *World Development Report 1984;* "In Kenya, Modernization, Drop in Breastfeeding and Low Contraceptive Use Bring Rising Fertility," *International Family Planning Perspectives,* Vol. 10, No. 4, 1984; Maleba Gomes, "Family Size and Education Attainment in Kenya," *Population and Development Review,* Vol. 10, No. 4, 1984.

40. Nancy Harris, former Regional Director, African Region, International Family Planning Assistance, Nairobi, Kenya, private communication, March 1985; see also Chapter 10 in this volume.

41. As reported in *Le Sahel,* February 6, 1985, and translated by U.S. Department of State, March 1985.

42. David Willis, "Price Tag on Slowing World Population Growth: $4 Billion a Year," *Christian Science Monitor,* August 16, 1984; Joseph Speidel, "Cost Implications of Population Stabilization," presented at the International Workshop on Cost-Effectiveness and Cost-Benefit Analysis in Family Planning Programs, St. Michael's, Md., August 17–20, 1981; R.A. Bulatao, draft memorandum to the World Bank, April 9, 1984.

43. Michael P. Todaro, *Economic Development in the Third World* (London: Langman Group, 1977); World Bank, *World Development Report 1983* (New York: Oxford University Press, 1983).

44. Schultz, *Investing in People.*

45. Organisation for Economic Co-operation and Development, *Development Cooperation* (Paris: 1984).

Chapter 10. Reversing Africa's Decline

1. Estimate of Africans fed with imported grain in 1984 based on import figures from U.S. Department of Agriculture (USDA), Foreign Agricultural Service, *Foreign Agriculture Circular* FG-8–84, Washington, D.C., May 1984, and on assumption that one ton of grain will feed roughly six people for a year; assessment of displaced people from United Nations, "Report on the Emergency Situation in Africa," New York, February 22, 1985; estimate of famine deaths from U.N. Economic Commission for Africa (ECA), "Second Special Memorandum by the ECA Conference of Ministers: International Action for Relaunching the Initiative for Long-Term Development and Economic Growth in Africa," Addis Ababa, April 25–29, 1985.

2. USDA, Economic Research Service (ERS), *World Indices of Agricultural and Food Production, 1950–84* (unpublished printout) (Washington, D.C.: 1985).

3. ECA, "Second Special Memorandum."

4. Paul Lewis, "Donor Nations Form Africa Fund With World Bank," *New York Times*, February 2, 1985; United Nations Office for Emergency Operations in Africa, *Africa Emergency Report*, April/May 1985. The special facility for sub-Saharan Africa is also discussed in World Bank, *Annual Report 1985* (Washington, D.C.: 1985).

5. Calculated from Population Reference Bureau, *1985 World Population Data Sheet* (Washington, D.C.: 1985).

6. U.N. projections cited in Thomas J. Goliber, "Sub-Saharan Africa: Population Pressures on Development," *Population Bulletin* (Washington, D.C.: Population Reference Bureau, February 1985).

7. Ibid.

8. Ibid.

9. Fred Sai, Senior Population Adviser, World Bank, Washington, D.C., private communication, October 2, 1985.

10. Private communications, April 30-May 5, 1985.

11. Population Institute, *Toward Population Stabilization: Findings From Project 1990* (New York: 1984).

12. Rodolfo A. Bulatao, *Expenditures on Population Programs in Developing Regions: Current Levels and Future Requirements*, Staff Working Paper No. 679 (Washington, D.C.: World Bank, 1985).

13. Private communications, April 30, 1985.

14. United Nations Food and Agriculture Organization (FAO), *Tropical Forest Resources*, Forestry Paper 30 (Rome: 1982).

15. Anne de Lattre and Arthur M. Fell, *The Club du Sahel: An Experiment in International Co-operation* (Paris: Organisation for Economic Co-operation and Development, 1984); Club du Sahel, "Food Self-Sufficiency and Ecological Balance in the Sahel Countries," Paris, May 27, 1982.

16. U.S. Agency for International Development (AID), Bureau for Africa, *Energy, Forestry and Natural Resources Activities in the Africa Region* (Washington, D.C: January 1984); John Spears, "Review of World Bank Financed Forestry Activity FY1984," World Bank, Washington, D.C., June 30, 1984.

17. Spears, "Review of World Bank Financed Forestry Activity."

18. FAO data cited in Office of Technology Assessment, U.S. Congress, *Technologies to Sustain Tropical Forest Resources* (Washington, D.C.: U.S. Government Printing Office, 1984).

19. Plantation share of fuelwood supply from Dennis Anderson and Robert Fishwick, *Fuelwood Consumption and Deforestation in African Countries*, Staff Working Paper No. 704 (Washington, D.C.: World Bank, 1984). For economic analysis of reforestation programs, see Kenneth Newcombe, *An Economic Justification for Rural Afforestation: the Case of Ethiopia*, Energy Department Paper No. 16 (Washington, D.C.: World Bank, 1984), and U.N. Development Program/World Bank Energy Sector Assessment Program, *Ethiopia: Issues and Options in the Energy Sector*, Report No. 4741-ET (Washington, D.C.: World Bank, 1984).

20. Anderson and Fishwick, *Fuelwood Consumption and Deforestation*.

21. J.B. Raintree and B. Lundgren, "Agroforestry Potentials for Biomass Production in Integrated Land Use Systems," presented at Biomass Energy Systems: Building Blocks for Sustainable Development, a conference sponsored by the World Resources Institute and the Rockefeller Brothers Fund, Airlie, Va., January 29-February 1, 1985.

22. T.M. Catterson, "AID Experience in the Forestry Sector in the Sahel—Opportunities for the Future," presented to the Meeting of the Steering Committee, CILSS/Club du Sahel, Paris, June 14–15, 1984.

23. Fred R. Weber, "Technical Update on Forestry Efforts in Africa," in AID, Bureau for Africa, *Report of Workshop on Forestry Program Evaluation* (Washington, D.C.: August 1984).

24. Dr. Y. Dommergues, "Using Biotechnologies for Improving the Forest Cover of the Sahelian and Sudanian Zones," presented to the World Bank, Washington, D.C., April 17, 1984; National Research Council, Board on Science and Technology for International Development, *Environmental Change in the West African Sahel* (Washington, D.C.: National Academy Press, 1983).

25. Michael Dow, National Research Council, private communication, Washington, D.C., March 27, 1985; Anderson and Fishwick, *Fuelwood Consumption and Deforestation*.

26. Weber, "Technical Update."

27. World Bank, *Accelerated Development in Sub-Saharan Africa* (Washington, D.C.: 1981).

28. Hans Hurni, Soil Conservation Research Project, Addis Ababa, private communications, January 9 and February 13, 1985.

29. Soil Conservation Research Project, *Compilation of Phase I Progress Reports* (Addis Ababa: June 1984).

30. Swedish International Development Authority, *Soil Conservation in Kenya, 1980 Review* (Stockholm: December 1980); "Soil Conservation in Kenya: An Interview with Carl-Gosta Wenner," *Ambio*, Vol. 12, No. 6, 1983.

31. William I. Jones and Roberto Egli, *Farming Systems in Africa*, Technical Paper Number 27 (Washington, D.C.: World Bank, 1984).

32. Michael Stocking, "Rates of Erosion and Sediment Yield in the African Environment," in D.E. Walling, S.S.D. Foster, and P. Wurzel, eds., *Challenges in African Hydrology and Water Resources* (Oxfordshire, U.K.: International Association of Hydrological Sciences, 1984).

33. Rattan Lal, *No-Till Farming*, Monograph No. 2 (Ibadan, Nigeria: International Institute of Tropical Agriculture, 1983).

34. International Institute of Tropical Agriculture (IITA), *Tasks for the Eighties: An Appraisal of Progress* (Ibadan, Nigeria: April 1983).

35. Jones and Egli, *Farming Systems*.

36. M.J. Swift, ed., "Soil Biological Processes and Tropical Soil Fertility: A Proposal for a Collaborative Programme of Research," *Biology International*, Special Issue—5, 1984.

37. Quoted in "Center Highlights," *News from CGIAR* (Washington, D.C.), December 1984.

38. Jones and Egli, *Farming Systems*. For a thorough introduction to agroforestry, see National Research Council, Board on Science and Technology for International Development, *Agroforestry in the West African Sahel* (Washington, D.C.: National Academy Press, 1984).

39. IITA, *Annual Report 1983* (Ibadan: 1984).

40. Peter Felker, Texas A&I University, cited in National Research Council, *Agroforestry*.

41. Ernest Stern, Senior Vice-President, Operations, "The Evolving Role of the Bank in the 1980s," presented to the Agriculture Symposium, World Bank, Washington, D.C., January 13, 1984.

42. IITA, *Tasks for the Eighties: A Long-Range Plan* (Ibadan, Nigeria: June 1981).

43. USDA, ERS, *World Indices*.

44. FAO, *Production Yearbook* (Rome: various years).

45. Ibid.

46. FAO, *Fertilizer Yearbook* (Rome: various years).

47. USDA, ERS, *World Indices*.

48. Jean Gorse, "Desertification in the Sahelian and Sudanian Zones of West Africa" (draft), World Bank, Washington, D.C., February 1985.

49. Robbie Mupawose, Secretary of Agriculture, Harare, Zimbabwe, private communication, April 30, 1985.

50. Peter Brumby, International Livestock Center for Africa (ILCA), Addis Ababa, private communication, April 1985; see also ILCA, *Annual Report 1983* (Addis Ababa: 1984).

51. Christel Palmberg, FAO, Rome, private communication, May 17, 1985.

52. See, for example, ECA, *ECA and Africa's Development 1983–2008* (Addis Ababa: April 1983), African Development Bank, "Desertification and Economic and Social Development in Africa," summary remarks at the 1985 Annual Meeting Symposium, Brazzaville, Congo, May 8, 1985, and Adebayo Adedeji, "Hunger and Poverty in Sub-Saharan Africa: The Immediate Focus," presented to the 1985 International Development Conference, Washington, D.C., March 20, 1985.

53. Flora Lewis, "A Risk for Africa," *New York Times*, March 18, 1985. For information on one such suggested youth corps, see David K. Willis, "European Youth Eager to Help in Third World," *Christian Science Monitor*, April 18, 1985.

Chapter 11. Redefining National Security

1. United States Arms Control and Disarmament Agency (ACDA), *World Military Expenditures and Arms Transfers 1985* (Washington, D.C.: 1985); income figures from World Bank, *World Development Report 1985* (New York: Oxford University Press, 1985).

2. Global military statistics from ACDA, *World Military Expenditures and Arms Transfers* (Washington, D.C.: various years); world economic output figures in 1960 from Herbert R. Block, *The Planetary Product in 1980* (Washington, D.C.: U.S. Department of State, 1981).

3. ACDA, *World Military Expenditures and Arms Transfers 1985;* Dan Gallik, international economist, ACDA, Washington, D.C., private communication, September 1985.

4. Quoted in June Kronholz, "Taking Up Arms: Third World's Buying of Weaponry Surges, Posing Risks, Burdens," *Wall Street Journal*, June 29, 1982.

5. ACDA, *World Military Expenditures and Arms Transfers* (various years).

6. ACDA, *World Military Expenditures and Arms Transfers 1985;* for further information on militarization in Africa, see Sanford J. Ungar, *Africa: The People and Politics of An Emerging Continent* (New York: Simon and Schuster, 1985).

7. Arms imports worldwide from ACDA, *World Military Expenditures and Arms Transfers* (various years); grain imports derived from U.S. Department of Agriculture (USDA), Economic Research Service (ERS), *World Indices of Agricultural and Food Production 1950–1984* (unpublished printout) (Washington, D.C.: 1985), and from International Monetary Fund (IMF), *International Financial Statistics Yearbook 1985* (Washington, D.C.: 1985).

8. ACDA, *World Military Expenditures and Arms Transfers 1985;* USDA, Foreign Agricultural Service, *Foreign Agriculture Circular* FG-13–85, Washington, D.C., October 1985; IMF, *International Financial Statistics Yearbook 1985*.

9. ACDA, *World Military Expenditures and Arms Transfers 1985*.

10. Sanford J. Ungar, "The Military Money Drain," *Bulletin of the Atomic Scientists*, September 1985.

11. Clifford D. May, "Africa's Men in Khaki Are Often a Law Unto Themselves," *New York Times*, October 6, 1985.

12. Colin Norman, *Knowledge and Power: The Global Research and Development Budget* (Washington, D.C.: Worldwatch Institute, June 1979). See also Ruth Leger Sivard, *World Military and Social Expenditures* (Washington, D.C.: World Priorities, 1985).

13. Norman, *Knowledge and Power*.

14. United States Census Bureau, *Statistical Abstract of the United States 1985* (Washington, D.C.: U.S. Government Printing Office, 1985); Office of Management and Budget, *The Budget of the United States Government* (Washington, D.C.: U.S. Government Printing Office, annual); data on the net interest paid on the federal debt from United States Government, *Economic Report of the President 1985* (Washington, D.C.: U.S. Government Printing Office, 1985).

15. Job loss estimates from Robert B. Reich, "Reagan's Hidden 'Industrial Policy'," *New York Times*, August 4, 1985, and from tables prepared for the Congressional Joint Economic Committee by Bureau of Labor Statistics, Office of Employment and Unemployment Analysis, United States Department of Labor, Washington, D.C., June 7, 1985.

16. Stanley H. Cohn, "Declining Soviet Capital Productivity and the Soviet Military Industrial Complex," in ACDA, *World Military Expenditures and Arms Transfers 1984* (Washington, D.C.: 1984).

17. Ed A. Hewitt, *Energy, Economics, and Foreign Policy in the Soviet Union* (Washington, D.C.: Brookings Institution, 1984).

18. Vera Rich, "Soil First," *Nature*, February 12, 1982.

19. Soviet water availability data from G.V. Voropayev et al., "The Problem of Redistribution of Water Resources in the Midlands Region of the USSR," *Soviet Geography*, December 1983; Philip P. Micklin, "The Vast Diversion of Soviet Rivers," *Environment*, March 1985; A.S. Kes' et al., "The Present State and Future Prospects of Using Local Water Resources in Central Asia and Southern Kazakhstan," *Soviet Geography*, June 1982.

20. British Petroleum Company, *BP Statistical Review of World Energy* (London: 1985).

21. Cohn, "Declining Soviet Capital Productivity."

22. Ibid.

23. Discussion of reforms in the Soviet Union in Leslie H. Gelb, " 'Gradual' Changes in the Soviet 5-Year Plan," *New York Times*, October 14, 1985. For a discussion of the effects of military spending on Soviet economy, see Stanley H. Cohn, *The Productivity of Soviet Investment and the Economic Burden of Defense* (Washington, D.C.: National Council for Soviet and East European Research, 1983), and Cohn, "Declining Soviet Capital Productivity." For a similar discussion of the impact of military spending on the U.S. economy, see Robert W. DeGrasse, Jr., *Military Expansion, Economic Decline: The Impact of Military Spending on U.S. Economic Performance* (Armonk, N.Y.: M.E. Sharpe, Inc., for Council on Economic Priorities, 1983).

24. Per capita income derived from income data for the Soviet Union from ACDA, *World Military Expenditures and Arms Transfers* (various years), and for Japan from IMF, *International Financial Statistics Yearbook 1985;* population data from Population Reference Bureau, *1985 World Population Data Sheet* (Washington, D.C.: 1985), and from United Nations, Department of International Economic and Social Affairs, *World Population and Its Age-Sex Composition By Country, 1950–2000* (New York: 1980).

25. Japanese net foreign assets derived from Japan Statistical Bureau, *Japan Statistical Yearbook* (Tokyo: 1965), from Bank of Japan, *Balance of Payments Monthly* (Tokyo: April 1973), from Bank of Japan, *External Assets and Liabilities of Japan* (Tokyo: April 1981), and from Laura Knoy, Institute for International Economics, Washington, D.C., private communication, September 1985; U.S. foreign

assets from U.S. Department of Commerce, *Historical Statistics of the United States Volume II* (Washington, D.C.: annual). See also E.S. Browning, "Gnomes of Tokyo: Japanese Set Up Role of Investing Overseas In Bonds, Real Estate," *Wall Street Journal*, August 15, 1985; David Hale, "U.S. As Debtor: A Threat to World Trade," *New York Times*, September 22, 1985; Peter T. Kilborn, "A Nation Living on Borrowed Money and, Perhaps, Time," *New York Times*, September 22, 1985.

26. Information on declining land productivity and declining per capita grain production from USDA, ERS, *World Indices*.

27. Mary Tobin, "Mexico Signs Debt Restructuring Plan," *Washington Post*, August 30, 1985; Robert J. McCartney, "New Loans to Mexico in Doubt," *Washington Post*, September 16, 1985; William Orme, "Mexico is Expected to Ask for Billions More," *Washington Post*, September 24, 1985. See also James L. Rowe, Jr, "Debt Noose Tightens Around Latin America," *Washington Post*, September 29, 1985.

28. Farmland productivity trends from USDA, ERS, *World Indices;* Sudan's debtor position described in "The Year After the Drought: How Much Recovery for Ethiopia and Sudan?" ERS, USDA, *Agricultural Outlook*, Washington, D.C., October 1985.

29. Collapse of the Peruvian anchovy fishery discussed in Erik Eckholm, *Losing Ground: Environmental Stress and World Food Prospects* (New York: W.W. Norton & Co., 1976); Alan Riding, "In Peru, a New Personality Attracts a Cult," *New York Times*, August 4, 1985; "Will Peru's Tough Talk Spark a Debtor's Revolt?" *Business Week*, August 12, 1985; James Brooke, "Peruvian President, at the U.N., Warns I.M.F. That Debt Repayment Must Be Eased," *New York Times*, September 24, 1985.

30. John M. Goshko, "U.S. Maps New Strategy In Debt Crisis," *Washington Post*, September 21, 1985; James L. Rowe, Jr., "Private Banks Urged to Boost Third World Loans," *Washington Post*, October 6, 1985.

31. García quoted in Jeffrey Sachs, "How To Save The Third World," *New Republic*, October 28, 1985; information on Brazil and Argentina in John Burgess, "Few Banks Rush To Aid Latin America," *Washington Post*, October 13, 1985.

32. Peter T. Kilborn, "Bank in Rockland Shut by the U.S. as Insolvent," *New York Times*, September 14, 1985; Nathaniel C. Nash, "Adjusting to 100 Failed Banks," *New York Times*, November 6, 1985.

33. Charles F. McCoy, "Out of Options: Farm Credit System, Buried in Bad Loans, Seeks Big U.S. Bailout," *Wall Street Journal*, September 4, 1985; "Blighted Ledgers: Farm Credit System Relies on Accounting That Hides Bad Loans," *Wall Street Journal*, October 7, 1985. For a discussion of the causes of financial stress in U.S. agriculture, see USDA, ERS, *The Current Financial Condition of Farmers and Farm Lenders* (Washington, D.C.: March 1985); information on Continental Illinois from Federal Deposit Insurance Corporation, "Permanent Assistance Program for Continental Illinois National Bank and Trust Company," Washington, D.C., July 26, 1984.

34. C. Fred Bergsten, "The Second Debt Crisis is Coming," *Challenge*, May/June 1985.

35. "China Maps Big Cuts in Military Strength," *Journal of Commerce*, July 31, 1985; "Deng's Military Build-Down," *Far Eastern Economic Review*, August 22, 1985.

36. ACDA, *World Military Expenditures and Arms Transfers 1985;* Alfred J. Watkins, "Argentine Debt: Playing by the Rules," *Report on the Americas*, July/August 1985.

37. Riding, "In Peru, a New Personality Attracts a Cult"; "The Young Are So Impetuous," *The Economist*, August 3, 1985.

38. Riding, "In Peru, a New Personality Attracts a Cult."

39. Estimate of famine deaths in Africa from U.N. Economic Commission for Africa, "Second Special Memorandum by the ECA Conference of Ministers: International Ac-

tion for Relaunching the Initiative for Long-Term Development and Economic Growth in Africa," Addis Ababa, April 25–29, 1985.

40. Alexander Cockburn, "Heed the SOS on Third World Finances," *Wall Street Journal,* September 12, 1985.

41: "Statement of Mr. Robert Wesson," in U.S. Senate, Committee on Foreign Relations, Subcommittee on African Affairs, *African Debt Crisis,* Hearing, October 24, 1985.

Index